WHAT THEY'RE SAYING ABOUT "*THEY SAY / I SAY*"

"Like a Swiss army knife for academic writing, '*They Say / I Say*' has long served as a multipurpose tool for students learning how to make the 'moves' that are second nature to more experienced writers. The fifth edition adds several useful implements to the knife, including new chapters with practical, how-to advice on revision and inquiry-driven research."

—**Steven Bailey, *Central Michigan University***

"It is so invigorating to have a concise, smart chapter on research writing that thinks past the 'standard' process we are all so used to reading and teaching."

—**Ana Cooke, *Penn State University***

"The text isn't just about writing arguments—it's about reading and evaluating arguments, understanding who is saying what and why. *That's* the heart of research and inquiry."

—**Kay Halasek, *The Ohio State University***

"The templates were beyond helpful. They give an excellent starting point from which to launch my writing and would oftentimes help me with the ·flow of my writing."

—**First Year Student, *College of Southern Nevada***

"Many students say that it is the first book they've found that actually helps them with writing in all disciplines."

—**Laura Sonderman, *Marshall University***

"A beautifully lucid way to approach argument—different from any rhetoric I've ever seen."

—**Anne-Marie Thomas, *Austin Community College, Riverside***

"This book demystifies rhetorical moves, tricks of the trade that many students are unsure about. It's reasonable, helpful, nicely written . . . and hey, it's true. I would have found it immensely helpful myself in high school

—**Mike Rose, *U***

"The argument of this book is important—that there are 'moves' to academic writing . . . and that knowledge of them can be generative. The template format is a good way to teach and demystify the moves that matter. I like this book a lot."

—David Bartholomae, *University of Pittsburgh*

"Students need to walk a fine line between their work and that of others, and this book helps them walk that line, providing specific methods and techniques for introducing, explaining, and integrating other voices with their own ideas."

—Libby Miles, *University of Vermont*

"A brilliant book. . . . It's like a membership card in the academic club."

—Eileen Seifert, *DePaul University*

"It offers students the formulas we, as academic writers, all carry in our heads."

—Karen Gardiner, *University of Alabama*

"The best tribute to *'They Say / I Say'* I've heard is this, from a student: 'This is one book I'm not selling back to the bookstore.' Nods all around the room. The students love this book."

—Christine Ross, *Quinnipiac University*

"What effect has *'They Say'* had on my students' writing? They are finally entering the Burkian Parlor of the university. This book uncovers the rhetorical conventions that transcend disciplinary boundaries, so that even freshmen, newcomers to the academy, are immediately able to join in the conversation."

—Margaret Weaver, *Missouri State University*

"It's the anti-composition text: Fun, creative, humorous, brilliant, effective."

—Perry Cumbie, *Durham Technical Community College*

"This book explains in clear detail what skilled writers take for granted."

—John Hyman, *American University*

FIFTH EDITION

"THEY SAY / I SAY"

The Moves That Matter in Academic Writing

GERALD GRAFF

CATHY BIRKENSTEIN

both of the University of Illinois at Chicago

UNIVERSITY OF NORTH

CAROLINA WILMINGTON

NORTON
CUSTOM

Copyright © 2021, 2018, 2017, 2014, 2010, 2009, 2006
by W. W. Norton & Company, Inc.

All rights reserved
Printed in the United States of America

Composition: KnowledgeWorks Global Ltd.
Manufacturing: LSC Communications, Crawfordsville

Permission to use copyrighted material is included in the credits section
of this book, which begins on page 521.

All rights reserved. No copyright (other than selection) is claimed by the publisher
for works included by permission of third-party licensors. For permission to reproduce
material contributed to this volume by its adopting school, inquiries should be directed
to the University of North Carolina Wilmington, Department of English.

ISBN: 978-0-393-44685-2

W. W. Norton & Company, Inc., 500 Fifth Avenue, New York, NY 10110
wwnorton.com
W. W. Norton & Company Ltd., 15 Carlisle Street, London W1D 3BS
1 2 3 4 5 6 7 8 9 0

For
Aaron David

CONTENTS

CONTENTS

PART 3. TYING IT ALL TOGETHER

PART 4. IN SPECIFIC ACADEMIC CONTEXTS

Contents

CONTENTS

Contents

PREFACE
TO THE FIFTH EDITION

SINCE IT WAS FIRST PUBLISHED over a decade ago, this book has been dedicated to the idea that our own views are most thoughtfully formed in conversation with the views of others, including views that differ from our own. When students work with one of this book's templates like "They say that _____, and I concede _____. But _____," they see their beliefs from another side and, in our view, are therefore able to produce more compelling arguments.

As the twenty-first century unfolds, however, the increasingly polarized state of our society is making it harder to listen to those who see things differently than we do. With the recent outbreak of the coronavirus pandemic, for instance, those for and against the seemingly simple act of wearing a protective face mask have come to occupy two noncommunicating universes. The wider such divisions become, the harder it is to find anyone who is willing to seriously consider viewpoints that oppose their own. Too often we either avoid difficult discussions altogether, or we talk only with like-minded people, who often reinforce our preexisting assumptions and insulate us from serious challenge.

In this fifth edition of our book, therefore, we continue to emphasize the importance of getting outside our isolated silos and listening to others, even when—especially when—we may not like what we hear.

WHAT'S NEW IN THIS EDITION

"But as Several Sources Suggest": Research as Conversation.
This new chapter, written with the help of librarian and social scientist Erin Ackerman, focuses on the research essay, as it is traditionally called, and on research writing more broadly. It suggests that the research paper is not just about amassing information, as is often assumed, but also about entering into conversation with other researchers. With a variety of templates and examples from academic writing, the chapter offers advice on such issues as how to craft a good research question (spoiler alert: it's one that can be debated), how to find relevant sources, how to synthesize sources into a common conversation, and how to locate online sources that are reliable and credible. The chapter concludes with an annotated student essay that shows how the advice we offer might look in a final piece of writing.

"What I Really Want to Say Is . . .": Revising Substantially.
This new chapter takes on one of the more formidable challenges faced by college students: how to move beyond superficial revision and improve a composition in a genuinely substantial way. It presents revision not as a matter of simply correcting spelling or moving a sentence or two but as a process students can use to discover what it is they really want to say. More specifically, the chapter encourages students to reread their writing with an eye to whether, for instance, they have accurately represented their sources, inadvertently contradicted themselves or lost their train of thought, or included "uh-oh" moments, as we refer to them, that are out of step with their larger intentions and aims.

New Exercises. Each main chapter (Chapters 1–15) now includes three exercises, which give students an opportunity to apply the chapter's advice. Instructors can either use these exercises for in-class work or assign them as homework. Many exercises include a short passage for reading and writing practice and also prompt students to join conversations on **theysayiblog.com.**

New Student Writing. This edition now includes three student essays in their entirety that model the moves taught in this book. Written from a variety of disciplinary perspectives and documented in MLA or APA style, these essays complement the chapters on writing in the disciplines. Annotated and shaded in gray, they can be found in the new Chapter 15 and the Readings section. This custom print book also includes essays written by students at your school.

WHAT'S ONLINE

"They Say / I Say" comes with more online options than ever—all of which are packaged automatically with all new copies of the book and are also available separately for a low cost. Visit **digital.wwnorton.com/theysay5** for access, or contact your Norton representative for more information or help with any of the resources below.

Ebooks, available for both *"They Say / I Say"* **and** *"They Say / I Say" with Readings,* **provide an enhanced reading experience.** Convenient and affordable, the Norton ebooks can be used on any device and let students highlight ideas, bookmark passages, take notes, and even listen to the text.

Online tutorials give students hands-on practice using the rhetorical moves that this book emphasizes. Each tutorial helps students analyze an essay with an eye to these "moves that matter" and then use the book's templates to craft a response.

InQuizitive for Writers delivers adaptive, game-like exercises to help students practice editing and working with sources, including fact-checking. InQuizitive for Writers includes *The Little Seagull Handbook*, so students get two books for the price of one with all new copies of *"They Say / I Say."*

Instructor's Guide includes expanded in-class activities, sample syllabi, summaries of each chapter and reading, and a chapter on using the online resources, including the tutorials and the book's blog.

"They Say / I Blog" provides current readings that use the rhetorical moves covered in the book, along with questions that prompt students to join conversations online. Updated twice a month by Laura J. Panning Davies of SUNY Cortland, the blog provides a rich archive of additional readings on important issues. Check it out at **theysayiblog.com**.

Resources for your learning management system (LMS) provide high-quality Norton content for your online, hybrid, or in-person course. Customizable resources include assignable writing prompts from **theysayiblog.com**, quizzes on editing and documentation, style guides, student essays, and more.

Even as we have updated *"They Say / I Say"* and added more online components, our basic goals remain unchanged: to help students master the all-too-rare skill of engaging closely with others, particularly those who challenge what we say. Our additions, that is, are meant to reinforce our long-standing goal of demystifying academic discourse by identifying its key moves in forms that students can put into practice. Given the deeply divided society we live in, this practice of engaging in dialogue and entertaining counterarguments seems more urgent than ever.

PREFACE

Demystifying Academic Conversation

———❧———

EXPERIENCED WRITING INSTRUCTORS have long recognized that writing well means entering into conversation with others. Academic writing in particular calls on writers not simply to express their own ideas but to do so as a response to what others have said. The first-year writing program at our own university, according to its mission statement, asks "students to participate in ongoing conversations about vitally important academic and public issues." A similar statement by another program holds that "intellectual writing is almost always composed in response to others' texts." These statements echo the ideas of rhetorical theorists like Kenneth Burke, Mikhail Bakhtin, and Wayne Booth as well as recent composition scholars like David Bartholomae, John Bean, Patricia Bizzell, Irene Clark, Greg Colomb, Lisa Ede, Peter Elbow, Joseph Harris, Andrea Lunsford, Elaine Maimon, Gary Olson, Mike Rose, John Swales and Christine Feak, Tilly Warnock, and others who argue that writing well means engaging the voices of others and letting them in turn engage us.

Yet despite this growing consensus that writing is a social, conversational act, helping student writers actually participate in these conversations remains a formidable challenge. This book aims to meet that challenge. Its goal is to demystify academic writing by isolating its basic moves, explaining them clearly, and representing them in the form of templates.

In this way, we hope to help students become active participants in the important conversations of the academic world and the wider public sphere.

HIGHLIGHTS

- *Shows that writing well means entering a conversation*, summarizing others ("they say") to set up one's own argument ("I say")
- *Demystifies academic writing*, showing students "the moves that matter" in language they can readily apply
- *Provides user-friendly templates* to help writers make those moves in their own writing
- *Shows that reading is a way of entering a conversation*—not just of passively absorbing information but of understanding and actively entering dialogues and debates

HOW THIS BOOK CAME TO BE

The original idea for this book grew out of our shared interest in democratizing academic culture. First, it grew out of arguments that Gerald Graff has been making throughout his career that schools and colleges need to invite students into the conversations and debates that surround them. More specifically, it is a practical, hands-on companion to his book *Clueless in Academe: How Schooling Obscures the Life of the Mind*, in which he looks at academic conversations from the perspective of those who find them mysterious and proposes ways in which such mystification can be overcome. Second, this book grew out of writing templates that Cathy Birkenstein developed in the 1990s for use in writing and literature courses she was teaching. Many students, she found, could readily grasp what it meant to support a thesis with evidence, to entertain a counterargument, to identify a textual contradiction, and ultimately to summarize and respond to challenging arguments, but they often had trouble putting these concepts into practice in their own writing. When Cathy sketched out templates on the board, however, giving her students some of the language and patterns that these sophisticated moves require, their writing—and even their quality of thought—significantly improved.

This book began, then, when we put our ideas together and realized that these templates might have the potential to open up and clarify academic conversation. We proceeded from the premise that all writers rely on certain stock formulas that they themselves didn't invent—and that many of these formulas are so commonly used that they can be represented in model templates that students can use to structure and even generate what they want to say.

As we developed a working draft of this book, we began using it in first-year writing courses that we teach at UIC. In class-room exercises and writing assignments, we found that students who otherwise struggled to organize their thoughts, or even to think of something to say, did much better when we provided them with templates like the following:

▸ In discussions of _____, a controversial issue is whether _____. While some argue that _____, others contend that _____.

▸ This is not to say that _____.

One virtue of such templates, we found, is that they focus writers' attention not just on what is being said but also on the *forms* that structure what is being said. In other words, they make students more conscious of the rhetorical patterns that are key to academic success but often pass under the classroom radar.

THE CENTRALITY OF "THEY SAY / I SAY"

The central rhetorical move that we focus on in this book is the "they say / I say" template that gives our book its title. In our view, this template represents the deep, underlying structure, the internal DNA as it were, of all effective argument. Effective persuasive writers do more than make well-supported claims ("I say"); they also map those claims relative to the claims of others ("they say").

Here, for example, the "they say / I say" pattern structures a passage from an essay by the media and technology critic Steven Johnson:

> For decades, we've worked under the assumption that mass culture follows a path declining steadily toward lowest-common-denominator standards, presumably because the "masses" want dumb, simple pleasures and big media companies try to give the masses what they want. But . . . the exact opposite is happening: the culture is getting more cognitively demanding, not less.
>
> Steven Johnson, "Watching TV Makes You Smarter"

In generating his own argument from something "they say," Johnson suggests *why* he needs to say what he is saying: to correct a popular misconception.

Even when writers do not explicitly identify the views they are responding to, as Johnson does, an implicit "they say" can often be discerned, as in the following passage by Zora Neale Hurston:

> I remember the day I became colored.
>
> ZORA NEALE HURSTON, "How It Feels to Be Colored Me"

In order to grasp Hurston's point here, we need to be able to reconstruct the implicit view she is responding to and questioning: that racial identity is an innate quality we are simply born with. On the contrary, Hurston suggests, our race is imposed on us by society—something we "become" by virtue of how we are treated.

As these examples suggest, the "they say / I say" model can improve not just student writing but student reading comprehension as well. Since reading and writing are deeply reciprocal activities, students who learn to make the rhetorical moves represented by the templates in this book figure to become more adept at identifying these same moves in the texts they read. And if we are right that effective arguments are always in dialogue with other arguments, then it follows that in order to understand the types of challenging texts assigned in college, students need to identify the views to which those texts are responding.

Working with the "they say / I say" model can also help with invention, finding something to say. In our experience, students best discover what they want to say not by thinking about a subject in an isolation booth but by reading texts, listening closely to what other writers say, and looking for an opening through which they can enter the conversation. In other words, listening closely to others and summarizing what they have to say can help writers generate their own ideas.

THE USEFULNESS OF TEMPLATES

Our templates also have a generative quality, prompting students to make moves in their writing that they might not otherwise make or even know they should make. The templates in this book can be particularly helpful for students who are unsure about what to say or who have trouble finding enough to say, often because they consider their own beliefs so self-evident that they need not be argued for. Students like this are often helped, we've found, when we give them a simple template like the following one for entertaining a counterargument (or planting a naysayer, as we call it in Chapter 6):

▸ Of course some might object that _____ . Although I concede that _____ , I still maintain that _____ .

What this particular template helps students do is make the seemingly counterintuitive move of questioning their own beliefs, of looking at them from the perspective of those who disagree. In so doing, templates can bring out aspects of students' thoughts that, as they themselves sometimes remark, they didn't even realize were there.

Other templates in this book help students make a host of sophisticated moves that they might not otherwise make: summarizing what someone else says, framing a quotation in one's own words, indicating the view that the writer is responding to, marking the shift from a source's view to the writer's own view, offering evidence for that view, entertaining and answering counterarguments, and explaining what is at stake in the first place. In showing students how to make such moves, templates do more than organize students' ideas; they help bring those ideas into existence.

"OK—BUT TEMPLATES?"

We are aware, of course, that some instructors may have reservations about templates. Some, for instance, may object that such formulaic devices represent a return to prescriptive forms of instruction that encourage passive learning or lead students to put their writing on automatic pilot.

This is an understandable reaction, we think, to kinds of rote instruction that have indeed encouraged passivity and drained writing of its creativity and dynamic relation to the social world. The trouble is that many students will never learn on their own to make the key intellectual moves that our templates represent. While seasoned writers pick up these moves unconsciously through their reading, many students do not. Consequently, we believe, students need to see these moves represented in the explicit ways that the templates provide.

The aim of the templates, then, is not to stifle critical thinking but to be direct with students about the key rhetorical moves that it comprises. Since we encourage students to modify and adapt the templates to the particularities of the arguments they are making, using such prefabricated formulas as learning tools need not result in writing and thinking that are themselves formulaic. Admittedly, no teaching tool can guarantee that students will engage in hard, rigorous thought. Our templates do, however, provide concrete prompts that can stimulate and shape such thought: What do "they say" about my topic? How would a naysayer respond to my argument? What is my evidence? Do I need to qualify my point? Who cares?

In fact, templates have a long and rich history. Public orators from ancient Greece and Rome through the European Renaissance studied rhetorical *topoi* or "commonplaces," model passages and formulas that represented the different strategies available to public speakers. In many respects, our templates echo this classical rhetorical tradition of imitating established models.

The journal *Nature* requires aspiring contributors to follow a guideline that is like a template on the opening page of their manuscript: "Two or three sentences explaining what the main result [of their study] reveals in direct comparison with what was thought to be the case previously, or how the main result adds to previous knowledge." In the field of education, a form designed by the education theorist Howard Gardner asks postdoctoral fellowship applicants to complete the following template: "Most scholars in the field believe _____ . As a result of my study, _____ ." That these two examples are geared toward postdoctoral fellows and veteran researchers shows that it is not only struggling undergraduates who can use help making these key rhetorical moves but experienced academics as well.

Templates have even been used in the teaching of personal narrative. The literary and educational theorist Jane Tompkins devised the following template to help student writers make the often difficult move from telling a story to explaining what it means: "X tells a story about _____ to make the point that _____ . My own experience with _____ yields a point that is similar / different / both similar and different. What I take away from my own experience with _____ is _____ . As a result, I conclude _____ ." We especially like this template because it suggests that "they say / I say" argument need not be mechanical, impersonal, or dry and that telling a story and making an argument are more compatible activities than many think.

WHY IT'S OK TO USE "I"

But wait—doesn't the "I" part of "they say / I say" flagrantly encourage the use of the first-person pronoun? Aren't we aware that some teachers prohibit students from using "I" or "we" on the grounds that these pronouns encourage ill-considered, subjective opinions rather than objective and reasoned arguments? Yes, we are aware of this first-person prohibition, but we think it has serious flaws. First, expressing ill-considered, subjective opinions is not necessarily the worst sin beginning writers can commit; it might be a starting point from which they can move on to more reasoned, less self-indulgent perspectives. Second, prohibiting students from using "I" is simply not an effective way of curbing students' subjectivity, since one can offer poorly argued, ill-supported opinions just as easily without it. Third and most important, prohibiting the first person tends to hamper students' ability not only to take strong positions but also to differentiate their own positions from those of others, as we point out in Chapter 5. To be sure, writers can resort to various circumlocutions—"it will here be argued," "the evidence suggests," "the truth is"—and these may be useful for avoiding a monotonous series of "I believe" sentences. But except for avoiding such monotony, we see no good reason why "I" should be set aside in persuasive writing. Rather than prohibit "I," then, we think a better tactic is to give students practice at using it well and learning its use, both by supporting their claims with evidence and by attending closely to alternative perspectives—to what "they" are saying.

HOW THIS BOOK IS ORGANIZED

Because of its centrality, we have allowed the "they say / I say" format to dictate the structure of this book. So while Part 1 addresses the art of listening to others, Part 2 addresses how to offer one's own response. Part 1 opens with the chapter

"Starting with What Others Are Saying," which explains why it is generally advisable to begin a text by citing others rather than plunging directly into one's own views. Subsequent chapters take up the arts of summarizing and quoting what these others have to say. Part 2 begins with a chapter on different ways of responding, followed by chapters on marking the shift between what "they say" and what "I say," on introducing and answering objections, and on answering the all-important questions "so what?" and "who cares?" Part 3, "Tying It All Together," includes a chapter on connection and coherence; one on academic language, which encourages students to draw on their everyday voice as a tool for writing; and others on the art of metacommentary and using templates to revise a text. Part 4 offers guidance for entering conversations in specific academic contexts, with chapters on entering class discussions, writing online, reading, and writing in literature courses, the sciences, and social sciences. Finally, we provide five readings and an index of templates.

WHAT THIS BOOK DOESN'T DO

There are some things that this book does not try to do. We do not, for instance, cover logical principles of argument, such as syllogisms, warrants, logical fallacies, or the differences between inductive and deductive reasoning. Although such concepts can be useful, we believe most of us learn the ins and outs of argumentative writing not by studying logical principles in the abstract but by plunging into actual discussions and debates, trying out different patterns of response, and in this way getting a sense of what works to persuade different audiences and what doesn't. In our view, people learn more about arguing from hearing someone say, "You miss my point. What I'm saying is not _____ but _____," or "I agree with you that _____ and would even add that _____," than they do from studying the differences between inductive and deductive reasoning. Such formulas give students an immediate sense of what it feels like to enter a public conversation in a way that studying abstract warrants and logical fallacies does not.

ENGAGING WITH THE IDEAS OF OTHERS

One central goal of this book is to demystify academic writing by returning it to its social and conversational roots. Although writing may require some degree of quiet and solitude, the "they say / I say" model shows students that they can best develop their arguments not just by looking inward but by doing what they often do in a good conversation with friends and family— listening carefully to what others are saying and engaging with other views.

This approach to writing therefore has an ethical dimension, since it asks writers not simply to keep proving and reasserting what they already believe but also to stretch what they believe by putting it up against beliefs that differ, sometimes radically, from their own. In an increasingly diverse, global society, this ability to engage with the ideas of others is especially crucial to democratic citizenship.

Gerald Graff
Cathy Birkenstein

INTRODUCTION

Entering the Conversation

THINK ABOUT AN ACTIVITY that you do particularly well: cooking, playing the piano, shooting a basketball, even something as basic as driving a car. If you reflect on this activity, you'll realize that once you mastered it you no longer had to give much conscious thought to the various moves that go into doing it. Performing this activity, in other words, depends on your having learned a series of complicated moves—moves that may seem mysterious or difficult to those who haven't yet learned them.

The same applies to writing. Often without consciously realizing it, accomplished writers routinely rely on a stock of established moves that are crucial for communicating sophisticated ideas. What makes writers masters of their trade is not only their ability to express interesting thoughts but their mastery of an inventory of basic moves that they probably picked up by reading a wide range of other accomplished writers. Less experienced writers, by contrast, are often unfamiliar with these basic moves and unsure how to make them in their own writing. Hence this book, which is intended as a short, user-friendly guide to the basic moves of academic writing.

One of our key premises is that these basic moves are so common that they can be represented in *templates* that you can use right away to structure and even generate your own writing. Perhaps the most distinctive feature of this book is its presentation of many such templates, designed to help you successfully enter not only the world of academic thinking and writing but also the wider worlds of civic discourse and work.

Instead of focusing solely on abstract principles of writing, then, this book offers model templates that help you put those principles directly into practice. Working with these templates will give you an immediate sense of how to engage in the kinds of critical thinking you are required to do at the college level and in the vocational and public spheres beyond.

Some of these templates represent simple but crucial moves, like those used to summarize some widely held belief:

▸ **Many Americans assume that _____.**

Others are more complicated:

▸ **On the one hand, _____. On the other hand, _____.**

▸ **Author X contradicts herself. At the same time that she argues _____, she also implies _____.**

▸ **I agree that _____. However, _____.**

▸ **This is not to say that _____.**

It is true, of course, that critical thinking and writing go deeper than any set of linguistic formulas, requiring that you question assumptions, develop strong claims, offer supporting reasons and evidence, consider opposing arguments, and so on. But these deeper habits of thought cannot be put into practice unless you have a language for expressing them in clear, organized ways.

STATE YOUR OWN IDEAS AS A
RESPONSE TO OTHERS

The single most important template that we focus on in this book is the "they say _____; I say _____" formula that gives our book its title. If there is any one point that we hope you will take away from this book, it is the importance not only of expressing your ideas ("I say") but of presenting those ideas as a *response to some other person or group* ("they say"). For us, the underlying structure of effective academic writing—and of responsible public discourse—resides not just in stating our own ideas but in listening closely to others around us, summarizing their views in a way that they will recognize, and responding with our own ideas in kind. Broadly speaking, academic writing is argumentative writing, and we believe that to argue well you need to do more than assert your own position. You need to enter a conversation, using what others say (or might say) as a launching pad or sounding board for your own views. For this reason, one of the main pieces of advice in this book is to write the voices of others into your text.

In our view, then, the best academic writing has one underlying feature: it is deeply engaged in some way with other people's views. Too often, however, academic writing is taught as a process of saying "true" or "smart" things in a vacuum, as if it were possible to argue effectively without being in conversation *with* someone else. If you have been taught to write a traditional five-paragraph essay, for example, you have learned how to develop a thesis and support it with evidence. This is good advice as far as it goes, but it leaves out the important fact that in the real world we don't make arguments without being provoked. Instead, we make arguments because someone has said or done something (or perhaps *not* said or done something) and we need to respond: "I can't see why you like the Lakers so much"; "I agree: it was a great film"; "That argument is contradictory." If it weren't for other people and our need to challenge, agree with, or otherwise respond to them, there would be no reason to argue at all.

"WHY ARE YOU TELLING ME THIS?"

To make an impact as a writer, then, you need to do more than make statements that are logical, well supported, and consistent. You must also find a way of entering into conversation with the views of others, with something "they say." The easiest and most common way writers do this is by *summarizing* what others say and then using it to set up what they want to say.

"But why," as a student of ours once asked, "do I always need to summarize the views of others to set up my own view? Why can't I just state my own view and be done with it?" Why indeed? After all, "they," whoever they may be, will have already had their say, so why do you have to *repeat* it? Furthermore, if they had their say in print, can't readers just go and read what was said themselves?

The answer is that if you don't identify the "they say" you're responding to, your own argument probably won't have a point. Readers will wonder what prompted you to say what you're saying and therefore motivated you to write. As the figure on the following page suggests, without a "they say," *what* you are saying may be clear to your audience, but *why* you are saying it won't be.

Even if we don't know what film he's referring to, it's easy to grasp what the speaker means here when he says that its characters are very complex. But it's hard to see why the speaker feels the need to say what he is saying. "Why," as one member

of his imagined audience wonders, "is he telling us this?" So the characters are complex—so what?

Now look at what happens to the same proposition when it is presented as a response to something "they say":

We hope you agree that the same claim—"the characters in the film are very complex"—becomes much stronger when presented as a response to a contrary view: that the film's characters "are sexist stereotypes." Unlike the speaker in the first cartoon, the speaker in the second has a clear goal or mission: to correct what he sees as a mistaken characterization.

THE AS-OPPOSED-TO-WHAT FACTOR

To put our point another way, framing your "I say" as a response to something "they say" gives your writing an element of contrast without which it won't make sense. It may be helpful to think of this crucial element as an "as-opposed-to-what factor" and, as you write, to continually ask yourself, "Who says otherwise?" and "Does anyone dispute it?" Behind the audience's "Yeah, so?" and "Why is he telling us this?" in the first cartoon above lie precisely these types of "As opposed to what?" questions. The speaker in the second cartoon, we think, is more satisfying because he answers these questions, helping us see his point that the film presents complex characters *rather than* simple sexist stereotypes.

HOW IT'S DONE

Many accomplished writers make explicit "they say" moves to set up and motivate their own arguments. One famous example is Martin Luther King Jr.'s "Letter from Birmingham Jail," which consists almost entirely of King's eloquent responses to a public statement by eight clergymen deploring the civil rights protests he was leading. The letter—which was written in 1963, while King was in prison for leading a demonstration against racial injustice in Birmingham—is structured almost entirely around a framework of summary and response, in which King summarizes and then answers their criticisms. In one typical passage, King writes as follows:

> You deplore the demonstrations taking place in Birmingham. But your statement, I am sorry to say, fails to express a similar concern for the conditions that brought about the demonstrations.
>
> MARTIN LUTHER KING JR., "Letter from Birmingham Jail"

King goes on to agree with his critics that "it is unfortunate that demonstrations are taking place in Birmingham," yet he hastens to add that "it is even more unfortunate that the city's white power structure left the Negro community with no alternative." King's letter is so thoroughly conversational, in fact, that it could be rewritten in the form of a dialogue or play.

King's critics:
King's response:
Critics:
Response:

Clearly, King would not have written his famous letter were it not for his critics, whose views he treats not as objections to his already-formed arguments but as the motivating source of those arguments, their central reason for being. He quotes not only what his critics have said ("Some have asked: 'Why didn't you give the new city administration time to act?'"), but also things they *might* have said ("One may well ask: 'How can you advocate breaking some laws and obeying others?'")—all to set the stage for what he himself wants to say.

A similar "they say / I say" exchange opens an essay about American patriotism by the social critic Katha Pollitt, who uses her own daughter's comment to represent the patriotic national fervor after the terrorist attacks of September 11, 2001.

> My daughter, who goes to Stuyvesant High School only blocks from the former World Trade Center, thinks we should fly the American flag out our window. Definitely not, I say: the flag stands for jingoism and vengeance and war. She tells me I'm wrong—the flag means standing together and honoring the dead and saying no to terrorism. In a way we're both right. . . .
>
> KATHA POLLITT, "Put Out No Flags"

As Pollitt's example shows, the "they" you respond to in crafting an argument need not be a famous author or someone known to your audience. It can be a family member, like Pollitt's daughter, or a friend or classmate who has made a provocative claim. It can even be something an individual or a group might say—or a side of yourself, something you once believed but no longer do, or something you partly believe but also doubt. The important thing is that the "they" (or "you" or "she") represent some wider group with which readers might identify—in Pollitt's case, those who patriotically believe in flying the flag. Pollitt's example also shows that responding to the views of others need not always involve unquali-fied opposition. By agreeing and disagreeing with her daughter, Pollitt enacts what we call the "yes and no" response, reconciling apparently incompatible views.

See Chapter 4 for more on agreeing, but with a difference.

While King and Pollitt both identify the views they are responding to, some authors do not explicitly state their views but instead allow the reader to infer them. See, for instance, if you can identify the implied or unnamed "they say" that the following claim is responding to:

> I like to think I have a certain advantage as a teacher of literature because when I was growing up I disliked and feared books.
> GERALD GRAFF, "Disliking Books at an Early Age"

In case you haven't figured it out already, the phantom "they say" here is the common belief that in order to be a good teacher of literature, one must have grown up liking and enjoying books.

COURT CONTROVERSY, BUT...

As you can see from these examples, many writers use the "they say / I say" format to challenge standard ways of thinking and thus to stir up controversy. This point may come as a shock to you if you have always had the impression that in order to succeed academically you need to play it safe and avoid controversy in your writing, making statements that nobody can possibly disagree with. Though this view of writing may appear logical, it is actually a recipe for flat, lifeless writing and for writing that fails to answer what we call the "so what?" and "who cares?" questions. "William Shakespeare wrote many famous plays and sonnets" may be a perfectly true statement, but precisely because nobody is likely to disagree with it, it goes without saying and thus would seem pointless if said.

But just because controversy is important doesn't mean you have to become an attack dog who automatically disagrees with everything others say. We think this is an important point to underscore because some who are not familiar with this book have gotten the impression from the title that our goal is to train writers simply to disparage whatever "they say."

LISTEN BEFORE YOU LEAP

There certainly are occasions when strong critique is needed. It's hard to live in a deeply polarized society like our current one and not feel the need at times to criticize what others think. But even the most justified critiques fall flat, we submit, unless we really listen to and understand the views we are criticizing:

▸ While I understand the impulse to _____, my own view is _____.

Even the most sympathetic audiences, after all, tend to feel manipulated by arguments that scapegoat and caricature the other side.

Furthermore, genuinely listening to views we disagree with can have the salutary effect of helping us see that beliefs we'd initially disdained may not be as thoroughly reprehensible as we'd imagined. Thus the type of "they say / I say" argument that we promote in this book can take the form of agreeing up to a point or, as the Pollitt example above illustrates, of both agreeing and disagreeing simultaneously, as in:

▸ While I agree with X that _____, I cannot accept her overall conclusion that _____.

▸ While X argues _____, and I argue _____, in a way we're both right.

Agreement cannot be ruled out, however:

▸ I agree with _____ that _____.

THE TEMPLATE OF TEMPLATES

There are many ways, then, to enter a conversation and respond to what "they say." But our discussion of ways to do so would be incomplete were we not to mention the most comprehensive way that writers enter conversations, which incorporates all the major moves discussed in this book:

▸ In recent discussions of _____, a controversial issue has been whether _____. On the one hand, some argue that _____. From this perspective, _____. On the other hand, however, others argue that _____. In the words of X, one of this view's main proponents, "_____." According to this view, _____. In sum, then, the issue is whether _____ or _____.

My own view is that _____. Though I concede that _____, I still maintain that _____. For example, _____. Although some might object that _____, I would reply that _____. The issue is important because _____.

This "template of templates," as we like to call it, represents the internal DNA of countless articles and even entire books. Writers commonly use a version of it not only to stake out their "they say" and "I say" at the start of their manuscript, but—just as important—to form the overarching blueprint that structures what they write over the entire length of their text.

Taking it line by line, this master template first helps you open your text by identifying an issue in some ongoing conversation or debate ("In recent discussions of _____, a controversial issue has been _____") and then map some of the voices in this controversy (by using the "on the one hand / on the other hand" structure). The template then helps you introduce a quotation ("In the words of X") and explain the quotation in your own words ("According to this view"). Then, in a new paragraph, it helps you state your own argument ("My own view is that"), qualify your argument ("Though I concede that"), and support your argument with evidence ("For example"). In addition, the template helps you make one of the most crucial moves in argumentative writing, what we call "planting a naysayer in your text," in which you summarize and then answer a likely objection to your own central claim ("Although it might be objected that _____, I reply _____"). Finally, this template helps you shift between general, overarching claims ("In sum, then") and smaller-scale, supporting claims ("For example").

Again, none of us is born knowing these moves, especially when it comes to academic writing—hence the need for this book.

BUT ISN'T THIS PLAGIARISM?

"But isn't this plagiarism?" at least one student each year will usually ask. "Well, is it?" we respond, turning the question around into one the entire class can profit from. "We are, after all, asking you to use language in your writing that isn't your own—language that you 'borrow' or, to put it less delicately, steal from other writers."

Often, a lively discussion ensues that raises important questions about authorial ownership and helps everyone better understand the frequently confusing line between plagiarism and the legitimate use of what others say and how they say it. Students are quick to see that no one person owns a conventional formula like "on the one hand / on the other hand." Phrases like "a controversial issue" are so commonly used and recycled that they are generic—community property that can be freely used without fear of committing plagiarism. It *is* plagiarism, however, if the words used to fill in the blanks of such formulas are borrowed from others without proper acknowledgment. In sum, then, while it is not plagiarism to recycle conventionally used formulas, it is a serious academic offense to take the substantive content from others' texts without citing the authors and giving them proper credit.

"OK—BUT TEMPLATES?"

Nevertheless, if you are like some of our students, your initial response to templates may be skepticism. At first, many of our students complain that using templates will take away their originality and creativity and make them all sound the same. "They'll turn us into writing robots," one of our students insisted. "I'm in college now," another student asserted. "This is third-grade-level stuff."

In our view, however, the templates in this book, far from being "third-grade-level stuff," represent the stock-in-trade of sophisticated thinking and writing, and they often require a great deal of practice and instruction to use successfully. As for the belief that preestablished forms undermine creativity, we think it rests on a very limited vision of what creativity is all about. In our view, the templates in this book will actually help your writing become *more* original and creative, not less. After all, even the most creative forms of expression depend on established patterns and structures. Most songwriters, for instance, rely on a time-honored verse-chorus-verse pattern, and few people would call Shakespeare uncreative because he didn't invent the sonnet or the dramatic forms that he used to such dazzling effect. Even the most avant-garde, cutting-edge artists like improvisational jazz musicians need to master the basic forms that their work improvises on, departs from, and goes beyond, or else their work will come across as uneducated child's play. Ultimately, then, creativity and originality lie not in the avoidance of established forms but in the imaginative use of them.

Furthermore, these templates do not dictate the *content* of what you say, which can be as original as you can make it, but only suggest a way of formatting *how* you say it. In addition, once you begin to feel comfortable with the templates in this book, you will be able to improvise creatively on them to fit new situations and purposes and find others in your reading. In other words, the templates offered here are learning tools to get you started, not structures set in stone. Once you get used to using them, you can even dispense with them altogether, for the rhetorical moves they model will be at your fingertips in an unconscious, instinctive way.

But if you still need proof that writing templates need not make you sound stiff and artificial, consider the following opening to an essay on the fast-food industry that we've included in Chapter 14:

> If ever there were a newspaper headline custom-made for Jay Leno's monologue, this was it. Kids taking on McDonald's this week, suing the company for making them fat. Isn't that like middle-aged men suing Porsche for making them get speeding tickets? Whatever happened to personal responsibility?
>
> I tend to sympathize with these portly fast-food patrons, though. Maybe that's because I used to be one of them.
>
> DAVID ZINCZENKO, "Don't Blame the Eater"

Although Zinczenko relies on a version of the "they say / I say" formula, his writing is anything but dry, robotic, or uncreative. While Zinczenko does not explicitly use the words "they say" and "I say," the template still gives the passage its underlying structure: "*They say* that kids suing fast-food companies for making them fat is a joke; but *I say* such lawsuits are justified."

PUTTING IN YOUR OAR

Though the immediate goal of this book is to help you become a better writer, at a deeper level it invites you to become a certain type of person: a critical, intellectual thinker who, instead of sitting passively on the sidelines, can participate in the debates and conversations of your world in an active and empowered way. Ultimately, this book invites you to become a critical thinker who can enter the types of conversations described eloquently by the philosopher Kenneth Burke in the following widely cited passage. Likening the world of intellectual exchange to a never-ending conversation at a party, Burke writes:

> You come late. When you arrive, others have long preceded you, and they are engaged in a heated discussion, a discussion too heated for them to pause and tell you exactly what it is about. . . . You listen for a while, until you decide that you have caught the tenor of the argument; then you put in your oar. Someone answers; you answer him; another comes to your defense; another aligns himself against you. . . . The hour grows late, you must depart. And you do depart, with the discussion still vigorously in progress.
>
> KENNETH BURKE, *The Philosophy of Literary Form*

What we like about this passage is its suggestion that stating an argument (putting in your oar) can only be done in conversation with others; that entering the dynamic world of ideas must be done not as isolated individuals but as social beings deeply connected to others.

This ability to enter complex, many-sided conversations has taken on a special urgency in today's polarized red state / blue state America, where the future for all of us may depend on our ability to put ourselves in the shoes of those who think very differently from us. The central piece of advice in this book—that we listen carefully to others, including those who disagree with us, and then engage with them thoughtfully and respectfully—can help us see beyond our own pet beliefs, which may not be shared by everyone. The mere act of crafting a sentence that begins "Of course, someone might object that _____" may not seem like a way to change the world; but it does have the potential to jog us out of our comfort zones, to get us thinking critically about our own beliefs, and even to change minds, our own included.

Exercises

1. Write two paragraphs in which you first summarize our rationale for the templates in this book and then articulate your own position in response. If you want, you can use the template below to organize your paragraphs, expanding and modifying it as necessary to fit what you want to say:

In the Introduction to *"They Say / I Say": The Moves That Matter in Academic Writing,* Gerald Graff and Cathy Birkenstein provide templates designed to _____. Specifically, Graff and Birkenstein argue that the types of writing templates they offer _____. As the authors themselves put it, "_____." Although some people believe _____, Graff and Birkenstein insist that _____. In sum, then, their view is that _____.

   I [agree / disagree / have mixed feelings]. In my view, the types of templates that the authors recommend _____. For instance, _____. In addition, _____. Some might object, of course, on the grounds that _____. Yet I would argue that _____. Overall, then, I believe _____ —an important point to make given _____.

2. Read the following paragraph from an essay by Emily Poe, written when she was a student at Furman University. Disregarding for the moment what Poe says, focus your attention on the phrases she uses to structure what she says (italicized here). Then write a new paragraph using Poe's as a model but replacing her topic, vegetarianism, with one of your own.

The term "vegetarian" tends to be synonymous with "tree-hugger" in many people's minds. *They see* vegetarianism as a cult that brainwashes its followers into eliminating an essential part of their daily diets for an abstract goal of "animal welfare." *However,* few vegetarians choose their lifestyle just to follow the crowd. *On the contrary,* many of these supposedly brainwashed people are actually independent thinkers, concerned citizens, and compassionate human beings. *For the truth is* that there are many very good reasons for giving up meat. Perhaps the best reasons are to improve the environment, to encourage humane treatment of livestock, or to enhance one's own health. *In this essay, then,* closely examining a vegetarian diet as compared to a meat-eater's diet will show that vegetarianism is clearly the better option for sustaining the Earth and all its inhabitants.

ONE

"THEY SAY"

Starting with What Others Are Saying

—▱—

NOT LONG AGO we attended a talk at an academic conference where the speaker's central claim seemed to be that a certain sociologist—call him Dr. X—had done very good work in a number of areas of the discipline. The speaker proceeded to illustrate his thesis by referring extensively and in great detail to various books and articles by Dr. X and by quoting long passages from them. The speaker was obviously both learned and impassioned, but as we listened to his talk, we found ourselves somewhat puzzled: the argument—that Dr. X's work was very important—was clear enough, but why did the speaker need to make it in the first place? Did anyone dispute it? Were there commentators in the field who had argued against X's work or challenged its value? Was the speaker's interpretation of what X had done somehow novel or revolutionary? Since the speaker gave no hint of an answer to any of these questions, we could only wonder why he was going on and on about X. It was only after the speaker finished and took questions from the audience that we got a clue: in response to one questioner, he referred to several critics who had

The hypothetical audience in the figure on p. 5 reacts similarly.

vigorously questioned Dr. X's ideas and convinced many sociologists that Dr. X's work was unsound.

This story illustrates an important lesson: that to give writing the most important thing of all—namely, a point—writers need to indicate clearly not only what their thesis is but also what larger conversation that thesis is responding to. Because our speaker failed to mention what others had said about Dr. X's work, he left his audience unsure about why he felt the need to say what he was saying. Perhaps the point was clear to other sociologists in the audience who were more familiar with the debates over Dr. X's work than we were. But even they, we bet, would have understood the speaker's point better if he'd sketched in some of the larger conversation his own claims were a part of and reminded the audience about what "they say."

This story also illustrates an important lesson about the *order* in which things are said: to keep an audience engaged, writers need to explain what they are responding to—either before offering that response or, at least, very early in the discussion. Delaying this explanation for more than one or two paragraphs in a very short essay or blog entry, three or four pages in a longer work, or more than ten or so pages in a book reverses the natural order in which readers process material—and in which writers think and develop ideas. After all, it seems very unlikely that our conference speaker first developed his defense of Dr. X and only later came across Dr. X's critics. As someone knowledgeable in his field, the speaker surely encountered the criticisms first and only then was compelled to respond and, as he saw it, set the record straight.

Therefore, when it comes to constructing an argument (whether orally or in writing), we offer you the following advice: remember that you are entering a conversation and therefore need to start with "what others are saying," as the title of this chapter recommends, and then introduce your own ideas as a response. Specifically, we suggest that you summarize what "they say" as soon as you can in your text and remind readers of it at strategic points as your text unfolds. Though it's true that not all texts follow this practice, we think it's important for all writers to master it before they depart from it.

This is not to say that you must start with a detailed list of everyone who has written on your subject before you offer your own ideas. Had our conference speaker gone to the opposite extreme and spent most of his talk summarizing Dr. X's critics with no hint of what he himself had to say, the audience probably would have had the same frustrated "why is he going on like this?" reaction. What we suggest, then, is that as soon as possible you state your own position and the one it's responding to *together*, and that you think of the two as a unit. It is generally best to summarize the ideas you're responding to briefly, at the start of your text, and to delay detailed elaboration until later. The point is to give your readers a quick preview of what is motivating your argument, not to drown them in details right away.

Starting with a summary of others' views may seem to contradict the common advice that writers should lead with their own thesis or claim. Although we agree that you shouldn't keep readers in suspense too long about your central argument, we also believe that you need to present that argument as part of some larger conversation, indicating something about the arguments of others that you are supporting, opposing, amending, complicating, or qualifying. One added benefit of summarizing others' views as soon as you can: you let those others do some of the work of framing and clarifying the issue you're writing about.

Consider, for example, how George Orwell starts his famous essay "Politics and the English Language" with what others are saying:

Most people who bother with the matter at all would admit that the English language is in a bad way, but it is generally assumed that we cannot by conscious action do anything about it. Our civilization is decadent and our language—so the argument runs—must inevitably share in the general collapse. . . .

[But] the process is reversible. Modern English . . . is full of bad habits . . . which can be avoided if one is willing to take the necessary trouble.

GEORGE ORWELL, "Politics and the English Language"

Orwell is basically saying, "Most people assume that we cannot do anything about the bad state of the English language. But I say we can."

Of course, there are many other powerful ways to begin. Instead of opening with someone else's views, you could start with an illustrative quotation, a revealing fact or statistic, or—as we do in this chapter—a relevant anecdote. If you choose one of these formats, however, be sure that it in some way illustrates the view you're addressing or leads you to that view directly, with a minimum of steps.

In opening this chapter, for example, we devote the first paragraph to an anecdote about the conference speaker and then move quickly at the start of the second paragraph to the misconception about writing exemplified by the speaker. In the following opening, from an opinion piece in the *New York Times Book Review*, Christina Nehring also moves quickly from an anecdote illustrating something she dislikes to her own claim—that book lovers think too highly of themselves:

"I'm a reader!" announced the yellow button. "How about you?" I looked at its bearer, a strapping young guy stalking my town's Festival of Books. "I'll bet you're a reader," he volunteered, as though we were two geniuses well met. "No," I replied. "Absolutely not," I wanted to yell, and fling my Barnes & Noble bag at his feet. Instead, I mumbled something apologetic and melted into the crowd.

There's a new piety in the air: the self-congratulation of book lovers.

CHRISTINA NEHRING, "Books Make You a Boring Person"

Nehring's anecdote is really a kind of "they say": book lovers keep telling themselves how great they are.

TEMPLATES FOR INTRODUCING WHAT "THEY SAY"

There are lots of conventional ways to introduce what others are saying. Here are some standard templates that we would have recommended to our conference speaker:

▸ A number of sociologists have recently suggested <u>that X's work has several fundamental problems.</u>

▸ It has become common today to dismiss _____.

▸ In their recent work, Y and Z have offered harsh critiques of _____ for _____.

TEMPLATES FOR INTRODUCING "STANDARD VIEWS"

The following templates can help you make what we call the "standard view" move, in which you introduce a view that has become so widely accepted that by now it is essentially the conventional way of thinking about a topic:

- Americans have always believed that <u>individual effort can triumph over circumstances</u>.

- Conventional wisdom has it that _____.

- Common sense seems to dictate that _____.

- The standard way of thinking about topic X has it that _____.

- It is often said that _____.

- My whole life I have heard it said that _____.

- You would think that _____.

- Many people assume that _____.

These templates are popular because they provide a quick and efficient way to perform one of the most common moves that writers make: challenging widely accepted beliefs, placing them on the examining table, and analyzing their strengths and weaknesses.

TEMPLATES FOR MAKING WHAT "THEY SAY" SOMETHING *YOU* SAY

Another way to introduce the views you're responding to is to present them as your own. That is, the "they say" that you respond to need not be a view held by others; it can be one that you yourself once held or one that you are ambivalent about:

- I've always believed that <u>museums are boring</u>.

- When I was a child, I used to think that _____.

▸ Although I should know better by now, I cannot help thinking that _____.

▸ At the same time that I believe _____, I also believe _____.

TEMPLATES FOR INTRODUCING
SOMETHING IMPLIED OR ASSUMED

Another sophisticated move a writer can make is to summarize a point that is not directly stated in what "they say" but is implied or assumed:

▸ Although none of them have ever said so directly, my teachers have often given me the impression that <u>education will open doors</u>.

▸ One implication of X's treatment of _____ is that _____.

▸ Although X does not say so directly, she apparently assumes that _____.

▸ While they rarely admit as much, _____ often take for granted that _____.

These are templates that can help you think analytically—to look beyond what others say explicitly and to consider their unstated assumptions, as well as the implications of their views.

TEMPLATES FOR INTRODUCING
AN ONGOING DEBATE

Sometimes you'll want to open by summarizing a debate that presents two or more views. This kind of opening demonstrates your awareness that there are conflicting ways to look at your subject, the clear mark of someone who knows the subject and therefore is likely to be a reliable, trustworthy guide. Furthermore, opening with a summary of a debate can help you explore the issue you are writing about before declaring your own view. In this way, you can use the writing process itself to help you discover where you stand instead of having to commit to a position before you are ready to do so.

Here is a basic template for opening with a debate:

> ▶ In discussions of X, one controversial issue has been _____.
> On the one hand, _____ argues _____. On the other
> hand, _____ contends _____. Others even maintain
> _____. My own view is _____.

The cognitive scientist Mark Aronoff uses this kind of template in an essay on the workings of the human brain:

> Theories of how the mind/brain works have been dominated for centuries by two opposing views. One, rationalism, sees the human mind as coming into this world more or less fully formed—preprogrammed, in modern terms. The other, empiricism, sees the mind of the newborn as largely unstructured, a blank slate.
>
> MARK ARONOFF, "Washington Sleeped Here"

A student writer, Michaela Cullington, uses a version of this template near the beginning of an essay to frame a debate over online writing abbreviations like "LOL" ("laughing out loud") and to indicate her own position in this debate:

> Some people believe that using these abbreviations is hindering the writing abilities of students, and others argue that texting is

actually having a positive effect on writing. In fact, it seems likely that texting has no significant effect on student writing.

    MICHAELA CULLINGTON, "Does Texting Affect Writing?"

Another way to open with a debate involves starting with a proposition many people agree with in order to highlight the point(s) on which they ultimately disagree:

> ▸ When it comes to the topic of _____, most of us will readily agree that _____. Where this agreement usually ends, however, is on the question of _____. Whereas some are convinced that _____, others maintain that _____.

The political writer Thomas Frank uses a variation on this move:

> That we are a nation divided is an almost universal lament of this bitter election year. However, the exact property that divides us—elemental though it is said to be—remains a matter of some controversy.
>
>   THOMAS FRANK, "American Psyche"

KEEP WHAT "THEY SAY" IN VIEW

We can't urge you too strongly to keep in mind what "they say" as you move through the rest of your text. After summarizing the ideas you are responding to at the outset, it's very important to continue to keep those ideas in view. Readers won't be able to follow your unfolding response, much less any complications you may offer, unless you keep reminding them what claims you are responding to.

In other words, even when presenting your own claims, you should keep returning to the motivating "they say." The longer and more complicated your text, the greater the chance that readers will forget what ideas originally motivated it—no matter how clearly you lay them out at the beginning. At strategic moments throughout your text, we recommend that you include what we call "return sentences." Here is an example:

> ▶ In conclusion, then, as I suggested earlier, defenders of _____ can't have it both ways. Their assertion that _____ is contradicted by their claim that _____.

We ourselves use such return sentences at every opportunity in this book to remind you of the view of writing that our book questions—that good writing means making true or smart or logical statements about a given subject with little or no reference to what others say about it.

By reminding readers of the ideas you're responding to, return sentences ensure that your text maintains a sense of mission and urgency from start to finish. In short, they frame your argument as a genuine response to others' views rather than just a set of observations about a given subject. The difference is huge. To be responsive to others and the conversation you're entering, you need to start with what others are saying and continue keeping it in the readers' view.

Exercises

1. Following is a list of topics people have debated. Working by yourself or with a partner, compose a "they say" argument

for each of these topics, using any of the templates from this chapter.

Example:
Self-driving vehicles. "Many people think that self-driving cars will make roads safer by reducing accidents caused by unavoidable human errors."

a. Free college tuition at public universities
b. Social media use among teenagers
c. The value of studying the humanities in college
d. Public-funded clean needle exchanges
e. Assigning homework in elementary school

When you finish, read aloud and compare your "they say" arguments with a partner or a small group. Which template moves were more challenging than others to use? Why do you think so?

2. Read the following passage from Kenneth Goldsmith's 2016 *Los Angeles Times* op-ed, "Go Ahead: Waste Time on the Internet."

The notion that the Internet is bad for you seems premised on the idea that the Internet is one thing—a monolith. In reality it's a befuddling mix of the stupid and the sublime, a shattered, contradictory, and fragmented medium. Internet detractors seem to miss this simple fact, which is why so many of their criticisms disintegrate under observation.

The way Internet pundits tell it, you'd think we stare for three hours at clickbait—those articles with hypersensational headlines—the way we once sat down and watched three hours of cartoons on Saturday morning TV. But most of us don't do any one thing on the Internet. Instead, we do many things, some of it frivolous, some of it heavy. Our time spent in front of the computer is a mixed time, a time that reflects our desires—as opposed to the time spent sitting in front of the television where we were fed shows we didn't necessarily enjoy. TV gave us few choices. Many of us truly did feel like we wasted our time—as our parents so often chided us—"rotting away" in front of the TV.

I keep reading—on screens—that in the age of screens we've lost our ability to concentrate, that we've become distracted. But when I look around me and see people riveted to their devices, I notice a great wealth of concentration, focus, and engagement.

a. Where in this passage do you see Goldsmith introducing what others are saying about the internet and the amount of time we spend on screens? What do you notice about the different ways Goldsmith introduces "they say" arguments?

b. Summarize Goldsmith's argument by using the following template for introducing an ongoing debate (p. 26):

In discussions of **how the internet affects people**, one controversial issue has been _____. On one hand, _____ argues _____. On the other hand, _____ contends _____. Others even maintain _____. My own view is _____.

3. Read over something you've written for one of your classes—a paragraph, a short response, or an essay—and then respond to the following questions. You can do this exercise with a partner or by yourself.

a. Where do you introduce what others are saying? Under-line or highlight where you include a "they say." If you can't find a "they say" in your writing, add one using one of the templates from this chapter.

b. How soon in your argument do you introduce these other views? Make sure that you include a "they say" early in your writing (in the first paragraph or two for a short response or essay). If the views you're responding to are buried later in your piece, revise your writing so that they appear earlier.

TWO

"HER POINT IS"

The Art of Summarizing

—◻—

IF IT IS TRUE, as we claim in this book, that to argue persuasively you need to be in dialogue with others, then summarizing others' arguments is central to your arsenal of basic moves. Because writers who make strong claims need to map their claims relative to those of other people, it is important to know how to summarize effectively what those other people say. (We're using the word "summarizing" here to refer to any information from others that you present in your own words, including that which you paraphrase.)

Many writers shy away from summarizing—perhaps because they don't want to take the trouble to go back to the text in question and wrestle with what it says, or because they fear that devoting too much time to other people's ideas will take away from their own. When assigned to write a response to an article, such writers might offer their own views on the article's *topic* while hardly mentioning what the article itself argues or says. At the opposite extreme are those who do nothing *but* summarize. Lacking confidence, perhaps, in their own ideas, these writers so overload their texts with summaries of others' ideas that their own voice gets lost. And since these summaries are not animated by the writers' own interests, they often read like mere lists of things that X thinks or Y says—with no clear focus.

As a general rule, a good summary requires balancing what the original author is saying with the writer's own focus. Generally speaking, a summary must at once be true to what the original author says while also emphasizing those aspects of what the author says that interest you, the writer. Striking this delicate balance can be tricky, since it means facing two ways at once: both outward (toward the author being summarized) and inward (toward yourself). Ultimately, it means being respectful of others but simultaneously structuring how you summarize them in light of your own text's central argument.

ON THE ONE HAND, PUT YOURSELF IN *THEIR* SHOES

To write a really good summary, you must be able to suspend your own beliefs for a time and put yourself in the shoes of someone else. This means playing what the writing theorist Peter Elbow calls the "believing game," in which you try to inhabit the worldview of those whose conversation you are joining—and whom you are perhaps even disagreeing with—and try to see their argument from their perspective. This ability to temporarily suspend one's own convictions is a hallmark of good actors, who must convincingly "become" characters whom in real life they may detest. As a writer, when you play the believing game well, readers should not be able to tell whether you agree or disagree with the ideas you are summarizing.

If, as a writer, you cannot or will not suspend your own beliefs in this way, you are likely to produce summaries that are so obviously biased that they undermine your credibility with readers. Consider the following summary:

> David Zinczenko's article "Don't Blame the Eater" is nothing more than an angry rant in which he accuses the fast-food companies of an evil conspiracy to make people fat. I disagree because these companies have to make money. . . .

If you review what Zinczenko actually says (pp. 199–202), you should immediately see that this summary amounts to an unfair distortion. While Zinczenko does argue that the practices of the fast-food industry have the *effect* of making people fat, his tone is never "angry," and he never goes so far as to suggest that the fast-food industry conspires to make people fat with deliberately evil intent.

Another telltale sign of this writer's failure to give Zinczenko a fair hearing is the hasty way he abandons the summary after only one sentence and rushes on to his own response. So eager is this writer to disagree that he not only caricatures what Zinczenko says but also gives the article a hasty, superficial reading. Granted, there are many writing situations in which, because of matters of proportion, a one- or two-sentence summary is precisely what you want. Indeed, as writing professor Karen Lunsford (whose own research focuses on argument theory) points out, it is standard in the natural and social sciences to summarize the work of others quickly, in one pithy sentence or phrase, as in the following example:

> Several studies (Crackle, 2012; Pop, 2007; Snap, 2006) suggest that these policies are harmless; moreover, other studies (Dick, 2011; Harry, 2007; Tom, 2005) argue that they even have benefits.

But if your assignment is to respond in writing to a single author, like Zinczenko, you will need to tell your readers enough about the argument so they can assess its merits on their own, independent of you.

When summarizing something you've read, be sure to provide a rigorous and thoughtful summary of the author's words, or you may fall prey to what we call "the closest cliché syndrome," in which what gets summarized is not the view the author in question has actually expressed but a familiar cliché that the writer mistakes for the author's view (sometimes because the writer believes it and mistakenly assumes the author must too). So, for example, Martin Luther King Jr.'s passionate defense of civil disobedience in "Letter from Birmingham Jail" might be summarized not as the defense of political protest that it actually is but as a plea for everyone to "just get along." Similarly, Zinczenko's critique of the fast-food industry might be summarized as a call for overweight people to take responsibility for their weight.

Whenever you enter into a conversation with others in your writing, then, it is extremely important that you go back to what those others have said, that you study it very closely, and that you not confuse it with something you already believe. Writers who fail to do this end up essentially conversing with imaginary others who are really only the products of their own biases and preconceptions.

ON THE OTHER HAND, KNOW WHERE *YOU* ARE GOING

Even as writing an effective summary requires you to temporarily adopt the worldview of another person, it does not mean ignoring your own view altogether. Paradoxically, at the same time that summarizing another text requires you to represent fairly what it says, it also requires that your own response exert a quiet influence. A good summary, in other words, has a focus or spin that allows the summary to fit with your own agenda while still being true to the text you are summarizing.

Thus if you are writing in response to the essay by Zinczenko, you should be able to see that an essay on the fast-food industry in general will call for a very different summary than will an essay on parenting, corporate regulation, or warning labels. If you want your essay to encompass all three topics, you'll need to subordinate these three issues to one of Zinczenko's general claims and then make sure this general claim directly sets up your own argument.

For example, suppose you want to argue that it is parents, not fast-food companies, who are to blame for children's obesity. To set up this argument, you will probably want to compose a summary that highlights what Zinczenko says about the fast-food industry *and parents*. Consider this sample:

In his article "Don't Blame the Eater," David Zinczenko blames the fast-food industry for fueling today's so-called obesity epidemic, not only by failing to provide adequate warning labels on its high-calorie foods but also by filling the nutritional void in children's lives left by their overtaxed working parents. With many parents working long hours and unable to supervise what their children eat, Zinczenko claims, children today are easily victimized by the low-cost, calorie-laden foods that the fast-food chains are all too eager to supply. When he was a young boy, for instance, and his single mother was away at work, he ate at Taco Bell, McDonald's, and other chains on a regular basis, and ended up overweight. Zinczenko's hope is that with the new spate of lawsuits against the food industry, other children with working parents will have healthier choices available to them, and that they will not, like him, become obese.

In my view, however, it is the parents, and not the food chains, who are responsible for their children's obesity. While it is true that many of today's parents work long hours, there are still several things that parents can do to guarantee that their children eat healthy foods. . . .

The summary in the first paragraph succeeds because it points in two directions at once—both toward Zinczenko's own text *and* toward the second paragraph, where the writer begins to establish her own argument. The opening sentence gives a sense of Zinczenko's general argument (that the fast-food chains are to blame for obesity), including his two main supporting claims (about warning labels and parents), but it ends with an emphasis on the writer's main concern: parental responsibility. In this way, the summary does justice to Zinczenko's arguments while also setting up the ensuing critique.

This advice—to summarize authors in light of your own agenda—may seem painfully obvious. But writers often summarize a given author on one issue even though their text actually focuses on another. To avoid this problem, you need to make sure that your "they say" and "I say" are well matched. In fact, aligning what they say with what you say is a good thing to work on when revising what you've written.

Often writers who summarize without regard to their own agenda fall prey to what might be called "list summaries," summaries that simply inventory the original author's various points but fail to focus those points around any larger overall claim. If you've ever heard a talk in which the points were connected only by words like "and then," "also," and "in addition," you

THE EFFECT OF A TYPICAL LIST SUMMARY

know how such lists can put listeners to sleep—as shown in the figure above. A typical list summary sounds like this:

> The author says many different things about his subject. *First* he says . . . *Then* he makes the point that . . . *In addition* he says . . . *And then* he writes . . . *Also* he shows that . . . *And then* he says . . .

It may be boring list summaries like this that give summaries in general a bad name and even prompt some instructors to discourage their students from summarizing at all.

Not all lists are bad, however. A list can be an excellent way to organize material—but only if, instead of being a miscellaneous grab bag, it is organized around a larger argument that informs each item listed. Many well-written summaries, for instance, list various points made by an author, sometimes itemizing those points ("First, she argues . . . ," "Second, she argues . . . ," "Third . . ."), and sometimes even itemizing those points in bullet form.

Many well-written arguments are organized in a list format as well. In "The New Liberal Arts," Sanford J. Ungar lists what he sees as seven common misperceptions that discourage college students from majoring in the liberal arts, the first of which begin:

> Misperception No. 1: A liberal-arts degree is a luxury that most families can no longer afford. . . .
> Misperception No. 2: College graduates are finding it harder to get good jobs with liberal-arts degrees. . . .
> Misperception No. 3: The liberal arts are particularly irrelevant for low-income and first-generation college students. They, more than their more-affluent peers, must focus on something more practical and marketable.
>
> SANFORD J. UNGAR, "The New Liberal Arts"

What makes Ungar's list so effective, and makes it stand out in contrast to the type of disorganized lists our cartoon parodies, is that it has a clear, overarching goal: to defend the liberal arts. Had Ungar's article lacked such a unifying agenda and instead been a miscellaneous grab bag, it almost assuredly would have lost its readers, who wouldn't have known what to focus on or what the final "message" or "takeaway" should be.

In conclusion, writing a good summary means not just representing an author's view accurately but doing so in a way that fits what you want to say, the larger point you want to make. On the one hand, it means playing Peter Elbow's believing game and doing justice to the source; if the summary ignores or misrepresents the source, its bias and unfairness will show. On the other hand, even as it does justice to the source, a summary has to have a slant or spin that prepares the way for your own claims. Once a summary enters your text, you should think of it as joint property—reflecting not just the source you are summarizing but your own perspective or take on it as well.

SUMMARIZING SATIRICALLY

Thus far in this chapter we have argued that, as a general rule, good summaries require a balance between what someone else has said and your own interests as a writer. Now, however, we want to address one exception to this rule: the satiric summary, in which writers deliberately give their own spin to someone else's argument in order to reveal a glaring shortcoming in it. Despite our previous comments that well-crafted summaries generally strike a balance between heeding what someone else has said and your own independent interests, the satiric mode can at times be a very effective form of critique because it lets the summarized argument condemn itself without overt editorializing by you, the writer.

One such satiric summary can be found in Sanford J. Ungar's essay "The New Liberal Arts," which we just mentioned. In his discussion of the "misperception," as he sees it, that a liberal arts education is "particularly irrelevant for low-income and first-generation college students," who "must focus on something more practical and marketable," Ungar restates this view as "another way of saying, really, that the rich folks will do the important thinking, and the lower classes will simply carry out their ideas." Few who would dissuade disadvantaged students from the liberal arts would actually state their position in this insulting way. But in taking their position to its logical conclusion, Ungar's satire suggests that this is precisely what their position amounts to.

USE SIGNAL VERBS THAT FIT THE ACTION

In introducing summaries, try to avoid bland formulas like "she says" or "they believe." Though language like this is sometimes serviceable enough, it often fails to reflect accurately what's been said. Using these weaker verbs may lead you to summarize the topic instead of the argument. In some cases, "he says" may even drain the passion out of the ideas you're summarizing.

We suspect that the habit of ignoring the action when summarizing stems from the mistaken belief we mentioned earlier, that writing is about playing it safe and not making waves, a matter of piling up truths and bits of knowledge rather than a dynamic process of doing things to and with other people. People who wouldn't hesitate to *say* "X totally misrepresented," "attacked," or "loved" something when chatting with friends will in their writing often opt for far tamer and even less accurate phrases like "X said."

But the authors you summarize at the college level seldom simply "say" or "discuss" things; they "urge," "emphasize," and "complain about" them. David Zinczenko, for example, doesn't just *say* that fast-food companies contribute to obesity; he *complains* or *protests* that they do; he *challenges*, *chastises*, and *indicts* those companies. The Declaration of Independence doesn't just *talk about* the treatment of the colonies by the British; it *protests against* it. To do justice to the authors you cite, we recommend that when summarizing—

or when introducing a quotation—you use vivid and precise signal verbs as often as possible. Though "he says" or "she believes" will sometimes be the most appropriate language for the occasion, your text will often be more accurate and lively if you tailor your verbs to suit the precise actions you're describing.

TEMPLATES FOR WRITING SUMMARIES

To introduce a summary, use one of the signal verbs above in a template like these:

▸ In her essay X, she advocates <u>a radical revision of the juvenile justice system.</u>

▸ They celebrate the fact that _____.

▸ _____, he admits.

When you tackle the summary itself, think about what else is important beyond the central claim of the argument. For example, what are the conversations the author is responding to? What kinds of evidence does the author's argument rely on? What are the implications of what the author says, both for your own argument and for the larger conversation?

Here is a template that you can use to develop your summary:

▸ X and Y, in their article _____, argue that _____. Their research, which demonstrates that _____, challenges the idea that _____. They use _____ to show _____. X and Y's argument speaks to _____ about the larger issue of _____.

VERBS FOR INTRODUCING
SUMMARIES AND QUOTATIONS

VERBS FOR MAKING A CLAIM

argue	insist
assert	observe
believe	remind us
claim	report
emphasize	suggest

VERBS FOR EXPRESSING AGREEMENT

acknowledge	do not deny
admire	endorse
admit	extol
agree	praise
celebrate	reaffirm
concede	support
corroborate	verify

VERBS FOR QUESTIONING OR DISAGREEING

complain	qualify
complicate	question
contend	refute
contradict	reject
deny	renounce
deplore the tendency to	repudiate

VERBS FOR MAKING RECOMMENDATIONS

advocate	implore
call for	plead
demand	recommend
encourage	urge
exhort	warn

Exercises

1. To get a feel for Peter Elbow's believing game, think about a debate you've heard recently—perhaps in class, at your workplace, or at home. Write a summary of one of the arguments you heard. Then write a summary of another position in the same debate. Give both your summaries to a classmate or two. See if they can tell which position you endorse. If you've succeeded, they won't be able to tell.

2. Read the following passage from "Our Manifesto to Fix America's Gun Laws," an argument written by the editorial board of the *Eagle Eye*, the student newspaper at Marjory Stoneman Douglas High School in Parkland, Florida, in response to the mass shooting that occurred there on February 14, 2018.

We have a unique platform not only as student journalists but also as survivors of a mass shooting. We are firsthand witnesses to the kind of devastation that gross incompetence and political inaction can produce. We cannot stand idly by as the country continues to be infected by a plague of gun violence that seeps into community after community and does irreparable damage to the hearts and minds of the American people....

The changes we propose:

Ban semi-automatic weapons that fire high-velocity rounds
Civilians shouldn't have access to the same weapons that soldiers do. That's a gross misuse of the second amendment …

Ban accessories that simulate automatic weapons
High-capacity magazines played a huge role in the shooting at our school. In only 10 minutes, 17 people were killed, and 17 others were injured. This is unacceptable …

Establish a database of gun sales and universal background checks
We believe that there should be a database recording which guns are sold in the United States, to whom, and of what caliber and capacity they are …

Raise the firearm purchase age to 21
In a few months from now, many of us will be turning 18. We will not be able to drink; we will not be able to rent a car. Most of us will still be living with our parents. We will not be able to purchase a handgun. And yet we will be able to purchase an AR-15 …

a. Do you think the list format is appropriate for this argument? Why or why not?
b. Write a one-sentence summary of this argument, using one of the verbs from the list on pages 43–44.
c. Compare your summary with a classmate's. What are the similarities and differences between them?

3. A student was asked to summarize an essay by writer Ben Adler, "Banning Plastic Bags Is Good for the World, Right?

Not So Fast." Here is the draft: "Ben Adler says that climate change is too big of a problem for any one person to solve."

a. How does this summary fall prey to the "closest cliché syndrome" (p. 35)?
b. What's a better verb to use than "say"? Why do you think so?

THREE

"AS HE HIMSELF PUTS IT"

The Art of Quoting

—⌐—

A KEY PREMISE OF THIS BOOK is that to launch an effective argument you need to write the arguments of others into your text. One of the best ways to do so is not only by summarizing what "they say," as suggested in Chapter 2, but also by quoting their exact words. Quoting someone else's words gives a tremendous amount of credibility to your summary and helps ensure that it is fair and accurate. In a sense, then, quotations function as a kind of proof of evidence, saying to readers: "Look, I'm not just making this up. She makes this claim, and here it is in her exact words."

Yet many writers make a host of mistakes when it comes to quoting, not the least of which is the failure to quote enough in the first place, if at all. Some writers quote too little— perhaps because they don't want to bother going back to the original text and looking up the author's exact words or because they think they can reconstruct the author's ideas from memory. At the opposite extreme are writers who so overquote that they end up with texts that are short on commentary of their own— maybe because they lack confidence in their ability to comment on the quotations, or because they don't fully understand what they've quoted and therefore have trouble explaining what the quotations mean.

But the main problem with quoting arises when writers assume that quotations speak for themselves. Because the meaning of a quotation is obvious to *them*, many writers assume that this meaning will also be obvious to their readers, when often it is not. Writers who make this mistake think that their job is done when they've chosen a quotation and inserted it into their text. They draft an essay, slap in a few quotations, and whammo, they're done. Such writers fail to see that quoting means more than simply enclosing what "they say" in quotation marks. In a way, quotations are orphans: words that have been taken from their original contexts and that need to be integrated into their new textual surroundings. This chapter offers two key ways to produce this sort of integration: (1) by choosing quotations wisely, with an eye to how well they support a particular part of your text, and (2) by surrounding every major quotation with a frame explaining whose words they are, what the quotation means, and how the quotation relates to your own text. The point we want to emphasize is that quoting what "they say" must always be connected with what *you* say.

QUOTE RELEVANT PASSAGES

Before you can select appropriate quotations, you need to have a sense of what you want to do with them—that is, how they will support your text at the particular point where you insert them. Be careful not to select quotations just for the sake of demonstrating that you've read the author's work; you need to make sure they support your own argument.

However, finding relevant quotations is not always easy. In fact, sometimes quotations that were initially relevant to your argument, or to a key point in it, become less so as your text changes during the process of writing and revising. Given the evolving and messy nature of writing, you may sometimes think that you've found the perfect quotation to support your argument, only to discover later on, as your text develops, that your focus has changed and the quotation no longer works. It can be somewhat misleading, then, to speak of finding your thesis and finding relevant quotations as two separate steps, one coming after the other. When you're deeply engaged in the writing and revising process, there is usually a great deal of back-and-forth between your argument and any quotations you select.

FRAME EVERY QUOTATION

Finding relevant quotations is only part of your job; you also need to present them in a way that makes their relevance and meaning clear to your readers. Since quotations do not speak for themselves, you need to build a frame around them in which you do that speaking for them.

Quotations that are inserted into a text without such a frame are sometimes called "dangling" quotations for the way they're left dangling without any explanation. One teacher we've worked with, Steve Benton, calls these "hit-and-run" quotations, likening them to car accidents in which the driver speeds away and avoids taking responsibility for the dent in your fender or the smashed taillights, as in the figure that follows.

DON'T BE A HIT-AND-RUN QUOTER.

What follows is a typical hit-and-run quotation by a student responding to an essay by Deborah Tannen, a linguistics professor and prominent author, who complains that academics value opposition over agreement:

> Deborah Tannen writes about academia. Academics believe "that intellectual inquiry is a metaphorical battle. Following from that is a second assumption that the best way to demonstrate intellectual prowess is to criticize, find fault, and attack."
>
> I agree with Tannen. Another point Tannen makes is that . . .

Since this student fails to introduce the quotation adequately or explain why he finds it worth quoting, readers will have a hard time reconstructing what Tannen argued. First, the student simply gives us the quotation from Tannen without telling us who Tannen is or even indicating that the quoted words are hers. In addition, the student does not explain what he takes Tannen to be saying or how her claims connect with his own. Instead, he simply abandons the quotation in his haste to zoom on to another point.

To adequately frame a quotation, you need to insert it into what we like to call a "quotation sandwich," with the statement introducing it serving as the top slice of bread and the explanation following it serving as the bottom slice. The introductory or lead-in claims should explain who is speaking and set up what the quotation says; the follow-up statements should explain why you consider the quotation to be important and what you take it to say.

TEMPLATES FOR INTRODUCING QUOTATIONS

▸ X states, "<u>Not all steroids should be banned from sports.</u>"

▸ As the prominent philosopher X puts it, "_____."

▸ According to X, "_____."

▸ X himself writes, "_____."

▸ In her book, _____, X maintains that "_____."

▸ Writing in the journal _____, X complains that "_____."

▸ In X's view, "_____."

▸ X agrees when she writes, "_____."

▸ X disagrees when he writes, "_____."

▸ X complicates matters further when she writes, "_____."

TEMPLATES FOR EXPLAINING QUOTATIONS

The one piece of advice about quoting that our students say they find most helpful is to get in the habit of following every major quotation by explaining what it means, using a template like one of the ones below.

▸ **Basically, X is warning <u>that the proposed solution will only make the problem worse</u>.**

▸ **In other words, X believes _____ .**

▸ **In making this comment, X urges us to _____ .**

▸ **X is corroborating the age-old adage that _____ .**

▸ **X's point is that _____ .**

▸ **The essence of X's argument is that _____ .**

When offering such explanations, it is important to use language that accurately reflects the spirit of the quoted passage. It is often serviceable enough in introducing a quotation to write "X states" or "X asserts," but in most cases you can add precision to your writing by introducing the quotation in more vivid terms. Since, in the example above, Tannen is clearly alarmed by the culture of "attack" that she describes, it would be more accurate to use language that reflects that alarm: "Tannen is alarmed that," "Tannen is disturbed by," "Tannen deplores," or (in our own formulation here) "Tannen complains."

See pp. 43–44 for a list of action verbs for summarizing what other say.

Consider, for example, how the earlier passage on Tannen might be revised using some of these moves:

Deborah Tannen, a prominent linguistics professor, complains that academia is too combative. Rather than really listening to others, Tannen insists, academics habitually try to prove one another wrong. As Tannen herself puts it, "We are all driven by our ideological assumption that intellectual inquiry is a metaphorical battle," that "the best way to demonstrate intellectual prowess is to criticize, find fault, and attack." In short, Tannen objects that academic communication tends to be a competition for supremacy in which loftier values like truth and consensus get lost.

Tannen's observations ring true to me because I have often felt that the academic pieces I read for class are negative and focus on proving another theorist wrong rather than stating a truth. . . .

This revision works, we think, because it frames or nests Tannen's words, integrating them and offering guidance about how they should be read. Instead of launching directly into the quoted words, as the previous draft had done, this revised version identifies Tannen ("a prominent linguistics professor") and clearly indicates that the quoted words are hers ("as Tannen herself puts it"). And instead of being presented without explanation as it was before, the quotation is now presented as an illustration of Tannen's point that, as the student helpfully puts it, "academics habitually try to prove one another wrong" and compete "for supremacy." In this way, the student explains the quotation while restating it in his own words, thereby making it clear that the quotation is being used purposefully instead of having been stuck in simply to pad the essay or the works-cited list.

BLEND THE AUTHOR'S WORDS
WITH YOUR OWN

This new framing material also works well because it accurately represents Tannen's words while giving those words the student's own spin. Instead of simply repeating Tannen word for word, the follow-up sentences echo just enough of her language

while still moving the discussion in the student's own direction. Tannen's "battle," "criticize," "find fault," and "attack," for
instance, get translated by the student into claims about how
"combative" Tannen thinks academics are and how she thinks
they "habitually try to prove one another wrong." In this way,
the framing creates a kind of hybrid mix of Tannen's words and
those of the writer.

CAN YOU OVERANALYZE A QUOTATION?

But is it possible to overexplain a quotation? And how do you
know when you've explained a quotation thoroughly enough?
After all, not all quotations require the same amount of explanatory framing, and there are no hard-and-fast rules for knowing
how much explanation any quotation needs. As a general rule,
the most explanatory framing is needed for quotations that may
be hard for readers to process: quotations that are long and
complex, that are filled with details or jargon, or that contain
hidden complexities.

And yet, though the particular situation usually dictates
when and how much to explain a quotation, we will still offer
one piece of advice: when in doubt, go for it. It is better to
risk being overly explicit about what you take a quotation to
mean than to leave the quotation dangling and your readers in
doubt. Indeed, we encourage you to provide such explanatory
framing even when writing to an audience that you know to be
familiar with the author being quoted and able to interpret your
quotations on their own. Even in such cases, readers need to see
how *you* interpret the quotation, since words—especially those
of controversial figures—can be interpreted in various ways
and used to support different, sometimes opposing, agendas.
Your readers need to see what you make of the material you've

quoted, if only to be sure that your reading of the material and theirs are on the same page.

HOW *NOT* TO INTRODUCE QUOTATIONS

We want to conclude this chapter by surveying some ways *not* to introduce quotations. Although some writers do so, you should not introduce quotations by saying something like "Orwell asserts an idea that" or "A quote by Shakespeare says." Introductory phrases like these are both redundant and misleading. In the first example, you could write either "Orwell asserts that" or "Orwell's assertion is that" rather than redundantly combining the two. The second example misleads readers, since it is the writer who is doing the quoting, not Shakespeare (as "a quote by Shakespeare" implies).

The templates in this book will help you avoid such mistakes. Once you have mastered templates like "as X puts it" or "in X's own words," you probably won't even have to think about them—and will be free to focus on the challenging ideas that templates help you frame.

Exercises

1. Find an essay that is posted on **theysayiblog.com**. Read the essay, and look closely to see how the writer has integrated quotations in the argument. How has the writer introduced the quotations in the argument? What, if anything, has the writer said to explain the quotations? How has the writer tied the quotations to the essay? Based on what you read in this chapter about how to sandwich quotations, what revisions would you suggest?

2. Below is a passage from Christine Michel Carter's 2019 *Harper's Bazaar* essay, "How Feminism Is Stifling Our Sons." In this essay, Carter points out how gender stereotypes are harmful to both girls and boys, and she argues that popular media needs to present more positive models of masculinity. Read this passage and choose a phrase or sentence to quote as a "they say" for an argument of your own. Use the templates from this chapter to sandwich this quote: introduce the quote, explain what it means, and connect it to your own ideas. Your entire response (the introduction, quote, explanation, and connection to your ideas) should be three or four sentences long.

We've committed so strongly to teaching girls they're equal to boys that we've forgotten to extend the message to the boys themselves in a healthy, inclusive way. Along with our focus on feminism, we need to embrace a new men's movement too—one that pays attention to the young boys who are discovering their manhood against a backdrop of hashtags and equality campaigns that tend to either overlook or vilify where masculinity fits in.

3. Read over something you've written for one of your classes. Have you quoted any sources? If so, highlight or underline all the quotations. How have you integrated each quotation into your own text? How have you introduced it? explained what it means? indicated how it relates to *your* text? If you haven't done all these things, revise your text to do so using the list of verbs for introducing summaries and quotations (pp. 43–44) and the templates for introducing quotations (p. 51) and explaining quotations (p. 51). If you haven't written anything with quotations, revise an academic text you've written so that it uses quotations.

FOUR

"YES / NO / OK, BUT"

Three Ways to Respond

THE FIRST THREE CHAPTERS of this book discuss the "they say" stage of writing, in which you devote your attention to the views of some other person or group. In this chapter, we move to the "I say" stage, in which you offer your own argument as a response to what "they" have said.

Moving to the "I say" stage can be daunting in academia, where it often may seem that you need to be an expert in a field to have an argument at all. Many students have told us that they have trouble entering some of the high-powered conversations that take place in college or graduate school because they do not know enough about the topic at hand or because, they say, they simply are not "smart enough." Yet often these same students, when given a chance to study in depth the contribution that some scholar has made in a given field, will turn around and say things like "I can see where she is coming from, how she makes her case by building on what other scholars have said. Perhaps if I had studied the situation longer, *I* could have come up with a similar argument." What these students come to realize is that good arguments are based not on knowledge that only a special class of experts has access to but on everyday habits of mind that can be isolated, identified, and used by almost anyone. Though there's certainly no substitute for expertise and for knowing as much as possible about one's topic, the arguments that finally win the day are built, as the title of this chapter suggests, on some very basic rhetorical patterns that most of us use on a daily basis.

There are a great many ways to respond to others' ideas, but this chapter concentrates on the three most common and recognizable ways: agreeing, disagreeing, or some combination of both. Although each way of responding is open to endless variation, we focus on these three because readers come to any text needing to learn fairly quickly where the writer stands, and they do this by placing the writer on a mental map consisting of a few familiar options: the writer agrees with those being responded to, disagrees with them, or presents some combination of both agreeing and disagreeing.

When writers take too long to declare their position relative to views they've summarized or quoted, readers get frustrated, wondering, "Is this guy agreeing or disagreeing? Is he *for* what this other person has said, *against* it, or what?" For this reason, this chapter's advice applies to reading as well as to writing. Especially with difficult texts, you need not only to find the position the writer is responding to—the "they say"—but also to determine whether the writer is agreeing with it, challenging it, or some mixture of the two.

ONLY *THREE* WAYS TO RESPOND?

Perhaps you'll worry that fitting your own response into one of these three categories will force you to oversimplify your argument or lessen its complexity, subtlety, or originality. This is certainly a serious concern for academics who are rightly skeptical of writing that is simplistic and reductive. We would argue, however, that the more complex and subtle your argument is, and the more it departs from the conventional ways people think, the more your readers will need to be able to place it on their mental map in order to process the complex details you present. That is, the complexity, subtlety, and originality of your response are more likely to stand out and be noticed if readers have a baseline sense of where you stand relative to any ideas you've cited. As you move through this chapter, we hope you'll agree that the forms of agreeing, disagreeing, and both agreeing and disagreeing that we discuss, far from being simplistic or one-dimensional, are able to accommodate a high degree of creative, complex thought.

It is always a good tactic to begin your response not by launching directly into a mass of details but by stating clearly whether you agree, disagree, or both, using a direct, no-nonsense formula such as: "I agree," "I disagree," or "I am of two minds. I agree that _____, but I cannot agree that _____." Once you have offered one of these straightforward statements (or one of the many variations discussed below), readers will have a strong grasp of your position and then be able to appreciate the complications you go on to offer as your response unfolds.

See p. 21 for suggestions on previewing where you stand.

Still, you may object that these three basic ways of responding don't cover all the options—that they ignore interpretive or analytical responses, for example. In other words, you might think that when you interpret a literary work, you don't necessarily agree or disagree with anything but simply explain the work's meaning, style, or structure. Many essays about literature and the arts, it might be said, take this form—they interpret a work's meaning, thus rendering matters of agreeing or disagreeing irrelevant.

We would argue, however, that the most interesting inter-pretations tend to be those that agree, disagree, or both—that instead of being offered solo, the best interpretations take strong stands relative to other interpretations. In fact, there would be no reason to offer an interpretation of a work of literature or art unless you were responding to the interpretations or possible interpretations of others. Even when you point out features or qualities of an artistic work that others have not noticed, you are implicitly disagreeing with what those interpreters have said by pointing out that they missed or overlooked something that, in your view, is important. In any effective interpretation, then, you need not only to state what you yourself take the work of art to mean but also to do so relative to the interpretations of other readers—be they professional scholars, teachers, class-mates, or even hypothetical readers (as in, "Although some readers might think that this poem is about _____, it is in fact about _____ ").

DISAGREE—AND EXPLAIN WHY

Disagreeing may seem like one of the simpler moves a writer can make, and it is often the first thing people associate with critical thinking. Disagreeing can also be the easiest way to generate an essay: find something you can disagree with in what has been said or might be said about your topic, summarize it, and argue with it. But disagreement in fact poses hidden challenges. You need to do more than simply assert that you disagree with a par-ticular view; you also have to offer persuasive reasons *why* you disagree. After all, disagreeing means more than adding "not" to what someone else has said, more than just saying, "Although they say women's rights are improving, I say women's rights are *not* improving." Such a response merely contradicts the view it responds to and fails to add anything interesting or new. To turn it into an argument, you need to give reasons to support what you say: because another's argument fails to take relevant factors into account; because it is based on faulty or incomplete evidence; because it rests on questionable assumptions; or because it uses flawed logic, is contradictory, or overlooks what you take to be the real issue. To move the conversation forward (and, indeed, to justify your very act of writing), you need to demonstrate that you have something to contribute.

You can even disagree by making what we call the "duh" move, in which you disagree not with the position itself but with the assumption that it is a new or stunning revelation. Here is an example of such a move, used to open an essay on the state of American schools:

> According to a recent report by some researchers at Stanford University, high school students with college aspirations "often lack crucial information on applying to college and on succeeding academically once they get there."
>
> Well, duh. . . . It shouldn't take a Stanford research team to tell us that when it comes to "succeeding academically," many students don't have a clue.
>
> GERALD GRAFF, "Trickle-Down Obfuscation"

Like all the other moves discussed in this book, the "duh" move can be tailored to meet the needs of almost any writing situation. If you find the expression "duh" too brash to use with your intended audience, you can always dispense with the term itself and write something like "It is true that _____; but we already knew that."

TEMPLATES FOR DISAGREEING, WITH REASONS

▸ X is mistaken because she overlooks <u>recent fossil discoveries in the South</u>.

▸ X's claim that _____ rests on the questionable assumption that _____.

▸ I disagree with X's view that _____ because, as recent research has shown, _____.

▸ X contradicts herself/can't have it both ways. On the one hand, she argues _____. On the other hand, she also says _____.

▸ By focusing on _____, X overlooks the deeper problem of _____.

You can also disagree by making what we call the "twist it" move, in which you agree with the evidence that someone else has presented but show through a twist of logic that this evidence actually supports your own, contrary position. For example:

> X argues for stricter gun control legislation, saying that the crime rate is on the rise and that we need to restrict the circulation of guns. I agree that the crime rate is on the rise, but that's precisely why I oppose stricter gun control legislation. We need to own guns to protect ourselves against criminals.

In this example of the "twist it" move, the writer agrees with X's claim that the crime rate is on the rise but then argues that this increasing crime rate is in fact a valid reason for *opposing* gun control legislation.

At times you might be reluctant to express disagreement, for any number of reasons—not wanting to be unpleasant, to hurt someone's feelings, or to make yourself vulnerable to being dis-agreed with in return. One of these reasons may in fact explain why the conference speaker we described at the start of Chapter 1 avoided mentioning the disagreement he had with other scholars until he was provoked to do so in the discussion that followed his talk.

As much as we understand such fears of conflict and have experienced them ourselves, we nevertheless believe it is better to state our disagreements in frank yet considerate ways than to deny them. After all, suppressing disagreements doesn't make them go away; it only pushes them underground, where they can fester in private unchecked. Nevertheless, disagreements do not need to take the form of personal put-downs. Further-more, there is usually no reason to take issue with *every* aspect of someone else's views. You can single out for criticism only those aspects of what someone else has said that are troubling and then agree with the rest—although such an approach, as we will see later in this chapter, leads to the somewhat more complicated terrain of both agreeing and disagreeing at the same time.

AGREE—BUT WITH A DIFFERENCE

Like disagreeing, agreeing is less simple than it may appear. Just as you need to avoid simply contradicting views you disagree with, you also need to do more than simply echo views you agree with. Even as you're agreeing, it's important to bring something new and fresh to the table, adding something that makes you a valuable participant in the conversation.

There are many moves that enable you to contribute something of your own to a conversation even as you agree with what someone else has said. You may point out some unnoticed evidence or line of reasoning that supports X's claims that X herself hadn't mentioned. You may cite some corroborating personal experience or a situation not mentioned by X that her views help readers understand. If X's views are particularly challenging or esoteric, what you bring to the table could be an accessible translation—an explanation for readers not already in the know. In other words, your text can usefully contribute to the conversation simply by pointing out unnoticed implications or explaining something that needs to be better understood.

Whatever mode of agreement you choose, the important thing is to open up some difference or contrast between your position and the one you're agreeing with rather than simply parroting what it says.

TEMPLATES FOR AGREEING

▸ I agree that <u>diversity in the student body is educationally valuable</u> because my experience <u>at Central University</u> confirms it.

▸ X is surely right about _____ because, as she may not be aware, recent studies have shown that _____.

▸ X's theory of _____ is extremely useful because it sheds light on the difficult problem of _____.

▸ Those unfamiliar with this school of thought may be interested to know that it basically boils down to _____.

Some writers avoid the practice of agreeing almost as much as others avoid disagreeing. In a culture like America's, which prizes originality, independence, and competitive individualism, writers sometimes don't like to admit that anyone else has made the same point, seemingly beating them to the punch. In our view, however, as long as you can support a position taken by someone else without merely restating what was said, there is no reason to worry about being "unoriginal." Indeed, there is good reason to rejoice when you agree with others since those others can lend credibility to your argument. While you don't want to present yourself as a mere copycat of someone else's views, you also need to avoid sounding like a lone voice in the wilderness.

But do be aware that whenever you agree with one person's view, you are likely disagreeing with someone else's. It is hard to align yourself with one position without at least implicitly positioning yourself against others. The psychologist Carol Gilligan does just that in an essay in which she agrees with scientists who argue that the human brain is "hard-wired" for cooperation but in so doing aligns herself against anyone who believes that the brain is wired for selfishness and competition:

These findings join a growing convergence of evidence across the human sciences leading to a revolutionary shift in consciousness. . . . If cooperation, typically associated with altruism and self-sacrifice, sets off the same signals of delight as pleasures commonly associated with hedonism and self-indulgence; if the opposition between selfish and selfless, self vs. relationship biologically makes no sense, then a new paradigm is necessary to reframe the very terms of the conversation.

CAROL GILLIGAN, "Sisterhood Is Pleasurable:
A Quiet Revolution in Psychology"

In agreeing with some scientists that "the opposition between selfish and selfless . . . makes no sense," Gilligan implicitly disagrees with anyone who thinks the opposition *does* make sense. Basically, what Gilligan says could be boiled down to a template:

▸ I agree that _____, a point that needs emphasizing since so many people still believe _____.

▸ If group X is right that _____, as I think they are, then we need to reassess the popular assumption that _____.

What such templates allow you to do, then, is to agree with one view while challenging another—a move that leads into the domain of agreeing and disagreeing simultaneously.

AGREE AND DISAGREE SIMULTANEOUSLY

This last option is often our favorite way of responding. One thing we particularly like about agreeing and disagreeing simultaneously is that it helps us get beyond the kind of "is too" / "is not" exchanges that often characterize the disputes of young children and the more polarized shouting matches of talk radio and TV.

Sanford J. Ungar makes precisely this move in his essay "The New Liberal Arts" when, in critiquing seven common "misperceptions" of liberal arts education, he concedes that several contain a grain of truth. For example, after summarizing "Misperception No. 2," that "college graduates are finding it harder to get good jobs with liberal-arts degrees," that few employers want to hire those with an "irrelevant major like philosophy or French," Ungar writes: "Yes, recent graduates have had difficulty in the job market. . . ." But then, after making this concession, Ungar insists that this difficulty affects graduates in all fields, not just those from the liberal arts. In this way, we think, Ungar paradoxically strengthens his case. By admitting that the opposing argument has a point, Ungar bolsters his credibility, presenting himself as a writer willing to acknowledge facts as they present themselves rather than one determined to cheerlead only for his own side.

TEMPLATES FOR AGREEING AND DISAGREEING SIMULTANEOUSLY

"Yes and no." "Yes, but . . ." "Although I agree up to a point, I still insist . . ." These are just some of the ways you can make your argument complicated and nuanced while maintaining a clear, reader-friendly framework. The parallel structure—"yes and no"; "on the one hand I agree, on the other I disagree" enables readers to place your argument on that map of positions we spoke of earlier in this chapter while still keeping your argument sufficiently complex.

Charles Murray's essay "Are Too Many People Going to College?" contains a good example of the "yes and no" move when, at the outset of his essay, Murray responds to what he sees as the prevailing wisdom about the liberal arts and college:

> We should not restrict the availability of a liberal education to a rarefied intellectual elite. More people should be going to college, not fewer.
>
> Yes and no. More people should be getting the basics of a liberal education. But for most students, the places to provide those basics are elementary and middle school.
>
> CHARLES MURRAY, "Are Too Many People Going to College?"

In other words, Murray is saying yes to more liberal arts but not to more college.

Another aspect we like about this "yes and no," "agree and disagree" option is that it can be tipped subtly toward agreement or disagreement, depending on where you lay your stress. If you want to emphasize the disagreement end of the spectrum, you would use a template like the one below:

▸ **Although I agree with X up to a point, I cannot accept his over-riding assumption that <u>religion is no longer a major force today</u>.**

Conversely, if you want to stress your agreement more than your disagreement, you would use a template like this one:

▸ **Although I disagree with much that X says, I fully endorse his final conclusion that _____ .**

The first template above might be called a "yes, but . . ." move, the second a "no, but . . ." move. Other versions include the following:

▸ **Though I concede that _____ , I still insist that _____ .**

▸ **X is right that _____ , but she seems on more dubious ground when she claims that _____ .**

▸ **While X is probably wrong when she claims that _____ , she is right that _____ .**

▸ **Whereas X provides ample evidence that _____ , Y and Z's research on _____ and _____ convinces me that _____ instead.**

Another classic way to agree and disagree at the same time is to make what we call an "I'm of two minds" or a "mixed feelings" move:

▸ I'm of two minds about X's claim that _____. On the one hand, I agree that _____. On the other hand, I'm not sure if _____.

▸ My feelings on the issue are mixed. I do support X's position that _____, but I find Y's argument about _____ and Z's research on _____ to be equally persuasive.

This move can be especially useful if you are responding to new or particularly challenging work and are as yet unsure where you stand. It also lends itself well to the kind of speculative investigation in which you weigh a position's pros and cons rather than come out decisively either for or against. But again, as we suggested earlier, whether you are agreeing, disagreeing, or both agreeing and disagreeing, you need to be as clear as possible, and making a frank statement that you are ambivalent is one way to be clear.

IS BEING UNDECIDED OK?

Nevertheless, writers often have as many concerns about expressing ambivalence as they do about expressing disagreement or agreement. Some worry that by expressing ambivalence they will come across as evasive, wishy-washy, or unsure of themselves. Others worry that their ambivalence will end up confusing readers who require decisive, clear-cut conclusions.

The truth is that in some cases these worries are legitimate. At times ambivalence can frustrate readers, leaving them with the feeling that you failed in your obligation to offer the guidance they expect from writers. At other times, however, acknowledging that a clear-cut resolution of an issue is impossible can demonstrate your sophistication as a writer. In an academic culture that values complex thought, forthrightly declaring that you have mixed feelings can be impressive, especially after having ruled out the one-dimensional positions on your issue taken by others in the conversation. Ultimately, then, how ambivalent you end up being comes down to a judgment call based on different readers' responses to your drafts, on your knowledge of your audience, and on the challenges of your particular argument and situation.

Exercises

1. Below is a passage from Chris Nowinski's 2019 *Vox* essay, "Youth Tackle Football Will Be Considered Unthinkable 50 Years from Now." In this essay, Nowinski (director of the Concussion Legacy Foundation and former college football player) argues that tackle football should be banned for kids under fourteen years old.

   a. Read the passage. Then respond to Nowinski's argument using one of the templates from this chapter: one that responds by agreeing and one that responds by disagreeing.
   b. Work with a partner to compare your responses. Which response do you think is the strongest, and why?

   The science is clearer than ever: Exposure data shows children as young as 9 are getting hit in the head more than 500 times in one season of youth tackle football. That should not feel normal to us. Think of the last time, outside of sports, you allowed your child to get hit hard in the head 25 times in a day. Better yet, when was the last time you were hit hard in the head?

Scientists are now beginning to understand the long-term consequences of all those hits. Chronic traumatic encephalopathy, or CTE, is a degenerative brain disease that was once thought to be confined only to "punch-drunk" boxers. Yet in the past decade, Boston University and Veterans Affairs researchers have diagnosed CTE in American football, soccer, ice hockey, and rugby players, along with other collision sport athletes....

Our society is committed to protecting children—that's why we ban smoking, remove children from homes with lead paint, and force parents to put their children in car seats. We should also protect children from unnecessary brain damage in youth sports.

2. Working together with a partner, write a response where you agree and disagree simultaneously—the "OK, but" move. You can write your response using the Nowinski passage above as your "they say," or you can respond to a reading posted on **theysayiblog.com**. Use the templates from this chapter to compose your response. Decide if you want to emphasize disagreement or agreement, and revise your response accordingly.

3. Read an essay that is posted on **theysayiblog.com**.

    a. Is the writer agreeing, disagreeing, or both? Where do you see the writer doing this? Point to a particular sentence or passage.

    b. How connected is the writer's argument ("I say") to the larger conversation ("they say")?

    c. If the writer is disagreeing, how considerate is the writer to the views being rebutted? Why do you think being considerate while disagreeing is important in academic writing?

FIVE

"AND YET"

Distinguishing What You Say from What They Say

—▢—

IF GOOD ACADEMIC WRITING involves putting yourself into dialogue with others, it is extremely important that readers be able to tell at every point when you are expressing your own view and when you are stating someone else's. This chapter takes up the problem of moving from what *they* say to what *you* say without confusing readers about who is saying what.

DETERMINE WHO IS SAYING WHAT IN THE TEXTS YOU READ

Before examining how to signal who is saying what in your own writing, let's look at how to recognize such signals when they appear in the texts you read—an especially important skill when it comes to the challenging works assigned in school. Frequently, when students have trouble understanding difficult texts, it is not just because the texts contain unfamiliar ideas or words but also because the texts rely on subtle clues to let readers know when a particular view should be attributed to the writer or to someone else. Especially with texts that present a true dialogue of perspectives, readers need to be alert to the often subtle markers that indicate whose voice the writer is speaking in.

Consider how the social critic and educator Gregory Mantsios uses these "voice markers," as they might be called, to distinguish the different perspectives in his essay on America's class inequalities:

> "We are all middle-class," or so it would seem. Our national consciousness, as shaped in large part by the media and our political leadership, provides us with a picture of ourselves as a nation of prosperity and opportunity with an ever expanding middle-class life-style. As a result, our class differences are muted and our collective character is homogenized.
>
> Yet class divisions are real and arguably the most significant factor in determining both our very being in the world and the nature of the society we live in.
>
> GREGORY MANTSIOS, "Rewards and Opportunities: The Politics and Economics of Class in the U.S."

Although Mantsios makes it look easy, he is actually making several sophisticated rhetorical moves here that help him distinguish the common view he opposes from his own position.

In the opening sentence, for instance, the phrase "or so it would seem" shows that Mantsios does not necessarily agree with the view he is describing, since writers normally don't present views they themselves hold as ones that only "seem" to be true. Mantsios also places this opening view in quotation marks to signal that it is not his own. He then further distances himself from the belief being summarized in the opening paragraph by attributing it to "our national consciousness, as shaped in large part by the media and our political leadership," and then further attributing to this "consciousness" a negative, undesirable "result": one in which "our class differences" get "muted" and "our collective character" gets "homogenized," stripped of its diversity and distinctness. Hence, even before Mantsios has declared his own position in the second paragraph, readers can get a pretty solid sense of where he probably stands.

Furthermore, the second paragraph opens with the word "Yet," indicating that Mantsios is now shifting to his own view (as opposed to the common view he has thus far been describing). Even the parallelism he sets up between the first and second paragraphs—between the first paragraph's claim that class differences do not exist and the second paragraph's claim that they do—helps throw into sharp relief the differences between the two voices. Finally, Mantsios's use of a direct, authoritative, declarative tone in the second paragraph also suggests a switch in voice. Although he does not use the words "I say" or "I argue," he clearly identifies the view he holds by presenting it not as one that merely *seems* to be true or that *others tell us* is true but as a view that *is* true or, as Mantsios puts it, "real."

Paying attention to these voice markers is an important aspect of reading comprehension. Readers who fail to notice these markers often take an author's summaries of what someone else believes to be an expression of what the author himself or herself believes. Thus, when we teach Mantsios's essay, some students invariably come away thinking that the statement "we are all middle-class" is Mantsios's own position rather than the perspective he is opposing, failing to see that in writing these words Mantsios acts as a kind of ventriloquist, mimicking what others say rather than directly expressing what he himself is thinking.

To see how important such voice markers are, consider what the Mantsios passage looks like if we remove them:

> We are all middle-class. . . . We are a nation of prosperity and opportunity with an ever expanding middle-class life-style. . . .
>
> Class divisions are real and arguably the most significant factor in determining both our very being in the world and the nature of the society we live in.

In contrast to the careful delineation between voices in Mantsios's original text, this unmarked version leaves it hard to tell where his voice begins and the voices of others end. With the markers removed, readers cannot tell that "We are all middle-class" represents a view the author opposes and that "Class divisions are real" represents what the author himself believes. Indeed, without the markers, especially the "yet," readers might well miss the fact that the second paragraph's claim that "Class divisions are real" contradicts the first paragraph's claim that "We are all middle-class."

TEMPLATES FOR SIGNALING WHO IS SAYING WHAT IN YOUR OWN WRITING

To avoid confusion in your own writing, make sure that at every point your readers can clearly tell who is saying what. To do so, you can use as voice-identifying devices many of the templates presented in previous chapters.

▸ Although X makes the best possible case for <u>universal, government-funded health care</u>, I <u>am not persuaded</u>.

▸ My view, however, contrary to what X has argued, is that _____.

▸ Adding to X's argument, I would point out that _____.

▸ According to both X and Y, _____.

▸ Politicians, X argues, should _____.

▸ Most athletes will tell you that _____.

BUT I'VE BEEN TOLD NOT TO USE "I"

Notice that the first three templates above use the first-person, as do many of the templates in this book, thereby contradicting the common advice about avoiding the first person in academic writing. Although you may have been told that the "I" word encourages subjective, self-indulgent opinions rather than well-grounded arguments, we believe that texts using "I" can be just as well supported—or just as self-indulgent—as those that don't. For us, well-supported arguments are grounded in persuasive reasons and evidence, not in the use or nonuse of any particular pronouns.

Furthermore, if you consistently avoid the first person in your writing, you will probably have trouble making the key move addressed in this chapter: differentiating your views from those of others or even offering your own views in the first place. But don't just take our word for it. See for yourself how freely the first person is used by the writers quoted in this book and by the writers assigned in your courses.

Nevertheless, certain occasions may warrant avoiding the first person and writing, for example, that "she is correct" instead of "I think that she is correct." Since it can be monotonous to read an unvarying series of "I" statements ("I believe . . . I think . . . I argue . . . "), it is a good idea to mix first-person assertions with ones like the following:

▸ **X is right that** <u>certain common patterns can be found in the communities</u>.

▸ **The evidence shows that _____ .**

▸ **X's assertion that _____ does not fit the facts.**

▸ **Anyone familiar with _____ should agree that _____ .**

One might even follow Mantsios's lead, as in the following template:

▸ **Yet _____ are real, and are arguably the most significant factor in _____ .**

On the whole, however, academic writing today, even in the sciences and social sciences, makes use of the first person fairly liberally.

ANOTHER TRICK FOR IDENTIFYING WHO IS SPEAKING

To alert readers about whose perspective you are describing at any given moment, you don't always have to use overt voice markers like "X argues" followed by a summary of the argument. Instead, you can alert readers about whose voice you're speaking in by *embedding* a reference to X's argument in your own sentences. Hence, instead of writing

> Liberals believe that cultural differences need to be respected. I have a problem with this view, however.

you might write

> I have a problem with *what liberals call cultural differences*.

> There is a major problem with the liberal doctrine of *so-called cultural differences*.

You can also embed references to something you yourself have previously said. So instead of writing two cumbersome sentences like

> Earlier in this chapter we coined the term "voice markers." We would argue that such markers are extremely important for reading comprehension.

you might write

> We would argue that "voice markers," as we identified them earlier, are extremely important for reading comprehension.

Embedded references like these allow you to economize your train of thought and refer to other perspectives without any major interruption.

TEMPLATES FOR EMBEDDING VOICE MARKERS

▸ **X overlooks what I consider an important point about** <u>cultural differences</u>**.**

▸ **My own view is that what X insists is a _____ is in fact a _____ .**

▸ **I wholeheartedly endorse what X calls _____ .**

▸ **These conclusions, which X discusses in _____ , add weight to the argument that _____ .**

When writers fail to use voice-marking devices like the ones discussed in this chapter, their summaries of others' views tend to become confused with their own ideas—and vice versa. When readers cannot tell if you are summarizing your own views or endorsing a certain phrase or label, they have to stop and think: "Wait. I thought the author disagreed with this claim. Has she actually been asserting this view all along?" or "Hmmm, I thought she would have objected to this kind of phrase. Is she actually endorsing it?" Getting in the habit of using voice markers will keep you from confusing your readers and help alert you to similar markers in the challenging texts you read.

Exercises

1. Look at the short passages below. Right now, it's unclear who is saying what. Use the templates from this chapter to revise these passages so they include voice markers that allow a reader to distinguish between the two voices.

Example:
Students who major in preprofessional programs like accounting or medical technology are trained for in-demand careers. Students who study the humanities learn valuable skills that prepare them for many jobs, including some that may not even exist today.

Revision:
<u>Well-meaning advisers</u> argue that students who major in preprofessional programs like accounting or medical technologies are trained for in-demand careers. <u>However, they overlook what I consider an important point</u>, that studying the humanities gives students valuable skills that prepare them for many jobs, including some that may not even exist today.

a. Fracking, or drilling deeply into the ground to reach natural gas, can contaminate drinking water in communities near the drilling operations. Natural gas is a cleaner form of energy than coal, and fracking is a cost-effective way to access the reserves of natural gas in the United States.

b. Charter schools give families in struggling school districts options to choose which schools their kids will attend. Charter schools, controlled by private individuals or corporations, divert essential funds away from the public education systems that serve all children.

2. To see how one writer signals when she is asserting her own views and when she is summarizing those of someone else, read the following passage from Anne-Marie Slaughter's essay "Why Women Still Can't Have It All." As you do so, identify those spots where Slaughter refers to the views of others and the signal phrases she uses to distinguish her views from theirs.

Seeking out a more balanced life is not a women's issue; balance would be better for us all. Bronnie Ware, an Australian blogger who worked for years in palliative care and is the author of the 2011 book *The Top Five Regrets of the Dying*, writes that the regret she heard most often was "I wish I'd had the courage to live a life true to myself, not the life others expected of me." The second-most common regret was "I wish I didn't work so hard." She writes: "This came from every male patient that I nursed. They missed their children's youth and their partner's companionship."

Juliette Kayyem, who several years ago left the Department of Homeland Security soon after her husband, David Barron, left a high position in the Justice Department, says their joint decision to leave Washington and return to Boston sprang from their desire to work on the "happiness project," meaning quality time with their three children. (She borrowed the term from her friend Gretchen Rubin, who wrote a best-selling book and now runs a blog with that name.)

It's time to embrace a national happiness project. As a daughter of Charlottesville, Virginia, the home of Thomas Jefferson and the university he founded, I grew up with the Declaration of Independence in my blood. Last I checked, he did not declare American independence in the name of life, liberty, and professional success. Let us rediscover the pursuit of happiness, and let us start at home.

3. Read over a draft of your own writing—a paragraph or an essay—and then respond to the following questions. How do you distinguish your own voice from the argument(s) you are summarizing, quoting, and responding to? How could you use a template from this chapter to clarify the distinction between *your* argument and *their* argument(s)? Where could you use first-person voice markers or embedded references in your writing?

SIX

"SKEPTICS MAY OBJECT"

Planting a Naysayer in Your Text

THE WRITER Jane Tompkins describes a pattern that repeats itself whenever she writes a book or an article. For the first couple of weeks when she sits down to write, things go relatively well. But then in the middle of the night, several weeks into the writing process, she'll wake up in a cold sweat, suddenly realizing that she has overlooked some major criticism that readers will surely make against her ideas. Her first thought, invariably, is that she will have to give up on the project or that she will have to throw out what she's written thus far and start over. Then she realizes that "this moment of doubt and panic is where my text really begins." She then revises what she's written in a way that incorporates the criticisms she's anticipated, and her text becomes stronger and more interesting as a result.

This little story contains an important lesson for all writers, experienced and inexperienced alike. It suggests that even though most of us are upset at the idea of someone criticizing our work, such criticisms can actually work to our advantage. Although it's naturally tempting to ignore criticism of our ideas, doing so may in fact be a big mistake, since our writing improves when we not only listen to these objections but also give them an explicit hearing in our writing. Indeed, no single device more quickly improves a piece of writing than planting a naysayer in the text—saying, for example, that "although some readers may object" to something in your argument, you "would reply that _____."

ANTICIPATE OBJECTIONS

But wait, you say. Isn't the advice to incorporate critical views a recipe for destroying your credibility and undermining your argument? Here you are, trying to say something that will hold up, and we want you to tell readers all the negative things someone might say against you?

Exactly. We *are* urging you to tell readers what others might say against you, but our point is that doing so will actually *enhance* your credibility, not undermine it. As we argue throughout this book, writing well does not mean piling up uncontroversial truths in a vacuum; it means engaging others in a dialogue or debate—not only by opening your text with a summary of what others *have* said, as we suggest in Chapter 1, but also by imagining what others *might* say against your argument as it unfolds. Once you see writing as an act of entering a conversation, you should also see how opposing arguments can work for you rather than against you.

Paradoxically, the more you give voice to your critics' objections, the more you tend to disarm those critics, especially if you go on to answer their objections in convincing ways. When you entertain a counterargument, you make a kind of preemptive strike, identifying problems with your argument before others can point them out for you. Furthermore, by entertaining counterarguments, you show respect for your readers, treating them not as gullible dupes who will believe anything you say but as independent, critical thinkers who are aware that your view is not the only one in town. In addition, by imagining what others might say against your claims, you come across as a generous, broad-minded person who is confident enough to be open to debate—like the writer in the figure on the following page.

Conversely, if you don't entertain counterarguments, you may very likely come across as closed-minded, as if you think your beliefs are beyond dispute. You might also leave important questions hanging and concerns about your arguments unaddressed. Finally, if you fail to plant a naysayer in your text, you may find that you have very little to say. Our own students often say that entertaining counterarguments makes it easier to generate enough text to meet their assignment's page-length requirements.

Planting a naysayer in your text is a relatively simple move, as you can see by looking at the following passage from a book by the writer Kim Chernin. Having spent some thirty pages complaining about the pressure on American women to be thin, Chernin inserts a whole chapter titled "The Skeptic," opening it as follows:

> At this point I would like to raise certain objections that have been inspired by the skeptic in me. She feels that I have been ignoring some of the most common assumptions we all make about our bodies and these she wishes to see addressed. For example: "You know perfectly well," she says to me, "that you feel better when you lose weight. You buy new clothes. You look at yourself more eagerly in the mirror. When someone invites you to a party you don't stop and ask yourself whether you want to go. You feel sexier. Admit it. You like yourself better."
>
> KIM CHERNIN, *The Obsession:*
> *Reflections on the Tyranny of Slenderness*

The remainder of Chernin's chapter consists of her answers to this inner skeptic. In the face of the skeptic's challenge to her book's central premise (that the pressure to diet seriously harms women's lives), Chernin responds neither by repressing the skeptic's critical voice nor by giving in to it and relinquishing her own position. Instead, she embraces that voice and writes it into her text. Note, too, that instead of dispatching this naysaying voice quickly, as many of us would be tempted to do, Chernin stays with it and devotes a full paragraph to it. By borrowing some of Chernin's language, we can come up with templates for entertaining virtually any objection.

TEMPLATES FOR ENTERTAINING OBJECTIONS

▸ **At this point I would like to raise some objections that have been inspired by the skeptic in me. She feels that I have been ignoring the complexities of the situation.**

▸ **Yet some readers may challenge my view by insisting that** _____.

▸ **Of course, many will probably disagree on the grounds that** _____.

Note that the objections in the above templates are attributed not to any specific person or group but to "skeptics," "readers," or "many." This kind of nameless, faceless naysayer is perfectly appropriate in many cases. But the ideas that motivate arguments and objections often can—and, where possible, should—be ascribed to a specific ideology or school of thought (for example, liberals, Christian fundamentalists, neopragmatists) rather than to anonymous anybodies. In other words, naysayers can be labeled, and you can add precision and impact to your writing by identifying what those labels are.

TEMPLATES FOR NAMING YOUR NAYSAYERS

▸ Here many *feminists* would probably object that <u>gender does influence language</u>.

▸ But *social Darwinists* would certainly take issue with the argument that _____.

▸ *Biologists*, of course, may want to question whether _____.

▸ Nevertheless, both *followers and critics of Malcolm X* will probably suggest otherwise and argue that _____.

To be sure, some people dislike such labels and may even resent having labels applied to themselves. Some feel that labels put individuals in boxes, stereotyping them and glossing over what makes each of us unique. And it's true that labels can be used inappropriately, in ways that ignore individuality and promote stereotypes. But since the life of ideas, including many of our most private thoughts, is conducted through groups and types rather than solitary individuals, intellectual exchange requires labels to give definition and serve as a convenient shorthand. If you categorically reject all labels, you give up an important resource and even mislead readers by presenting yourself and others as having no connection to anyone else. You also miss an opportunity to generalize the importance and relevance of your work to some larger conversation. When you attribute a position you are summarizing to liberalism, say, or historical materialism, your argument is no longer just about your own solitary views but also about the intersection of broad ideas and habits of mind that many readers may already have a stake in.

The way to minimize the problem of stereotyping, then, is not to categorically reject labels but to refine and qualify their use, as the following templates demonstrate:

▸ Although not all *Christians* think alike, some of them will probably dispute my claim that _____.

▸ *Non-native English speakers* are so diverse in their views that it's hard to generalize about them, but some are likely to object on the grounds that _____.

Another way to avoid needless stereotyping is to qualify labels carefully, substituting "pro bono lawyers" for "lawyers" in general, for example, or "quantitative sociologists" for all "social scientists," and so on.

TEMPLATES FOR INTRODUCING OBJECTIONS INFORMALLY

Objections can also be introduced in more informal ways. For instance, you can frame objections in the form of questions:

▸ But is my proposal realistic? What are the chances of its actually being adopted?

▸ Yet is it necessarily true that _____? Is it always the case, as I have been suggesting, that _____?

▸ However, does the evidence I've cited prove conclusively that _____?

You can also let your naysayer speak directly:

▸ **"Impossible," some will say. "You must be reading the research selectively."**

Moves like this allow you to cut directly to the skeptical voice itself, as the singer-songwriter Joe Jackson does in the following excerpt from a *New York Times* article complaining about the restrictions on public smoking in New York City bars and restaurants:

> I like a couple of cigarettes or a cigar with a drink, and like many other people, I only smoke in bars or nightclubs. Now I can't go to any of my old haunts. Bartenders who were friends have turned into cops, forcing me outside to shiver in the cold and curse under my breath. . . . It's no fun. Smokers are being demonized and victimized all out of proportion.
>
> "Get over it," say the anti-smokers. "You're the minority." I thought a great city was a place where all kinds of minorities could thrive. . . . "Smoking kills," they say. As an occasional smoker with otherwise healthy habits, I'll take my chances. Health consciousness is important, but so are pleasure and freedom of choice.
>
> JOE JACKSON, "Want to Smoke? Go to Hamburg"

Jackson could have begun his second paragraph, in which he shifts from his own voice to that of his imagined naysayer, more formally, as follows: "Of course anti-smokers will object that since we smokers are in the minority, we should simply stop complaining and quietly make the sacrifices we are being called on to make for the larger social good." Or "Anti-smokers might insist, however, that the smoking minority should submit to the nonsmoking majority." We think, though, that Jackson gets the job done in a far more lively way with the more colloquial form he chooses. Borrowing a standard move of playwrights and novelists, Jackson cuts directly to the objectors' view and then to his own retort, then back to the objectors' view and then to his own retort again, thereby creating a kind of dialogue or miniature play within his own text. This move works well for Jackson but only because he uses quotation marks and other voice markers to make clear at every point whose voice he is in.

See Chapter 5 for more advice on using voice markers.

REPRESENT OBJECTIONS FAIRLY

Once you've decided to introduce a differing or opposing view into your writing, your work has only just begun, since you still need to represent and explain that view with fairness and generosity. Although it is tempting to give opposing views short shrift, to hurry past them, or even to mock them, doing so is usually counterproductive. When writers make the best case they can for their critics (playing Peter Elbow's "believing game"), they actually bolster their credibility with readers rather than undermine it. They make readers think, "This is a writer I can trust."

See pp. 33–34 for more on the believing game.

We recommend, then, that whenever you entertain objections in your writing, you stay with them for several sentences or even paragraphs and take them as seriously as possible. We also recommend that you read your summary of opposing views with an outsider's eye: put yourself in the shoes of someone who disagrees with you and ask if such a reader would recognize himself in your summary. Would that reader think you have taken his views seriously, as beliefs that reasonable people might hold? Or would he detect a mocking tone or an oversimplification of his views?

There will always be certain objections, to be sure, that you believe do not deserve to be represented, just as there will be objections that seem so unworthy of respect that they inspire ridicule. Remember, however, that if you do choose to mock a view that you oppose, you are likely to alienate those readers who don't already agree with you—likely the very readers you want to reach. Also be aware that in mocking another's view you may contribute to a hostile argument culture in which someone may ridicule you in return.

ANSWER OBJECTIONS

Do be aware that when you represent objections successfully, you still need to be able to answer those objections persuasively. After all, when you write objections into a text, you take the risk that readers will find those objections more convincing than the argument you yourself are advancing. In the editorial quoted above, for example, Joe Jackson takes the risk that readers will identify more with the anti-smoking view he summarizes than with the pro-smoking position he endorses.

This is precisely what Benjamin Franklin describes happening to himself in *The Autobiography of Benjamin Franklin* (1793), when he recalls being converted to Deism (a religion that exalts reason over spirituality) by reading *anti*-Deist books. When he encountered the views of Deists being negatively summarized by authors who opposed them, Franklin explains, he ended up finding the Deist position more persuasive. To avoid having this kind of unintentional reverse effect on readers, you need to do your best to make sure that any counter-arguments you address are not more convincing than your own claims. It is good to address objections in your writing but only if you are able to overcome them.

One surefire way to *fail* to overcome an objection is to dismiss it out of hand—saying, for example, "That's just wrong." The difference between such a response (which offers no supporting reasons whatsoever) and the types of nuanced responses we're promoting in this book is the difference between bullying your readers and genuinely persuading them.

Often the best way to overcome an objection is not to try to refute it completely but to agree with part of it while challenging only the part you dispute. In other words, in answering counterarguments, it is often best to say "yes, but" or "yes See pp. 63–66 for more on agreeing, with a difference. and no," treating the counterview as an opportunity to revise and refine your own position. Rather than build your argument into an impenetrable fortress, it is often best to make concessions while still standing your ground, as Kim Chernin does in the following response to the counter-argument quoted above. While in the voice of the "skeptic," Chernin writes: "Admit it. You like yourself better when you've lost weight." In response, Chernin replies as follows:

Can I deny these things? No woman who has managed to lose weight would wish to argue with this. Most people feel better about themselves when they become slender. And yet, upon reflection, it seems to me that there is something precarious about this well-being. After all, 98 percent of people who lose weight gain it back. Indeed, 90 percent of those who have dieted "successfully" gain back more than they ever lost. Then, of course, we can no longer bear to look at ourselves in the mirror.

In this way, Chernin shows how you can use a counterview to improve and refine your overall argument by making a concession. Even as she concedes that losing weight feels good in the short run, she argues that in the long run the weight always returns, making the dieter far more miserable.

TEMPLATES FOR MAKING CONCESSIONS WHILE STILL STANDING YOUR GROUND

▸ Although I grant that <u>the book is poorly organized</u>, I still maintain that <u>it raises an important issue</u>.

▸ Proponents of X are right to argue that _____. But they exaggerate when they claim that _____.

▸ While it is true that _____, it does not necessarily follow that _____.

▸ On the one hand, I agree with X that _____. But on the other hand, I still insist that _____.

Templates like these show that answering naysayers' objections does not have to be an all-or-nothing affair in which either you definitely refute your critics or they definitely refute you. Often the most productive engagements among differing views end with a combined vision that incorporates elements of each one.

But what if you've tried out all the possible answers you can think of to an objection you've anticipated and you *still* have a nagging feeling that the objection is more convincing than your argument itself? In that case, the best remedy is to go back and make some fundamental revisions to your argument, even reversing your position completely if need be. Although finding out late in the game that you aren't fully convinced by your own argument can be painful, it can actually make your final text more intellectually honest, challenging, and serious. After all, the goal of writing is not to keep proving that whatever you initially said is right, but to stretch the limits of your thinking. So if planting a strong naysayer in your text forces you to change your mind, that's not a bad thing. Some would argue that that is what the academic world is all about.

Exercises

1. Read the following passage from "A People's Democratic Platform" by the cultural critic Eric Schlosser. As you'll see, he hasn't planted any naysayers in this text. Do it for him. Insert a brief paragraph stating an objection to his argument and then responding to the objection as he might.

   The United States must declare an end to the war on drugs. This war has filled the nation's prisons with poor drug addicts and small-time drug dealers. It has created a multibillion-dollar black market, enriched organized crime groups and promoted the corruption of government officials throughout the world. And it has not stemmed the widespread use of illegal drugs. By any rational measure, this war has been a total failure.

   We must develop public policies on substance abuse that are guided not by moral righteousness or political expediency but by common sense. The United States should immediately decriminalize the cultivation and possession of small amounts of marijuana for personal use. Marijuana should no longer be classified as a Schedule I narcotic, and those who seek to use marijuana as medicine should no longer face criminal sanctions. We must shift our entire approach to drug abuse from the criminal justice system to the public health system. Congress should appoint an independent commission to study the harm-reduction policies that have been adopted in Switzerland, Spain, Portugal, and the Netherlands. The commission should recommend policies for the United States based on one important criterion: what works.

In a nation where pharmaceutical companies advertise powerful antidepressants on billboards and where alcohol companies run amusing beer ads during the Super Bowl, the idea of a "drug-free society" is absurd. Like the rest of American society, our drug policy would greatly benefit from less punishment and more compassion.

2. Think of a debate you recently had with a friend or classmate. Compose a one-sentence summary of your argument. Then, by yourself or with a partner, brainstorm a list of possible objections or alternative perspectives on the issue. Pick one, and use it to write a naysayer objection that responds to your argument. Use the templates in this chapter to introduce and respond to this naysayer fairly.

3. Read over something you've written that makes an argument. Work with a partner to review your draft to see if you've anticipated and responded to any objections. Use these questions to guide your review: Have you anticipated all the likely objections to your argument? Whom, if anyone, have you attributed the objections to? Have you represented the objections fairly? Have you answered them well enough, or do you think you now need to qualify your own argument? Does the introduction of the naysayer strengthen your argument? Why or why not?

SEVEN

"SO WHAT? WHO CARES?"

Saying Why It Matters

—⟨◻⟩—

BASEBALL IS THE NATIONAL PASTIME. Bernini was the best sculptor of the baroque period. All writing is conversational. So what? Who cares? Why does any of this matter?

How many times have you had reason to ask these questions? Regardless of how interesting a topic may be to you as a writer, readers always need to know what is at stake in a text and why they should care. All too often, however, these questions are left unanswered—mainly because writers and speakers assume that audiences will know the answers already or will figure them out on their own. As a result, students come away from lectures feeling like outsiders to what they've heard, just as many of us feel left hanging after talks we've attended. The problem is not necessarily that the speakers lack a clear, well-focused thesis or that the thesis is inadequately supported with evidence. Instead, the problem is that the speakers don't address the crucial question of why their arguments matter.

That this question is so often left unaddressed is unfortunate since the speakers generally *could* offer interesting, engaging answers. When pressed, for instance, most academics will tell you that their lectures and articles matter because they address some belief that needs to be corrected or updated—and because their arguments have important, real-world consequences. Yet many academics fail to identify these reasons and consequences explicitly in what they say and write. Rather than assume that audiences will know why their claims matter, all writers need to answer the "so what?" and "who cares?" questions up front. Not everyone can claim to have a cure for cancer or a solution to end poverty. But writers who fail to show that others *should* care or already *do* care about their claims will ultimately lose their audiences' interest.

This chapter focuses on various moves that you can make to answer the "who cares?" and "so what?" questions in your own writing. In one sense, the two questions get at the same thing: the relevance or importance of what you are saying. Yet they get at this significance in different ways. Whereas "who cares?" literally asks you to identify a person or group who cares about your claims, "so what?" asks about the real-world applications and consequences of those claims—what difference it would make if they were accepted. We'll look first at ways of making clear who cares.

"WHO CARES?"

To see how one writer answers the "who cares?" question, consider the following passage from the science writer Denise Grady. Writing in the *New York Times*, she explains some of the latest research into fat cells:

> Scientists used to think body fat and the cells it was made of were pretty much inert, just an oily storage compartment. But within the past decade research has shown that fat cells act like chemical factories and that body fat is potent stuff: a highly active

tissue that secretes hormones and other substances with profound and sometimes harmful effects. . . .

In recent years, biologists have begun calling fat an "endocrine organ," comparing it to glands like the thyroid and pituitary, which also release hormones straight into the bloodstream.

DENISE GRADY, "The Secret Life of a Potent Cell"

Notice how Grady's writing reflects the central advice we give in this book, offering a clear claim and also framing that claim as a response to what someone else has said. In so doing, Grady immediately identifies at least one group with a stake in the new research that sees fat as "active," "potent stuff": namely, the scientific community, which formerly believed that body fat is inert. By referring to these scientists, Grady implicitly acknowledges that her text is part of a larger conversation and shows who besides herself has an interest in what she says.

Consider, however, how the passage would read had Grady left out what "scientists used to think" and simply explained the new findings in isolation:

> Within the past few decades research has shown that fat cells act like chemical factories and that body fat is potent stuff: a highly active tissue that secretes hormones and other substances. In recent years, biologists have begun calling fat an "endocrine organ," comparing it to glands like the thyroid and pituitary, which also release hormones straight into the bloodstream.

Though this statement is clear and easy to follow, it lacks any indication that anyone needs to hear it. OK, one thinks while reading this passage, fat is an active, potent thing. Sounds plausible enough; no reason to think it's not true. But does anyone really care? Who, if anyone, is interested?

TEMPLATES FOR INDICATING WHO CARES

To address "who cares?" questions in your own writing, we suggest using templates like the following, which echo Grady in refuting earlier thinking:

▸ <u>Parents</u> used to think <u>yelling at their kids was necessary</u>. But recently <u>experts</u> suggest that <u>it can be counterproductive</u>.

▸ This interpretation challenges the work of those critics who have long assumed that _____.

▸ These findings challenge the work of earlier researchers, who tended to assume that _____.

▸ Recent studies like these shed new light on _____, which previous studies had not addressed.

Grady might have been more explicit by writing the "who cares?" question directly into her text, as in the following template:

▸ But who really cares? Who besides me and a handful of recent researchers has a stake in these claims? At the very least, the researchers who formerly believed _____ should care.

To gain greater authority as a writer, it can help to name specific people or groups who have a stake in your claims and to go into some detail about their views:

▸ Researchers have long assumed that _____. For instance, one eminent scholar of cell biology, _____, assumed in _____, her seminal work on cell structures and functions, that fat cells _____. As _____ herself put it, "_____" (2012). Another leading scientist, _____, argued that fat cells "_____" (2011). Ultimately, when it came to the nature of fat, the basic assumption was that _____.

But a new body of research shows that fat cells are far more complex and that _____.

In other cases, you might refer to certain people or groups who *should* care about your claims:

▸ If sports enthusiasts stopped to think about it, many of them might simply assume that the most successful athletes _____. However, new research shows _____.

▸ These findings challenge neoliberals' common assumption that _____.

▸ At first glance, teenagers might say _____. But on closer inspection _____.

As these templates suggest, answering the "who cares?" question involves establishing the type of contrast between what others say and what you say that is central to this book. Ultimately, such templates help you create a dramatic tension or clash of views in your writing that readers will feel invested in and want to see resolved.

"SO WHAT?"

Although answering the "who cares?" question is crucial, in many cases it is not enough, especially if you are writing for general readers who don't necessarily have a strong investment in the particular clash of views you are setting up. In the case of Grady's argument about fat cells, such readers may still wonder why it matters that some researchers think fat cells are active, while others think they're inert. Or, to move to a different field of study, American literature, *so what* if some scholars disagree about Huck Finn's relationship with the runaway slave Jim in Mark Twain's *Adventures of Huckleberry Finn*? Why should anyone besides a few specialists in the field care about such disputes? What, if anything, hinges on them?

The best way to answer such questions about the larger consequences of your claims is to appeal to something that your audience already figures to care about. Whereas the "who cares?" question asks you to identify an interested person or group, the "so what?" question asks you to link your argument to some larger matter that readers already deem important. Thus, in analyzing *Huckleberry Finn*, a writer could argue that seemingly narrow disputes about the hero's relationship with Jim actually shed light on whether Twain's canonical, widely read novel is a critique of racism in America or is itself marred by it.

Let's see how Grady invokes such broad, general concerns in her article on fat cells. Her first move is to link researchers' interest in fat cells to a general concern with obesity and health:

> Researchers trying to decipher the biology of fat cells hope to find new ways to help people get rid of excess fat or, at least, prevent obesity from destroying their health. In an increasingly obese world, their efforts have taken on added importance.

Further showing why readers should care, Grady's next move is to demonstrate the even broader relevance and urgency of her subject matter:

> Internationally, more than a billion people are overweight. Obesity and two illnesses linked to it, heart disease and high blood pressure, are on the World Health Organization's list of the top 10 global health risks. In the United States, 65 percent of adults weigh too much,

compared with about 56 percent a decade ago, and government researchers blame obesity for at least 300,000 deaths a year.

What Grady implicitly says here is "Look, dear reader, you may think that these questions about the nature of fat cells I've been pursuing have little to do with everyday life. In fact, however, these questions are extremely important—particularly in our 'increasingly obese world' in which we need to prevent obesity from destroying our health."

Notice that Grady's phrase "in an increasingly _____ world" can be adapted as a strategic move to address the "so what?" question in other fields as well. For example, a sociologist analyzing back-to-nature movements of the past thirty years might make the following statement:

> In a world increasingly dominated by cell phones and sophisticated computer technologies, these attempts to return to nature appear futile.

This type of move can be readily applied to other disciplines because no matter how much disciplines may differ from one another, the need to justify the importance of one's concerns is common to them all.

TEMPLATES FOR ESTABLISHING WHY YOUR CLAIMS MATTER

▸ *Huckleberry Finn* matters / is important because it is one of the most widely taught novels in the American school system.

▸ Although X may seem trivial, it is in fact crucial in terms of today's concern over _____.

▸ Ultimately, what is at stake here is _____.

▸ These findings have important implications for the broader domain of _____.

▸ If we are right about _____, then major consequences follow for _____.

▸ These conclusions/This discovery will have significant applications in _____ as well as in _____.

Finally, you can also treat the "so what?" question as a related aspect of the "who cares?" question:

▸ Although X may seem of concern to only a small group of _____, it should in fact concern anyone who cares about _____.

All these templates help you hook your readers. By suggesting the real-world applications of your claims, the templates not only demonstrate that others care about your claims but also tell your readers why *they* should care. Again, it bears repeating that simply stating and proving your thesis isn't enough. You also need to frame it in a way that helps readers care about it.

WHAT ABOUT READERS WHO ALREADY KNOW WHY IT MATTERS?

At this point, you might wonder if you need to answer the "who cares?" and "so what?" questions in *everything* you write. Is it really necessary to address these questions if you're proposing something so obviously consequential as, say, a treatment for autism or a program to eliminate illiteracy? Isn't it obvious that everyone cares about such problems? Does it really need to be spelled out? And what about when you're writing for audiences who you know are already interested in your claims and who understand perfectly well why they're important? In other words, do you always need to address the "so what?" and "who cares?" questions?

As a rule, yes—although it's true that you can't keep answering them forever and at a certain point must say enough is enough. Although a determined skeptic can infinitely ask why something matters—"Why should I care about earning a salary? And why should I care about supporting a family?"—you have to stop answering at some point in your text. Nevertheless, we urge you to go as far as possible in answering such questions. If you take it for granted that readers will somehow intuit the answers to "so what?" and "who cares?" on their own, you may make your work seem less interesting than it actually is, and you run the risk that readers will dismiss your text as irrelevant and unimportant. By contrast, when you are careful to explain who cares and why, it's a little like bringing a cheerleading squad into your text. And though some expert readers might already know why your claims matter, even they need to be reminded. Thus the safest move is to be as explicit as possible in answering the "so what?" question, even for those already in the know. When you step back from the text and explain why it matters, you are urging your audience to keep reading, pay attention, and care.

Exercises

1. Below are two claims. Who might have a stake in these arguments? Use the templates in this chapter to answer in

one or two sentences the "who cares?" question for both arguments.

   a. The benefits of online shopping don't justify the environmental consequences of shipping items purchased online.
   b. The federal government should fund universal health care.

2. Here are two more claims. What are the possible real-world consequences of these arguments? Use the templates in this chapter to answer, in one or two sentences, the "so what?" question for both arguments.

   a. Violent video games do not cause mass shootings.
   b. Because all combat roles are now open to women, both men and women should be required to register for the Selective Service.

3. Read the following passage from Elizabeth Silkes's 2020 essay, "Cultural Heritage Reminds Us of Our Shared Humanity. That's Why Threats against Them Are So Dangerous," found on **theysayiblog.com**. Where do you see Silkes answering the "so what?" and "who cares?" questions? Who does she say should care about preserving cultural sites, and why should they?

The destruction of cultural sites—from libraries to places of worship to museums—is ultimately about erasing a people's entire history. During the Bosnian war in the early 1990s, Serb and Croat forces destroyed or damaged hundreds of mosques in their efforts to rid the region of Muslims. In Zvornik, which had been a historic Muslim trading post on the Drina River, so many traces of the town's past had been eliminated that Brano Grujic, the Serb-installed mayor there, could falsely boast in 1993 that "there were never any mosques in Zvornik." As Helen Walasek, the author of *Bosnia and the Destruction of Cultural Heritage*, writes, sites such as archives and museums were targeted in part because they reflected Bosnia's pluralistic past. Such attacks were aimed at "eradicating any trace of Bosnia-Herzegovina's historic diversity and traditions of coexistence."...

The current conversation around preservation of cultural heritage in the Middle East comes at a critical time for the region, when conflict and atrocity have put a number of marginalized cultures at risk....

While cultural heritage is not the only way we form bonds with others, it is one of the most powerful and effective means of doing so across barriers. It is heartening to see the public outcry at this latest threat, but the risk to cultural sites during conflict remains extraordinarily high. This is especially so given the limited funding for multilateral organizations dedicated to their protection such as UNESCO, from which the United States formally withdrew a year ago. If our children and our children's children cannot access the most fundamental aspects of our own histories and those of others, they will never be able to identify the common threads that bind us all. And it is only through this binding that we can tap into—and act on—our shared humanity.

4. Read over the draft of an essay you are working on. Work with a partner to identify the answers to the "so what?" and "who cares?" questions for your argument. Then revise your draft to say why your argument matters by using the following template:

My point here, that _____, should interest those who _____. Beyond this limited audience, however, my point should speak to anyone who cares about the larger issue of _____.

EIGHT

"AS A RESULT"

Connecting the Parts

—◻—

WE ONCE HAD A STUDENT named Billy, whose characteristic sentence pattern went something like this:

> Spot is a good dog. He has fleas.

"Connect your sentences," we urged in the margins of Billy's papers. "What does Spot's being good have to do with his fleas? These two statements seem unrelated. Can you connect them in some logical way?" When comments like these yielded no results, we tried inking in suggested connections for him:

> Spot is a good dog, *but* he has fleas.
> Spot is a good dog, *even though* he has fleas.

But our message failed to get across, and Billy's disconnected sentence pattern persisted to the end of the semester.

And yet Billy did focus well on his subjects. When he mentioned Spot the dog (or Plato or any other topic) in one sentence, we could count on Spot (or Plato) being the topic of the following sentence as well. This was not the case with some of Billy's classmates, who sometimes changed topic from sentence to sentence or even from clause to clause within a single sentence. But because Billy neglected to mark his connections, his writing was as frustrating to read as theirs. In all these cases, we had to struggle to figure out on our own how the sentences and paragraphs connected or failed to connect with one another.

What makes such writers so hard to read, in other words, is that they never gesture back to what they have just said or forward to what they plan to say. "Never look back" might be their motto, almost as if they see writing as a process of thinking of something to say about a topic and writing it down, then thinking of something else to say about the topic and writing that down, too, and on and on until they've filled the assigned number of pages and can hand the paper in. Each sentence basically starts a new thought rather than growing out of or extending the thought of the previous sentence.

When Billy talked about his writing habits, he acknowledged that he never went back and read what he had written. Indeed, he told us that, other than using his computer software to check for spelling errors and make sure that his tenses were all aligned, he never actually reread what he wrote before turning it in. As Billy seemed to picture it, writing was something one did while sitting at a computer, whereas reading was a separate activity generally reserved for an easy chair, book in hand. It had never occurred to Billy that to write a good sentence he had to think about how it connected to those that came before and after; that he had to think hard about how that sentence fit into the sentences that surrounded it. Each sentence for Billy existed in a sort of tunnel isolated from every other sentence on the page. He never bothered to fit all the parts of his essay together because he apparently thought of writing as a matter of piling up information or observations rather than building a sustained argument. What we suggest in this chapter, then, is that you converse not only with others in your writing but with yourself: that you establish clear relations between one statement and the next by connecting those statements.

This chapter addresses the issue of how to connect all the parts of your writing. The best compositions establish a sense of momentum and direction by making explicit connections among their different parts, so that what is said in one sentence (or paragraph) both sets up what is to come and is clearly informed by what has already been said. When you write a sentence, you create an expectation in the reader's mind that the next sentence will in some way echo and extend it, even if—*especially if*—that next sentence takes your argument in a new direction.

It may help to think of each sentence you write as having arms that reach backward and forward, as the figure below suggests. When your sentences reach outward like this, they establish connections that help your writing flow smoothly in a way readers appreciate. Conversely, when writing lacks such connections and moves in fits and starts, readers repeatedly have to go back over the sentences and guess at the connections on their own. To prevent such disconnection and make your writing flow, we advise

YOUR
LAST
SENTENCE

YOUR SENTENCE

YOUR
NEXT
SENTENCE

following a "do-it-yourself" principle, which means that it is your job as a writer to do the hard work of making the connections rather than, as Billy did, leaving this work to your readers.

This chapter offers several strategies you can use to put this principle into action: (1) using transition terms (like "therefore" and "as a result"); (2) adding pointing words (like "this" or "such"); (3) developing a set of key terms and phrases for each text you write; and (4) repeating yourself, but with a difference—a move that involves repeating what you've said, but with enough variation to avoid being redundant. All these moves require that you always look back and, in crafting any one sentence, think hard about those that precede it.

Notice how we ourselves have used such connecting devices thus far in this chapter. The second paragraph of this chapter, for example, opens with the transitional "And yet," signaling a change in direction, while the opening sentence of the third includes the phrase "in other words," telling you to expect a restatement of a point we've just made. If you look through this book, you should be able to find many sentences that contain some word or phrase that explicitly hooks them back to something said earlier, to something about to be said, or both. And many sentences in *this* chapter repeat key terms related to the idea of connection: "connect," "disconnect," "link," "relate," "forward," and "backward."

USE TRANSITIONS

For readers to follow your train of thought, you need not only to connect your sentences and paragraphs to each other but also to mark the kind of connection you are making. One of the easiest ways to make this move is to use *transitions* (from the Latin root *trans*, "across"), which help you cross from one point to another in your text. Transitions are usually placed at or near the start of sentences so they can signal to readers where your text is going: in the same direction it has been moving or in a new direction. More specifically, transitions tell readers whether your text is echoing a previous sentence or paragraph ("in other words"), adding something to it ("in addition"), offering an example of it ("for example"), generalizing from it ("as a result"), or modifying it ("and yet").

The following is a list of commonly used transitions, categorized according to their different functions:

ADDITION

also	in fact
and	indeed
besides	moreover
furthermore	so too
in addition	

ELABORATION

actually	to put it another way
by extension	to put it bluntly
in other words	to put it succinctly
in short	ultimately
that is	

EXAMPLE

after all	for instance
as an illustration	specifically
consider	to take a case in point
for example	

CAUSE AND EFFECT

accordingly	so
as a result	then
consequently	therefore
hence	thus
since	

COMPARISON

along the same lines	likewise
in the same way	similarly

CONTRAST

although	nevertheless
but	nonetheless
by contrast	on the contrary
conversely	on the other hand
despite	regardless
even though	whereas
however	while
in contrast	yet

CONCESSION

admittedly	naturally
although it is true	of course
granted	to be sure

CONCLUSION

as a result	in sum
consequently	therefore
hence	thus
in conclusion	to sum up
in short	to summarize

Ideally, transitions should operate so unobtrusively in a piece of writing that they recede into the background and readers do not even notice that they are there. It's a bit like what happens when drivers use their turn signals before turning right or left: just as other drivers recognize such signals almost unconsciously, readers should process transition terms with a minimum of thought. But even though such terms should function unobtrusively in your writing, they can be among the most powerful tools in your vocabulary. Think how your heart sinks when someone, immediately after praising you, begins a sentence with "but" or "however." No matter what follows, you know it won't be good.

Notice that some transitions can help you not only move from one sentence to another but also combine two or more sentences into one. Combining sentences in this way helps prevent the choppy, staccato effect that arises when too many short sentences are strung together, one after the other. For instance, to combine Billy's two choppy sentences ("Spot is a good dog. He has fleas.") into one, better-flowing sentence, we suggested that he rewrite them as "Spot is a good dog, *even though* he has fleas."

Transitions like these not only guide readers through the twists and turns of your argument but also help ensure that you *have* an argument in the first place. In fact, we think of words like "but," "yet," "nevertheless," "besides," and others as argument words, since it's hard to use them without making some kind of argument. The word "therefore," for instance, commits you to making sure that the claims preceding it lead logically to the conclusion that it introduces. "For example" also assumes an argument, since it requires the material you are introducing to stand as an instance or proof of some preceding generalization. As a result, the more you use transitions, the more you'll be able not only to connect the parts of your text but also to construct a strong argument in the first place. And if you draw on them frequently enough, using them should eventually become second nature.

To be sure, it is possible to overuse transitions, so take time to read over your drafts carefully and eliminate any transitions that are unnecessary. But following the maxim that you need to learn the basic moves of argument before you can deliberately depart from them, we advise you not to forgo explicit transition terms until you've first mastered their use. In all our years of teaching, we've read countless essays that suffered from having few or no transitions, but we cannot recall one in which the transitions were overused. Seasoned writers sometimes omit explicit transitions but only because they rely heavily on the other types of connecting devices that we turn to in the rest of this chapter.

Before doing so, however, let us warn you about inserting transitions without really thinking through their meanings—using "therefore," say, when your text's logic actually requires "nevertheless" or "however." So beware. Choosing transition terms should involve a bit of mental sweat, since the whole point of using them is to make your writing *more* reader-friendly, not less. The only thing more frustrating than reading Billy-style passages like "Spot is a good dog. He has fleas" is reading mis-connected sentences like "Spot is a good dog. For example, he has fleas."

USE POINTING WORDS

Another way to connect the parts of your argument is by using pointing words—which, as their name implies, point or refer backward to some concept in the previous sentence. The most common of these pointing words include "this," "these," "that," "those," "their," and "such" (as in "these pointing words" near the start of this sentence) and simple pronouns like "his," "he," "her," "she," "it," and "their." Such terms help you create the flow we spoke of earlier that enables readers to move effortlessly through your text. In a sense, these terms are like an invisible hand reaching out of your sentence, grabbing what's needed in the previous sentences and pulling it along.

Like transitions, however, pointing words need to be used carefully. It's dangerously easy to insert pointing words into your text that don't refer to a clearly defined object, assuming that because the object you have in mind is clear to you it will also be clear to your readers. For example, consider the use of "this" in the following passage:

> Alexis de Tocqueville was highly critical of democratic socie-
> ties, which he saw as tending toward mob rule. At the same time,
> he accorded democratic societies grudging respect. *This* is seen in
> Tocqueville's statement that . . .

When "this" is used in such a way it becomes an ambiguous or free-floating pointer, since readers can't tell if it refers to Tocqueville's critical attitude toward democratic societies, his grudging respect for them, or some combination of both. "This what?" readers mutter as they go back over such passages and try to figure them out. It's also tempting to try to cheat with pointing words, hoping that they will conceal or make up for conceptual confusions that may lurk in your argument. By referring to a fuzzy idea as "this" or "that," you might hope the fuzziness will somehow come across as clearer than it is.

You can fix problems caused by a free-floating pointer by making sure there is one and only one possible object in the vicinity that the pointer could be referring to. It also often helps to name the object the pointer is referring to at the same time that you point to it, replacing the bald "this" in the example above with a more precise phrase like "this ambivalence toward democratic societies" or "this grudging respect."

REPEAT KEY TERMS AND PHRASES

A third strategy for connecting the parts of your argument is to develop a constellation of key terms and phrases, including their synonyms and antonyms, that you repeat throughout your text. When used effectively, your key terms should be items that readers could extract from your text in order to get a solid sense of your topic. Playing with key terms also can be a good way to come up with a title and appropriate section headings for your text.

Notice how often Martin Luther King Jr. uses the keywords "criticism," "statement," "answer," and "correspondence" in the opening paragraph of his famous "Letter from Birmingham Jail":

> Dear Fellow Clergymen:
>
> While confined here in the Birmingham city jail, I came across your recent *statement* calling my present activities "unwise and untimely." Seldom do I pause to *answer criticism* of my work and ideas. If I sought to *answer* all the *criticisms* that cross my desk, my secretaries would have little time for anything other than *such correspondence* in the course of the day, and I would have no time for constructive work. But since I feel that you are men of genuine good will and that your *criticisms* are sincerely set forth, I want to try to *answer* your *statement* in what I hope will be patient and reasonable terms.
>
> MARTIN LUTHER KING JR., "Letter from Birmingham Jail"

Even though King uses the terms "criticism" and "answer" three times each and "statement" twice, the effect is not overly repetitive. In fact, these key terms help build a sense of momentum in the paragraph and bind it together.

For another example of the effective use of key terms, consider the following passage, in which the historian Susan Douglas develops a constellation of sharply contrasting key terms around the concept of "cultural schizophrenics": women like herself who, Douglas claims, have mixed feelings about the images of ideal femininity with which they are constantly bombarded by the media:

> In a variety of ways, the mass media helped make us the cultural schizophrenics we are today, women who rebel against yet submit to prevailing images about what a desirable, worthwhile woman should be. . . . [T]he mass media has engendered in many women a kind of cultural identity crisis. We are ambivalent toward femininity on the one hand and feminism on the other. Pulled in opposite directions—told we were equal, yet told we were subordinate; told we could change history but told we were trapped by history—we got the bends at an early age, and we've never gotten rid of them.
>
> When I open *Vogue*, for example, I am simultaneously infuriated and seduced. . . . I adore the materialism; I despise the materialism. . . . I want to look beautiful; I think wanting to look beautiful is about the most dumb-ass goal you could have. The magazine stokes my desire; the magazine triggers my bile. And this doesn't only happen when I'm reading *Vogue*; it happens all the time. . . . On the one hand, on the other hand—that's not just me—that's what it means to be a woman in America.
>
> To explain this schizophrenia . . .
>
> SUSAN DOUGLAS, Where the Girls Are:
Growing Up Female with the Mass Media

In this passage, Douglas establishes "schizophrenia" as a key concept and then echoes it through synonyms like "identity crisis," "ambivalent," "the bends"—and even demonstrates it through a series of contrasting words and phrases:

rebel against / submit
told we were equal / told we were subordinate
told we could change history / told we were trapped by history
infuriated / seduced
I adore / I despise
I want / I think wanting . . . is about the most dumb-ass goal
stokes my desire / triggers my bile
on the one hand / on the other hand

These contrasting phrases help flesh out Douglas's claim that women are being pulled in two directions at once. In so doing, they bind the passage together into a unified whole that, despite its complexity and sophistication, stays focused over its entire length.

REPEAT YOURSELF—BUT WITH A DIFFERENCE

The last technique we offer for connecting the parts of your text involves repeating yourself, but with a difference—which basically means saying the same thing you've just said but in a slightly different way that avoids sounding monotonous. To effectively connect the parts of your argument and keep it moving forward, be careful not to leap from one idea to a different idea or introduce new ideas cold. Instead, try to build bridges between your ideas by echoing what you've just said while simultaneously moving your text into new territory.

Several of the connecting devices discussed in this chapter are ways of repeating yourself in this special way. Key terms, pointing terms, and even many transitions can be used in a way that not only brings something forward from the previous sentence but in some way alters it, too. When Douglas, for instance, uses the key term "ambivalent" to echo her earlier reference to schizophrenics, she is repeating herself with a difference—repeating the same concept but with a different word that adds new associations.

In addition, when you use transition phrases like "in other words" and "to put it another way," you repeat yourself with a difference, since these phrases help you restate earlier claims but in a different register. When you open a sentence with "in other words," you are basically telling your readers that in case they didn't fully understand what you meant in the last sentence, you are now coming at it again from a slightly different angle, or that since you're presenting a very important idea, you're not going to skip over it quickly but will explore it further to make sure your readers grasp all its aspects.

We would even go so far as to suggest that after your first sentence, almost every sentence you write should refer back to previous statements in some way. Whether you are writing a "furthermore" comment that adds to what you have just said or a "for example" statement that illustrates it, each sentence should echo at least one element of the previous sentence in some discernible way. Even when your text changes direction and requires transitions like "in contrast," "however," or "but," you still need to mark that shift by linking the sentence to the one just before it, as in the following example:

> Cheyenne loved basketball. Nevertheless, she feared her height would put her at a disadvantage.

These sentences work because even though the second sentence changes course and qualifies the first, it still echoes key concepts from the first. Not only does "she" echo "Cheyenne," since both refer to the same person, but "feared" echoes "loved" by establishing the contrast mandated by the term "nevertheless." "Nevertheless," then, is not an excuse for changing subjects radically. It too requires repetition to help readers shift gears with you and follow your train of thought.

Repetition, in short, is the central means by which you can move from point A to point B in a text. To introduce one last analogy, think of the way experienced rock climbers move up a steep slope. Instead of jumping or lurching from one handhold to the next, good climbers get a secure handhold on the position they have established before reaching for the next ledge. The same thing applies to writing. To move smoothly from point to point in your argument, you need to firmly ground what you say in what you've already said. In this way, your writing remains focused while simultaneously moving forward.

"But hold on," you may be thinking. "Isn't repetition precisely what sophisticated writers should avoid, on the grounds that it will make their writing sound simplistic—as if they are belaboring the obvious?" Yes and no. On the one hand, writers certainly can run into trouble if they merely repeat themselves and nothing more. On the other hand, repetition is key to creating continuity in writing. It is impossible to stay on track in a piece of writing if you don't repeat your points throughout the length of the text. Furthermore, writers would never make an impact on readers if they didn't repeat their main points often enough to reinforce those points and make them stand out above subordinate points. The trick therefore is not to avoid repeating yourself but to repeat yourself in varied and interesting enough ways that you advance your argument without sounding tedious.

Exercises

1. The statements below aren't yet connected to each other. Use any of the transitions listed on pages 111 and 112 to connect them. You can combine the statements into one sentence, or you can keep them as two separate sentences, adding or deleting words. Once you're done, compare your responses with a partner's. How does your choice of transition words affect the meaning of the statements?

   a. Herd immunity is established when 93 percent of a population is vaccinated. Vaccinations can wear off in early adolescence.
   b. Writing can look like an individual pursuit. It requires other people. Other people help writers imagine how their audience will understand and respond to their claims.
   c. Some ski resorts have begun to diversify their operations to increase year-round profitability. Some have added zip lines that draw in people in the summer months.

2. Read the following passage from the MIT professor Sherry Turkle's essay "Stop Googling. Let's Talk." Annotate the connecting devices you see. Underline the transitions, circle the key terms, and put boxes around the pointing terms.

   Across generations, technology is implicated in this assault on empathy. We've gotten used to being connected all the time, but we have found ways around conversation—at least from conversation that is open-ended and spontaneous, in which we play with ideas and allow ourselves to be fully present and vulnerable. But it is in this type of conversation—where we learn to make eye contact, to become aware of another person's posture and tone, to comfort one another and respectfully challenge one another—that empathy and intimacy flourish. In these conversations, we learn who we are.

Of course, we can find empathic conversations today, but the trend line is clear. It's not only that we turn away from talking face to face to chat online. It's that we don't allow these conversations to happen in the first place because we keep our phones in the landscape.

In our hearts, we know this, and now research is catching up with our intuitions. We face a significant choice. It is not about giving up our phones but about using them with greater intention. Conversation is there for us to reclaim. For the failing connections of our digital world, it is the talking cure.

3. Read over something you've written with an eye for the devices you've used to connect the parts. Working either by yourself or with a partner, do the following:

   a. Underline all the transitions, pointing terms, key terms, and repetitions.

   b. Describe the patterns you see. Do you rely on certain devices more than others?

   c. Locate a passage that could use better connections. Revise it using the devices introduced in this chapter. Is it easier to read now?

NINE

"YOU MEAN I CAN JUST SAY IT THAT WAY?"

Academic Writing Doesn't Mean Setting Aside Your Own Voice

WE WISH WE HAD A DOLLAR for each time a student has asked us a version of the above question. It usually comes when the student is visiting us during our office hours, seeking advice about how to improve a draft of an essay. When we ask the student to tell us in simple words the point being made in the essay, the student will almost invariably produce a statement that is far clearer and more incisive than anything in the draft.

"Write that down," we will urge. "What you just said is sooo much better than anything you wrote in your draft. We suggest going home and revising your paper in a way that makes that claim the focal point of your essay."

"Really?" our student will ask, looking surprised. "You mean I can just say it that way?"

"Sure. Why not?"

"Well, saying it that way seems just so elementary—so obvious. I mean, I don't want to sound stupid."

The goal of this chapter is to counteract this common misconception: that relying in college on the straightforward, down-to-earth language you use every day will make you sound stupid; that to impress your teachers you need to set aside your everyday voice and write in a way that is hard to understand.

It's easy to see how this misconception took hold, since academic writing is notoriously obscure. Students can't be blamed for such obscurity when much of the writing they're assigned to read is so hard to understand—as we can see in the following sentence from a science paper that linguist Steven Pinker quotes in his essay "Why Academics Stink at Writing":

> Participants read assertions whose veracity was either affirmed or denied by the subsequent presentation of an assessment word.

After struggling to determine what the writer of this sentence was trying to say, Pinker finally decided it was probably something as simple as this:

> Participants read sentences, each followed by the word *true* or *false*.

Had the author revised the original statement by tapping into more relaxed, everyday language, as Pinker did in revising it, much of this struggle could have been avoided. In our view, then, mastering academic writing does not mean completely abandoning your normal voice for one that's stiff, convoluted, or pompous, as students often assume. Instead, it means creating a new voice that draws on the voice you already have.

This is not to suggest that any language you use among friends has a place in academic writing. Nor is it to suggest that you may fall back on your everyday voice as an excuse to remain in your comfort zone and avoid learning the rigorous forms and habits that characterize academic culture. After all, learning new words and rhetorical moves is a major part of getting an education. We do, however, wish to suggest that everyday language can often enliven such moves and even enhance your precision in using academic terminology. In our view, then, it is a mistake to assume that the academic and everyday are completely separate languages that can never be used together. Ultimately, we suggest, academic writing is often at its best when it combines what we call "everydayspeak" and "academicspeak."

BLEND ACADEMIC AND COLLOQUIAL STYLES

In fact, we would point out that many academics are highly successful writers who themselves blend everyday and academic styles. Note, for example, how Judith Fetterley, a prominent scholar in the field of literary studies, blends academic and everyday ways of talking in the following passage on the novelist Willa Cather:

> As Merrill Skaggs has put it, "[Cather] is neurotically controlling and self-conscious about her work, but she knows at all points what she is doing. Above all else, she is self-conscious."
>
> Without question, Cather was a control freak.
>
> JUDITH FETTERLEY, "Willa Cather and the
Question of Sympathy: An Unofficial Story"

In this passage, Fetterley makes use of what is probably the most common technique for blending academic and everyday language: she puts them side by side, juxtaposing "neurotically controlling" and "self-conscious" from a quoted source with her own colloquial term,

See p. 291 for an essay that mixes colloquial and academic styles.

"control freak." In this way, Fetterley lightens a potentially dry subject and makes it more accessible and even entertaining.

A TRANSLATION RECIPE

But Fetterley does more than simply put academicspeak and everydayspeak side by side. She takes a step further by translating the one into the other. By translating Skaggs's polysyllabic description of Cather as "neurotically controlling and self-conscious" into the succinct, if blunt, "control freak," Fetterley shows how rarefied, academic ways of talking and more familiar language can not only coexist but can also actually enhance one another—her informal "control freak" serving to explain the formal language that precedes it.

To be sure, slangy, colloquial expressions like "control freak" may be far more common in the humanities than in the sciences, and even in the humanities such casual usages are a recent development. Fifty years ago academic writing in all disciplines was the linguistic equivalent of a black-tie affair. But as times have changed, so has the range of options open to academic writers—so much so that it is not surprising to find writers in all fields using colloquial expressions and referring to movies, music, and other forms of popular culture.

Indeed, Fetterley's passage offers a simple recipe for mixing styles that we encourage you to try out in your own writing: first state the point in academic language, and then translate the point into everyday language. Everyone knows that academic terms like "neurotically controlling" and "self-conscious"—and others you might encounter like "subject position" or "bifurcate"—can be hard to understand. But this translation recipe, we think, eases such difficulties by making the academic familiar. Here is one way you might translate academicspeak into everydayspeak:

▸ **Scholar X argues, "_____." In other words, _____.**

Instead of "In other words," you might try variations like the following:

▸ **Essentially, X argues _____.**

▸ **X's point, succinctly put, is that _____.**

▸ **Plainly put, _____.**

Following Fetterley's lead and making moves like these can help you not only demystify challenging academic material but also reinterpret it, showing you understand it (and helping readers understand it) by putting it into your own terms.

SELF-TRANSLATION

But this translation recipe need not be limited to clarifying the ideas of others. It can also be used to clarify your own complex ideas, as the following passage by the philosopher Rebecca Goldstein illustrates:

> We can hardly get through our lives—in fact, it's hard to get through a week—without considering what makes specific actions right and others wrong and debating with ourselves whether that is a difference that must compel the actions we choose. (Okay, it's wrong! I get it! But why should I care?)
>
> REBECCA GOLDSTEIN, *Plato at the Googleplex:*
> *Why Philosophy Won't Go Away*

Though Goldstein's first sentence may require several rereadings, it is one that most of us, with varying degrees of effort, can come to understand: that we all wrestle regularly with the challenging philosophical questions of what the ethics of a given situation are and whether those ethics should alter our behavior. But instead of leaving us entirely on our own to figure out what she is saying, Goldstein helps us out in her closing parenthetical remarks, which translate the abstractions of her first sentence into the kind of concrete everydayspeak that runs through our heads.

Yet another example of self-translation—one that actually uses the word "translation"—can be found on the opening page of a book by scholar Helen Sword:

> There is a massive gap between what most readers consider to be good writing and what academics typically produce and publish. I'm not talking about the kinds of formal strictures necessarily imposed

by journal editors—article length, citation style, and the like—but about a deeper, duller kind of disciplinary monotony, a compulsive proclivity for discursive obscurantism and circumambulatory diction (translation: an addiction to big words and soggy syntax).

HELEN SWORD, *Stylish Academic Writing*

In this passage, Sword gives her own unique twist to the translation technique we've been discussing. After a stream of difficult polysyllabic words—"a compulsive proclivity for discursive obscurantism and circumambulatory diction"—she then concludes by translating these words into everydayspeak: "an addiction to big words and soggy syntax." The effect is to dramatize her larger point: the "massive gap between what most readers consider to be good writing and what academics typically produce and publish."

FAMOUS EXAMPLES

Even notoriously difficult thinkers could be said to use the translation practice we have been advocating in this chapter, as the following famous and widely quoted claims illustrate:

I think, therefore I am.
—RENÉ DESCARTES

The master's tools will never dismantle the master's house.
—AUDRE LORDE

The medium is the message.
—MARSHALL MCLUHAN

Form follows function.
—LOUIS SULLIVAN

These sentences can be read almost as sound bites—short, catchy statements that express a more complex idea. Though the term "sound bite" is usually used to refer to mindless media simplifications, the succinct statements above show what valuable work they can do. These distillations are admittedly reductive in that they do not capture all the nuances of the more complex ideas they represent. But consider their power to stick in the minds of readers. Without these memorable translations, we wonder if these authors' ideas would have achieved such widespread circulation.

Consider Descartes' "I think, therefore I am," for example, which comes embedded in the following passage, in which Descartes is struggling to find a philosophical foundation for absolute truth in the face of skeptical doctrines that doubt that anything can be known for certain. After putting himself in the shoes of a radical skeptic and imagining what it would be like to believe all apparent truths to be false, Descartes "immediately ... observed," he writes:

> whilst I thus wished to think that all was false, it was absolutely
> necessary that I, who thus thought, should be somewhat; and as I
> observed that this truth, I think, therefore I am (*cogito ergo sum*),
> was so certain and of such evidence that no ground of doubt, however
> extravagant, could be alleged by the sceptics capable of shaking it, I concluded that I might, without scruple, accept it as the
> first principle of the philosophy of which I was in search.
>
> RENÉ DESCARTES, "Discourse on the Method, Part IV"

Had Descartes been less probing and scrupulous, we speculate, he would have stopped writing and ended the passage after the statement "it was absolutely necessary that I, who thus thought, should be somewhat." After all, the passage up to this point contains all the basic ingredients that the rest of it goes on to explain, the simpler, more accessible formulation

"I think, therefore I am" being merely a reformulation of this earlier material. But just imagine if Descartes had decided that his job as a writer was finished after his initial claim and had failed to add the more accessible phrase "I think, therefore I am." We suspect this idea of his would not have become one of the most famous touchstones of Western philosophy.

EVERYDAY LANGUAGE AS A THINKING TOOL

As the examples in this chapter suggest, then, translating academic language into everydayspeak can be an indispensable tool for clarifying and underscoring ideas for readers. But at an even more basic level, such translation can be an indispensable means for you as a writer to clarify your ideas to yourself. In other words, translating academicspeak into everydayspeak can function as a thinking tool that enables you to discover what you are trying to say to begin with.

For as writing theorists often note, writing is generally not a process in which we start with a fully formed idea in our heads that we then simply transcribe in an unchanged state onto the page. On the contrary, writing is more often a means of discovery in which we use the writing process to figure out what our idea is. This is why writers are often surprised to find that what they end up with on the page is quite different from what they thought it would be when they started. What we are trying to say here is that everydayspeak is often crucial for this discovery process, that translating your ideas into more common, simpler terms can help you figure out what your ideas really are, as opposed to what you initially imagined they were. Even Descartes, for example, may not have had the formulation "I think, therefore I am" in mind before he wrote the passage above; instead, he may have arrived at it as he worked through the writing process.

We ourselves have been reminded of this point when engaged in our own writing. One major benefit of writing collaboratively, as the two of us do, is that it repeatedly forces us to explain in simpler terms our less-than-clear ideas when one of us doesn't already know what the other means. In the process of writing and revising this book, for instance, we were always turning to each other after reading something the other had written and asking a version of the "Can you explain that more simply?" question that we described asking our students in our office in this chapter's opening anecdote: "What do you mean?" "I don't get it—can you explain?" "Huh!?" Sometimes, when the idea is finally stated in plain, everyday terms, we realize that it doesn't make sense or that it amounts to nothing more than a cliché—or that we have something worth pursuing. It's as if using everyday language to talk through a draft—as any writer can do by asking others to critique a draft—shines a bright light on our writing to expose its strengths and weaknesses.

STILL NOT CONVINCED?

To be sure, not everyone will be as enthusiastic as we are about the benefits of everydayspeak. Many will insist that, while some fields in the humanities may be open to everyday language, colloquial expressions, and slang, most fields in the sciences are not. And some people in both the humanities and the sciences will argue that some ideas simply can't be done justice to in everyday language. "Theory X," they will say, "is just too complex to be explained in simple terms," or "You have to be in the field to understand it." Perhaps so. But at least one distinguished scientist, the celebrated atomic physicist Enrico Fermi, thought otherwise. Fermi, it is said, believed that all faculty in his field should teach basic physics to undergraduates, because having to explain the science in relatively plain English helped clarify their thinking. This last point can be stated as a rule of thumb: if you can't explain it to your aunt Franny, chances are you don't understand it yourself.

Furthermore, when writers tell themselves that their ideas are just too complex to be explained to nonspecialists, they risk fooling themselves into thinking that they are making more sense than they actually are. Translating academicspeak into everydayspeak functions as a kind of baloney detector, a way of keeping us honest when we're in danger of getting carried away by our own verbosity.

CODE-MESHING

"But come on," some may say. "Get real! Academic writing must, in many cases, mean setting aside our own voices." Sure, it may be fine to translate challenging academic ideas into plain everyday language, as Goldstein, Sword, and Descartes do above, when it's a language that your audience will understand and find acceptable. But what if your everyday language— the one you use when you're most relaxed, with family and friends—is filled with slang and questionable grammar? And what if your everyday language is an ethnic or regional dialect— or a different language altogether? Is there really a place for such language in academic, professional, or public writing?

Yes and no. On the one hand, there are many situations— like when you're applying for a job or submitting a proposal to be read by an official screening body—in which it's probably safest to write in "standard" English. On the other hand, the line between language that might confuse audiences and language that engages or challenges them is not always obvious. Nor is the line between foreign words that readers don't already know and those that readers might happily learn. After all, standard written English is more open and inclusive than it may at first appear. And readers often appreciate writers who take risks and mix things up.

Many prominent writers mix standard written English with other dialects or languages, employing a practice that cultural and linguistic theorists Vershawn Ashanti Young and Suresh Canagarajah call "code-meshing." For instance, in the titles of two of her books, *Talkin and Testifyin: The Language of Black America* and *Black Talk: Words and Phrases From the Hood to the Amen Corner*, the language scholar Geneva Smitherman mixes African American vernacular phrases with more scholarly language in order to suggest, as she explicitly argues in these books, that black vernacular English is as legitimate a variety of language as standard English. Here are three typical passages:

In Black America, the oral tradition has served as a fundamental vehicle for gittin ovah. That tradition preserves the Afro-American heritage and reflects the collective spirit of the race.

Blacks are quick to ridicule "educated fools," people who done gone to school and read all dem books and still don't know nothin!

It is a socially approved verbal strategy for black rappers to talk about how bad they is.

GENEVA SMITHERMAN, *Talkin and Testifyin:
The Language of Black America*

In these examples, Smitherman blends the types of terms we expect in scholarly writing like "oral tradition" and "fundamental vehicle" with Black vernacular phrases like "gittin ovah." She even blends the standard English spelling of words with African American English variants like "dem" and "ovah" in a way that evokes how some speakers of African American English sound. Some might object to these unconventional practices, but this is precisely Smitherman's point: that our habitual language practices need to be opened up, and that the number of participants in the academic conversation needs to be expanded.

Along similar lines, the writer and activist Gloria Anzaldúa mixes standard English with what she calls Chicano Spanish to make a political point about the suppression of the Spanish language in the United States. In one typical passage, she writes:

> From this racial, ideological, cultural, and biological cross-pollinization, an "alien" consciousness is presently in the making— a new *mestiza* consciousness, *una conciencia de mujer.*
>
> GLORIA ANZALDÚA,
Borderlands / La Frontera: The New Mestiza

Anzaldúa gets her point across not only through *what* she says but also through the *way* she says it, showing that the new hybrid, or "*mestiza* consciousness," that she celebrates is, as she puts it, "presently in the making." Ultimately, such code-meshing suggests that languages, like the people who speak them, are not distinct, separate islands.

Because there are so many options in writing, then, there is no need to ever feel limited in your choice of words. You can always experiment with your language and improve it. Depending on your audience and purpose, and how much risk you're willing to take, you can dress up your language, dress it down, or some combination of both. You could even recast the title of this book, *"They Say / I Say,"* as a teenager might say it: "She Goes / I'm Like."

We hope you agree with us, then, that to succeed as a college writer, you need not always set aside your everyday voice, even when that voice may initially seem unwelcome in the academic world. It is by blending everyday language with standard written English that what counts as "standard" changes and the range of possibilities open to academic writers continues to grow.

Exercises

1. Take a paragraph from this book and dress it down, rewriting it in informal colloquial language. Then rewrite the same paragraph again by dressing it up, making it much more formal. Then rewrite the paragraph in a way that blends the two styles. Share your paragraphs with a classmate and discuss which versions are most effective and why.

2. Find something you've written for a course, and study it to see whether you've used any of your own everyday expressions, any words or structures that are not "academic." If by chance you don't find any, see if there's a place or two where shifting into more casual or unexpected language would help you make a point, get your reader's attention, or just add liveliness to your text. Be sure to keep your audience and purpose in mind, and use language that will be appropriate to both.

3. Below is a short passage from Stephanie Owen and Isabel Sawhill's report, "Should Everyone Go to College?" Use one of the translation templates on page 127 to translate the academic language in the underlined sentence into everyday language. Compare your response with a classmate.

We all know that, on average, college graduates make significantly more money over their lifetimes than those with only a high school education. What gets less attention is the fact that not all college degrees or college graduates are equal. <u>There is enormous variation in the so-called return to education depending on factors such as institution attended, field of study, whether a student graduates, and post-graduation occupation.</u>

4. Find a reading on **theysayiblog.com** that blends academic and everyday styles, such as James Hatch's 2019 essay, "My Semester with the Snowflakes." Identify a sentence or passage where you see the author mixing everyday and academic language. Explain how this blending affects the overall argument. How did you react as a reader?

TEN

"BUT DON'T GET ME WRONG"
The Art of Metacommentary

—◻—

WHEN WE TELL PEOPLE that we are writing a chapter on the art of metacommentary, they often give us a puzzled look and tell us that they have no idea what "metacommentary" is. "We know what commentary is," they'll sometimes say, "but what does it mean when it's *meta?*" Our answer is that whether or not they know the term, they practice the art of metacommentary on a daily basis whenever they make a point of explaining something they've said or written: "What I meant to say was _____," "My point was not _____, but _____," or "You're probably not going to like what I'm about to say, but _____." In such cases, they are not offering new points but telling an audience how to interpret what they have already said or are about to say. In short, then, metacommentary is a way of commenting on your claims and telling others how—and how not—to think about them.

It may help to think of metacommentary as being like the chorus in a Greek play that stands to the side of the drama unfolding on the stage and explains its meaning to the audience—or like a voice-over narrator who comments on and explains the action in a television show or movie. Think of metacommentary as a sort of second text that stands alongside your main text and explains what it means. In the main text you say something; in the metatext you guide your readers in interpreting and processing what you've said.

What we are suggesting, then, is that you think of your text as two texts joined at the hip: a main text in which you make your argument and another in which you "work" your ideas, distinguishing your views from others they may be confused with, anticipating and answering objections, connecting one point to another, explaining why your claim might be controversial, and so forth. The figure below demonstrates what we mean.

THE MAIN TEXT SAYS SOMETHING. THE METATEXT TELLS READERS HOW—AND HOW NOT—TO THINK ABOUT IT.

USE METACOMMENTARY TO CLARIFY
AND ELABORATE

But why do you need metacommentary to tell readers what you mean and guide them through your text? Can't you just clearly say what you mean up front? The answer is that no matter how clear and precise your writing is, readers can still fail to understand it in any number of ways. Even the best writers can provoke reactions in readers that they didn't intend, and even good readers can get lost in a complicated argument or fail to see how one point connects with another. Readers may also fail to see what follows from your argument, or they may follow your reasoning and examples yet fail to see the larger conclusion you draw from them. They may fail to see your argument's overall significance or mistake what you are saying for a related argument that they have heard before but that you want to distance yourself from. As a result, no matter how straightforward a writer you are, readers still need you to help them grasp what you really mean. Because the written word is prone to so much mischief and can be interpreted in so many different ways, we need metacommentary to keep misinterpretations and other communication misfires at bay.

Another reason to master the art of metacommentary is that it will help you develop your ideas and generate more text. If you have ever had trouble producing the required number of pages for a writing project, metacommentary can help you add both length and depth to your writing. We've seen many students who try to produce a five-page paper sputter to a halt at two or three pages, complaining they've said everything they can think of about their topic. "I've stated my thesis and presented my reasons and evidence," students have told us. "What else is there to do?" It's almost as if such writers have generated a thesis and don't know what to do with it. When these students learn to use metacommentary, however, they get more out of their ideas and write longer, more substantial texts. In sum, metacommentary can help you extract the full potential from your ideas, drawing out important implications, explaining ideas from different perspectives, and so forth.

So even when you may think you've said everything possible in an argument, try inserting the following types of metacommentary:

▸ In other words, <u>she doesn't realize how right she is</u>.

▸ What _____ really means is _____.

▸ My point is not _____ but _____.

▸ Ultimately, then, my goal is to demonstrate that _____.

Ideally, such metacommentary should help you recognize some implications of your ideas that you didn't initially realize were there.

Let's look at how the cultural critic Neil Postman uses metacommentary in the following passage describing the shift in American culture when it began to move from print and reading to television and movies:

> *It is my intention in this book to show* that a great . . . shift has taken place in America, with the result that the content of much of our public discourse has become dangerous nonsense. *With this in view, my task in the chapters ahead is* straightforward. *I must, first, demonstrate* how, under the governance of the printing

press, discourse in America was different from what it is now—
generally coherent, serious and rational; *and then* how, under the
governance of television, it has become shriveled and absurd.
But to avoid the possibility that my analysis will be interpreted as
standard-brand academic whimpering, a kind of elitist complaint
against "junk" on television, *I must first explain that* . . . I appreciate junk as much as the next fellow, *and I know full well that* the
printing press has generated enough of it to fill the Grand Canyon
to overflowing. Television is not old enough to have matched
printing's output of junk.

NEIL POSTMAN, *Amusing Ourselves to Death:*
Public Discourse in the Age of Show Business

To see what we mean by metacommentary, look at the phrases
above that we have italicized. With these moves, Postman
essentially stands apart from his main ideas to help readers
follow and understand what he is arguing.

He previews what he will argue: *It is my intention in this book*
to show . . .

He spells out how he will make his argument: *With this in*
view, my task in the chapters ahead is . . . *I must, first, dem-*
onstrate . . . *and then* . . .

He distinguishes his argument from other arguments it may
easily be confused with: *But to avoid the possibility that my*
analysis will be interpreted as . . . *I must first explain that* . . .

TITLES AS METACOMMENTARY

Even the title of Postman's book, *Amusing Ourselves to Death:*
Public Discourse in the Age of Show Business, functions as a form of

metacommentary since, like all titles, it stands apart from the text itself and tells readers the book's main point: that the very pleasure provided by contemporary show business is destructive.

Titles, in fact, are one of the most important forms of metacommentary, functioning rather like carnival barkers telling passersby what they can expect if they go inside. Subtitles, too, function as metacommentary, further explaining or elaborating on the main title. The subtitle of this book, for example, not only explains that it is about "the moves that matter in academic writing" but also indicates that "they say / I say" is one of these moves. Thinking of a title as metacommentary can actually help you develop sharper titles, ones that, like Postman's, give readers a hint of what your argument will be. Contrast such titles with unhelpfully open-ended ones, like "Shakespeare" or "Steroids" or "English Essay" or essays with no titles at all. Essays with vague titles (or no titles) send the message that the writer has simply not bothered to reflect on what is being said and is uninterested in guiding or orienting readers.

USE OTHER MOVES AS METACOMMENTARY

Many of the other moves covered in this book function as metacommentary: entertaining objections, adding transitions, framing quotations, answering "so what?" and "who cares?" When you entertain objections, you stand outside of your text and imagine what a critic might say; when you add transitions, you essentially explain the relationship between various claims. And when you answer the "so what?" and "who cares?" questions, you look beyond your central argument and explain who should be interested in it and why.

TEMPLATES FOR INTRODUCING
METACOMMENTARY

TO WARD OFF POTENTIAL MISUNDERSTANDINGS

The following moves help you differentiate certain views from ones they might be mistaken for:

▶ Essentially, I am arguing not that <u>we should give up the policy</u> but that we should monitor effects far more closely.

▶ This is not to say _____ , but rather _____ .

▶ X is concerned less with _____ than with _____ .

TO ELABORATE ON A PREVIOUS IDEA

The following moves elaborate on a previous point, saying to readers: "In case you didn't get it the first time, I'll try saying the same thing in a different way."

▶ In other words, _____ .

▶ To put it another way, _____ .

▶ What X is saying here is that _____ .

TO PROVIDE A ROAD MAP TO YOUR TEXT

This move orients readers, clarifying where you have been and where you are going—and making it easier for them to process and follow your text:

▶ Chapter 2 explores _____ , while Chapter 3 examines _____ .

▶ Having just argued that _____ , I want now to complicate the point by _____ .

TO MOVE FROM A GENERAL CLAIM TO A SPECIFIC EXAMPLE

These moves help you explain a general point by providing a concrete example that illustrates what you're saying:

▸ For example, _____.

▸ _____, for instance, demonstrates _____.

▸ Consider _____, for example.

▸ To take a case in point, _____.

TO INDICATE THAT A CLAIM IS MORE, LESS, OR EQUALLY IMPORTANT

The following templates help you give relative emphasis to the claim that you are introducing, showing whether that claim is of more or less weight than the previous one or equal to it:

▸ Even more important, _____.

▸ But above all, _____.

▸ Incidentally, we will briefly note, _____.

▸ Just as important, _____.

▸ Equally, _____.

▸ Finally, _____.

TO EXPLAIN A CLAIM WHEN YOU ANTICIPATE OBJECTIONS

Here's a template to help you anticipate and respond to possible objections:

Chapter 6 has more templates for anticipating objections.

▸ Although some readers may object that _____, I would answer that _____.

TO GUIDE READERS TO YOUR MOST GENERAL POINT

These moves show that you are wrapping things up and tying up various subpoints previously made:

▸ In sum, then, _____.

▸ My conclusion, then, is that _____.

▸ In short, _____.

In this chapter we have tried to show that the most persuasive writing often doubles back and comments on its own claims in ways that help readers negotiate and process them. Instead of simply piling claim upon claim, effective writers are constantly "stage-managing" how their claims will be received. It's true, of course, that to be persuasive a text has to have strong claims to argue in the first place. But even the strongest arguments will flounder unless writers use metacommentary to prevent potential misreadings and make their arguments shine.

Exercises

1. Complete each of the following metacommentary templates in any way that makes sense:
    a. In making a case for raising the minimum wage, I am not saying that _____.
    b. But my argument will do more than prove that one particular industrial chemical has certain toxic properties. In this essay, I will also _____.
    c. My point about the national obsession with sports reinforces the belief held by many _____ that _____.

d. I believe, therefore, that the war is completely unjustified. But let me back up and explain how I arrived at this conclusion: _____. In this way, I came to believe that this war is a big mistake.

2. Read the following passage from Pau Gasol's 2018 essay, "An Open Letter about Female Coaches." You can find the link to the full essay on **theysayiblog.com**. Underline where Gasol uses the moves of metacommentary to guide his readers through the main text of his argument. Does the author use any of the chapter's templates (see p. 144)? How do you think the author's use of metacommentary enhances (or harms) his writing?

The reason I wanted to start by telling you about my parents, is that their story makes me think about today's NBA. Specifically about how, in the 72-year history of the league, there has never been a female head coach. Even more specifically, it makes me think of Becky Hammon: a coach who has been the topic of much conversation lately, and who I've had the opportunity to play for in San Antonio.

But if you think I'm writing this to argue why Becky is qualified to be an NBA head coach . . . well, you're mistaken. That part is obvious: One, she was an accomplished player—with an elite point guard's mind for the game. And two, she has been a successful assistant for arguably the greatest coach in the game. What more do you need? But like I said—I'm not here to make that argument. Arguing on Coach Hammon's behalf would feel patronizing. To me, it would be strange if NBA teams were not interested in her as a head coach.

3. Read over the draft of an essay, and try the following:

    a. Locate a passage that needs more clarification or elaboration. Revise it using the metacommentary templates included in this chapter.

    b. Add in "road map" metacommentary to help your reader follow your text, using the template on page 144.

    c. Compose a title and subtitle that function as metacommentary on your whole argument.

ELEVEN

"WHAT I REALLY WANT TO SAY IS"
Revising Substantially

—◻—

ONE OF THE MOST common frustrations teachers have—we've had it, too—is that students do not revise in any substantial way. As one of our colleagues put it, "I ask my classes to do a substantial revision of an essay they've turned in, emphasis on the word 'substantial,' but invariably little is changed in what I get back. Students hand in the original essay with a word changed here and there, a few spelling errors corrected, and a comma or two added. . . . I feel like all my advice is for nothing." We suspect, however, that in most cases when students do merely superficial revisions, it's not because they are indifferent or lazy, as some teachers may assume, but because they aren't sure what a good revision looks like. Like even many seasoned writers, these students would *like* to revise more thoroughly, but when they reread what they've written, they have trouble seeing where it can be improved—and how. What they lack is not just a reliable picture in their head of what their draft could be but also reliable strategies for getting there. In this chapter we supply ten such revision strategies and a revision checklist (see pp. 165–70) that are designed to work in virtually any academic setting, regardless of assignment, instructor, discipline, or course.

1. THINK GLOBALLY

Perhaps the best strategy for revising your writing in a substantial way is to think globally, as we might put it, about your draft. This involves stepping back from your writing and looking at the big picture, asking yourself what, finally, you are trying to say. You might ask: Do I have a central argument, or do I just ramble and talk *about* my subject? And if I do have a central argument, does that argument make sense? Is it coherent and unified, or do I go off on tangents or even contradict myself? Do I logically link the parts, tying them together with clear connections between them all, developing a continuous line of argument over my essay's entire length? Does my evidence match my central argument and, as we put it in our revision checklist, is it clear what is motivating my argument—why it needs to be made in the first place? That is, do I present my argument as an entry into some larger conversation or debate, as a response to something "they say"? Have I included the strongest possible objections that can be made against my argument or answered any counterarguments in a superficial way? In the end, might any such counterarguments I address be more convincing to readers—or even to me—than my own argument?

It was big questions like these that inspired a student several years ago to radically revise an essay she'd written on the Iraq War, transforming it from a series of disconnected observations about the war into a sharply focused critique of the view that the war promoted democracy. Her first draft had been a mere collection of scattered claims, all presented as if they were of equal importance: Iraq had no weapons of mass destruction. The United States has the strongest military. Saddam Hussein was evil. Many Americans and Iraqis were killed. The war increased terrorism. And so forth. But her final draft nicely subordinated all its points to a larger "they say / I say" thesis: though Saddam Hussein is an evil dictator, it makes no sense to wage war on Iraq's innocent people. The final version was virtually a different essay.

We open with this suggestion to think globally not just because it is perhaps the central way to substantially revise an essay but also because it is so frequently neglected. Because writing is often associated with local, sentence-level mechanics and grammar, some writers picture revision as a small-scale matter of dotting an occasional "i" and crossing an occasional "t." What often gets overlooked, as writing expert Nancy Sommers points out, are "strategies for handling the whole essay," ones that would help writers "reorder lines of reasoning or ask questions about their purposes and readers." It would be as if a jewelry appraiser were to assess a gem only by studying its smallest, microscopic details and never holding it back to form an overall impression.

Revising globally, then, may mean changing the way we think. It asks us to move beyond microlevel edits, beyond

The messiness of the revision process.

merely tweaking or refining an existing argument. At its best, revision is a messy process that often helps us discover what our argument is in the first place. In fact, a good way to test how substantial your revisions are is to ask how much you learned about your argument through the revision process.

2. BUT STILL SWEAT THE SMALL STUFF

But just because the global level is very important in revising, it doesn't mean that local, surface-level issues—word choice, sentence structure, grammar, style, and so forth—aren't very important too. After all, everything you write is composed of countless small-scale decisions, and if you improve enough of them your next draft has a chance of constituting a significant revision. Also, it is always possible that changing just a single word will help you radically resee your central argument and lead to major, global changes. So while we suggest you think of global revisions as more important than microlevel ones, in practice the two levels are deeply interdependent. Although writers are often told to start out by focusing on their big idea—getting that big idea down on paper and only at a later stage worrying about small-scale mechanics—seasoned writers often move back and forth between the two levels throughout the revision process.

To see how we sweat the small stuff, consider the photo on the facing page of revisions we made on our last paragraph, none of which significantly alter the paragraph's central point. The central point—about the importance of small edits and their connection to big edits—is recognizable from the one draft to the other. And yet we like to think that, taken together, these edits make the passage much more readable. The mere decision alone to move this section up in the chapter and make it the

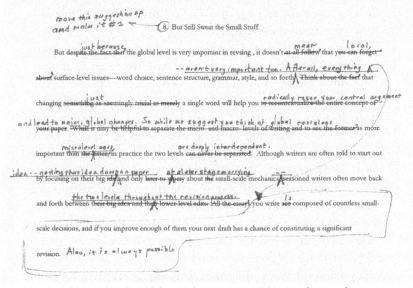

move this suggestion up and make it #2

(8.) But Still Sweat the Small Stuff

But despite the fact that [*just because*] the global level is very important in revising, it doesn't at all follow [*mean*] that you can forget [*local,*] about surface-level issues—word choice, sentence structure, grammar, style, and so forth. Think about the fact that [*—aren't very important too. After all, everything*] changing something as seemingly trivial as merely [*just*] a single word will help you to recontextualize the entire concept of [*radically reser your central argument*] your paper. While it may be helpful to separate the micro- and macro- levels of writing and to see the former [*and lead to major, global changes. So while we suggest you think of global revisions*] as more important than the latter, in practice the two levels can never be separated [*microlevel ones, are deeply interdependent.*] Although writers are often told to start out by focusing on their big idea and only later to worry about the small-scale mechanics, seasoned writers often move back [*idea -- getting that idea down on paper at a later stage worrying*] and forth between their big idea and their lower-level edits. All the essays you write are composed of countless small- [*the two levels throughout the revision process. Is*] scale decisions, and if you improve enough of them your next draft has a chance of constituting a significant revision. [*Also, it is always possible*]

second strategy listed has a big impact. The reader no longer needs to struggle to recall what we'd said several items back about thinking globally. We now have just said it.

3. READ YOUR OWN WRITING

But it is difficult to make any revisions, global or local, unless you do something even more fundamental, which is simply to read what you've written and then ideally reread and reread it again. It is very hard to set the revision process in motion if you don't do at least one initial read-through of your draft, and then do as many additional read-throughs as needed to get a solid grasp of the material with which you're dealing. As Donald Murray explains in *A Writer Teaches Writing*, "The writer reads and rereads and rereads, standing far back and reading quickly from a distance, moving in close and reading slowly line-by-line, reading again and again. . . ."

But why, you might wonder, should you read your own writing? You, after all, are the one who wrote it, so if anyone must know what your text says, shouldn't it be you? The answer is that, precisely because you're the author, you're too close to your text to know what it says. As writers, we tend to be so invested in what we've written that we need to find ways of stepping back from our text to gain some critical distance.

Perhaps the central way of gaining such distance is by reading the draft from an outsider's perspective—as if, instead of being the author, you were some other person who is on the lookout for logical glitches and inconsistencies, for better ways of stating a point, for parts that are hard to follow, for claims and subclaims that need more explanation, or for how your argument might be vulnerable to critique. You might also try reading your text aloud to yourself—or even try using text-to-speech technology on your computer or phone. And it never hurts, if you have time, to set your draft aside for a few days so that when you return to it you can reread it with fresh eyes.

4. AND HAVE OTHERS READ YOUR WRITING, TOO

Of course there are other ways to get critical distance on your work and see it from an outsider's perspective. One of the best ways is to show your work to someone who is willing to read it—a fellow student, family member, friend, or tutor—and ask for feedback. Teachers, in fact, may ask you to pair up with another student to comment on each other's work. It's a great way to get a sense of audience: how your text will be processed and received when it goes out into the world. In seeking out such readers, we often naturally gravitate toward those who share our opinions and predilections. But don't underestimate the value of readers who may know little about your subject or disagree with your position. Often, the more readers differ from you, the more likely they will be able to see things that you yourself could not have thought of.

5. GO BACK TO THE TEXT

While developing a deep familiarity with your own writing is essential in any revision process, developing a deep famil-iarity with your sources is also very important. It's surprising how often errors are introduced when we haven't read the text we're responding to carefully enough and start writing about it before we really understand it. It's also surprising how often errors are introduced when we fail to check and double-check our quotations against the originals and thus mistranscribe them in our texts. If we are right that the most persuasive writing responds to something that others have said, then writing that misquotes or misrepresents what those others say, as we suggested in Chapter 2 (see particularly our comments on the "closest cliché syndrome"), will be built on a false foundation.

If you're anything like us, however, you might not like going back to your source. At times we don't want to go back to a source because we don't want to take the time to unpack its difficult, challenging language. At other times, we don't want to return to a source because we fear, deep down, that it doesn't quite say what we want it to say. When this happens, there is always a danger of creating a straw man: distorting what an author says in order to pursue our own agenda, transforming the author into a mere projection of ourselves. In this respect, accurately representing what "they say" is not just an intellectual obligation but a moral one as well.

As an example, let's turn to Rosa, a student who wanted to write an essay defending the practice of meditation. In her first draft, Rosa made a strong case that meditation promotes democratic politics, but she misconstrued her essay's central source, a scholarly article by Dean Mathiowetz that reads:

Meditation Is Good for Nothing

> Does meditation bring political benefits in the sense of strengthening citizenship or democracy? Taking the Zen phrase "meditation doesn't work—it's good for nothing" as my point of departure . . . I argue that meditation can foster significant dimensions of democratic citizenship. . . .

Mathiowetz's argument here is that meditation can in fact "foster significant dimensions of democratic citizenship"—or, as he goes on to claim, that, paradoxically, because "meditation . . . is good for nothing," it can help citizens and politicians detach from their self-interested passions and biases and find common ground. Yet Rosa presented Mathiowetz as saying that meditation is literally "good for nothing" and has no political or civic benefits.

When Rosa realized her mistake, she was inspired to do a revision. And the following week, she produced a much improved draft that opens as follows:

Many people think that meditation is a waste of time. According to these skeptics, meditation is a useless activity that is only for self-absorbed flakes who have no concern for the give-and-take of politics. But I disagree. As Dean Mathiowetz argues, the very uselessness of meditation makes it a valuable political tool. It can make us less polarized—better able to listen to one another and move beyond our rigid political views, and more committed to the common good.

In this way, Rosa was able to continue using Mathiowetz as a central source in her essay but without distorting his position. Instead of casting him as a naysayer in her essay who opposes meditation, she now presents Mathiowetz as the pro-meditation ally he really is.

6. DOES YOUR EXAMPLE SAY WHAT YOU SAY IT SAYS?

Offering an example to support your argument is such a natural, familiar part of writing that it may seem easy. And yet providing examples is often a challenge, largely because of the kind of disconnection issues we discussed in Chapter 8. When giving an example—which might take the form of a statistic, a quotation, evidence, or a story or anecdote—writers often discover that the example gets away from them. That is, the example they provide turns out not to support the point they want it to support and may even contradict it. So in revising your drafts, pay special attention to whether your example actually supports your argument, whether your example and what it is supposed to exemplify are united.

A student named Jacob needed help with this issue in an essay he'd written about how, as his title put it, "We All Need to Become More Green." In an attempt to provide a model example of someone who, in Jacob's words, has admirably "stopped using toxic, traditional household cleaners" that harm the environment, Jacob cites the case of his mother:

> My mother is a perfect example. She cares a lot about the environment and has always opposed chemicals. She frequently uses cleaning products in our house that are environmentally friendly but claims they never work. She once spent almost a hundred dollars on eco-friendly cleaners for our house but ended up throwing most of them out and returning to the toxic products she's always used. Nothing ever changes. She keeps using the old-fashioned cleaners but complaining about them.

Although each sentence here is admirably clear, Jacob ran into the classic problem of his thesis being out of sync with his example. Instead of showing that we should all stop using toxic cleaners, the story of his mother actually shows just how hard giving up such cleaners can be.

With Jacob's permission, his instructor circulated his essay to his class and asked how it might be revised. One student proposed that Jacob modify his thesis so that it asserts not just that we should all be more green, but that, to echo Kermit the Frog, "it's not easy being green," which, the student added, might be a fun new title for Jacob's essay. In his next draft, however, Jacob did decide to modify his argument, but in a different way by claiming that nobody, not even his deeply committed mother, will ever be able to become fully green if they don't lower their expectations about cleanliness.

7. KEEP ASKING "AS OPPOSED TO WHAT?"

Throughout this book we suggest that writers start "with what others are saying," as the subtitle of Chapter 1 puts it, and that they use this "they say" to motivate their "I say." But writers often neglect this important rhetorical move. They get so caught up in making their claims that they forget even the truest, most accurate, and well-supported claim will seem pointless if they fail to answer the all-important "as opposed to what?" or "who says otherwise?" question.

We sometimes forget to ask these questions ourselves. For example, it was only after years of writing and rewriting this very book that we realized there was an important "they say" or "as opposed to what?" contrast buried in our manuscript that we needed to draw out. At the end of a passage describing our templates as "one of the novel features of this book," we'd written:

> This book offers model templates to help you put key principles of writing directly into practice.

When we reread this sentence, we felt that it was missing something, that it sounded flat and uninspired. But why? After experimenting with different versions of the sentence, none of which seemed to help, we realized we weren't following our own advice. "There's no 'they say' here," Cathy announced. "Nothing we push off against, no 'as opposed to what.'" With this in mind, we embarked on another round of revisions and eventually came up with the following contrast, which now appears on page 2 of this edition:

Instead of focusing solely on abstract principles of writing, then, this book offers model templates to help you put those principles directly into practice.

Why did we prefer this version? Because its new material, which we've underlined, not only establishes that we offer templates but also indicates why: to depart from and, we hope, improve upon writing instruction that focuses only on "abstract principles." Had this sentence been all we changed, however, it would not have amounted to the type of "substantial" revision we've been saying is so important. But as often happens in the revision process, this one revision led to several others, setting in motion a series of revisions that significantly transformed our core argument. As we went back and reread the parts of the book we'd already written, we found several ways to extend the contrast we draw above between our templates and more abstract approaches. In the preface and introduction, we added two sections—"OK, but Templates?," and "What This Book Doesn't Do"—which help us further explain our template-based approach by contrasting it with what it isn't.

8. MOVE IT UP!

In her memoir *The Vanity Fair Diaries*, the magazine's former editor, Tina Brown, describes "the rewarding moment" in editing a manuscript

> when you see that the whole thing should start on page nine and flip the penultimate paragraph to the top of the piece, and all you want to do is call the writer immediately and tell him or her why. (73)

Brown's premise here is simple: *where* you say something matters, and the more important the point, the more it needs to be moved to "the top of the piece," where it will better get your reader's attention and infuse all you say that follows.

Imagine, after all, how frustrating it is for readers to have to slog through a lengthy text that doesn't state what its big point is until the very end, which is precisely what happens in Charles R. Morris's 333-page book, *A Rabble of Dead Money: The Great Crash and the Global Depression: 1929–1939*. Although Morris demonstrates impressive knowledge of the Great Depression and its historical era, he doesn't declare his central argument— that, contrary to what most people assume, "the 1929 stock market crash . . . did not cause the Depression"—until page 313. Had Morris foregrounded this point early in the book and used it to structure all that followed, readers wouldn't have been left wondering where he was going for the first three hundred pages: "Why is Morris telling us this?" "What's his big point?" "And this matters because . . . ?"

Delays of this kind are so common among writers that journalists long ago coined a term for it: "burying the lead" (or "lede," as it is sometimes spelled). Because writing is not a smoothly linear process of adding one perfectly polished paragraph on top of another until the last word is written, writers often don't know what their most important, or "lead," point will be until late in the writing process. As our cartoon on page 151 suggests, it is common for writers to start out thinking that their big idea will be one thing, only to realize later, just as they think their work is finished, that a different point needs to take center stage. When this happens, the best remedy, as Brown suggests, is to "flip" that point up "to the top of the piece," near the opening, and edit the rest so that your belatedly discovered argument informs your entire text from start to finish.

9. TAKE YOUR "UH-OH" MOMENTS SERIOUSLY

In our view, the best writers are always on the lookout for places in their writing that take their argument in the wrong direction. Especially when reading their work with a skeptical eye, as we suggested earlier, these self-critical writers keep looking for unanticipated implications in their writing that, for one reason or another, they are not comfortable with. As you reread your drafts, then, we suggest that you listen for any little voices in your head that say, "Uh-oh, what have I done? As I was arguing _____, I accidentally suggested _____." "Uh-oh" moments, as they might be called, can often be upsetting. But if you're willing to put in the time and to experiment with different solutions, you can head off such problems in your draft and possibly even turn them to your advantage.

Gerald had several such "uh-oh" moments as he was writing "Hidden Intellectualism" (see p. 291), in which he makes the counterintuitive claim that schools should be organized like sports. One, for instance, came when he was arguing that the worlds of academic intellectual culture and of popular sports are more similar than one might assume. He had written:

> [T]he real intellectual world, the one that existed in the big world beyond school, is organized very much like the world of team sports, with rival texts, rival interpretations and evaluations of texts, . . . and elaborate team competitions in which "fans" of writers, intellectual systems, methodologies, and -isms contend against one another. (295)

"Oh, no," Gerald thought to himself as he reread this passage. "Couldn't someone misunderstand me? Couldn't someone think that in saying schools should be organized like sports,

I'm promoting the ugly side of sports, the side that's filled with petty one-upmanship and, at times, even violence? How can I argue that schools should imitate the contentious domain of sports when schools already have too much small-minded and destructive competition?"

For a while, Gerald was disturbed enough by thoughts like these that he was tempted to simply eliminate the comparison he makes between sports and school. But after wrestling with the problem, he realized that he was defending sports not at their worst but at their best. As a result, the next chance he got, Gerald sat down with his manuscript and added the following new material, which explains that sports not only promote rivalry but

> also satisfy the thirst for community. When you entered sports debates, you became part of a community that was not limited to your family and friends, but was national and public. (295)

In this way, Gerald was able to use his "uh-oh" moment to enhance his argument. What began as a serious problem ended up helping him discover an aspect of his own argument that he hadn't seen before: that schooling should emulate not the uglier side of sports but the side that encourages camaraderie and broad, public excitement.

10. DON'T LET THE MESS SHOW

At several points in this chapter we have suggested that revising your writing in a global, substantial way is often a messy undertaking. In this final section, however, we want to suggest that to create a coherent, unified, and reader-friendly text, you need to *hide* this very mess. In other words, when you find any problems in your text, you need to do what is often a lot of hard work to correct them and make it look as if they never existed. If, for instance, you find a problem with your thesis, you need to not only reframe your thesis but also make sure that all your supporting claims, evidence, and examples, as we suggested above, match that thesis, erasing any confusing disconnects between your thesis and the rest of your text. Along similar lines, if you find that a section of your text doesn't make sense, you need to revise it until it does or eliminate that section altogether, making sure that the material that had preceded and followed the deleted material is well stitched together. And for a final example, if you realize that your best argument is buried too far back in your essay, you need not only to "move it up," as we suggested above, but also revise your entire draft so that it looks as if that best argument is what you had originally planned to say.

Joseph M. Williams and Lawrence McEnerney, writing experts, make a version of this point:

> If you find that the sentence from your conclusion is more insightful than the one from your introduction, then you have to revise your introduction to make it seem that you had this sentence in mind all along (even though when you started drafting the paper you may have had no idea how you were going to end it).

This advice holds true, we think, not just for introductions and conclusions but for virtually every part of a text. Even if you discover that your best claim appears mid-essay, you need to engage in a little smoke and mirrors, revising in a way that makes "it seem that you had" this claim in mind from the very outset, even though you hadn't.

A REVISION CHECKLIST

The checklist that follows is keyed both to this chapter on revision and to the writing advice throughout this book. It is composed of a series of questions designed to help you when rereading and revising your drafts.

Is Your Revision Really Substantial?

Look over the revisions you've made to your draft before turning it in and ask yourself if you have made enough changes to seriously improve it. If you've merely changed a few words or phrases, then you probably haven't addressed these larger issues: How coherent is your argument? Does your argument enter in dialogue with a motivating "they say"? Does your argument address a naysayer's counterargument? Is your argument consistent or contradictory?

Did you reread your draft several times and perhaps show it to other readers for feedback? If so, do you adequately respond to any concerns these readers raised, including ones possibly expressed to you by your instructor or a classmate?

Are the parts of your composition in the most effective order, or do some need to be moved? If you rearranged any of your text, have you revised the remaining material to avoid letting the "mess" show? (See pp. 163–64)

How Well Do You Represent What Others Say?

Do you start with what "they say"? If not, try revising to do so. See pages 23–28 for templates that can help.

Is it clear what is motivating your argument—why it needs to be made in the first place? If not, see pages 23–26 for templates that can help.

Do you summarize what others have said? If so, have you represented their views accurately—and adequately? Can you improve your summaries, perhaps by going back to the text and rereading the source you're summarizing?

Do you quote others? Have you carefully checked your quotations against the original sources? Do you frame each quotation in a way that integrates it into your text, explaining the quotation in your own words, and have you carefully considered whether the quotation actually supports your argument? (See pp. 49–51 for tips on creating a "quotation sandwich.")

Look at the verbs you use to introduce summaries and quotations, and consider how well they fit the action you're describing. If you've used all-purpose signal verbs such as X "said" or "believes," are there other such phrases that might be more precise, such as X "complains" or "predicts"? (See pp. 43–44 for a list of such signal verbs.)

Have you documented all of the sources you mention, both in parenthetical notations in the body of your text and at the end in a works-cited or references list?

Do you remind readers of the "they say" you're responding to throughout your text, or do you get off track and inadvertently start responding to a different "they say"? Can you revise so as to respond more continuously throughout the entire length of your text? (See pp. 27–28 for advice on using return sentences to keep your argument focused.)

How Effective Is What *You* Say?

Is it clear how you are responding to your "they say"? Is it clear what your position is—*agree, disagree, or a combination of both*—or might readers be unsure and need clarification? Do you use signal verbs that fit your position and clear language ("I question whether . . ." or "I'm of two minds about . . .")? (See Chapter 4 for three ways to respond and Chapter 5 for help in distinguishing the "I say" from "they say.")

If you disagree with the "they say" you're responding to, do you give reasons why in a way that moves the conversation forward, or do you merely contradict the "they say"? If you agree with the "they say," do you "agree with a difference," adding something of your own to the conversation? (For help with this move, see pp. 63–64.) And finally, if you both agree and disagree with your "they say," do you do so without contradicting yourself or seeming evasive? (See Chapter 4 for help in responding in these three different ways.)

Are your "I say" and "they say" clearly connected? Do your argument and the argument you are responding to address the same issue, or does a switch occur that takes you on a tangent? Do you use the same key terms for explaining both? (See pp. 116 for our discussion of key terms.)

What reasons—evidence, data, or examples—do you offer to support your "I say"? Do your reasons actually support your position, or is there a mismatch between them? Could a naysayer use your reasons against you to support a contrary position, and if so, could you defend your reasoning by summarizing and answering this objection? (See Chapter 6 for tips on doing so).

Will readers be able to distinguish what you say from what others say? Do you use voice markers ("My own view, however, is . . ." or "Skeptics, however, would disagree . . .") to mark the shift from the views of others to your own view and back? (See Chapter 5 for advice about using voice markers to make that distinction clear.)

Have You Introduced Any Naysayers?

Have you acknowledged likely objections to your argument? If so, have you represented these objections fairly—and responded to them persuasively? *If not,* think about what other perspectives exist on your topic, and incorporate them into your draft. (See Chapter 6 for tips on planting and responding to naysayers in your text.)

Have You Used Metacommentary?

How well, if at all, do you stand back from your writing and clarify what you do and don't mean? Might your argument be improved if you did a better job of explaining what you mean—or *don't* mean—with phrases like "in other words," "don't get me wrong," or "what I'm really trying to say here is . . ." (See Chapter 10 for examples of how to reinforce your argument with metacommentary.)

Do you have a helpful title? Does your title merely identify your topic, or does it successfully point to the position you take on that topic? Is your title lively and engaging, and might a subtitle help indicate your position?

Have You Tied It All Together?

Can readers follow your argument from one sentence, paragraph, and section to the next? Can readers see how each successive point is joined together in service of your overall argument? Are there any tangents that need to be brought in line with your larger train of thought or perhaps eliminated altogether?

Do you use transition phrases like "however," "in addition," and "in other words," which clarify how your ideas relate to one another? Are these phrases the right ones for your purposes—or do you use "however," say, when you really mean "also" or "in addition"? (See pp. 111–12 for a list of transitions.)

Do you use pointing words like "this" and "that," which help you gesture backward in your text and lead readers from one point to the next? If so, is it always clear what "this" and "that" refer to, or do you need to add nouns (e.g., "this book" or "this tendency to exaggerate") to avoid ambiguity? (See pp. 114–16 for tips on using pointing words to connect parts of your argument.)

Have you used what we call "repetition with a difference" to help connect parts of your argument? That is, do you succeed in *saying the same thing but in a slightly different way each time, which helps you move your argument forward and avoid being monotonous?* (See pp. 118–20 for help with this move).

Have You Shown Why Your Argument Matters?

Do you make clear why your argument is important—and why your readers should care? Might your draft be improved by using templates like "My critique here is important because_____" or "The stakes in how we answer this question are high, given that _____"? (See Chapter 7 for advice on addressing the "so what? and "who cares?" questions.)

Exercises

1. Read over a draft of your writing, and think about it globally. Explain to yourself the "big picture" of your argument using the following template: "Aha! Now I see! What I'm really trying to say is not, as I initially thought, _____ but _____." Use your response to write yourself a revision plan. Name two important things you need to do so that your argument matches what you're "really trying to say."

2. Read over a draft of your writing, paying particular attention to how you use sources.

   a. Go back to your sources to check how accurately you are using them. Confirm that your summaries and paraphrases are fair representations of the sources' arguments. Have you transcribed your quotations correctly? Have you properly cited all your sources?

   b. Look critically at the examples—quotations, evidence, anecdotes, and so forth—that you use to support your claims. Ask yourself, "Does this example support my argument?" Revise your writing to unify your argument and examples.

3. Read a draft of your writing out loud or listen to it using text-to-speech technology.

   a. As you read or listen, mark the places in the text that are hard to follow. Then go back to these places and revise them. Could you use better transitions? Might metacommentary help? Could you use more voice markers, such as "In Smith's opinion . . ." or "She argues . . ."?

   b. As you read or listen, also mark the places in the text where you find yourself saying "uh-oh" because your words or their implications don't reflect your underlying intentions. Then go back to these "uh-oh" moments to clarify your intentions. Consider using a template like "This is not to suggest . . . It is, however, to suggest . . ."

TWELVE

"I TAKE YOUR POINT"

Entering Class Discussions

HAVE YOU EVER been in a class discussion that feels less like a genuine meeting of the minds than like a series of discrete, disconnected monologues? You make a comment, say, that seems provocative to you, but the classmate who speaks after you makes no reference to what you said, instead going off in an entirely different direction. Then the classmate who speaks next makes no reference either to you or to anyone else, making it seem as if everyone in the conversation is more interested in their own ideas than in actually conversing with anyone else.

We like to think that the principles this book advances can help improve class discussions, which increasingly include various forms of online communication. Particularly important for class discussion is the point that our own ideas become more cogent and powerful the more responsive we are to others and the more we frame our claims not in isolation but as responses to what others before us have said. Ultimately, then, a good face-to-face classroom discussion (or online communication) doesn't just happen spontaneously. It requires the same sorts of disciplined moves and practices used in many writing situations, particularly that of identifying to what and to whom you are responding.

FRAME YOUR COMMENTS AS A RESPONSE
TO SOMETHING THAT HAS ALREADY BEEN SAID

The single most important thing you need to do when joining a class discussion is to link what you are about to say to something that has already been said.

> ▸ I really liked Aaron's point about <u>the two sides being closer than they seem</u>. I'd add that <u>both seem rather moderate</u>.

> ▸ I take your point, Nadia, that _____. Still . . .

> ▸ Though Kayla and Ryan seem to be at odds about _____, they may actually not be all that far apart.

In framing your comments this way, it is usually best to name both the person and the idea you're responding to. If you name the person alone ("I agree with Aaron because _____"), it may not be clear to listeners what part of what Aaron said you are referring to. Conversely, if you only summarize what Aaron said without naming him, you'll probably leave your classmates wondering whose comments you're referring to.

But won't you sound stilted and deeply redundant in class if you try to restate the point your classmate just made? After all, in the case of the first template above, the entire class will have just heard Aaron's point about the two sides being closer than they seem. Why, then, would you need to restate it?

We agree that in oral situations it does often sound artificial to restate what others just said precisely because they just said it. It would be awkward if on being asked to pass the salt at lunch, one were to reply: "If I understand you correctly, you have asked me to pass the salt. Yes, I can, and here it is." But in oral discussions about complicated issues that are open to multiple interpretations, we usually do need to resummarize what others have said to make sure that everyone is on the same page. Since Aaron may have made several points when he spoke and may have been followed by other commentators, the class will probably need you to summarize which point of his you are referring to. And even if Aaron made only one point, restating that point is helpful not only to remind the group what his point was (since some may have missed or forgotten it) but also to make sure that he, you, and others have interpreted his point in the same way.

TO CHANGE THE SUBJECT, INDICATE EXPLICITLY THAT YOU ARE DOING SO

It is fine to try to change the conversation's direction. There's just one catch: you need to make clear to listeners that this is what you are doing. For example:

▸ So far we have been talking about <u>the characters in the film</u>. But isn't the real issue here <u>the cinematography</u>?

▸ I'd like to change the subject to one that hasn't yet been addressed.

You can try to change the subject without indicating that you are doing so. But you risk that your comment will come across as irrelevant rather than as a thoughtful contribution that moves the conversation forward.

BE EVEN MORE EXPLICIT
THAN YOU WOULD BE IN WRITING

Because listeners in an oral discussion can't go back and reread what you just said, they are more easily overloaded than are readers of a print text. For this reason, in a class discussion you will do well to take some extra steps to help listeners follow your train of thought. (1) When you make a comment, limit yourself to one point only, though you can elaborate on this point, fleshing it out with examples and evidence. If you feel you must make two points, either unite them under one larger umbrella point, or make one point first and save the other for later. Trying to bundle two or more claims into one comment can result in neither getting the attention it deserves. (2) Use metacommentary to highlight your key point so that listeners can readily grasp it.

▶ In other words, what I'm trying to get at here is _____.

▶ My point is this: _____.

▶ My point, though, is not _____ but _____.

▶ This distinction is important because _____.

Exercises

1. Choose a text you've read in class, and discuss the text's argument in a small group. Use these questions to start your conversation:

   a. Whom (or what) is the writer responding to?

b. What perspectives does the writer include, and what perspectives are missing?

c. Why does this argument matter?

2. Listen carefully to a class discussion, either in this class or another one of your courses. Notice what moves from this chapter your classmates and your instructor make:

   a. How do they frame their comments to link their ideas to something that has already been said?

   b. How do they change the direction of the conversation?

   c. How do they use metacommentary to clarify their points?

   Reflect on the conversation as a whole. Were the people in the conversation responsive to one another's ideas, or did the conversation feel more like a series of unconnected points? Explain one strategy from this chapter that would improve class discussions.

3. In your next class discussion, try using use these strategies to help your classmates follow your ideas:

   a. Write down your thoughts before you say them.

   b. Limit yourself to just one point per comment.

   c. Use metacommentary to highlight your key idea.

   How did these strategies help clarify your ideas? How did they help you listen more attentively to others? How did they invite others to respond? What was challenging about this exercise?

THIRTEEN

DON'T MAKE THEM SCROLL UP

Entering Online Conversations

—⌐⌐—

THE INTERNET HAS TRANSFORMED COMMUNICATION in more ways than we can count. With just a few taps on a keyboard, we can be connected with what others have said not only throughout history, but right now, in the most remote places. Almost instantaneously, communities can be created that are powerful enough to change the world. In addition, virtually the moment we voice an opinion online, we can get responses from supporters and critics alike, while any links we provide to sources can connect readers to voices they might otherwise never have known about and to conversations they might never have been able to join.

Because of this connectivity, the internet lends itself perfectly to the type of conversational writing at the core of this book. Just the other day, we were on a discussion board in which one of the participants wrote to another, let's call him X, in a form that could have provided a template for this textbook: "Fascinating point about _____, X. I'd never thought of it that way before. I'd always thought that _____, but if you're right, then that would explain why _____."

IDENTIFY WHAT YOU'RE RESPONDING TO

Unfortunately, not all online writers make clear who or what prompted them to write. As a result, too many online exchanges end up being not true conversations but a series of statements without clear relationships to one another. All too often, it's hard to tell if the writer is building on what someone else has said, challenging it, or trying to change the discussion topic altogether. So although the digital world may connect us far more rapidly and with far more people than ever, it doesn't always encourage a genuine meeting of minds.

We've seen this type of confusion in the writing our own students submit to online discussions. Even students who use the "they say / I say" framework routinely and effectively in the essays they write often neglect to make those same moves online. While our students engage enthusiastically in online discussions, their posts are often all "I say" with little or no "they say." As a result, they end up talking past rather than to one another.

What is happening here, we suspect, is that the easy accessibility made possible by the internet makes slowing down and summarizing or even identifying what others say seem unnecessary. Why repeat the views you are responding to, writers seem to assume, when readers can easily find them by simply scrolling up or clicking on a link?

The problem with this way of thinking is that readers won't always take the time to track down the comments you're responding to, assuming they can figure out what those comments are to begin with. And even when readers do make the effort to find the comments you're responding to, they may not be sure what aspect or part of those comments you're referring to

or how you interpret them. Ultimately, when you fail to identify your "they say," you leave readers guessing, like someone
listening to one side of a phone conversation trying to piece
together what's being said at the other end.

It's true, of course, that there are some situations online
where summarizing what you're responding to would indeed
be redundant. When, for instance, you're replying to a friend's
text asking, "Meet in front of the theater at 7?" a mere "OK"
suffices, whereas a more elaborate response—"With regard to
your suggestion that we meet in front of the theater at 7, my
answer is yes"—would be not only redundant but also downright bizarre. But in more complex academic conversations
where the ideas are challenging, many people are involved,
and there is therefore a greater chance of misunderstanding,
you do need to clarify whom and what you're responding to.

To see how hard it can be to make sense of a post that
fails to identify the "they say" it is responding to, consider the
following example from an online class discussion devoted to
Nicholas Carr's article "Is Google Making Us Stupid?":

> Blogs and social media allow us to reach many people all at once. The internet makes us more efficient.

When we first read this post, we could see that this writer was making a claim about the efficiency of the internet, but we weren't sure what the claim had to do with Carr or with any of the other comments in the discussion. After all, the writer never names Carr or anyone else in the conversation. Nor does she use templates such as "Like Carr, I believe _____" or "What X overlooks is _____" to indicate whether she's agreeing or disagreeing with Carr or with one of her classmates. Indeed, we couldn't tell if the writer had even read Carr or any of the other posts, or if she was just expressing her own views on the topic.

We suspect, however, that in arguing that the internet is making us more efficient, this writer was probably trying to refute Carr's argument that the internet is, as Carr puts it in his title, "making us stupid." Then again, she could also have been criticizing someone who agreed with Carr—or, conversely, siding with someone else who disagreed with Carr.

It would have been better if she had used the "they say / I say" framework taught in this book, opening not with her own "I say," as she did but with the "they say" that's motivated her to respond, perhaps using one of the following templates:

▸ **X argues that _____.**

▸ **Like X, Y would have us believe that _____.**

▸ **In challenging X's argument that _____, Y asserts that _____.**

It would also have helped if, in her "I say," she had identified the "they say" she is addressing, using a template like one of these:

▸ **But what X overlooks is that _____.**

▸ **What both X and Y fail to see is that _____.**

▸ **Z's point is well taken. Like him, I contend that _____ is not, as X insists, _____ but _____.**

Here's one way this writer might have responded:

> Carr argues that Google is undermining our ability to think and read deeply. But far from making people "stupid," as Carr puts it in his title, the internet, in my view, is making people more efficient. What Carr ignores is how blogs and social media allow us to reach many people at once.

This version makes clear that the writer is not just making a claim out of the blue but that she also had a reason for making her claim: to take a position in a conversation or debate.

TECHNOLOGY WON'T DO ALL THE WORK

But still, you might wonder, doesn't the internet enable writers to connect so directly with others that summarizing their claims is unnecessary? Granted, the internet does provide several unique ways of referring to what others are saying, like linking and embedding, that help us connect to what others are saying. But as the following examples show, these techniques don't mean that technology will do all the work for you.

LINKING TO WHAT "THEY SAY"

One way the internet makes it especially easy to connect directly with others is by allowing us to insert a link to what others have said into our own text. Anything with a URL can be linked to—blog posts, magazine articles, *Facebook* posts, and so forth. Readers can then click on the words to which you've attached the link and be taken directly to that page, as we can see in the following comment in another online class discussion about how the internet affects our brains:

> In his essay "Is Google Making Us Stupid?" Nicholas Carr argues that the kind of skimming we do when we read online destroys deep reading and thinking. But I would argue the opposite: that all the complex information we're exposed to online actually makes us read and think more deeply.

By including a link to Carr's essay, this writer gives her readers direct access to Carr's arguments, allowing them to assess how well she has summarized and responded to what he wrote. But the reason the writer's post succeeds is that she introduces the link to Carr's essay, summarizes what she takes Carr to be saying, and gives her response to it.

Here are a few templates for framing a link:

▸ As X mentions in <u>this article</u>, " _____."

▸ In making <u>this comment</u>, X warns that _____.

▸ Economists often assume _____; however, <u>new research</u> by X suggests _____.

JUXTAPOSING YOUR "THEY SAY"
WITH YOUR "I SAY"

Another way that online forums enhance our ability to connect with others is by allowing readers to respond—not only to the original article or post but also to one another through what we might call "juxtaposition." On many online forums, when you reply to someone else's comment, your response appears below the original comment and indented slightly, so that it is visually clear whom you're responding to. This means that, in many cases, your "they say" and "I say" are presented almost as a single conversational unit, as the following example from the online discussion of Carr's article illustrates:

> Lee, 4/12/20, 3:02 PM
>
> Carr argues that the internet has harmed us by making it hard for us to read without breaks to look at other things. That might be true, but overall I think it has improved our lives by giving us access to so many different viewpoints.

>> Cody, 4/12/20, 5:15 PM
>>
>> Like Lee, I think the internet has improved our lives more than it's hurt them. I would add that it's enabled us to form and participate in political communities online that make people way more politically engaged.

Twitter also allows for this type of close proximity, by enabling you to embed someone else's tweet inside your own. For instance, consider the following tweet:

> **Jade T. Moore** @JadeTMoore
>
> @willwst I agree—access to books is a social justice issue.
>
> > **William West** @willwst
> >
> > Every child has the right to access to a school library.

Cody's response in the discussion board and Jade's on *Twitter* are effective not only because the platforms connect Cody and Jade to their "they say" but also because they take the time to make those connections clear. Cody connects his comment to his "they say" by including the words "Like Lee" and restating Lee's view, while Jade does so by including West's *Twitter* handle, @willwst, and the words "I agree." Sure, the technology does some of the work, by making the responses to comments directly available for readers to see—no scrolling or searching involved. But it can't do it all. Imagine if Cody, for instance, had merely written, "We're able to form and participate in political communities online that make people way more politically engaged." Or if Jade hadn't included an "I agree" with her comment. As readers, we'd have been left scratching our heads, unable to tell what Cody's claim had to do with Lee's claim, or what Jade's claim had to do with William's, despite how close together these claims are on the screen.

Digital communication, then, does shrink the world, as is often said, allowing us to connect with others in ways we couldn't before. But technology doesn't relieve writers of the need to use the "they say / I say" framework. A central premise of this book is that this framework is a rhetorical move that transcends the differences between all types of writing. Whether you're writing online or off, if you want others to listen to what you say, you'd better pay attention to what they think, and start with what they say. However limited your space, whatever your format, and whatever the technology, you can always find a way to identify and summarize your "they say."

Exercises

1. Look back at some of your old posts on a social media site, a class discussion board, or some other website. How well did you let other readers know whom and what you were responding to and what your own position was? What kinds of moves did you make? Does that site have any conventions or special features that you used? Revise one of your posts using the strategies described in this chapter so that your post more clearly follows the "they say / I say" format.

2. Choose an online forum (e.g., *Facebook*, *Twitter*, **theysayiblog.com**), and analyze how the site encourages users to enter conversations in response to others:

   a. Is it easy to tell whom and what people are responding to? Why or why not?

   b. What features, structures, or norms specific to that forum (e.g., embedding, hashtags, linking, etc.) influence how users formulate their "they say"?

c. Find a post that you think follows the "they say / I say" format. Describe how the writer uses the forum's specific features as well as templates from this book to clarify whom and what are being responded to.

3. Go to the blog that accompanies this book, **theysayiblog.com**. Examine some of the exchanges that appear there and evaluate the quality of the responses. For example, how well do the participants in these exchanges summarize one another's claims before making their own responses? How would you characterize the discussion? How well do people listen to one another? How do these online discussions compare with the face-to-face discussions you have in class? What advantages do each offer? Go to other blogs or forums on topics that interest you, and ask these same questions.

FOURTEEN

WHAT'S MOTIVATING THIS WRITER?

Reading for the Conversation

"W HAT IS THE AUTHOR'S ARGUMENT? What is the author trying to say?" For many years, these were the first questions we would ask our classes in a discussion of an assigned reading. The discussion that resulted was often halting, as our students struggled to get a handle on the argument, but eventually, after some awkward silences, the class would come up with something we could all agree was an accurate summary of the author's main thesis. Even after we'd gotten over that hurdle, however, the discussion would often still seem forced and would limp along as we all struggled with the question that naturally arose next: now that we had determined what the author was saying, what did we ourselves have to say?

For a long time we didn't worry much about these halting discussions, justifying them to ourselves as the predictable result of assigning difficult, challenging readings. Several years ago, however, as we started writing this book and began thinking about writing as the art of entering conversations, we latched on to the idea of leading with some different questions: "What other argument(s) is the writer responding to?" "Is the writer disagreeing or agreeing with something, and if so, what?" "What is motivating the writer's argument?" "Are there other ideas that you have encountered in this class or elsewhere that might be pertinent?" The results were often striking. The discussions that followed tended to be far livelier and to draw in a greater number of students. We were still asking students to look for the main argument, but we were now asking them to see that argument as a response to some other argument that provoked it, gave it a reason for being, and helped all of us see why we should care about it.

What had happened, we realized, was that by changing the opening question, we changed the way our students approached reading and perhaps the way they thought about academic work in general. Instead of thinking of the argument of a text as an isolated entity, they now thought of that argument as one that responded to and provoked other arguments. Since they were now dealing not with *one* argument but at least *two* (the author's argument and the one[s] being responded to), they now had alternative ways of seeing the topic at hand. This meant that instead of just trying to understand the view presented by the author, they were more able to question that view intelligently and engage in the type of discussion and debate that is the hallmark of a college education. In our discussions, animated debates often arose between students who found the author's argument convincing and others who were more convinced by the view it was challenging. In the best of these debates, the binary positions would be questioned by other students, who suggested each was too simple, that both might be right or that a third alternative was possible. Still other students might object that the discussion thus far had missed the author's real point and suggest that we all go back to the text and pay closer attention to what it actually said.

We eventually realized that the move from reading for the author's argument in isolation to reading for how the author's argument is in conversation with the arguments of others helps readers become active, critical readers rather than passive recipients of knowledge. On some level, reading for the conversation is more rigorous and demanding than reading for what one author says. It asks that you determine not only what the author thinks but also how what the author thinks fits with what others think and ultimately with what you yourself think. Yet on another level, reading this way is a lot simpler and more familiar than reading for the thesis alone, since it returns writing to the familiar, everyday act of communicating with other people about real issues.

DECIPHERING THE CONVERSATION

We suggest, then, that when assigned a reading, you imagine the author not as sitting alone in an empty room hunched over a desk or staring at a screen but as sitting in a crowded coffee shop talking to and engaging with others who are making claims. In other words, imagine an ongoing, multisided conversation in which all participants (including the author) are trying to persuade others to agree or at least to take their positions seriously.

The trick in reading for the conversation is to figure out *what views the author is responding to* and *what the author's own argument is*—or, to put it in the terms used in this book, to determine the "they say" and how the author responds to it. One of the challenges in reading for the "they say" and "I say" can be figuring out which is which, since it may not be obvious when writers are summarizing others and when they are speaking for themselves. Readers need to be alert for any changes in voice that a writer might make, since instead of using explicit road-mapping phrases like "although many believe," authors may simply summarize the view that they want to engage with and indicate only subtly that it is not their own.

Consider again the opening to the selection by David Zinczenko on page 199:

> If ever there were a newspaper headline custom-made for Jay Leno's monologue, this was it. Kids taking on McDonald's this week, suing the company for making them fat. Isn't that like middle-aged men suing Porsche for making them get speeding tickets? Whatever happened to personal responsibility?
>
> I tend to sympathize with these portly fast-food patrons, though. Maybe that's because I used to be one of them.
>
> DAVID ZINCZENKO, "Don't Blame the Eater"

Whenever we teach this passage, some students inevitably assume that Zinczenko must be espousing the view expressed in his first paragraph: that suing McDonald's is ridiculous. When their reading is challenged by their classmates, these students point to the page and reply, "Look. It's right here on the page. This is what Zinczenko wrote. These are his exact words." The assumption these students are making is that if something appears on the page, the author must endorse it. In fact, however, we ventriloquize views that we don't believe in, and may in fact passionately disagree with, all the time. The central clues that Zinczenko disagrees with the view expressed in his opening paragraph come in the second paragraph, when he finally offers a first-person declaration and

See Chapter 6 for more discussion of naysayers.

uses a contrastive transition, "though," thereby resolving any questions about where he stands.

WHEN THE "THEY SAY" IS UNSTATED

Another challenge can be identifying the "they say" when it is not explicitly identified. Whereas Zinczenko offers an up-front summary of the view he is responding to, other writers assume that their readers are so familiar with these views that they need not name or summarize them. In such cases, you the reader have to reconstruct the unstated "they say" that is motivating the text through a process of inference.

See, for instance, if you can reconstruct the position that Tamara Draut is challenging in the opening paragraph of her essay "The Growing College Gap":

> "The first in her family to graduate from college." How many times have we heard that phrase, or one like it, used to describe a successful American with a modest background? In today's United States, a four-year degree has become the all-but-official ticket to middle-class security. But if your parents don't have much money or higher education in their own right, the road to college—and beyond—looks increasingly treacherous. Despite a sharp increase in the proportion of high school graduates going on to some form of postsecondary education, socio-economic status continues to exert a powerful influence on college admission and completion; in fact, gaps in enrollment by class and race, after declining in the 1960s and 1970s, are once again as wide as they were thirty years ago, and getting wider, even as college has become far more crucial to lifetime fortunes.
>
> TAMARA DRAUT, "The Growing College Gap"

You might think that the "they say" here is embedded in the third sentence: they say (or we all think) that a four-year degree is "the all-but-official ticket to middle-class security," and you might assume that Draut will go on to disagree.

If you read the passage this way, however, you would be mistaken. Draut is not questioning whether a college degree has become the "ticket to middle-class security" but whether most Americans can obtain that ticket, whether college is within the financial reach of most American families. You may have been thrown off by the "but" following the statement that college has become a prerequisite for middle-class security. However, unlike the "though" in Zinczenko's opening, this "but" does not signal that Draut will be disagreeing with the view she has just summarized, a view that in fact she takes as a given. What Draut disagrees with is that this ticket to middle-class security is still readily available to the middle and working classes.

Were one to imagine Draut in a room talking with others with strong views on this topic, one would need to picture her challenging not those who think college is a ticket to financial security (something she agrees with and takes for granted) but those who think the doors of college are open to anyone willing to put forth the effort to walk through them. The view that Draut is challenging, then, is not summarized in her opening. Instead, she assumes that readers are already so familiar with this view that it need not be stated.

Draut's example suggests that in texts where the central "they say" is not immediately identified, you have to construct it yourself based on the clues the text provides. You have to start by locating the writer's thesis and then imagine some of the arguments that might be made against it. What would it look like to disagree with this view? In Draut's case, it is relatively easy to construct a counterargument: it is the familiar faith in the

American Dream of equal opportunity when it comes to access to college. Figuring out the counterargument not only reveals what motivated Draut as a writer but also helps you respond to her essay as an active, critical reader. Constructing this counter-argument can also help you recognize how Draut challenges your own views, questioning opinions that you previously took for granted.

WHEN THE "THEY SAY" IS ABOUT SOMETHING "NOBODY HAS TALKED ABOUT"

Another challenge in reading for the conversation is that writ-ers sometimes build their arguments by responding to a *lack* of discussion. These writers build their case not by playing off views that can be identified (like faith in the American Dream or the idea that we are responsible for our body weight) but by pointing to something others have overlooked. As the writing theorists John M. Swales and Christine B. Feak point out, one effective way to "create a research space" and "establish a niche" in the academic world is "by indicating a gap in . . . previous research." Much research in the sciences and humanities takes this "Nobody has noticed X" form.

In such cases, the writer may be responding to scientists, for example, who have overlooked an obscure plant that offers insights into global warming or to literary critics who have been so busy focusing on the lead character in a play that they have overlooked something important about the minor characters.

READING PARTICULARLY CHALLENGING TEXTS

Sometimes it is difficult to figure out the views that writers are responding to, not because these writers do not identify those views but because their language and the concepts they are dealing with are particularly challenging. Consider, for instance, the first two sentences of *Gender Trouble: Feminism and the Subversion of Identity*, a book by the feminist philosopher and literary theorist Judith Butler, thought by many to be a particularly difficult academic writer:

> Contemporary feminist debates over the meaning of gender lead time and again to a certain sense of trouble, as if the indeterminacy of gender might eventually culminate in the failure of feminism. Perhaps trouble need not carry such a negative valence.
>
> JUDITH BUTLER, Gender Trouble:
Feminism and the Subversion of Identity

There are many reasons readers may stumble over this relatively short passage, not the least of which is that Butler does not explicitly indicate where her own view begins and the view she is responding to ends. Unlike Zinczenko, Butler does not use the first-person "I" or a phrase such as "in my own view" to show that the position in the second sentence is her own. Nor does Butler offer a clear transition such as "but" or "however" at the start of the second sentence to indicate, as Zinczenko does with "though," that in the second sentence she is questioning the argument she has summarized in the first. And finally, like many academic writers, Butler uses abstract, challenging words that many readers may need to look up, like "indeterminacy" (the quality of being impossible to define or pin down), "culminate" (finally result in), and "negative valence" (a term borrowed from chemistry, roughly denoting "negative significance" or "meaning"). For all these reasons, we can imagine many readers feeling intimidated before they reach the third sentence of Butler's book.

But readers who break down this passage into its essential parts will find that it is actually a lucid piece of writing that conforms to the classic "they say / I say" pattern. Though it can be difficult to spot the clashing arguments in the two sentences, close analysis reveals that the first sentence offers a way of looking at a certain type of "trouble" in the realm of feminist politics that is being challenged in the second.

To understand difficult passages of this kind, you need to translate them into your own words—to build a bridge, in effect, between the passage's unfamiliar terms and ones more familiar to you. Building such a bridge should help you connect what you already know to what the author is saying—and will then help you move from reading to writing, providing you with some of the language you will need to summarize the text. One major challenge in translating the author's words into your own, however, is to stay true to what the author is actually saying, avoiding what we call "the closest cliché syndrome," in which one mistakes a commonplace idea for an author's more complex one (mistaking Butler's critique of the concept of "woman," for instance, for the common idea that women must have equal rights). The work of complex writers like Butler, who frequently challenge conventional thinking, cannot always be collapsed into the types of ideas most of us are already familiar with. Therefore, when you translate, do not try to fit the ideas of such writers into your preexisting beliefs, but instead allow your own views to be challenged. In building a bridge to the writers you read, it is often necessary to meet those writers more than halfway.

So what, then, does Butler's opening say? Translating Butler's words into terms that are easier to understand, we can see that the first sentence says that for many feminists today,

For more on translating, see Chapter 9.

For more on the closest cliché syndrome, see Chapter 2.

"the indeterminacy of gender"—the inability to define the essence of sexual identity—spells the end of feminism; that for many feminists the inability to define "gender," presumably the building block of the feminist movement, means serious "trouble" for feminist politics. In contrast, the second sentence suggests that this same "trouble" need not be thought of in such "negative" terms, that the inability to define femininity, or "gender trouble" as Butler calls it in her book's title, may not be such a bad thing—and, as she goes on to argue in the pages that follow, may even be something that feminist activists can profit from. In other words, Butler suggests, highlighting uncertainties about masculinity and femininity can be a powerful feminist tool.

Pulling all these inferences together, then, the opening sentences can be translated as follows: "While many contemporary feminists believe that uncertainty about what it means to be a woman will undermine feminist politics, I, Judith Butler, believe that this uncertainty can actually help strengthen feminist politics." Translating Butler's point into our own book's basic move: "They say that if we cannot define 'woman,' feminism is in big trouble. But I say that this type of trouble is precisely what feminism needs." Despite its difficulty, then, we hope you agree that this initially intimidating passage does make sense if you stay with it.

We hope it is clear that critical reading is a two-way street. It is just as much about being open to the way that writers can challenge you, maybe even transform you, as it is about questioning those writers. And if you translate a writer's argument into your own words as you read, you should allow the text to take you outside the ideas that you already hold and to introduce you to new terms and concepts. Even if you end up disagreeing with an author, you first have to show that you have really listened to what is being said, have fully grasped the arguments, and can accurately summarize those arguments. Without such deep, attentive listening, any critique you make will be superficial and decidedly *uncritical*. It will be a critique that says more about you than about the writer or idea you're supposedly responding to.

In this chapter we have tried to show that reading for the conversation means looking not just for the thesis of a text in isolation but for the view or views that motivate that thesis—the "they say." We have also tried to show that reading for the conversation means being alert for the different strategies writers use to engage the view(s) that are motivating them, since not all writers engage other perspectives in the same way. Some writers explicitly identify and summarize a view they are responding to at the outset of their text and then return to it frequently as their text unfolds. Some refer only obliquely to a view that is motivating them, assuming that readers will be able to reconstruct that view on their own. Other writers may not explicitly distinguish their own view from the views they are questioning in ways that all of us find clear, leaving some readers to wonder whether a given view is the writer's own or one that is being challenged. And some writers push off against the "they say" that is motivating them in a challenging academic language that requires readers to translate what they are saying into more accessible, everyday terms. In sum, then, though most persuasive writers do follow a conversational "they say / I say" pattern, they do so in a great variety of ways. What this means for readers is that they need to be armed with various strategies for detecting the conversations in what they read, even when those conversations are not self-evident.

Exercises

1. Read Michelle Alexander's "The New Jim Crow" (pp. 298–311). Use the strategies described in this chapter to examine the conversation at the heart of her essay. Write a paragraph explaining what is motivating Alexander. What views of the US criminal justice system—and American culture—does Alexander think need correcting?
2. Annotate the concluding section of Michelle Alexander's essay, found on pages 298–311. Write "TS" in the margins where you see Alexander summarizing a "they say." Write "IS" in the margins where you see her asserting her own "I say" position. Circle the voice markers you see in the text.
3. Read over a draft of your own writing, and choose an important text you rely on in it. Reread that text, and then do the following:

   a. Ask yourself, "What view is motivating the author of this text?" Highlight where you see the writer naming or hinting at this motivating viewpoint.

   b. Examine how you use the text to motivate your own argument. Have you presented its argument thoroughly and accurately? Have you aligned the text clearly with your own "I say" position, showing whether it supports your position, challenges it, or some combination of both? If not, revise how you frame, summarize, or interpret this source accordingly.

Don't Blame the Eater

DAVID ZINCZENKO

———▢———

IF EVER THERE WERE a newspaper headline custom-made for Jay Leno's* monologue, this was it. Kids taking on McDonald's this week, suing the company for making them fat. Isn't that like middle-aged men suing Porsche for making them get speeding tickets? Whatever happened to personal responsibility?

I tend to sympathize with these portly fast-food patrons, though. Maybe that's because I used to be one of them.

I grew up as a typical mid-1980s latchkey kid. My parents were split up, my dad off trying to rebuild his life, my mom working long hours to make the monthly bills. Lunch and dinner, for me, was a daily choice between

———

DAVID ZINCZENKO, who was for many years the editor-in-chief of the fitness magazine *Men's Health*, is founder and CEO of Galvanized Brands, a global health and wellness media company. This piece was first published on the Op-Ed page of the *New York Times* on November 23, 2002.

***Jay Leno** Comedian and former host of NBC's *The Tonight Show*.

McDonald's, Taco Bell, Kentucky Fried Chicken, or Pizza Hut. Then as now, these were the only available options for an American kid to get an affordable meal. By age 15, I had packed 212 pounds of torpid teenage tallow on my once lanky 5-foot-10 frame.

Then I got lucky. I went to college, joined the Navy Reserves and got involved with a health magazine. I learned how to manage my diet. But most of the teenagers who live, as I once did, on a fast-food diet won't turn their lives around: they've crossed under the golden arches to a likely fate of lifetime obesity. And the problem isn't just theirs—it's all of ours.

Before 1994, diabetes in children was generally caused by a genetic disorder—only about 5 percent of childhood cases were obesity-related, or Type 2, diabetes. Today, according to the National Institutes of Health, Type 2 diabetes accounts for at least 30 percent of all new childhood cases of diabetes in this country.

5

For tips on saying why it matters, see Chapter 7.

Not surprisingly, money spent to treat diabetes has skyrocketed, too. The Centers for Disease Control and Prevention estimate that diabetes accounted for $2.6 billion in health care costs in 1969. Today's number is an unbelievable $100 billion a year.

Shouldn't we know better than to eat two meals a day in fast-food restaurants? That's one argument. But where, exactly, are consumers—particularly teenagers—supposed to find alternatives? Drive down any thoroughfare in America, and I guarantee you'll see one of our country's more than 13,000 McDonald's restaurants. Now, drive back up the block and try to find someplace to buy a grapefruit.

Complicating the lack of alternatives is the lack of information about what, exactly, we're consuming. There are no calorie information charts on fast-food packaging, the way there are on grocery items. Advertisements don't carry warning labels the way tobacco ads do. Prepared foods aren't covered under Food and Drug Administration labeling laws. Some fast-food purveyors will provide calorie information on request, but even that can be hard to understand.

For example, one company's Web site lists its chicken salad as containing 150 calories; the almonds and noodles that come with it (an additional 190 calories) are listed separately. Add a serving of the 280-calorie dressing, and you've got a healthy lunch alternative that comes in at 620 calories. But that's not all. Read the small print on the back of the dressing packet and you'll realize it actually contains 2.5 servings. If you pour what you've been served, you're suddenly up around 1,040 calories, which is half of the government's recommended daily calorie intake. And that doesn't take into account that 450-calorie super-size Coke.

Make fun if you will of these kids launching lawsuits against   10
the fast-food industry, but don't be surprised if you're the next plaintiff. As with the tobacco industry, it may be only a matter of time before state governments begin to see a direct line between the $1 billion that McDonald's and Burger King spend each year on advertising and their own swelling health care costs.

And I'd say the industry is vulnerable. Fast-food companies are marketing to children a product with proven health hazards and no warning labels. They would do well to protect themselves, and their customers, by providing the nutrition information people need to make informed choices about their products. Without such warnings, we'll see more sick, obese children and more angry, litigious parents. I say, let the deep-fried chips fall where they may.

FIFTEEN

"BUT AS SEVERAL SOURCES SUGGEST"

Research as Conversation

—⌐◻┐—

So, you've been asked to write a research essay. What exactly does that mean? What is your instructor asking you to do?

The best answer to these questions, of course, will always come from your instructors and from any assignment prompt or prompts that they may provide. Although most instructors will want a traditional paper or essay, some will want a webpage, podcast, or a poster that includes a visual component and may even be produced collaboratively with your classmates. Yet other instructors will urge you to produce what is often referred to as a "literature review," in which you summarize a variety of sources on a topic ("literature," in this case, referring not to poems and novels but to published commentary, such as the literature on the French Revolution). Chances are, however, if you've been assigned this book, your instructor will want whatever final project you produce to follow our "they say / I say" model. In our opinion, even the best literature reviews are not just disconnected summaries of various sources but coherent, unified documents that highlight the connections among these sources, framing—and very often entering—the conversation among them. As a result, though we speak throughout this chapter about "the research essay," we hope you'll be able to translate what we say about the conversational pattern at the heart of such essays to any alternative versions of the genre you may be producing. Regardless of what form it takes, the research essay, as we conceive it, is always about entering into conversation with others.

This might mean rethinking some common assumptions. In high school, you may have been asked to write research essays that involve reading various sources on a topic, learning as much as you could about it, and then reporting on what you learned in an essay or oral report. As a result, you may have formed the impression that the research essay is a kind of "data dump," as it is often called, in which you gather a lot of data or information and then dump it into some prescribed number of pages. College-level research, however, as compositionist Joseph Bizup points out, generally means *doing something* with the information you gather, which for us above all means using it to take a stance in response to other researchers. "Sources," in this model, are not merely storehouses of information that you cite, usually to support a thesis, but conversationalists like you who hold views that need to be challenged, agreed with, or some combination of both (for more on these three ways of responding, see Chapter 4). For this reason, we believe that the best research essays rely on the same "they say / I say" format that we've been describing for academic writing in general.

That being said, it does not follow that the college research essay and your standard college writing assignment are one and the same. As we illustrate below, the research paper poses special challenges, one of which has to do with its greater length; in most courses, including first-year writing, it is usually the longest paper you'll be asked to write. How do you fill all those pages? How do you develop an argument or thesis that you can focus on over your essay's entire length? And what about all the sources (articles, book chapters, and so forth) you need to find? How do you find sources that are relevant and credible? How do you select sources from among the often overwhelming number available on the internet? And perhaps most pressing of all, how do you find sources that you can fit together or synthesize as part of a common dialogue or debate?

Given how daunting such challenges can be, we have broken them down into the following issues, to be addressed one at a time.

DEVELOP A GOOD RESEARCH QUESTION

One big challenge of the research essay is navigating the sheer volume of sources that the internet makes available on almost any topic you want to write about. Students often come to our offices in a panic, having found many more sources than they can possibly read in a single semester. We reassure them, however, that they don't have to read everything that's been written on their topic, that they aren't expected to become experts on the subject (though nobody will complain if they do). Their goal instead should be to use a certain number of sources to develop some fundamental skills of intellectual inquiry, the central one of which, as we said before, is to enter a debate or conversation, terms that, as we suggest in our preface, are deeply related.

But still, students will ask, which sources do we focus on? How do we reduce a huge pile of sources to a manageable number? Our answer is pretty much the same one most writing instructors will give you: by coming up with a good research question. A good research question will help you cut through the clutter by identifying which sources are most important to you and how you'll approach them.

But what is a good research question?

In our view, you probably won't be surprised to hear, a good research question identifies a controversy, posing an issue that people can agree or disagree about. In other words, a good research question does more than identify a general topic, about which everything—and, hence, ultimately nothing—can be said. Instead, it focuses on a debate or conversation that both narrows down your sources and helps you integrate or synthesize those sources under a common umbrella issue. Consider these examples:

▸ Why did X happen? Was it, as _____ argues, because of _____ or, as _____ contends, because of _____?

▸ What should we do about X? Should we _____, as _____ urges, or _____, as _____ argues?

▸ Is X as harmful as _____ insists, or does it have benefits, as _____ claims?

▸ Is it true, as some assert, that _____?

▸ What is the relationship between _____ and _____? Is it X, as most assume, or could it be Y, as one source suggests?

In addition, good research questions often come by tapping into your own personal interests:

▸ Throughout the many years that I have taken an interest in _____, I, probably like most people, have assumed that _____. When I researched the topic for this essay, however, I was surprised to discover that _____.

▸ X argues _____. In my experience, however, _____.

Templates like these are tailor-made for sources, helping you put writers who may not even mention one another into a dialogue as part of a common conversation. But remember, a good research question is not something you can nail down once and for all at the start of your project. It is something you revise, refine, and in some cases radically alter as you work with your sources and better identify the unifying issue that you and they are concerned with.

To appreciate how important a research question is, consider how a hypothetical research paper that lacks one might open:

Robotics

Robotics is a very interesting topic in today's society. According to author X, human beings since time immemorial have been making tools to help them accomplish tasks, and in many respects artificial intelligence and robotics are no different. Authors Y and Z suggest that many companies are exploring robotics for ways it can help them make more money, and robots are a central concern in a lot of literature, film, and popular culture. The classic novel *Frankenstein* is basically about a robot. One study by author Z shows that young people take a special interest in robots, but many older people do, too.

Authors have touched on many different aspects of robotics. For example . . .

The problem with research papers like this is that they are untethered to any specific question or issue and therefore tend to lack direction, coming across as dumping grounds or grab bags of information without any unifying thread. As a result, such papers often take the form of a series of "and then" state-ments with references to sources sprinkled in—not unlike the "list summaries" we complained about in Chapter 2.

A controversial question or issue can remedy this type of unfocused writing. Compare, for example, the opening above with the opening to an essay reproduced in full at the end of this chapter by student writer Jason Smith:

> In recent years, many commentators have suggested that robots will take over most jobs in the next fifty years and leave the human workforce out in the cold. Experts even argue that this takeover is already happening. This paper challenges this alarm-ist way of thinking. The evidence, I argue, suggests that robots are not eliminating human jobs. In fact, they are creating new jobs.
>
> JASON SMITH, *Roe Butt, Cy Borg, Ann Droid:*
> *Hint, They're Not Taking Your Job*

Note here that Smith addresses the same topic—robots—as the hypothetical writer above, but he narrows it to the ques-tion of whether robots are likely to replace human workers. As a result, everything in this opening, as in the remainder of Smith's essay, is quietly devoted to this controversial question. Smith's title alone indicates that he is not going to just *talk about* robots but instead enter a conversation over whether or not robots should be feared.

You might also note here that Smith does not state his research question explicitly. But some exemplary writers do, as the environmental journalist Ben Alder illustrates when, in his very title, he asks, "Banning Plastic Bags Is Great for the World, Right? Not So Fast." In this way, Adler reaches out directly to his readers and draws them in, helping them invest in the conversation he's entering.

LET ONE GOOD SOURCE LEAD TO ANOTHER

Thus far we've suggested that a controversial question is central to academic research. But here you might wonder where a controversial question comes from. How do you find a question or issue that different people—you and your sources—disagree about? By looking in your sources themselves.

Sources frequently respond to other sources, either to confirm what those other sources are saying, contradict it, or some combination of both, as in:

▸ **X is far too pessimistic in her prediction that _____.**

▸ **Authors X and Y focus on the wrong issue. The issue is not _____ but _____.**

▸ **I agree with X in her critique of the view that _____, but _____.**

In such ways, sources are connected together in an intertextual network of conversation that the best researchers are always alert for. One major challenge of the research paper is to locate one of these conversations in your sources and then frame and enter that conversation.

This is no easy task. Nevertheless, you may be heartened to know that a single source alone can point you in the right direction. That is, just one effective source can provide you with a controversial issue or question that you can use in your own paper—as long as you appropriately credit the source, of course. If you're interested in writing about the environmental or green movement, for instance, you wouldn't have to go very far in Adler's article alone to find such a controversy, since Adler starts identifying positions he agrees and disagrees with as early as his third paragraph. You could also track down some of these sources—which online writing often makes easy when it provides clickable links—and read them next. You might also want to search to see if any of the sources Adler mentions extended the conversation by responding to Adler after his article was published, perhaps by using the Cited By function, which we discuss below (p. 213).

Using one source in this way to find other sources actually has a name. It's called "citation chaining" (or "reference mining") and involves following the trail of a conversation or debate from one source to another, in much the same way as you might follow a trail of bread crumbs. To start such a chain, you might ask questions like these: "In the material I have read, whom are the authors in dialogue with? Who are their 'they says'? What other sources are mentioned in this material that I might follow up on? Are there other texts these sources refer to that could be useful to me?"

BEWARE OF CONFIRMATION BIAS

Before you start searching for sources, though, it is important to understand what you're searching for—and *not* searching for. You're not just looking for sources that support your own viewpoint. Sure, you'll need some, or even many, sources that support your beliefs. But if you look only for the sources that you agree with, you will miss one of the central points of research—and of education itself—which is to get outside yourself and learn from different perspectives. Put another way, you could fall prey to so-called confirmation bias, the tendency to seek out and emphasize whatever confirms your preexisting beliefs and to ignore complicating and contradictory evidence.

Tips for Avoiding Confirmation Bias

• Try searching journal databases (like *JSTOR* for the humanities or *EBSCO* for the hard sciences) instead of relying solely on the internet search engine you usually use. This is an important step, because the most commonly used search engines prioritize results based on what they have learned about you from previous searches and are thus prone to reinforcing what you already believe. For this reason, when you do use your favorite search engine, try scrolling down in the list of entries that come up rather than relying solely on the first one or two that appear.

• Seek out sources with a variety of perspectives. Do all your sources agree or toe the same general line? Do they come from the same websites, journals, or group of authors?

• If you have trouble finding opposing points of view, try returning to the sources you agree with to see if they mention authors they differ from.

• Become your own naysayer. Ask yourself, "If I had to challenge or critique my own argument, what would I say? What is the strongest objection that could be made against my position?"

• But above all else, be sure to treat other perspectives with an open mind. Play the "believing game," as we discuss in Chapter 2, in which you try to understand what they are saying on their own terms before rushing to judgment.

APPRECIATE SCHOLARLY SOURCES

Some students might shy away from scholarly sources since they are usually a harder read than their nonscholarly counterparts. But such sources have many benefits, not least of which that they make chaining or tracking conversations relatively easy.

Unlike most popular and journalistic sources, academic sources provide all the citation information you need to track down any source or sources that have been referred to. That is, scholarly sources are scholarly precisely because they draw so heavily on other sources and include key elements like works-cited pages, references, or bibliographies that tell you exactly where those other sources can be found.

Our goal here, however, is not to cover all the ins-and-outs of scholarly documentation (MLA and APA style, endnotes, footnotes, parenthetical notes, works-cited lists, and so forth). Nor is our goal to explain how these distinctive documentation features of academic writing differ from one discipline to another. There are many excellent writer's handbooks and websites out there that provide this type of intricate instruction. And yet our discussion of research would be incomplete if it didn't underscore how helpful it is that scholarly writers tell you exactly which sources they are responding to in any particular passage and that they end their publications with all the documentation information you need to track these sources down.

In this way, scholarly, academic writers (like you!) are remarkably transparent, taking pains to identify their sources in ways that popular, journalistic, and literary writers do not. So, for instance, when Michelle Alexander, in the excerpt included in this book from *The New Jim Crow: Mass Incarceration in the Age of Colorblindness*, cites studies, she includes note numbers that direct readers to the precise studies she's referring to. One of her sentences on page 306, for instance, runs as follows:

> Studies show that people of all colors *use and sell* drugs at remarkably similar rates.[9]

To locate these studies, all you need to do is flip to the end of Alexander's text and look for endnote 9, which cites several reports, such as the US Department of Health and Human Services and the National Household Survey on Drug Abuse. So, for example, if you were examining illegal drug use in your community compared to national averages, you could turn to the sources cited by Alexander for relevant data. Through devices like these, scholarly writers are remarkably transparent, inviting any reader to independently assess the conversation that they are engaged in.

But looking inside a scholarly source is not the only way to piece together or "chain" a debate or conversation. Because it is unlikely that any one scholarly source will be the last word in a published conversation, you might want to find out if any other sources have responded to your source, something you can do by using the handy Cited By or Cited Reference functions provided by *Google Scholar*, and journal repositories like *JSTOR* or *EBSCO*. For example, when we keyed in "Michelle Alexander, *The New Jim Crow*" into *Google Scholar*, here's what we got:

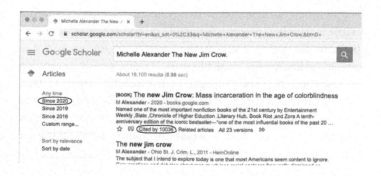

Librarians are usually more than happy to help you use this function. But the upshot is that, the number to the right of "Cited by" tells you that Alexander's book has inspired a tremendous amount of discussion, having been cited in no less than 10,036 other publications—far too many sources for you to possibly sort through. But no need to despair. By clicking on the "Cited by" link itself, you can do a more focused search by checking the box, "Search within citing articles," and then entering into the new search bar keywords tailored to your particular interests, as in: "presidential election, voter suppression, Black Lives Matter, Donald Trump." When we keyed in these more precise terms, we were able to reduce our list of 10,000+ publications to 1,480 results. And when we sorted by date, selecting, for example, only articles published "Since 2020," we further reduced that number to an even more manageable 86 that can be scanned for relevant titles.

EVALUATE YOUR SOURCES

Whether a source converges around a common question or issue is only one consideration when evaluating a source. Another factor is whether a source is reliable or not, which is often difficult to determine. Even as the internet greatly expands the amount of knowledge available to us, it is notoriously susceptible to misinformation and propaganda that look like objective fact. In their research article, "Lateral Reading: Reading Less and Learning More When Evaluating Digital Information," Sam Wineburg and Sarah McGrew of the Stanford History Education Group, found that even professional historians accustomed to online searches "often fell victim to easily manipulated features of websites such as official-looking logos and domain names."

So even as the internet has made academic research easier in many ways, it makes it hard to tell if what you are looking at is or isn't reliable. How are you to sort out one type of text from the other? How can you tell whether a source you're looking at has been discredited? One common answer is to restrict your searches to a type of scholarly writing we discussed earlier: the type that appears in academic journals and university presses that rely on the peer-review process of only publishing submissions that have been approved by other expert scholars.

Despite its merits, however, this approach excludes such indispensable venues as the *New York Times* and the *Wall Street Journal*, and general interest magazines like *Harper's* and the *Atlantic*, not to mention many popular books and most of what appears on the internet. Limiting yourself only to peer-reviewed sources is especially difficult when writing about current events and contemporary issues, which tend to be the purview of news periodicals.

For this reason, you might want to know about a second approach for determining whether a source is credible: the strategy that Wineburg and McGrew recommend of "reading laterally," which involves cross-checking all sources. Wineburg and McGrew suggest that in doing online research, we imitate professional fact-checkers, who tend to be more adept than even experienced academics at evaluating web sources. While most researchers, according to Wineburg and McGrew, "read vertically, staying within a website to evaluate its reliability," fact-checkers "read laterally," looking not just at what the source itself says but at what other sources say about it, too. In contrast to vertical readers, these savvy researchers are able to more accurately determine whether any group sponsors the website and who might have a financial stake in its claims.

Fact-checkers are also able to more accurately assess whether a website has a bias that needs to be taken into account and whether it promotes suspicious information.

Tips for Researching Like a Fact-Checker

- Open a browser tab and window and type in the website's name along with key terms like "funding," "credibility," and "bias." Hit Search and see what comes up.

- Go to the *Wikipedia* pages for the authors or website you're investigating, and consider following up on the links at the bottom of the page under "References," "Notes and References," and "Internal Links."

- Cross-check any claims presented by the source that strike you as improbable. In other words, when you come across claims that sound suspect, try investigating further to see if the claim is supported or refuted by other sources. That one source treats as factual what another source treats as questionable can, after all, be an excellent starting point for a paper.

- And again, if you're using a popular search engine, be sure not to rely exclusively on the first two or three results that come up but to scroll down to the lower items. Remember that the results given in nonscholarly search engines are based on your previous searches and are designed to get clicks.

If we could add anything to Wineburg's and McGrew's suggestions here, it would be to not underestimate how interesting in itself reading laterally like this can be. You may just find that investigating whether a given source is reliable is so fascinating that you just have to make it the central question that your research paper addresses, as in:

▶ While many observers seem to find website X trustworthy, others are suspicious of X because of _____ . I, however, am of two minds about this site and argue that we need to use this website with great caution.

▶ X challenges the reliability of Blog Y on the grounds that _____ _____ . My own view is _____ .

Templates like these can form the basis of a dynamite research paper. After all, throughout this chapter we have insisted that strong research writing requires a good controversial question, and it is hard to think of a controversial question that is better and more fundamental than whether the sources we rely on can be trusted.

DON'T LET ALL THOSE VOICES DERAIL YOU

Avoiding tangents is important in any piece of writing. As we explained in Chapter 8, regardless of the nature of the assignment, you need to stay focused throughout the entire length of your paper.

And yet, as we suggested at the start of this chapter, staying focused throughout a research paper can be especially challenging. This is not just because the research paper is relatively long but also because it requires you to synthesize a large number of sources that rarely come prepackaged in a ready-made conversation. In some cases, the sources you collect will not directly mention or address the others, and most will have an agenda that differs from your own. As a result, it can be difficult to reduce all your sources to a common conversation or issue and all too easy to let them throw you off track.

To see how one student manages to stay focused on his central research question over the full course of his research paper, let's return to the essay by student writer Jason Smith (pp. 222–31). As we noted earlier, Smith does an excellent job stating his central question—whether or not robots threaten to eliminate human jobs—at the start of his essay and even in his title. What we now want to note is that he does an equally good job staying focused on this issue while piloting through numerous sources.

On page 225, for instance, Smith opens one of his paragraphs with the following:

> A second alarming view of robots taking home the paycheck comes from . . . McKinsey Quarterly. . . .

This topic sentence, which introduces a new article, may look unremarkably simple. Nevertheless, this sentence does something that is actually quite difficult: it puts this new article in dialogue not only with the previous article that Smith had just addressed but also with the controversial question that Smith established in his opening paragraph a full three pages earlier. How can we tell that this sentence makes all these connections? In part because it relies on the same key terms, or their synonyms and antonyms, that Smith has already established in his preceding pages: terms like "robots," "alarmist," "fear," "taking over," "paycheck," "work," "employments," "workforce," and "jobs." Even the seemingly inconsequential word "second" makes connections, suggesting a parallel between this "second" article and the previous one that Smith addressed, suggesting that both adopt an "alarming view of robots taking home the paycheck." If you need help with such moves, you might want to do the exercises below, which are designed to help.

In this chapter, we've given you, we hope, some useful tips on how to write the college research essay. But as the chapter draws to a conclusion, we'd like to step back from this how-to discussion and say a word about what such research, as we see it, is essentially all about. For some students, the research essay may seem to be just one more pointless hoop that some authority is asking them to jump through. But for us, it's the highest expression of the conversational approach to writing that we discuss in this book, an opportunity to take off the training wheels and contribute to a conversation that instead of being preestablished by your instructor, you independently find and frame yourself. In this way, the academic research essay is far from merely academic in the negative sense. It is a chance to practice a set of skills that you can use the rest of your life: going out into the community, finding a space for yourself, and making a contribution of your own.

Exercises

1. Read Ayana Elizabeth Johnson's 2020 essay, "To Save the Climate, Look to the Oceans," on **theysayiblog.com** in light of the techniques addressed in this chapter. Working with a partner or a small group, answer the following questions:

   a. What do you take Johnson's central research question to be? What debate does that question frame or set up? Choose one of the templates from this chapter that corresponds with Johnson's question and then state that question using the template's language.

b. Look at the sources Johnson includes in her essay, which are hyperlinked, and analyze what Johnson does with each one. Does the source support or challenge her position? And how do you know? How does Johnson synthesize that source into her essay's central debate question?

c. Choose one of the sources Johnson includes and read it "laterally," as the term is used in this chapter, to evaluate its credibility. "Fact-check" the source to determine its commitments and biases. In the end, do you think the source is reliable? Why or why not?

d. Use *Google Scholar* to determine who has cited Johnson's essay and what conversations or debates her essay is part of. How might you enter this conversation in a research essay of your own?

2. Take a section of Johnson's essay and annotate it in the same ways that we annotated Jason Smith's essay (pp. 222–31). Identify as many "moves that matter" as you can, noting, for instance, how Johnson

- entertains counterarguments

- sets up a debate or conversation

- synthesizes sources to a common issue

- uses transition terms

- uses pointing words

- uses voice markers

- repeats herself with a difference

- includes metacommentary

- develops a constellation of key terms and phrases

- frames, or "sandwiches," quotations

3. To get going on a research essay, try the following steps:

Decide on a general topic for your essay, and then, working with a classmate, use the templates on page 206 to come up with at least two different research questions that address that topic. Analyze each question with your classmate, weighing its strengths and weaknesses until you decide which question you prefer.

Then, having decided on a question, continue working with your partner to develop a list of eight to ten key terms and phrases that you can use both in your paper itself and to search for sources on the internet.

After you've gathered your sources and written a draft of your paper, have a classmate read your draft to determine if it exhibits any of the confirmation bias discussed in this chapter. Do you use sources only to support your position, or do you bring in a variety of perspectives, including those of naysayers? Do other perspectives come to mind that could—or should— also be included in your text? Work together to either track down sources that represent any excluded perspectives or come up with language of your own to represent them, as in, "It is sometimes said that . . ."

Finally, have your partner evaluate how well you integrate or synthesize your sources. Are all your sources aligned with one another and with your essay's central debate question or issue? Can you come up with strategies to heighten the alignment and eliminate any misalignment?

Roe Butt, Cy Borg, Ann Droid: Hint, They're Not Taking Your Job

JASON SMITH

—▫—

IN RECENT YEARS, many commentators have suggested that robots will take over most jobs in the next fifty years and leave the human workforce out in the cold. Experts even argue that this takeover is already happening. This paper challenges this alarmist way of thinking. The evidence, I argue, suggests that robots are not eliminating human jobs. In fact, they are creating new jobs. Throughout history, such innovative tools didn't end work but increased it.

JASON SMITH wrote this essay for his first-year writing course at Atlantic Cape Community College, where he is pursuing a general studies associate's degree in science. This essay was nominated for the Norton Writer's Prize and is documented in MLA style.

To be sure, in periods when innovations take hold, workers tend to fear their own dislocation. For example, as researcher James Lacey notes, during the industrialization of the French silk industry, "French weavers threw their wooden shoes (sabots) into textile machines to make them break down. (Thus the term sabotage.)." However, it is likely that those displaced workers found other jobs—as auto mechanics, gas station attendants, and car makers, for example—just as those who worked in carriage houses and were replaced by the automobile did. Changes happen in every industry over time: the airplane replaced the train, for example, and lightbulbs replaced the need for the candlemaker, but in every era, many displaced workers found new professions. A well-defined pattern is beginning to emerge here—all technological advances bring with them new opportunities.

Predictions about the downfall of the workforce due to technological innovation have been happening for nearly a century. Jeff Borland notes that "in the 1930s, John Maynard Keynes envisaged that innovations such as electricity would produce a world where people spent most of their time on leisure." Later, during the 1930s, as Richard Freeman notes, "US President Franklin D. Roosevelt blamed unemployment on his country's failure to employ the surplus labor created by the efficiency of its industrial processes." He also points out that

> Makes a concession to the "they say" that actually bolsters his "I say."

> Summarizes some "they say" sources from the past.

in the early 1960s, widespread fears that automation was eliminating thousands of jobs per week led the Kennedy and Johnson administrations to examine the link between productivity growth and employment.

Despite those worries and failed projections, studies done in the 1960s through the 1990s (a period that includes the advent of the modern computer) proclaimed the demise of work.

Previews the first of two "they say" sources to be addressed.

Two more recent studies demonstrate contemporary arguments for the impact robots will have on our future. *Race against the Machine*, a book by Erik Brynjolfsson and Andrew McAfee, focuses on the results of their study of the recovery from the Great Recession of 2008. In his TED talk based on the book, McAfee uses a chart that presents a dramatic correlation between productivity and the labor force and notes that his research with coauthor Brynjolfsson reveals that from 2008 through 2011, while the US working-age population increased, the actual number of available jobs declined, even though the economy was recovering during that time frame and productivity actually increased (00:0:51–1:56). Their inevitable conclusion, according to McAfee, is that robots are already replacing the human workforce.

Answers this first "they say," integrating sources.

However, the data gathered in *Race against the Machine* is shortsighted. Had the study continued only three more years, the authors would have seen the graph's job curve return to normal values. After any recession, the rebound in employment has always taken longer than the rebound in the GDP, for several reasons. Manufacturers reduce their inventories, which makes it look like fewer people are producing more. In a recession, the remaining workers always find ways to pick up the slack left behind by laid-off workers, often through the use of overtime, which is cheaper in the short run than hiring new workers or rehiring those laid off. Once again, the greater productivity stems from existing workers, not automation. The most recent recession, moreover, produced some unusual employment data. Part-time workers are not counted as full-time employees, yet their work output is included in the overall productivity numbers.

A second alarming view of robots taking home the paycheck comes from Michael Chui and colleagues in a *McKinsey Quarterly* article titled "Where Machines Could Replace Humans—and Where They Can't." They write:

> Summarizes and answers the second "they say," integrating yet more sources.

> Last year, we showed that currently demonstrated technologies could automate 45 percent of the activities people are paid to perform and that about 60 percent of all occupations could see 30 percent or more of their constituent activities automated, again with technologies available today.

The problem with this report is its use of probability for its logic: just because a thing *can* be done does not mean it *will* be done. As Gillian White points out in her reporting on a study by two economists, "The authors note that just because an industry can automate doesn't mean that it will." Costs in every case must be examined, as well as return on investment. Theoretical predictions only go so far; there is a real-world cost/benefit analysis that must be applied to each of these possible robot advancements. In addition, Chui and colleagues overlook arguments that it will require more humans to maintain and build robots than they replace (Metz).

In fact, convincing, well-researched papers that examine data over a much greater time span find there is no evidence of a robot takeover. These studies indicate that the opposite is true. For example, Jeff Borland and Michael Coelli, two Australian researchers, published an exhaustive study in 2017 that found that

> (i) the total amount of work available [in Australia] has not decreased following the introduction of computer-based technologies; and (ii) the pace of structural change and job turnover in the labor market has not accelerated with the increasing application of computer-based technologies. A review of recent studies that claim computer-based technologies may be about to cause widespread job destruction establishes several major flaws with these predictions. (377)

Continues to answer this second "they say," integrating even more sources.

Borland and Coelli found that fears about job losses have happened often throughout history: "Our suggested explanation for why techno-phobia has such a grip on popular imagination is a human bias to believe that 'we live in special times'" (377). In other words, we think that our particular era is unique—that now is truly the time that robots will take over our jobs—but such a scenario doesn't come to pass.

There are more practical reasons why robots will not replace humans in many fields, especially those areas of work that require direct interaction with humans. In his *Tech.Co* article "5 Reasons Why Robots Will Never Fully Replace Humans," Lanre Onibalusi notes that robots cannot "understand irrational thought," cannot "understand context," and "lack creative problem solving" abilities and that "people prefer to talk with a human." Additionally, as Ryan Nakashima reports, behind almost every form of robotization is an army of technocrats. This army of workers is considered the "dirty little secret" behind the artificially intelligent robot. Whether it be the hundreds of programmers or the vast numbers of call-center operators required to carry the load, robots require human helpers. It seems that robots simply cannot understand context, and enormous numbers of analysts are required to try to reteach an automated system every time it fails to understand a request

> Engages more sources in support of the "I say."

from a customer (Nakashima). In fact, according to a recent *New York Times* article, grocery retailers who have started using robots report that "the robots are good for their workers. They free up employees from mundane and sometimes injury-prone jobs like unloading delivery trucks to focus on more fulfilling tasks like helping customers" (Corkery). In this case, as in others, robots help increase productivity rather than replace humans.

Some of these alarmists argue that as robots become smarter, laws must be instituted to guard against a massive upheaval, or even elimination, of the human workforce. The problem with this preemptive approach is that no one can possibly imagine where or when those laws should exist or how to apply them. The normal course of events is to first have solid evidence that some event is "bad" and later proceed to legislate. For example, those who oppose self-driving cars, another kind of robot, call for governmental restrictions on them, but before such vehicles are on the road, there's no reason to fear them. In fact, they require human help. Many have heard of the self-driving truck that hauled two thousand cases of beer 120 miles in Colorado without a driver at the wheel (Isaac). What was not revealed was that there was a full police escort for the entire route and that the vehicle was incapable of negotiating the on- and off-ramps. I will admit that during the writing of this paper, a self-driving-car fatality

Addresses a final naysayer.

did occur when an Arizona woman was struck and killed by a driverless vehicle owned by Uber. Uber immediately suspended all driverless test vehicles in the United States and Canada, and the following week Nvidia suspended all tests with the same product (Sage). Perhaps here is an example of a worthy event triggering the possibility of new laws, but an overall ban on automation itself in the workforce seems hasty.

As Jeff Borland has astutely observed, "The tale of new technologies causing the death of work is the prophecy that keeps on giving." It is sensational, alarmist, and grossly premature. I agree with those who believe society should not worry about robots taking away all the jobs. Most of the predictions for the future are countered by past facts. The reality is that all new technologies bring about new avenues of invention, experimentation, and work and that much of the new technology requires the intervention of humans. It is therefore unnecessary for governments to regulate robots to protect jobs.

> Succinctly recaps the essay's "I say" position.

WORKS CITED

Borland, Jeff. "Why We Are Still Convinced Robots Will Take Our Jobs despite the Evidence." *The Conversation*, 25 Nov. 2017, theconversation.com/why-we-are-still-convinced -robots-will-take-our-jobs-despite-the-evidence-87188.

Borland, Jeff, and Michael Coelli. "Are Robots Taking Our
    Jobs?" *The Australian Economic Review*, vol. 50, no. 4, 2017,
    pp. 377–97. *Wiley Online Library*, https://doi.org/10.1111
    /1467-8462.12245.
Brynjolfsson, Erik, and Andrew McAfee. *Race against the Machine*.
    Digital Frontier Press, 2011.
Chui, Michael, et al. "Where Machines Could Replace Humans—
    and Where They Can't (Yet)." *McKinsey Quarterly*, July 2016,
    www.mckinsey.com/business-functions/digital-mckinsey/our
    -insights/where-machines-could-replace-humans-and-where
    -they-cant-yet.
Corkery, Michael. "Should Robots Have a Face?" *The New York
    Times*, 26 Feb. 2020, www.nytimes.com/2020/02/26/business
    /robots-retail-jobs.html.
Freeman, Richard B. "Who Owns the Robots Rules the World."
    IZA World of Labor, May 2015, wol.iza.org/articles/who-owns
    -the-robots-rules-the-world/long.
Isaac, Mike. "Self-Driving Truck's First Mission: A 120-Mile Beer
    Run." *The New York Times*, 25 Oct. 2016, www.nytimes
    .com/2016/10/26/technology/self-driving-trucks-first-mission-a
    -beer-run.html.
Lacey, James. Comment on "Should Governments Limit
    Corporations' Abilities to Replace Human Workers with
    Technology?" *Quora*, 1 Jan. 2017, www.quora.com/Should
    -governments-limit-corporations-abilities-to-replace-human
    -workers-with-technology.
McAfee, Andrew. "Race against the Machine." *YouTube*,
    uploaded by TedxBoston, 17 July 2012, www.youtube.com
    /watch?v=QfMGyCk3XTw.
Metz, Cade. "Robots Will Steal Our Jobs, but They'll Give Us
    New Ones." *Wired*, 24 Aug. 2015, wired.com/2015/08/robots
    -will-steal-jobs-theyll-give-us-new-ones.
Nakashima, Ryan. "AI's Dirty Little Secret: It's Powered by
    People." *AP News*, 5 Mar. 2018, apnews.com/1f58465e55d643
    ea84e51713f35ad214.

Onibalusi, Lanre. "5 Reasons Why Robots Will Never Fully Replace Humans." *Tech.Co*, 2 Aug. 2017, tech.co/robots-replace-humans -work-2017-08.

Sage, Alexandria, and Sonam Rai. "Nvidia Halts Self-Driving Tests in Wake of Uber Accident." *Reuters*, 27 Mar. 2018, www.reuters.com/article/us-autos-selfdriving-nvidia /nvidia-halts-self-driving-tests-in-wake-of-uber-accident -idUSKBN1H32E0.

White, Gillian B. "How Many Robots Does It Take to Replace a Human Job?" *The Atlantic*, 30 Mar. 2017, www.theatlantic .com/business/archive/2017/03/work-automation/521364.

SIXTEEN

"ON CLOSER EXAMINATION"

Entering Conversations about Literature

In Chinua Achebe's novel *Things Fall Apart*, Okonkwo, the main character, is a tragic hero.

So what? Who cares?

Why does this typical way of opening an essay on a literary work leave readers wondering, "Why are you telling me this?" Because, in our view, such statements leave it unclear who would say otherwise. Would anyone deny that the main character of Achebe's novel is a tragic hero? Is there some other view of the subject that this writer is responding to? Since no such alternative interpretation is indicated, the reader thinks, "OK, Okonkwo is a tragic hero—as opposed to what?"

Now compare this opening with another possible one:

> Several members of our class have argued that Okonkwo, the main character of *Things Fall Apart*, is a hateful villain. My own view, however, is that, while it is true that Okonkwo commits villainous acts, he is ultimately a tragic hero—a flawed but ultimately sympathetic figure.

We hope you agree that the second version, which responds to what someone else says about Okonkwo, makes for more engaging writing than the first. Since the first version fails to present itself as a response to any alternative view of its subject, it comes at readers out of the blue, leaving them wondering why it needs to be said at all.

As we stress in this book, it is the views of others and our desire to respond to these views that gives our writing its underlying motivation and helps readers see why what we say matters, why others should care, and why we need to say it in the first place. In this chapter we suggest that this same principle applies to writing about literature. Literary critics, after all, don't make assertions about literary works out of the blue. Rather, they contribute to discussions and debates about the meaning and significance of literary works, some of which may continue for years and even centuries.

Indeed, this commitment to discussion animates most literature courses, in which students discuss and debate assigned works in class before writing papers about them. The premise is that engaging with classmates and teachers enables us to make discoveries about the work that we might not arrive at in simply reading the work alone.

We suggest that you think of writing about literature as a natural extension of such in-class discussions, listening carefully to others and using what they say to set up and motivate what you have to say.

START WITH WHAT OTHERS ARE SAYING

But in writing about literature, where do views to respond to—"they say"s—come from? Many sources. Published literary criticism is perhaps the most obvious:

- Critic X complains that author Y's story is compromised by his _____ perspective. While there's some truth to this critique, I argue that critic X overlooks _____.

- According to critic A, novel X suggests _____. I agree, but would add that _____.

But the view that you respond to in writing about literature can be far closer to home than published literary criticism. As our opening example illustrates, it can be something said about the literary work by a classmate or teacher:

- Several members of our class have suggested that the final message of play X is _____. I agree up to a point, but I still think that _____.

Another tactic is to start with something you yourself thought about the work that on second thought you now want to revise:

- On first reading play Z, I thought it was an uncritical celebration of _____. After rereading the play and discussing it in class, however, I see that it is more critical of _____ than I originally thought.

You can even respond to something that hasn't actually been said about the work but might hypothetically be said:

- It might be said that poem Y is chiefly about _____. But the problem with this reading, in my view, is _____.

- Though religious readers might be tempted to analyze poem X as a parable about _____, a closer examination suggests that the poem is in fact _____.

Sometimes the "they say" that you respond to in writing about a literary work can be found in the work itself, as distinct from what some critic or other reader has said *about* the work. Much great literary criticism responds directly to the literary work, summarizing some aspect of the work's form or content and then assessing it, in much the same way you can do in response to a persuasive essay:

▶ Ultimately, as I read it, *The Scarlet Letter* seems to say _____. I have trouble accepting this proposition, however, on the grounds that _____.

One of the more powerful ways of responding to a literary work is to address any contradictions or inconsistencies:

▶ At the beginning of the poem, we encounter the generalization, seemingly introducing the poem's message, that "_____." But this statement is then contradicted by the suggestion made later in the poem that "_____." This opens up a significant inconsistency in the text: is it suggesting _____ or, on the contrary, _____?

▶ At several places in novel X, author Y leads us to understand that the story's central point is that _____. Yet elsewhere the text suggests _____, indicating that Y may be ambivalent on this issue.

If you review the above templates, you'll notice that each does what a good discussion, lecture, or essay does: it makes an argument about some aspect of a work that can be interpreted in various ways. Instead of just making a claim about the work in isolation—character X is a tragic hero; sonnet Y is about the loss of a loved one—these templates put one claim as a response to another, making clear what motivated the argument to begin with. They thus act as conversation starters that can invite or even provoke other readers to respond with their own interpretations and judgments.

FIGURING OUT
WHAT A LITERARY WORK "MEANS"

In order to enter conversations and debates about literature, you need to meet the time-honored challenge of being able to read and make sense of literary works, understanding and analyzing what the text says. On the one hand, like the types of persuasive essays we focus on throughout this book, literary works make arguments their authors want to convey, things they are for and against, ideas they want to endorse or condemn. On the other hand, discovering "the argument" of a literary work—what it's "saying"—can be a special challenge because, unlike persuasive essays, literary works usually do not spell out their arguments explicitly. Though poets, novelists, and playwrights may have the same level of conviction as persuasive writers, rarely do they step out from behind the pages of their texts and say, "OK, folks, this is what it all means. What I'm trying to say in a nutshell is _____." That is, since literary texts do not include an explicit thesis statement identifying their main point, it's left up to us as readers to figure it out.

Because literary works tend to avoid such explicitness, their meanings often need to be teased out from the clues they provide: from the dialogue between characters, the plot, the imagery and symbolism, and the kind of language the author uses. In fact, it is this absence of overt argument that makes literature so endlessly debatable—and explains why scholars and critics argue so much about what literary works mean in ways similar to the classroom discussions that you have likely participated in as a student.

The Elusive Literary Author

Indeed, not even the use of the first person "I" in a literary work is an indication that you have located the author's own position or stance, as it usually is in an essay. When David Zinczenko, for example, in his essay "Don't Blame the Eater" (pp. 199–202) writes, "I tend to sympathize with these portly fast-food patrons" who file lawsuits against the fast-food industry, we can be confident that the "I" is Zinczenko himself and that the position he expresses is his own and informs everything else in his essay. But we cannot assume that the "I" who addresses us in a work of fiction or poetry is necessarily the author, for the person who "I" refers to is a fictional character—and one who may be unreliable and untrustworthy.

Take, for example, the first sentence of Edgar Allan Poe's short story "The Cask of Amontillado":

> The thousand injuries of Fortunato I had borne as I best could, but when he ventured upon insult I vowed revenge.

As soon becomes clear in the story, the "I" who speaks as the narrator here is not Poe himself but an insanely vengeful murderer whose words must be seen through to get at the point of Poe's story.

Instead of a readily identifiable position, literary works often present the perspectives of a number of different characters and leave it to readers to determine which if any speaks for the author. Thus when we encounter the seemingly eloquent lines in *Hamlet* "To thine own self be true, . . . / And canst thou not be false to any man," we can't assume, as we might if we encountered this statement in an essay, that it represents the author's own view. For these words are uttered by Polonius, a character whom Shakespeare presents as a tedious, cliché-spouting bore—not someone he leads us to trust. After all, part of Hamlet's problem is that it's not clear to him what being "true" to his own self would require him to do.

This elusive quality of literary texts helps explain why some of our students complain about the challenge of finding the "hidden meaning," as they sometimes call it, let alone summarizing that meaning in the way assignments often require. Sure, some students say, they enjoy reading literature for pleasure. But analyzing literature in school for its "meaning" or "symbolism"—that's another matter. Some even say that the requirement that they hunt for meanings and symbols robs literature of its fun.

In fact, as most students come to recognize, analyzing meanings, symbols, and other elements should enhance rather than stifle the pleasure we get from reading literature. But it can indeed be hard to figure out what literary works mean. How do we determine the point of stories and poems when the authors, unlike essayists like Zinczenko, do not tell us explicitly what they are trying to say? How do you go from a fictional event or poetic image (an insane man committing murder, two roads that diverge in the woods) or from a dialogue between fictional characters ("Frankly, my dear, I don't give a damn") to what these events, images, or lines of dialogue mean?

Look for Conflict *in* the Work

There is no simple recipe for figuring out what a literary work means, but one tactic that seems to help our own students is to look for the conflict or debate in the literary work itself and then ask what the text is leading us to think about that conflict. Asking these questions—what is the conflict in the work and which side, if any, should we favor?—will help you think about and formulate a position on what the work means. And since such claims are often ones that literary scholars argue about, thinking about the conflict *in* a literary work will often lead you to discussions and debates *about* the work that you can then respond to in your writing. Because literary authors don't tell us explicitly what the text means, it's always going to be *arguable*—and your task in writing about a literary work is to argue for what *you* think it means. Here are two templates to help get you started responding to other interpretations:

▸ It might be argued that in the clash between characters **X** and **Y** in play **Z**, the author wants us to favor character **Y**, since she is presented as the play's heroine. I contend, however, that _____.

▸ Several critics seem to assume that poem **X** endorses the values of discipline and rationality represented by the image of _____ over those of play and emotion represented by the image of _____. I agree, but with the following caveat: that the poem ultimately sees both values as equally important and even suggests that ideally they should complement one another.

This tactic of looking for the conflicts in literary works is part of a long tradition of critical thought that sees conflict as central to literature. In ancient Greece, Aristotle argued that conflict between characters or forces underlies the plots of tragic dramas such as *Oedipus*. Indeed, the ancient Greek word *agon*, which means antagonism, conflict, or debate, leaves its traces in the term "protagonist," the hero or leading character of a narrative work who comes into conflict with other characters or with the fates. And Plato noted the pervasiveness of conflict in literature when he banished poets from his ideal community on the grounds that their works depict endless conflict and division.

This emphasis on the centrality of conflict in literature has been echoed by modern theorists like the New Critics of the 1940s and '50s, who focused on such tensions and paradoxes as good and evil or innocence and experience—and more recently by poststructuralists and political theorists who see literature, like society, as saturated by such polarities as male/female, gay/straight, white/Black, and so on. Writers today continue to recognize conflict as the engine of good storytelling. As the Hollywood screenwriter Robert McKee puts it, "Nothing moves forward in a story except through conflict."

Building on this idea that conflict is central to literature, we suggest the following four questions to help you understand and formulate your own position on any literary work:

1. What is the central conflict?
2. Which side—if any—does the text seem to favor?
3. What's your evidence? How might others interpret the evidence differently?
4. What's your opinion of the text?

WHAT IS THE CENTRAL CONFLICT?

Conflicts tend to manifest themselves in different ways in different literary genres. In works that take a narrative or story form (novels, short stories, and plays), the central conflict will often be represented in an actual debate between characters. These debates between characters will often reflect larger questions and debates in the society or historical era in which they were written, over such issues as the responsibility of rulers, the consequences of capitalism and consumerism, or the struggle for gender equality. Sometimes these debates will be located within an individual character, appearing as a struggle in someone caught between conflicting or incompatible choices. Whatever form they may take, these debates can provide you with points of entry into the issues raised by the work, its historical context, and its author's vision of the world.

One narrative work that lends itself to such an approach is Flannery O'Connor's 1961 short story "Everything That Rises Must Converge." The story presents a running debate between a mother and her son, Julian, about the civil rights movement for racial equality that had erupted in the American South at the time the story was written, with Julian defending the outlook of this movement and his mother defending the South's traditional racial hierarchy. The story raises the debatable question of which character we should side with: Julian, his mother, both, or neither?

WHICH SIDE—IF ANY—DOES THE TEXT SEEM TO FAVOR?

When we teach this story, most of our students first assume the story sides with Julian's outlook, which to them as northern, urban college students in the twenty-first century seems the obviously enlightened position. Who, after all, could fail to see that the mother's views are backward and racist? As our class discussions unfold, however, most students come to reject this view as a misreading, one based more on their own views than on what's in the text. Sooner or later, someone points out that in several places Julian is presented in highly critical ways—and that his apparently progressive sympathy for racial integration rests on arid intellectual abstractions and a hypocritical lack of self-knowledge, in contrast with his mother's heartfelt loyalty to her roots. Eventually another possible interpretation surfaces, that both characters suffer from a common malady: that they're living in a mental bubble that keeps them from being able to see themselves as they really are.

The writing assignment we often give builds on this class discussion by offering students the following template for thinking about which character, if any, the text leads them to favor:

▸ **Some might argue that when it comes to the conflict between Julian and his mother over _____ , our sympathies should lie with _____ . My own view is that _____ .**

WHAT'S YOUR EVIDENCE?

In entering the types of discussions and debates modeled by the above template, how do you determine where your "sympathies should lie"? More generally, how do you arrive at and justify an interpretation of what a literary text says?

The answer lies in the *evidence* provided by the work: its images, dialogue, plot, historical references, tone, stylistic details, and so forth.

It is important to remember, however, that evidence is not set in stone. Students sometimes assume that there exists some fixed code that unlocks the meaning of literary works, symbols, images, and other evidence. Characters die? This must mean that they are being condemned. A stairway appears? A symbol for upward mobility. A garden? Must be something sexual.

But evidence itself is open to interpretation and thus to debate. The mother's death in O'Connor's story, for instance, *could* be seen as evidence that we are supposed to disapprove of her as someone whose racial views are regressive and on the way out. On the other hand, her death may instead be evidence that she is to be seen as a heroic martyr too good for this cruel, harsh world. What a character's death means, then, depends on how that character is treated in the work, positively or negatively, which in turn may be subject to debate.

As we've repeatedly emphasized in this book, others will often disagree with you and may even use the same evidence you do to support interpretations that are contrary to your own. As with other objects of study, literary works are like the famous ambiguous drawing that can be seen as either a duck or a rabbit, depending how one views it.

Since the same piece of evidence in a literary work will often support differing, even opposing interpretations, you need to argue for what you think the evidence shows—and to acknowledge that others may read that evidence differently.

In writing about literature, then, you need to show that the evidence you are citing supports your interpretation and to anticipate other alternative ones:

▶ Although some might read the metaphor of _____ in this poem as evidence that, for author X, modern technology undermines community traditions and values, I see it as _____.

To present evidence in such a "they say / I say" way, you need to be alert for how others may read the work differently than you—and even use this very same evidence in support of an opposing interpretation:

▶ Some might claim that evidence X suggests _____, but I argue that, on the contrary, it suggests _____.

▶ I agree with my classmate _____ that the image of _____ in novel Y is evidence of childhood innocence that has been lost. Unlike _____, however, I think this loss of innocence is to be read not as a tragic event but as a necessary, even helpful, stage in human development.

Are Some Interpretations Simply Wrong?

No matter how flexible and open to debate evidence might be, not all interpretations we arrive at using that evidence are equally valid. And some interpretations are simply unsupported by that evidence. Let us illustrate.

As we noted earlier, some of our students first favored Julian over his mother. One student, let's call her Nancy, cited as evidence a passage early in the story in which Julian is compared to Saint Sebastian, a Christian martyr who is said to have exhibited exceptional faith under extreme suffering and persecution. As the mother stood preparing for Julian to take her to her weekly swimming class, Julian is described as standing "pinned to the door frame, waiting like Saint Sebastian for the arrows to begin piercing him."

Thinking this passage proves that Julian is the more sympathetic character, Nancy pointed to other evidence as well, including the following passage:

> [Julian] was free of prejudice and unafraid to face facts. Most miraculous of all, instead of being blinded by love for [his mother] as she was for him, he had cut himself emotionally free of her and could see her with complete objectivity. He was not dominated by his mother.

Citing passages like this in her essay, Nancy concluded: "Julian represents the future of society, a nonracist and an educated thinker."

After rereading the story, however, and hearing other students' views, Nancy came to realize that the passages she had cited—comparing Julian to a saint, suggesting that he is racially progressive, and that he is "free of" his mother and "objective" about her—were all intended ironically. Julian congratulates *himself* for being saint-like, free of prejudice, and objective, but the story ultimately implies that he deludes himself.

How did the supporters of the ironic reading convince Nancy to revise her initial reading—to see it as wrong, unsupported by the evidence? First, they pointed to the glaring discrepancy between the situations and kinds of suffering endured by Julian and Saint Sebastian. Could anyone be serious, they asked, in comparing something as mundane as being forced to wait a few minutes to go to the YMCA to a martyr dying for his faith? No, they answered, and the jarring incongruity of the events being compared, they argued, suggests that Julian, far from saint-like, is presented in this passage as an impatient, ungrateful, undutiful son. In addition, students pointed out that the gap between Julian's self-image as a progressive man of "complete objectivity" and "facts," "free of [his mother]," and the blubbering young man crying "Mama, Mama!" with "guilt and sorrow" at the end of the story suggests that Julian's righteous, high-minded image of himself is not to be taken at face value.

At this point you may be wondering, How can we say that some interpretations of literature must be ruled out as *wrong*? Isn't the great thing about interpreting literary works—in contrast to scientific texts—that there are no wrong answers? Are we saying that there is one "correct" way to read a literary work—the one way the work itself tells us we "should" read it?

No, we aren't saying that there is only one way to read a literary work. If we believed there were, we would not be offering a method of literary analysis based on multiple interpretations and debate. But yes, acknowledging that literary interpretations are open to debate is not to say that a work can mean anything we want it to mean, as if all interpretations are equally good. In our view, and that of most literature teachers, some interpretations are better than others—more persuasively reasoned and better grounded in the evidence of the text.

If we maintain that all interpretations are equally valid, we risk confusing the perspective of the work's author with our own, as did the students who confused their own views on the civil rights movement of the 1960s with Flannery O'Connor's. Such misreadings are reminiscent of what we call "the closest cliché syndrome," where what's summarized is not the view the author actually expresses but a familiar cliché—or, in O'Connor's case, a certain social belief—that the writer believes and mistakenly assumes the author must too. The view that there are no wrong answers in literary interpretation encourages a kind of solipsism that erases the difference between us and others and transforms everything we encounter into a version of ourselves.

See p. 35 for more on the closest cliché syndrome.

As the literary theorist Robert Scholes puts it, reading, conceived "as a submission to the intentions of another is the first step" to understanding what a literary work is saying. For "if we do not postulate the existence of [an author] behind the verbal text," we will "simply project our own subjective modes of thought and desire upon the text." In other words, unless we do the best we can to get at what authors are saying, we will never truly recognize their ideas except as some version of our own. Scholes acknowledges that good reading often involves going beyond the author's intention, pointing out contradictions and ideological blind spots, but he argues that we must recognize the author's intention *before* we can try to see beyond it in these ways.

WHAT'S YOUR OPINION OF THE TEXT?

In accord with the principle that we must try to understand the text on its own terms before responding to it, we have thus far in this chapter focused on how to understand and unpack what literary texts say and do. Our approach to get at what they say involves looking for the central conflict in the work and then asking yourself how the author uses various types of evidence (characters, dialogue, imagery, events, plot, etc.) to guide you in thinking about that conflict. Ultimately, your job as a reader of literature is to be open to a work as its author presents it, or else your reading will fail to see what makes that work worth reading and thinking about.

But once you have reached a good understanding of the work, it is time to allow your own opinion to come into play. Offering your own interpretation of a work and opening that interpretation to response are crucial steps in any act of literary analysis, but they are not the end of the process. The final step involves offering your own insight into or critique of the work and its vision, assessing whether, as you see it, it is morally justified or questionable, unified or contradictory, historically regressive or progressive, and so forth. For example:

> Though she is one of the most respected Southern authors of the American literary canon, Flannery O'Connor continually deni-grates the one character in her 1961 story who represents the civil rights movement and in so doing disparages progressive ideas that I believe deserve a far more sympathetic hearing.

Offering a critique, however, doesn't necessarily mean finding fault:

> Some criticize O'Connor's story by suggesting that it has a politi-cally regressive agenda. But I see the story as a laudable critique of politics as such. In my view, O'Connor's story rightly criticizes the polarization of political conflicts—North vs. South, liberal vs. conservative, and the like—and suggests that they need to come together: to "converge," as O'Connor's title implies, through reli-gious love, understanding, and forgiveness.

We realize that the prospect of critiquing a literary work can be daunting. Indeed, simply stating what you think an author is saying can be intimidating, since it means going out on a limb, asserting something about highly respected figures—works that are often complex, contradictory, and connected to larger historical movements. Nevertheless, if you can master these challenges, you may find that figuring out what a literary work is saying, offering an opinion about it, and entering into conversation and debate with others about such questions is what makes literature matter. And if you do it well, what *you* say will invite its own response: your "I say" will become someone else's "they say," and the conversation will go on and on.

SEVENTEEN

"THE DATA SUGGEST"

Writing in the Sciences

CHRISTOPHER GILLEN

———▯———

CHARLES DARWIN DESCRIBED *On the Origin of Species* as "one long argument." In *Dialogue Concerning the Two Chief World Systems*, Galileo Galilei cast his argument for a sun-centered solar system as a series of conversations. As these historical examples show, scientific writing is fundamentally argumentative. Like all academic writers, scientists make and defend claims. They address disagreements and explore unanswered questions. They propose novel mechanisms and new theories. And they advance certain explanations and reject others. Though their vocabulary may be more technical and their emphasis more numerical, science writers use the same

———

CHRISTOPHER GILLEN is a professor of biology at Kenyon College and the faculty director of the Kenyon Institute in Biomedical and Scientific Writing. He teaches courses in animal physiology, biology of exercise, and introductory biology, all stressing the critical reading of primary research articles.

rhetorical moves as other academic writers. Consider the following example from a book about the laws of physics:

> The common refrain that is heard in elementary discussions of quantum mechanics is that a physical object is in some sense both a wave and a particle, with its wave nature apparent when you measure a wave property such as wavelength, and its particle nature apparent when you measure a particle property such as position. But this is, at best, misleading and, at worst, wrong.
>
> V. J. STENGER, *The Comprehensible Cosmos*

The "they say / I say" structure of this passage is unmistakable: they say that objects have properties of both waves and particles; I say they are wrong. This example is not a lonely argumentative passage cherry-picked from an otherwise non-argumentative text. Rather, Stenger's entire book makes the argument that is foreshadowed by its title, *The Comprehensible Cosmos*: that although some might see the universe as hopelessly complex, it is essentially understandable.

Here's another argumentative passage, this one from a research article about the role of lactic acid in muscle fatigue:

> In contrast to the often suggested role for acidosis as a cause of muscle fatigue, it is shown that in muscles where force was depressed by high $[K^+]_o$, acidification by lactic acid produced a pronounced recovery of force.
>
> O. B. NIELSEN, F. DE PAOLI, AND K. OVERGAARD,
> "Protective Effects of Lactic Acid on Force Production in
> Rat Skeletal Muscle," *Journal of Physiology*

In other words: many scientists think that lactic acid causes muscle fatigue, but our evidence shows that it actually promotes recovery. Notice that the authors frame their claim with a version of the "they say / I say" formula: "Although previous work suggests _____, our data argue _____." This basic move and its many variations are widespread in scientific writing. The essential argumentative moves taught in this book transcend disciplines, and the sciences are no exception. The examples in this chapter were written by professional scientists, but they show moves that are appropriate in any writing that addresses scientific issues.

Despite the importance of argument in scientific writing, newcomers to the genre often see it solely as a means for communicating uncontroversial, objective facts. It's easy to see how this view arises. The objective tone of scientific writing can obscure its argumentative nature, and many textbooks reinforce a nonargumentative vision of science when they focus on accepted conclusions and ignore ongoing controversies. And because science writers base their arguments on empirical data, a good portion of many scientific texts *does* serve the purpose of delivering uncontested facts.

However, scientific writing often does more than just report facts. Data are crucial to scientific argumentation, but they are by no means the end of the story. Given important new data, scientists assess their quality, draw conclusions from them, and ponder their implications. They synthesize the new data with existing information, propose novel theories, and design the next experiments. In short, scientific progress depends on the insight and creativity that scientists bring to their data. The thrill of doing science, and writing about it, comes from the ongoing struggle to use data to better understand our world.

START WITH THE DATA

Data are the fundamental currency of scientific argument. Scientists develop hypotheses from existing data and then test those by comparing their predictions to new experimental data. Summarizing data is therefore a basic move in science writing. Because data can often be interpreted in different ways, describing the data opens the door to critical analysis, creating opportunities to critique previous interpretations and develop new ones.

Describing data requires more than simply reporting numbers and conclusions. Rather than jumping straight to the punch line—to what X concluded—it is important first to describe the hypotheses, methods, and results that led to the conclusion: "To test the hypothesis that _____, X measured _____ and found that _____. Therefore, X concluded _____." In the following sections, we explore the three key rhetorical moves for describing the data that underpin a scientific argument: presenting the prevailing theories, explaining methodologies, and summarizing findings.

Present the Prevailing Theories

Readers must understand the prevailing theories that a study responds to before they can fully appreciate the details. So before diving into specifics, place the work in context by describing the prevailing theories and hypotheses. In the following passage from a journal article about insect respiration, the authors discuss an explanation for discontinuous gas exchange (DGC), a phenomenon where insects periodically close valves on their breathing tubes:

See how a computer scientist describes a prevailing theory on p. 328.

Lighton (1996, 1998; see also Lighton and Berrigan, 1995) noted the prevalence of DGC in fossorial insects, which inhabit microclimates where CO_2 levels may be relatively high. Consequently, Lighton proposed the chthonic hypothesis, which suggests that

DGC originated as a mechanism to improve gas exchange while at the same time minimizing respiratory water loss.

A. G. Gibbs and R. A. Johnson, "The Role of Discontinuous Gas Exchange in Insects: The Chthonic Hypothesis Does Not Hold Water," *Journal of Experimental Biology*

Notice that Gibbs and Johnson not only describe Lighton's hypothesis but also recap the evidence that supports it. By presenting this evidence, Gibbs and Johnson set the stage for engaging with Lighton's ideas. For example, they might question the chthonic hypothesis by pointing out shortcomings of the data or flaws in its interpretation. Or they might suggest new approaches that could verify the hypothesis. The point is that by incorporating a discussion of experimental findings into their summary of Lighton's hypothesis, Gibbs and Johnson open the door to a conversation with Lighton.

Here are some templates for presenting the data that underpin prevailing explanations:

▸ **Experiments showing _____ and _____ have led scientists to propose _____ .**

▸ **Although most scientists attribute _____ to _____ , X's result _____ leads to the possibility that _____ .**

Explain the Methods

Even as we've argued that scientific arguments hinge on data, it's important to note that the quality of data varies depending on how they were collected. Data obtained with sloppy techniques or poorly designed experiments could lead to faulty conclusions. Therefore, it's crucial to explain the methods used to collect data. In order for readers to evaluate a method, you'll need to indicate its purpose, as the following passage from a journal article about the evolution of bird digestive systems demonstrates:

> To test the hypothesis that flowerpiercers have converged with hummingbirds in digestive traits, we compared the activity of intestinal enzymes and the gut nominal area of cinnamon-bellied flowerpiercers (*Diglossa baritula*) with those of eleven hummingbird species.
>
> J. E. Schondube and C. Martinez del Rio,
> "Sugar and Protein Digestion in Flowerpiercers and
> Hummingbirds: A Comparative Test of Adaptive Convergence,"
> *Journal of Comparative Physiology*

You need to indicate purpose whether describing your own work or that of others. Here are a couple of templates for doing so:

▸ **Smith and colleagues evaluated** _____ **to determine whether** ____.

▸ **Because** _____ **does not account for** _____, **we instead used** _____.

Summarize the Findings

Scientific data often come in the form of numbers. Your task when presenting numerical data is to provide the context readers need to understand the numbers—by giving supporting information and making comparisons. In the following passage from a book about the interaction between organisms and their environments, Turner uses numerical data to support an argument about the role of the sun's energy on Earth:

> The potential rate of energy transfer from the Sun to Earth is prodigious—about 600 W m^{-2}, averaged throughout the year. Of this, only a relatively small fraction, on the order of 1–2 percent,

is captured by green plants. The rest, if it is not reflected back into space, is available to do other things. The excess can be considerable: although some natural surfaces reflect as much as 95% of the incoming solar beam, many natural surfaces reflect much less (Table 3.2), on average about 15–20 percent. The remaining absorbed energy is then capable of doing work, like heating up surfaces, moving water and air masses around to drive weather and climate, evaporating water, and so forth.

J. S. TURNER, The Extended Organism

Turner supports his point that a huge amount of the sun's energy is directly converted to work on Earth by quoting an actual value (600) with units of measurement (W m^{-2}, watts per square meter). Readers need the units to evaluate the value; 600 watts per square inch is very different from 600 W m^{-2}. Turner then makes comparisons using percent values, saying that only 1 to 2 percent of the total energy that reaches Earth is trapped by plants. Finally, Turner describes the data's variability by reporting comparisons as ranges—1 to 2 percent and 15 to 20 percent—rather than single values.

Supporting information—such as units of measurement, sample size (n), and amount of variability—helps readers assess the data. In general, the reliability of data improves as its sample size increases and its variability decreases. Supporting information can be concisely presented as:

▶ _____ ± _____ *(mean ± variability)* _____ *(units)*, $n =$ _____ *(sample size)*.

For example: before training, resting heart rate of the subjects was 56 ± 7 beats per minute, $n = 12$. Here's another way to give supporting information:

▸ We measured _____ (*sample size*) subjects, and the average
response was _____ (*mean with units*) with a range of
_____ (*lower value*) to _____ (*upper value*).

To help readers understand the data, make comparisons with values from the same study or from other similar work. Here are some templates for making comparisons:

▸ Before training, average running speed was _____ ±
_____ kilometers per hour, _____ kilometers per hour
slower than running speed after training.

▸ We found athletes' heart rates to be _____ ± _____ %
lower than nonathletes'.

▸ The subjects in X's study completed the maze in _____ ±
_____ seconds, _____ seconds slower than those in
Y's study.

You will sometimes need to present qualitative data, such as that found in some images and photographs, which cannot be reduced to numbers. Qualitative data must be described precisely with words. In the passage below from a review article about connections between cellular protein localization and cell growth, the author describes the exact locations of three proteins, Scrib, Dlg, and Lgl:

> Epithelial cells accumulate different proteins on their apical (top) and basolateral (bottom) surfaces. . . . Scrib and Dlg are localized at the septate junctions along the lateral cell surface, whereas Lgl coats vesicles that are found both in the cytoplasm and "docked" at the lateral surface of the cell.
>
> M. PEIFER, "Travel Bulletin—Traffic Jams
> Cause Tumors," *Science*

EXPLAIN WHAT THE DATA MEAN

Once you summarize experiments and results, you need to say what the data mean. Consider the following passage from a study in which scientists fertilized plots of tropical rainforest with nitrogen (N) and / or phosphorus (P):

> Although our data suggest that the mechanisms driving the observed respiratory responses to increased N and P may be different, the large CO_2 losses stimulated by N and P fertilization suggest that knowledge of such patterns and their effects on soil CO_2 efflux is critical for understanding the role of tropical forests in a rapidly changing global C [carbon] cycle.
>
> C. C. CLEVELAND AND A. R. TOWNSEND, "Nutrient Additions to a Tropical Rain Forest Drive Substantial Soil Carbon Dioxide Losses to the Atmosphere," *Proceedings of the National Academy of Sciences*

Notice that in discussing the implications of their data, Cleveland and Townsend use language—including the verbs "suggest" and "may be"—that denotes their level of confidence in what they say about the data.

Whether you are summarizing what others say about their data or offering your own interpretation, pay attention to the verbs that connect data to interpretations.

To signify a moderate level of confidence:

▸ The data *suggest / hint / imply* _____.

To express a greater degree of certainty:

▸ Our results *show / demonstrate* _____.

Almost never will you use the verb "prove" in reference to a single study, because even very powerful evidence generally falls short of proof unless other studies support the same conclusion.

Scientific consensus arises when multiple studies point toward the same conclusion; conversely, contradictions among studies often signal research questions that need further work. For these reasons, you may need to compare one study's findings to those of another study. Here, too, you'll need to choose your verbs carefully:

▸ Our data *support / confirm / verify* the work of X by showing that _____.

▸ By demonstrating _____, X's work *extends* the findings of Y.

▸ The results of X *contradict / refute* Y's conclusion that _____.

▸ X's findings *call into question* the widely accepted theory that _____.

▸ Our data *are consistent with* X's hypothesis that _____.

MAKE YOUR OWN ARGUMENTS

Now we turn toward the part of scientific writing where you express your own opinions. One challenge is that the statements of other scientists about their methods and results usually must be accepted. You probably can't argue, for example, that "X and Y claim to have studied six elephants, but I think they actually only studied four." However, it might be fair to say, "X and Y studied only six elephants, and this small sample size casts doubts on their conclusions." The second statement doesn't question what the scientists did or found but instead examines how the findings are interpreted.

When developing your own arguments—the "I say"—you will often start by assessing the interpretations of other scientists. Consider the following example from a review article about the beneficial acclimation hypothesis (BAH), the idea that organisms exposed to a particular environment become better suited to that environment than unexposed animals:

> To the surprise of most physiologists, all empirical examinations of the BAH have rejected its generality. However, we suggest that these examinations are neither direct nor complete tests of the functional benefit of acclimation.
>
> R. S. WILSON AND C. E. FRANKLIN, "Testing the Beneficial Acclimation Hypothesis," *Trends in Ecology & Evolution*

Wilson and Franklin use a version of the "twist it" move: they acknowledge the data collected by other physiologists but question how those data have been interpreted, creating an opportunity to offer their own interpretation.

For more on the "twist it" move, see p. 62.

You might ask whether we should question how other scientists interpret their own work. Having conducted a study, aren't they in the best position to evaluate it? Perhaps, but as the above example demonstrates, other scientists might see the work from a different perspective or through more objective eyes. And, in fact, the culture of science depends on vigorous debate in which scientists defend their own findings and challenge those of others—a give-and-take that helps improve science's reliability. So expressing a critical view about someone else's work is an integral part of the scientific process. Let's examine some of the basic moves for entering scientific conversations: agreeing, with a difference; disagreeing and explaining why; simultaneously agreeing and disagreeing; anticipating objections; and saying why it matters.

Agree, but with a Difference

Scientific research passes through several levels of critical analysis before being published. Scientists get feedback when they discuss work with colleagues, present findings at conferences, and receive reviews of their manuscripts. So the juiciest debates may have been resolved before publication, and you may find little to disagree with in the published literature of a research field. Yet even if you agree with what you've read, there are still ways to join the conversation—and reasons to do so.

One approach is to suggest that further work should be done:

▸ **Now that _____ has been established, scientists will likely turn their attention toward _____.**

▸ **X's work leads to the question of _____. Therefore, we investigated _____.**

▸ **To see whether these findings apply to _____, we propose to _____.**

Another way to agree and at the same time jump into the conversation is to concur with a finding and then propose a mechanism that explains it. In the following sentence from a review article about dietary deficiencies, the author agrees with a previous finding and offers a probable explanation:

> Inadequate dietary intakes of vitamins and minerals are widespread, most likely due to excessive consumption of energy-rich, micronutrient-poor, refined food.
>
> B. AMES, "Low Micronutrient Intake
> May Accelerate the Degenerative Diseases of Aging through
> Allocation of Scarce Micronutrients by Triage,"
> *Proceedings of the National Academy of Sciences*

Here are some templates for explaining an experimental result:

▸ **One explanation for X's finding of** _____ **is that** _____.
  An alternative explanation is _____.

▸ **The difference between** _____ **and** _____ **is probably
  due to** _____.

Disagree—and Explain Why

Although scientific consensus is common, healthy disagreement is not unusual. While measurements conducted by different teams of scientists under the same conditions should produce the same result, scientists often disagree about which techniques are most appropriate, how well an experimental design tests a hypothesis, and how results should be interpreted. To illustrate such disagreement, let's return to the debate about whether or not lactic acid is beneficial during exercise. In the following passage, Lamb and Stephenson are responding to work by Kristensen and colleagues, which argues that lactic acid might be beneficial to resting muscle but not to active muscle:

> The argument put forward by Kristensen and colleagues (12) . . .
> is not valid because it is based on observations made with isolated
> whole soleus muscles that were stimulated at such a high rate that
> >60% of the preparation would have rapidly become completely
> anoxic (4). . . . Furthermore, there is no reason to expect that
> adding more H+ to that already being generated by the muscle
> activity should in any way be advantageous. It is a bit like open-
> ing up the carburetor on a car to let in too much air or throwing

gasoline over the engine and then concluding that air and gasoline are deleterious to engine performance.

G. D. LAMB AND D. G. STEPHENSON,
"Point: Lactic Acid Accumulation Is an Advantage during
Muscle Activity," *Journal of Applied Physiology*

Lamb and Stephenson bring experimental detail to bear on their disagreement with Kristensen and colleagues. First, they criticize methodology, arguing that the high muscle stimulation rate used by Kristensen and colleagues created very low oxygen levels (anoxia). They also criticize the logic of the experimental design, arguing that adding more acid (H+) to a muscle that is already producing it isn't informative. It's also worth noting how they drive home their point, likening Kristensen and colleagues' methodology to flooding an engine with air or gasoline. Even in technical scientific writing, you don't need to set aside your own voice completely.

In considering the work of others, look for instances where the experimental design and methodology fail to adequately test a hypothesis:

▸ **The work of Y and Z appears to show that _____, but their experimental design does not control for _____.**

Also, consider the possibility that results do not lead to the stated conclusions:

▸ **While X and Y claim that _____, their finding of _____ actually shows that _____.**

OK, But . . .

Science tends to progress incrementally. New work may refine or extend previous work but doesn't often completely overturn it.

For this reason, science writers frequently agree up to a point and then express some disagreement. In the following example from a commentary about methods for assessing how proteins interact, the authors acknowledge the value of the two-hybrid studies, but they also point out their shortcomings:

> The two-hybrid studies that produced the protein interaction map for *D. melanogaster* (12) provide a valuable genome-wide view of protein interactions but have a number of shortcomings (13). Even if the protein-protein interactions were determined with high accuracy, the resulting network would still require careful interpretation to extract its underlying biological meaning. Specifically, the map is a representation of all possible interactions, but one would only expect some fraction to be operating at any given time.
>
> J. J. Rice, A. Kershenbaum, and G. Stolovitzky,
> "Lasting Impressions: Motifs in Protein-Protein Maps
> May Provide Footprints of Evolutionary Events,"
> *Proceedings of the National Academy of Sciences*

Delineating the boundaries or limitations of a study is a good way to agree up to a point. Here are templates for doing so:

- ▸ While X's work clearly demonstrates _____, _____ will be required before we can determine whether _____.

- ▸ Although Y and Z present firm evidence for _____, their data cannot be used to argue that _____.

- ▸ In summary, our studies show that _____, but the issue of _____ remains unresolved.

Anticipate Objections

Skepticism is a key ingredient in the scientific process. Before an explanation is accepted, scientists demand convincing evidence and assess whether alternative explanations have been thoroughly explored, so it's essential that scientists consider possible objections to their ideas before presenting them. In the following example from a book about the origin of the universe, Tyson and Goldsmith first admit that some might doubt the existence of the poorly understood "dark matter" that physicists have proposed, and then they go on to respond to the skeptics:

> Unrelenting skeptics might compare the dark matter of today with the hypothetical, now defunct "ether," proposed centuries ago as the weightless, transparent medium through which light moved. . . . But dark matter ignorance differs fundamentally from ether ignorance. While ether amounted to a placeholder for our incomplete understanding, the existence of dark matter derives not from mere presumption but from the observed effects of its gravity on visible matter.
>
> N. D. TYSON AND D. GOLDSMITH,
> *Origins: Fourteen Billion Years of Cosmic Evolution*

Anticipating objections in your own writing will help you clarify and address potential criticisms. Consider objections to your overall approach, as well as to specific aspects of your interpretations. Here are some templates for doing so:

▸ **Scientists who take a _____ (*reductionist / integrative / biochemical / computational / statistical*) approach might view our results differently.**

▸ This interpretation of the data might be criticized by X, who has argued that _____.

▸ Some may argue that this experimental design fails to account for _____.

Say Why It Matters

Though individual studies can be narrowly focused, science ultimately seeks to answer big questions and produce useful technologies. So it's essential when you enter a scientific conversation to say why the work—and your arguments about it—matter. The following passage from a commentary on a research article notes two implications of work that evaluated the shape of electron orbitals:

> The classic textbook shape of electron orbitals has now been directly observed. As well as confirming the established theory, this work may be a first step to understanding high-temperature superconductivity.
>
> C. J. HUMPHREYS, "Electrons Seen in Orbit," *Nature*

Humphreys argues that the study confirms an established theory and that it may lead to better understanding in another area. When thinking about the broad significance of a study, consider both the practical applications and the impact on future scientific work:

▸ These results open the door to studies that _____.

▸ The methodologies developed by X will be useful for _____.

▸ Our findings are the first step toward _____.

▶ Further work in this area may lead to the development of
_____ .

READING AS A WAY OF ENTERING
SCIENTIFIC CONVERSATIONS

In science, as in other disciplines, you'll often start with work done by others, and therefore you will need to critically evaluate their work. To that end, you'll need to probe how well their data support their interpretations. Doing so will lead you toward your own interpretations—your ticket into an ongoing scientific conversation. Here are some questions that will help you read and respond to scientific research:

How well do the methods test the hypothesis?

- Is the sample size adequate?
- Is the experimental design valid? Were the proper controls performed?
- What are the limitations of the methodology?
- Are other techniques available?

How fairly have the results been interpreted?

- How well do the results support the stated conclusion?
- Has the data's variability been adequately considered?
- Do other findings verify (or contradict) the conclusion?
- What other experiments could test the conclusion?

What are the broader implications of the work, and why does it matter?

- Can the results be generalized beyond the system that was studied?

- What are the work's practical implications?

- What questions arise from the work?

- Which experiments should be done next?

The examples in this chapter show that scientists do more than simply collect facts; they also interpret those facts and make arguments about their meaning. On the frontiers of science, where we are probing questions that are just beyond our capacity to answer, the data are inevitably incomplete and controversy is to be expected. Writing about science presents the opportunity to add your own arguments to the ongoing discussion.

EIGHTEEN

"ANALYZE THIS"

Writing in the Social Sciences

ERIN ACKERMAN

—🖳—

SOCIAL SCIENCE is the study of people—how they behave
and relate to one another, and the organizations and institutions that facilitate these interactions. People are complicated,
so any study of human behavior is at best partial, taking into
account some elements of what people do and why, but not
always explaining those actions definitively. As a result, it is
the subject of constant conversation and argument.

Consider some of the topics studied in the social sciences:
minimum wage laws, immigration policy, health care, what causes
aggressive behavior, employment discrimination. Got an opinion
on any of these topics? You aren't alone. But in the writing you do
as a student of the social sciences, you need to write about more

---

ERIN ACKERMAN is the social sciences librarian at the College of New
Jersey and formerly taught political science at John Jay College, City
University of New York. Her research and teaching interests include
American law and politics, women and law, and information literacy
in the social sciences.

than just your opinions. Good writing in the social sciences, as in other academic disciplines, requires that you demonstrate that you have examined what you think and why. The best way to do that is to bring your views into conversation with those expressed by others and to test what you and others think against a review of evidence. In other words, you'll need to start with what others say and then present what you say as a response.

Consider the following example from an op-ed in the *New York Times* by two psychology professors:

> Is video game addiction a real thing?
>
> It's certainly common to hear parents complain that their children are "addicted" to video games. Some researchers even claim that these games are comparable to illegal drugs in terms of their influence on the brain—that they are "digital heroin" (the neuroscientist Peter C. Whybrow) or "digital pharmakeia" (the neuroscientist Andrew Doan). The American Psychiatric Association has identified internet gaming disorder as a possible psychiatric illness, and the World Health Organization has proposed including "gaming disorder" in its catalog of mental diseases, along with drug and alcohol addiction.
>
> This is all terribly misguided. Playing video games is not addictive in any meaningful sense. It is normal behavior that, while perhaps in many cases a waste of time, is not damaging or disruptive of lives in the way drug or alcohol use can be.
>
> CHRISTOPHER J. FERGUSON AND PATRICK MARKEY,
"Video Games Aren't Addictive"

In other words, "they" (parents, other researchers, health organizations) say that the video games are addictive, whereas Ferguson and Markey disagree. In the rest of the op-ed, they argue that video game critics have misinterpreted the evidence and are not being very precise with what counts as "addiction."

This chapter explores some of the basic moves social science writers make. Writing in the social sciences often takes the form of a research paper that generally includes several core components: a strong introduction and thesis, a literature review, and the writer's own analysis, including presentation of evidence/data and consideration of implications. The introduction sets out the thesis, or point, of the paper, briefly explaining the topic or question you are investigating and previewing what you will say in your paper and how it fits into the preexisting conversation. The literature review summarizes what has already been said on your topic. Your analysis allows you to present evidence (the information, or data, about human behavior that you are measuring or testing against what other people have said), to explain the conclusions you have drawn based on your investigation, and to discuss the implications of your research. Do you agree, disagree, or some combination of both with what has been said by others? What reasons can you give for why you feel that way? And so what? Who should be interested in what you have to say, and why?

You may get other types of writing assignments in the social sciences, such as preparing a policy memo, writing a legal brief, or designing a grant or research proposal. While there may be differences from the research papers in terms of the format and audience for these assignments, the purposes of sections of the research paper and the moves discussed here will help you with those assignments as well.

THE INTRODUCTION AND THESIS:
"THIS PAPER CHALLENGES . . ."

Your introduction sets forth what you plan to say in your essay. You might evaluate the work of earlier scholars or certain widely held assumptions and find them incorrect when measured against new events or data. Alternatively, you might point out that an author's work is largely correct but that it could use some qualifications or be extended in some way. Or you might identify a gap in our knowledge—we know a great deal about topic X but almost nothing about some other closely related topic. In each of these instances, your introduction needs to cover both "they say" and "I say" perspectives. If you stop after the "they say," your readers won't know what you are bringing to the conversation. Similarly, if you were to jump right to the "I say" portion of your argument, readers might wonder why you need to say anything at all.

Sometimes you join the conversation at a point where the discussion seems settled. One or more views about a topic have become so widely accepted among a group of scholars or society at large that these views are essentially the conventional way of thinking about the topic. You may wish to offer new reasons to support this interpretation, or you may wish to call these standard views into question. To do so, you must first introduce and identify these widely held beliefs and then present your own view. In fact, much of the writing in the social sciences takes the form of calling into question that which we think we already know. Consider the following example from an article in the *Journal of Economic Perspectives*:

> Fifteen years ago, Milton Friedman's 1957 treatise A *Theory of the Consumption Function* seemed badly dated. Dynamic optimization theory had not been employed much in economics when Friedman wrote, and utility theory was still comparatively primitive, so his statement of the "permanent income hypothesis" never actually specified a formal mathematical model of behavior derived explicitly from utility maximization. . . . [W]hen other economists subsequently

found multiperiod maximizing models that could be solved explicitly, the implications of those models differed sharply from Friedman's intuitive description of his "model." Furthermore, empirical tests in the 1970s and 1980s often rejected these rigorous versions of the permanent income hypothesis in favor of an alternative hypothesis that many households simply spent all of their current income.

Today, with the benefit of a further round of mathematical (and computational) advances, Friedman's (1957) original analysis looks more prescient than primitive.

CHRISTOPHER D. CARROLL, "A Theory of Consumption
Function, with and without Liquidity Constraints,"
Journal of Economic Perspectives

This introduction makes clear that Carroll will defend Milton Friedman against some major criticisms of his work. Carroll mentions what has been said about Friedman's work and then goes on to say that the critiques turn out to be wrong and to suggest that Friedman's work reemerges as persuasive. A template of Carroll's introduction might look something like this: "Economics research in the last fifteen years suggested Friedman's 1957 treatise was _____ because _____. In other words, they say that Friedman's work is not accurate because of _____, _____, and _____. Recent research convinces me, however, that Friedman's work makes sense."

In some cases, however, there may not be a strong consensus among experts on a topic. You might enter the ongoing debate by casting your vote with one side or another or by offering an alternative view. In the following example, Sheri Berman identifies two competing accounts of how to explain world events in the twentieth century and then puts forth a third view:

Conventional wisdom about twentieth-century ideologies rests on two simple narratives. One focuses on the struggle for dominance between democracy and its alternatives. . . . The other narrative focuses on the competition between free-market capitalism and its rivals. . . . Both of these narratives obviously contain some truth. . . . Yet both only tell part of the story, which is why their common conclusion—neoliberalism as the "end of History"—is unsatisfying and misleading.

What the two conventional narratives fail to mention is that a third struggle was also going on: between those ideologies that believed in the primacy of economics and those that believed in the primacy of politics.

SHERI BERMAN, "The Primacy of Economics versus the Primacy of Politics: Understanding the Ideological Dynamics of the Twentieth Century," *Perspectives on Politics*

After identifying the two competing narratives, Berman suggests a third view—and later goes on to argue that this third view explains current debates over globalization. A template for this type of introduction might look something like this: "In recent discussions of _____, a controversial aspect has been _____. On the one hand, some argue that _____. On the other hand, others argue that _____. Neither of these arguments, however, considers the alternative view that _____."

Given the complexity of many of the issues studied in the social sciences, however, you may sometimes agree *and* disagree with existing views—pointing out things that you believe are correct or have merit, while disagreeing with or refining other points. In the example below, anthropologist Sally Engle Merry agrees with another scholar about something that is a key trait of modern society but argues that this trait has a different origin than the other author identifies:

For more on different ways of responding, see Chapter 4.

Although I agree with Rose that an increasing emphasis on governing the soul is characteristic of modern society, I see the transformation not as evolutionary but as the product of social mobilization and political struggle.

> SALLY ENGLE MERRY, "Rights, Religion, and Community:
> Approaches to Violence against Women in the
> Context of Globalization," *Law and Society Review*

Here are some templates for agreeing and disagreeing:

▸ Although I agree with X up to a point, I cannot accept his overall conclusion that _____.

▸ Although I disagree with X on _____ and _____, I agree with her conclusion that _____.

▸ Political scientists studying _____ have argued that it is caused by _____. While _____ contributes to the problem, _____ is also an important factor.

▸ While noting _____, I contend _____.

In the process of examining people from different angles, social scientists sometimes identify gaps—areas that have not been explored in previous research.

In the following example, several sociologists identify such a gap:

Family scholars have long argued that the study of dating deserves more attention (Klemer, 1971), as dating is an important part of the life course at any age and often a precursor to marriage (Levesque & Caron, 2004). . . .

The central research questions we seek to answer with this study are whether and how the significance of particular dating rituals are patterned by gender and race simultaneously. We use a racially diverse data set of traditional-aged college students from a variety of college contexts. Understanding gender and racial differences in the assessment of dating rituals helps us explore the extent to which relationship activities are given similar importance across institutional and cultural lines. Most of the studies that inform our knowledge of dating and relationships are unable to draw conclusions regarding racial differences because the sample is Caucasian (e.g., Bogle, 2008), or primarily so (e.g., Manning & Smock, 2005). Race has been recently argued to be an often-overlooked variable in studies examining social psychological processes because of the prevalence of sample limitations as well as habitual oversight in the literature (Hunt, Jackson, Powell, & Steelman, 2000). Additionally, a failure to examine both gender and race prevents assessment of whether gendered beliefs are shared across groups. Gauging the extent of differences in beliefs among different population subgroups is critical to advancing the study of relationship dynamics (see Weaver & Ganong, 2004).

PAMELA BRABOY JACKSON, SIBYL KLEINER, CLAUDIA GEIST, AND KARA CEBULKO, "Conventions of Courtship: Gender and Race Differences in the Significance of Dating Rituals," *Journal of Family Issues*

Jackson and her coauthors note that while other scholars have said that studying dating is important and have examined some aspects of dating, we have little information about whether attitudes about dating activities (such as sexual intimacy, gift exchange, and meeting the family) vary across groups by gender and race. Their study aims to fill this gap in our understanding of relationships.

Here are some templates for introducing gaps in the existing research:

▸ **Studies of X have indicated _____. It is not clear, however, that this conclusion applies to _____.**

▸ **_____ often take for granted that _____. Few have investigated this assumption, however.**

▸ **X's work tells us a great deal about _____. Can this work be generalized to _____?**

▸ **Our understanding of _____ remains incomplete because previous work has not examined _____.**

Again, a good introduction indicates what you have to say in the larger context of what others have said. Throughout the rest of your paper, you will move back and forth between the "they say" and the "I say," adding more details.

THE LITERATURE REVIEW: "PRIOR RESEARCH INDICATES . . ."

The point of a literature review is to establish the state of knowledge on your topic. Before you (and your reader) can properly consider an issue, you need to understand the conversation about your topic that has already taken place (and is likely still in progress). In the literature review, you explain what "they say" in more detail, summarizing, paraphrasing, or quoting the viewpoints to which you are responding. But you need to balance what they are saying with your own focus. You need to characterize someone else's work fairly and accurately but set up the points you yourself want to make by selecting the details that are relevant to your own perspective and observations.

It is common in the social sciences to summarize several arguments in a single paragraph or even a single sentence, grouping several sources together by their important ideas or other attributes. The example below cites some key findings and conclusions of psychological research that should be of interest to motivated college students looking to improve their academic performance:

> Some people may associate sacrificing hours of sleep with being studious, but the reality is that sleep deprivation can hurt your cognitive functioning without your being aware of it (e.g., becoming worse at paying attention and remembering things; Goel, Rao, Durmer, & Dinges, 2009; Pilcher & Walters, 1997).... Sleep affects learning and memory by organizing and consolidating memories from the day (Diekelmann & Born, 2010; Rasch & Born, 2013), which can lead to better problem-solving ability and creativity (Verleger, Rose, Wagner, Yordanova, & Kolev, 2013).
>
> ADAM L. PUTNAM, VICTOR W. SUNGKHASETTEE, AND
> HENRY L. ROEDIGER, III, "Optimizing Learning in College:
> Tips from Cognitive Psychology," *Perspectives on
> Psychological Science*

A template for this paragraph might look like this: "Students believe _____, but researchers disagree because _____. According to researchers, negative consequences of sleep deprivation include _____. The research shows that a positive effect of sleep is _____, which improves _____."

Such summaries are brief, bringing together relevant arguments by several scholars to provide an overview of scholarly work on a particular topic. In writing such a summary, you need to ask yourself how the authors themselves might describe their positions and also consider what in their work is relevant for the point you wish to make. This kind of summary is especially appropriate when you have a large amount of research material on a topic and want to identify the major strands of a debate or to show how the work of one author builds on that of another. Here are some templates for overview summaries:

▸ In addressing the question of _____, researchers have considered several explanations for _____. X argues that _____. According to Y and Z, another plausible explanation is _____.

▸ What is the effect of _____ on _____? Previous work on _____ by X and by Y and Z supports _____.

▸ Scholars point to the role of _____ in _____.

▸ Existing research on _____ presents convincing evidence of _____.

Sometimes you may need to say more about the works you cite. On a midterm or final exam, for example, you may need to demonstrate that you have a deep familiarity with a particular work. And in some disciplines of the social sciences, longer, more detailed literature reviews are the standard. Your instructor and any assigned articles are your best guides for the length and level of detail of your literature review. Other times, the work of certain authors is especially important for your argument, and therefore you need to provide more details to explain what these authors have said. See how political scientists Hahrie Han and Lisa Argyle, in a report for the Ford Foundation, summarize an argument that is central to their investigation of improving democratic participation:

> [A]t the root of declining rates of participation is the sense that people do not feel like their participation matters. People do not feel like they have any real reason or opportunity to exercise voice in the political process. People's sense of agency is in decline, especially given negative or incomplete experiences of government in their lives.
>
> This lack of caring comes as no surprise when we examine research showing that most people have negative or, at best, incomplete experiences of the role of government in their lives. Suzanne Mettler, for instance, finds that many middle-class people who benefit from different government programs—ranging from education savings accounts to welfare to tax credits—believe that they "have not used a government social program." In addition, other scholars find a trend towards increasing privatization of public goods and political processes in the twenty-first century. As a result, government is what Mettler calls a "submerged state," since the role of government in people's lives is effectively submerged from view.
>
> HAHRIE HAN AND LISA ARGYLE, "A Program Review of the Promoting Electoral Reform and Democratic Participation (PERDP) Initiative of the Ford Foundation"

Note that Han and Argyle start by identifying the broad problem of lack of participation and then explain how Mettler's work describes how middle-class people may be unaware of the role of government in their lives, leading Mettler to argue for the idea of the "submerged state."

You may want to include direct quotations of what others have said, as Han and Argyle do. Using exact words helps you demonstrate that you are representing the author fairly. But you cannot simply insert a quotation; you need to explain to your readers what it means for your point. Consider the following example drawn from a political science book on the debate over tort reform:

> The essence of *agenda setting* was well enunciated by E. E. Schattschneider: "In politics as in everything else, it makes a great difference whose game we play" (1960, 47). In short, the ability to define or control the rules, terms, or perceived options in a contest over policy greatly affects the prospects for winning.
>
> WILLIAM HALTOM AND MICHAEL MCCANN,
Distorting the Law: Politics, Media, and the Litigation Crisis

Notice how Haltom and McCann first quote Schattschneider and then explain in their own words how political agenda setting can be thought of as a game, with winners and losers.

Remember that whenever you summarize, quote, or paraphrase the work of others, credit must be given in the form of a citation to the original work. The words may be your own, but if the idea comes from someone else you must give credit to the original work. There are several formats for documenting sources. Consult your instructor for help choosing which citation style to use.

THE ANALYSIS

The literature review covers what others have said on your topic. The analysis allows you to present and support your own response. In the introduction you indicate whether you agree, disagree, or some combination of both with what others have said. You will want to expand on how you have formed your opinion and why others should care about your topic.

"The Data Indicate . . ."

The social sciences use evidence to develop and test explanations. This evidence is often referred to as data. Data can be quantitative or qualitative and can come from a number of sources. You might use statistics related to GDP growth, unemployment, voting rates, or demographics. You might report results from an experiment or simulation. Or you could use surveys, interviews, or other first-person accounts.

Regardless of the type of data used, it is important to do three things: define your data, indicate where you got the data, and then say what you have done with your data. For a chapter in their book assessing media coverage of female candidates, political scientists Danny Hayes and Jennifer Lawless explain how they assembled a data set:

> From the perspective of campaign professionals and voters, local newspaper coverage remains the most important news source during House campaigns....
>
> We began by selecting the appropriate newspaper for each House race in 2010 and 2014.... [W]e identified every news story during the thirty days leading up to the election that mentioned at least one of the two major-party candidates....
>
> Our data collection efforts produced 10,375 stories about 1,550 candidates who received at least some local news coverage in either the 2010 or 2014 midterms....
>
> Coders read the full text of each article and recorded several pieces of information. First, they tracked the number of times a candidate's sex or gender was mentioned.... Second, we recorded the number of explicit references to candidate traits, both positive and negative (e.g., "capable" and "ineffective")....
>
> Third, we tracked every time an issue was mentioned in connection with a candidate.... We then classified issues in two ways:

(1) We assigned each issue to one of the eight broad categories...
and (2) we classified a subset of the topics as "women's" or "men's"
issues.

DANNY HAYES AND JENNIFER L. LAWLESS, *Women on the Run:*
Gender, Media, and Political Campaigns in a Polarized Era

Hayes and Lawless explain how they collected their data—local
newspaper coverage of congressional candidates—and explain
how they coded and classified the coverage to allow them to
perform statistical analysis of the news pieces. While you probably won't collect 10,000-plus news items for a class project, you
could collect information (such as media coverage, interview
responses, or legal briefs) and analyze and sort them to identify
patterns such as repeated words and ideas.

If your data are quantitative, you also need to explain
them. Sociologist Jonathan Horowitz's research concludes
that job quality influences personal assessments of well-being
by "improving social life, altering class identification, affecting
physical health, and increasing amounts of leisure time." See
how he introduces the data he analyzes:

In this study, I use data from the General Social Survey (GSS) and
structural equation modeling to test relationships between job quality and subjective well-being. The GSS is a nationally representative
sample of adults in the United States that asks a large number of
questions about experiences at work (Smith et al., 2010). In particular, the GSS introduced a new battery of questions titled "Quality
of Working Life" in 2002 (and repeated in 2006 and 2010) which
includes multiple questions about several job quality dimensions.

JONATHAN HOROWITZ, "Dimensions of Job Quality,
Mechanisms, and Subjective Well-Being in the United States,"
Sociological Forum

Here are some templates for discussing data:

▸ In order to test the hypothesis that _____, we assessed _____. Our calculations suggest _____.

▸ I used _____ to investigate _____. The results of this investigation indicate _____.

"But Others May Object . . ."

No matter how strongly your data support your argument, there are almost surely other perspectives (and thus other data) that you need to acknowledge. By considering possible objections to your argument and taking them seriously, you demonstrate that you've done your work and that you're aware of other perspectives—and most important, you present your own argument as part of an ongoing conversation.

See p. 298 for a selection from *The New Jim Crow*. See how law professor Michelle Alexander acknowledges that there may be objections to her argument describing trends in mass incarceration as "the new Jim Crow."

> Some might argue that as disturbing as this system appears to be, there is nothing particularly new about mass incarceration; it is merely a continuation of past drug wars and biased law enforcement practices. Racial bias in our criminal justice system is simply an old problem that has gotten worse, and the social excommunication of "criminals" has a long history; it is not a recent invention. There is some merit to this argument.
>
> MICHELLE ALEXANDER, *The New Jim Crow: Mass Incarceration in the Age of Colorblindness*

Alexander imagines a conversation with people who might be skeptical about her argument, particularly her claim that this represents a "new" development. And she responds that they are correct, to a point. After acknowledging her agreement with the assessment of historical racial bias in the criminal justice system, she goes on in the rest of her chapter to explain that the expanded scope and consequences of contemporary mass incarceration have caused dramatic differences in society.

Someone may object because there are related phenomena that your analysis does not explain or because you do not have the right data to investigate a particular question. Or perhaps someone may object to assumptions underlying your argument or how you handled your data. Here are some templates for considering naysayers:

▸ _____ might object that _____ .

▸ Is my claim realistic? I have argued _____ , but readers may question _____ .

▸ My explanation accounts for _____ but does not explain _____ . This is because _____ .

"Why Should We Care?"

Who should care about your research, and why? Since the social sciences attempt to explain human behavior, it is important to consider how your research affects the assumptions we make about human behavior. In addition, you might offer recommendations for how other social scientists might continue to explore an issue, or what actions policy makers should take.

In the following example, sociologist Devah Pager identifies the implications of her study of the way having a criminal record affects a person applying for jobs:

> [I]n terms of policy implications, this research has troubling conclusions. In our frenzy of locking people up, our "crime control"

policies may in fact exacerbate the very conditions that lead to crime in the first place. Research consistently shows that finding quality steady employment is one of the strongest predictors of desistance from crime (Shover 1996; Sampson and Laub 1993; Uggen 2000). The fact that a criminal record severely limits employment opportunities—particularly among blacks—suggests that these individuals are left with few viable alternatives.

> DEVAH PAGER, "The Mark of a Criminal Record,"
> American Journal of Sociology

Pager's conclusion that a criminal record negatively affects employment chances creates a vicious circle, she says: steady employment discourages recidivism, but a criminal record makes it harder to get a job.

In answering the "so what?" question, you need to explain why your readers should care. Although sometimes the implications of your work may be so broad that they would be of interest to almost anyone, it's never a bad idea to identify explicitly any groups of people who will find your work important.

Templates for establishing why your claims matter:

▸ **X is important because _____.**

▸ **Ultimately, what is at stake here is _____.**

▸ **The finding that _____ should be of interest to _____ because _____.**

As noted at the beginning of this chapter, the complexity of people allows us to look at their behavior from many different viewpoints. Much has been, and will be, said about how and why people do the things they do. As a result, we can look at writing in the social sciences as an ongoing conversation. When you join this conversation, the "they say / I say" framework will help you figure out what has already been said ("they say") and what you can add ("I say"). The components of social science writing presented in this chapter are tools to help you join that conversation.

READINGS

Hidden Intellectualism

GERALD GRAFF

EVERYONE KNOWS SOME YOUNG PERSON who is impressively "street smart" but does poorly in school. What a waste, we think, that one who is so intelligent about so many things in life seems unable to apply that intelligence to academic work. What doesn't occur to us, though, is that schools and colleges might be at fault for missing the opportunity to tap into such street smarts and channel them into good academic work.

Nor do we consider one of the major reasons why schools and colleges overlook the intellectual potential of street smarts: the fact that we associate those street smarts with anti-intellectual concerns. We associate the educated life, the life of the mind, too narrowly and exclusively with subjects and texts that we consider inherently weighty and academic. We assume that it's possible to wax intellectual about Plato, Shakespeare,

---

GERALD GRAFF, a coauthor of this book, is a professor of English and education at the University of Illinois at Chicago. He is a past president of the Modern Language Association, the world's largest professional association of university scholars and teachers. This essay is adapted from his 2003 book, *Clueless in Academe: How Schooling Obscures the Life of the Mind.*

the French Revolution, and nuclear fission, but not about cars, dating, fashion, sports, TV, or video games.

The trouble with this assumption is that no necessary connection has ever been established between any text or subject See pp. 60–63 for tips on disagreeing, with reasons. and the educational depth and weight of the discussion it can generate. Real intellectuals turn any subject, however lightweight it may seem, into grist for their mill through the thoughtful questions they bring to it, whereas a dullard will find a way to drain the interest out of the richest subject. That's why a George Orwell writing on the cultural meanings of penny postcards is infinitely more substantial than the cogitations of many professors on Shakespeare or globalization (104–16).

Students do need to read models of intellectually challenging writing—and Orwell is a great one—if they are to become intellectuals themselves. But they would be more prone to take on intellectual identities if we encouraged them to do so at first on subjects that interest them rather than ones that interest us.

I offer my own adolescent experience as a case in point. Until I 5 entered college, I hated books and cared only for sports. The only reading I cared to do or could do was sports magazines, on which I became hooked, becoming a regular reader of *Sport* magazine in the late forties, *Sports Illustrated* when it began publishing in 1954, and the annual magazine guides to professional baseball, football, and basketball. I also loved the sports novels for boys of John R. Tunis and Clair Bee and autobiographies of sports stars like Joe DiMaggio's *Lucky to Be a Yankee* and Bob Feller's *Strikeout Story*. In short, I was your typical teenage anti-intellectual—or so I believed for a long time. I have recently come to think, however, that my preference for sports over schoolwork was not anti-intellectualism so much as intellectualism by other means.

In the Chicago neighborhood I grew up in, which had become a melting pot after World War II, our block was solidly middle class, but just a block away—doubtless concentrated there by the real estate companies—were African Americans, Native Americans, and "hillbilly" whites who had recently fled postwar joblessness in the South and Appalachia. Negotiating this class boundary was a tricky matter. On the one hand, it was necessary to maintain the boundary between "clean-cut" boys like me and working-class "hoods," as we called them, which meant that it was good to be openly smart in a bookish sort of way. On the other hand, I was desperate for the approval of the hoods, whom I encountered daily on the playing field and in the neighborhood, and for this purpose it was not at all good to be book-smart. The hoods would turn on you if they sensed you were putting on airs over them: "Who you lookin' at, smart ass?" as a leather-jacketed youth once said to me as he relieved me of my pocket change along with my self-respect.

I grew up torn, then, between the need to prove I was smart and the fear of a beating if I proved it too well; between the need not to jeopardize my respectable future and the need to impress the hoods. As I lived it, the conflict came down to a choice between being physically tough and being verbal. For a boy in my neighborhood and elementary school, only being "tough" earned you complete legitimacy. I still recall endless, complicated debates in this period with my closest pals over who was "the toughest guy in the school." If you were less than negligible as a fighter, as I was, you settled for the next best thing, which was to be inarticulate, carefully hiding telltale marks of literacy like correct grammar and pronunciation.

In one way, then, it would be hard to imagine an adolescence more thoroughly anti-intellectual than mine. Yet in retrospect, I see that it's more complicated, that I and the 1950s themselves were not simply hostile toward intellectualism, but divided and ambivalent. When Marilyn Monroe married the playwright Arthur Miller in 1956 after divorcing the retired baseball star

Joe DiMaggio, the symbolic triumph of geek over jock suggested the way the wind was blowing. Even Elvis, according to his biographer Peter Guralnick, turns out to have supported Adlai over Ike in the presidential election of 1956. "I don't dig the intellectual bit," he told reporters. "But I'm telling you, man, he knows the most" (327).

Though I too thought I did not "dig the intellectual bit," I see now that I was unwittingly in training for it. The germs had actually been planted in the seemingly philistine debates about which boys were the toughest. I see now that in the interminable analysis of sports teams, movies, and toughness that my friends and I engaged in—a type of analysis, needless to say, that the real toughs would never have stooped to—I was already betraying an allegiance to the egghead world. I was practicing being an intellectual before I knew that was what I wanted to be.

It was in these discussions with friends about toughness and sports, I think, and in my reading of sports books and magazines, that I began to learn the rudiments of the intellectual life: how to make an argument, weigh different kinds of evidence, move between particulars and generalizations, summarize the views of others, and enter a conversation about ideas. It was in reading and arguing about sports and toughness that I experienced what it felt like to propose a generalization, restate and respond to a counterargument, and perform other intellectualizing operations, including composing the kind of sentences I am writing now.

Only much later did it dawn on me that the sports world was more compelling than school because it was *more intellectual than school,* not less. Sports after all was full of challenging arguments, debates, problems for analysis, and intricate statistics that you could care about, as school conspicuously was not. I believe that street smarts beat out book smarts in our culture not because street smarts are nonintellectual, as we generally suppose, but because they satisfy an intellectual thirst more thoroughly than school culture, which seems pale and unreal.

They also satisfy the thirst for community. When you entered sports debates, you became part of a community that was not limited to your family and friends, but was national and public. Whereas schoolwork isolated you from others, the pennant race or Ted Williams's .400 batting average was something you could talk about with people you had never met. Sports introduced you not only to a culture steeped in argument, but to a public argument culture that transcended the personal. I can't blame my schools for failing to make intellectual culture resemble the Super Bowl, but I do fault them for failing to learn anything from the sports and entertainment worlds about how to organize and represent intellectual culture, how to exploit its gamelike element and turn it into arresting public spectacle that might have competed more successfully for my youthful attention.

For here is another thing that never dawned on me and is still kept hidden from students, with tragic results: that the real intellectual world, the one that existed in the big world beyond school, is organized very much like the world of team sports, with rival texts, rival interpretations and evaluations of texts, rival theories of why they should be read and taught, and elaborate team competitions in which "fans" of writers, intellectual systems, methodologies, and -isms contend against each other.

To be sure, school contained plenty of competition, which became more invidious as one moved up the ladder (and has become even more so today with the advent of high-stakes testing). In this competition, points were scored not by making arguments, but by a show of information or vast reading, by grade-grubbing, or other forms of one-upmanship. School competition, in short, reproduced the less attractive features of sports culture without those that create close bonds and community.

And in distancing themselves from anything as enjoyable and absorbing as sports, my schools missed the opportunity to capitalize on an element of drama and conflict that the intellectual world shares with sports. Consequently, I failed to see the parallels between the sports and academic worlds that could have helped me cross more readily from one argument culture to the other.

Sports is only one of the domains whose potential for literacy training (and not only for males) is seriously underestimated by educators, who see sports as competing with academic development rather than a route to it. But if this argument suggests why it is a good idea to assign readings and topics that are close to students' existing interests, it also suggests the limits of this tactic. For students who get excited about the chance to write about their passion for cars will often write as poorly and unreflectively on that topic as on Shakespeare or Plato. Here is the flip side of what I pointed out before: that there's no necessary relation between the degree of interest a student shows in a text or subject and the quality of thought or expression such a student manifests in writing or talking about it. The challenge, as college professor Ned Laff has put it, "is not simply to exploit students' nonacademic interests, but to get them to see those interests through academic eyes."

To say that students need to see their interests "through academic eyes" is to say that street smarts are not enough. Making students' nonacademic interests an object of academic study is useful, then, for getting students' attention and overcoming their boredom and alienation, but this tactic won't in itself necessarily move them closer to an academically rigorous treatment of those interests. On the other hand, inviting students to write about cars, sports, or clothing fashions does not have to be a pedagogical cop-out as long as students are required to see these interests "through academic eyes," that is, to think and write about cars, sports, and fashions in a reflective, analytical way, one that sees them as microcosms of what is going on in the wider culture.

If I am right, then schools and colleges are missing an opportunity when they do not encourage students to take their nonacademic interests as objects of academic study. It is self-defeating to decline to introduce any text or subject that figures to engage students who will otherwise tune out academic work entirely. If a student cannot get interested in Mill's *On Liberty* but will read *Sports Illustrated* or *Vogue* or the hip-hop magazine *Source* with absorption, this is a strong argument for assigning the magazines over the classic. It's a good bet that if students get hooked on reading and writing by doing term papers on *Source*, they will eventually get to *On Liberty*. But even if they don't, the magazine reading will make them more literate and reflective than they would be otherwise. So it makes pedagogical sense to develop classroom units on sports, cars, fashions, rap music, and other such topics. Give me the student anytime who writes a sharply argued, sociologically acute analysis of an issue in *Source* over the student who writes a lifeless explication of *Hamlet* or Socrates' *Apology*.

Works Cited

DiMaggio, Joe. *Lucky to Be a Yankee.* Bantam, 1949.

Feller, Bob. *Strikeout Story.* Bantam, 1948.

Guralnick, Peter. *Last Train to Memphis: The Rise of Elvis Presley.* Little, Brown, 1994.

Orwell, George. *A Collection of Essays.* Harcourt, 1953.

The New Jim Crow: Mass Incarceration in the Age of Colorblindness

MICHELLE ALEXANDER

—▫—

JARVIOUS COTTON CANNOT VOTE. Like his father, grand-father, great-grandfather, and great-great-grandfather, he has been denied the right to participate in our electoral democracy. Cotton's family tree tells the story of several generations of black men who were born in the United States but who were denied the most basic freedom that democracy promises—the freedom to vote for those who will make the rules and laws that govern one's life. Cotton's great-great-grandfather could not vote as a slave. His great-grandfather was beaten to death by the Ku Klux Klan for attempting to vote. His grandfather

———

MICHELLE ALEXANDER is a lawyer and scholar known for her work to protect civil rights. She has taught at Stanford Law School and Ohio State University's law school, and she currently teaches at Union Theological Seminary in New York City. She is a contributing opinion writer for the *New York Times* and has written opinion pieces for many other publications. She is the author of *The New Jim Crow: Mass Incarceration in the Age of Colorblindness* (2010); this selection is from the book's introduction, and it is documented in Chicago style.

was prevented from voting by Klan intimidation. His father was barred from voting by poll taxes and literacy tests. Today, Jarvious Cotton cannot vote because he, like many black men in the United States, has been labeled a felon and is currently on parole.[1]

Cotton's story illustrates, in many respects, the old adage "The more things change, the more they remain the same." In each generation, new tactics have been used for achieving the same goals—goals shared by the Founding Fathers. Denying African Americans citizenship was deemed essential to the formation of the original union. Hundreds of years later, America is still not an egalitarian democracy. The arguments and rationalizations that have been trotted out in support of racial exclusion and discrimination in its various forms have changed and evolved, but the outcome has remained largely the same. An extraordinary percentage of black men in the United States are legally barred from voting today, just as they have been throughout most of American history. They are also subject to legalized discrimination in employment, housing, education, public benefits, and jury service, just as their parents, grandparents, and great-grandparents once were.

What has changed since the collapse of Jim Crow has less to do with the basic structure of our society than with the language we use to justify it. In the era of colorblindness, it is no longer socially permissible to use race, explicitly, as a justification for discrimination, exclusion, and social contempt. So we don't. Rather than rely on race, we use our criminal justice system to label people of color "criminals" and then engage in all the practices we supposedly left behind. Today it is perfectly legal to discriminate against criminals in nearly all the ways that it was once legal to discriminate against African Americans. Once you're labeled a felon, the old forms of discrimination— employment discrimination, housing discrimination, denial of the right to vote, denial of educational opportunity, denial of food stamps and other public benefits, and exclusion from jury service—are suddenly legal. As a criminal, you have scarcely more rights, and arguably less respect, than a black man living in Alabama at the height of Jim Crow. We have not ended racial caste in America; we have merely redesigned it.

I reached [these conclusions] reluctantly. Ten years ago, I would have argued strenuously against the central claim made here—namely, that something akin to a racial caste system currently exists in the United States. Indeed, if Barack Obama had been elected president back then, I would have argued that his election marked the nation's triumph over racial caste—the final nail in the coffin of Jim Crow. My elation would have been tempered by the distance yet to be traveled to reach the promised land of racial justice in America, but my conviction that nothing remotely similar to Jim Crow exists in this country would have been steadfast.

See pp. 24–25 for tips on making what "they say" something you say.

Today my elation over Obama's election is tempered by a far more sobering awareness. As an African American woman, with three young children who will never know a world in which a black man could not be president of the United States, I was beyond thrilled on election night. Yet when I walked out of the election night party, full of hope and enthusiasm, I was immediately reminded of the harsh realities of the New Jim Crow. A black man was on his knees in the gutter, hands cuffed behind his back, as several police officers stood around him talking, joking, and ignoring his human existence. People poured out of the building; many stared for a moment at the black man cowering in the street, and then averted their gaze. What did the election of Barack Obama mean for him?

Like many civil rights lawyers, I was inspired to attend law school by the civil rights victories of the 1950s and 1960s. Even in the face of growing social and political opposition to remedial policies such as affirmative action, I clung to the notion that the evils of Jim Crow are behind us and that, while we have a long way to go to fulfill the dream of an egalitarian, multiracial democracy, we have made real progress and are now struggling to hold on to the gains of the past. I thought my job as a civil rights lawyer was to join with the allies of racial progress to resist attacks on affirmative action and to eliminate the vestiges of Jim Crow segregation, including our still separate and unequal system of education. I understood the problems plaguing poor communities of color, including problems associated with crime and rising incarceration rates, to be a function of poverty and lack of access to quality education—the continuing legacy of slavery and Jim Crow. Never did I seriously consider the possibility that a new racial caste system was operating in this country. The new system had been developed and implemented swiftly, and it was largely invisible, even to people, like me, who spent most of their waking hours fighting for justice.

I first encountered the idea of a new racial caste system more than a decade ago, when a bright orange poster caught my eye. I was rushing to catch the bus, and I noticed a sign stapled to a telephone pole that screamed in large bold print: THE DRUG WAR IS THE NEW JIM CROW. I paused for a moment and skimmed the text of the flyer. Some radical group was holding a community meeting about police brutality, the new three-strikes law in California, and the expansion of America's prison system. The meeting was being held at a small community church a few blocks away; it had seating capacity for no more than fifty people. I sighed, and muttered to myself something like, "Yeah, the criminal justice system is racist in many ways, but it really doesn't help to make such an absurd comparison. People will just think you're crazy." I then crossed the street and hopped on the bus. I was headed to my new job, director of the Racial Justice Project of the American Civil Liberties Union (ACLU) in Northern California.

When I began my work at the ACLU, I assumed that the criminal justice system had problems of racial bias, much in the same way that all major institutions in our society are plagued with problems associated with conscious and unconscious bias. As a lawyer who had litigated numerous class-action employment-discrimination cases, I understood well the many ways in which racial stereotyping can permeate subjective decision-making processes at all levels of an organization, with devastating consequences. I was familiar with the challenges associated with reforming institutions in which racial stratification is thought to be normal—the natural consequence of differences in education, culture, motivation, and, some still believe, innate ability. While at the ACLU, I shifted my focus from employment discrimination to criminal justice reform and dedicated myself to the task of working with others to identify and eliminate racial bias whenever and wherever it reared its ugly head.

By the time I left the ACLU, I had come to suspect that I was wrong about the criminal justice system. It was not just another institution infected with racial bias but rather a different beast entirely. The activists who posted the sign on the telephone pole were not crazy; nor were the smattering of lawyers and advocates around the country who were beginning to connect the dots between our current system of mass incarceration and earlier forms of social control. Quite belatedly, I came to see that mass incarceration in the United States had, in fact, emerged as a stunningly comprehensive and well-disguised system of racialized social control that functions in a manner strikingly similar to Jim Crow.

In my experience, people who have been incarcerated 10
rarely have difficulty identifying the parallels between these
systems of social control. Once they are released, they are often
denied the right to vote, excluded from juries, and relegated
to a racially segregated and subordinated existence. Through
a web of laws, regulations, and informal rules, all of which are
powerfully reinforced by social stigma, they are confined to the
margins of mainstream society and denied access to the mainstream economy. They are legally denied the ability to obtain
employment, housing, and public benefits—much as African
Americans were once forced into a segregated, second-class
citizenship in the Jim Crow era.

Those of us who have viewed that world from a comfortable distance—yet sympathize with the plight of the so-called
underclass—tend to interpret the experience of those caught
up in the criminal justice system primarily through the lens of
popularized social science, attributing the staggering increase in
incarceration rates in communities of color to the predictable,
though unfortunate, consequences of poverty, racial segregation, unequal educational opportunities, and the presumed realities of the drug market, including the mistaken belief that most
drug dealers are black or brown. Occasionally, in the course of
my work, someone would make a remark suggesting that perhaps the War on Drugs is a racist conspiracy to put blacks back
in their place. This type of remark was invariably accompanied
by nervous laughter, intended to convey the impression that
although the idea had crossed their minds, it was not an idea
a reasonable person would take seriously.

Most people assume the War on Drugs was launched in
response to the crisis caused by crack cocaine in inner-city
neighborhoods. This view holds that the racial disparities in
drug convictions and sentences, as well as the rapid explosion

of the prison population, reflect nothing more than the government's zealous—but benign—efforts to address rampant drug crime in poor, minority neighborhoods. This view, while understandable, given the sensational media coverage of crack in the 1980s and 1990s, is simply wrong.

While it is true that the publicity surrounding crack cocaine led to a dramatic increase in funding for the drug war (as well as to sentencing policies that greatly exacerbated racial disparities in incarceration rates), there is no truth to the notion that the War on Drugs was launched in response to crack cocaine. President Ronald Reagan officially announced the current drug war in 1982, before crack became an issue in the media or a crisis in poor black neighborhoods. A few years after the drug war was declared, crack began to spread rapidly in the poor black neighborhoods of Los Angeles and later emerged in cities across the country.[2] The Reagan administration hired staff to publicize the emergence of crack cocaine in 1985 as part of a strategic effort to build public and legislative support for the war. The media campaign was an extraordinary success. Almost overnight, the media was saturated with images of black "crack whores," "crack dealers," and "crack babies"—images that seemed to confirm the worst negative racial stereotypes about impoverished inner-city residents. The media bonanza surrounding the "new demon drug" helped to catapult the War on Drugs from an ambitious federal policy to an actual war.

See p. 93 for tips on making concessions while still standing your ground.

The timing of the crack crisis helped to fuel conspiracy theories and general speculation in poor black communities that the War on Drugs was part of a genocidal plan by the government to destroy black people in the United States. From the outset, stories circulated on the street that crack and other drugs were being brought into black neighborhoods by the CIA. Eventually, even the Urban League came to take the claims of genocide seriously. In its 1990 report "The State of Black America," it stated: "There is at least one concept that must be recognized if one is to see the pervasive and insidious nature of the drug problem for the African American community. Though difficult to accept, that is the concept of genocide."[3] While the conspiracy theories were initially dismissed as far-fetched, if not downright loony, the word on the street turned out to be right, at least to a point. The CIA admitted in 1998 that guerrilla armies it actively supported in Nicaragua were smuggling illegal drugs into the United States—drugs that were making their way onto the streets of inner-city black neighborhoods in the form of crack cocaine. The CIA also admitted that, in the midst of the War on Drugs, it blocked law enforcement efforts to investigate illegal drug networks that were helping to fund its covert war in Nicaragua.[4]

It bears emphasis that the CIA never admitted (nor has any evidence been revealed to support the claim) that it intentionally sought the destruction of the black community by allowing illegal drugs to be smuggled into the United States. Nonetheless, conspiracy theorists surely must be forgiven for their bold accusation of genocide, in light of the devastation wrought by crack cocaine and the drug war, and the odd coincidence that an illegal drug crisis suddenly appeared in the black community after—not before—a drug war had been declared. In fact, the War on Drugs began at a time when illegal drug use was on the decline.[5] During this same time period, however, a war was declared, causing arrests and convictions for drug offenses to skyrocket, especially among people of color.

The impact of the drug war has been astounding. In less than thirty years, the US penal population exploded from around 300,000 to more than 2 million, with drug convictions accounting for the majority of the increase.[6] The United States now has the highest rate of incarceration in the world, dwarfing the rates of nearly every developed country, even surpassing those in highly repressive regimes like Russia, China, and Iran. In Germany, 93 people are in prison for every 100,000 adults and children. In the United States, the rate is roughly eight times that, or 750 per 100,000.[7]

The racial dimension of mass incarceration is its most striking feature. No other country in the world imprisons so many of its racial or ethnic minorities. The United States imprisons a larger percentage of its black population than South Africa did at the height of apartheid. In Washington, DC, our nation's capital, it is estimated that three out of four young black men (and nearly all those in the poorest neighborhoods) can expect to serve time in prison.[8] Similar rates of incarceration can be found in black communities across America.

These stark racial disparities cannot be explained by rates of drug crime. Studies show that people of all colors *use and sell* illegal drugs at remarkably similar rates.[9] If there are significant differences in the surveys to be found, they frequently suggest that whites, particularly white youth, are more likely to engage in drug crime than people of color.[10] That is not what one would guess, however, when entering our nation's prisons and jails, which are overflowing with black and brown drug offenders. In some states, black men have been admitted to prison on drug charges at rates twenty to fifty times greater than those of white men.[11] And in major cities wracked by the drug war, as many as 80 percent of young African American men now have criminal records and are thus subject to legalized discrimination for the rest of their lives.[12] These young men are part of a growing undercaste, permanently locked up and locked out of mainstream society.

• • •

The language of caste may well seem foreign or unfamiliar to some. Public discussions about racial caste in America are relatively rare. We avoid talking about caste in our society because we are ashamed of our racial history. We also avoid talking about race. We even avoid talking about class. Conversations about class are resisted in part because there is a tendency to imagine that one's class reflects upon one's character. What is key to America's understanding of class is the persistent belief—despite all evidence to the contrary—that anyone, with the proper discipline and drive, can move from a lower class to a higher class. We recognize that mobility may be difficult, but the key to our collective self-image is the assumption that mobility is always possible, so failure to move up reflects on one's character. By extension, the failure of a race or ethnic group to move up reflects very poorly on the group as a whole.

What is completely missed in the rare public debates today 20 about the plight of African Americans is that a huge percentage of them are not free to move up at all. It is not just that they lack opportunity, attend poor schools, or are plagued by poverty. They are barred by law from doing so. And the major institutions with which they come into contact are designed to prevent their mobility. To put the matter starkly: the current system of control permanently locks a huge percentage of the African American community out of the mainstream society and economy. The system operates through our criminal justice institutions, but it functions more like a caste system than a system of crime control. Viewed from this perspective, the so-called underclass is better understood as an *undercaste*—a lower caste of individuals who are permanently barred by law and custom from mainstream society. Although this new system of racialized social control purports to be colorblind, it creates and maintains racial hierarchy much as earlier systems of control did. Like Jim Crow (and slavery), mass incarceration operates as a tightly networked system of laws, policies, customs, and institutions that operate collectively to ensure the subordinate status of a group defined largely by race.

. . .

Skepticism about the claims made here is warranted. There are important differences, to be sure, among mass incarceration, Jim Crow, and slavery—the three major racialized systems of control adopted in the United States to date. Failure to acknowledge the relevant differences, as well as their implications, would be a disservice to racial justice discourse. Many of the differences are not as dramatic as they initially appear, however; others serve to illustrate the ways in which systems of racialized social control have managed to morph, evolve, and adapt to changes in the political, social, and legal context

See Chapter 7 for tips on establishing why your claim matters.

over time. Ultimately, I believe that the similarities between these systems of control overwhelm the differences and that mass incarceration, like its predecessors, has been largely immunized from legal challenge. If this claim is substantially correct, the implications for racial justice advocacy are profound.

With the benefit of hindsight, surely we can see that piecemeal policy reform or litigation alone would have been a futile approach to dismantling Jim Crow segregation. While those strategies certainly had their place, the Civil Rights Act of 1964 and the concomitant cultural shift would never have occurred without the cultivation of a critical political consciousness in the African American community and the widespread, strategic activism that flowed from it. Likewise, the notion that the *New* Jim Crow can ever be dismantled through traditional litigation and policy-reform strategies that are wholly disconnected from a major social movement seems fundamentally misguided.

Such a movement is impossible, though, if those most committed to abolishing racial hierarchy continue to talk and behave as if a state-sponsored racial caste system no longer exists. If we continue to tell ourselves the popular myths about racial progress or, worse yet, if we say to ourselves that the problem of mass incarceration is just too big, too daunting for us to do anything about and that we should instead direct our energies to battles that might be more easily won, history will judge us harshly. A human rights nightmare is occurring on our watch.

A new social consensus must be forged about race and the role of race in defining the basic structure of our society, if we hope ever to abolish the New Jim Crow. This new consensus must begin with dialogue, a conversation that fosters a critical consciousness, a key prerequisite to effective social action. My writing is an attempt to ensure that the conversation does not end with nervous laughter.

NOTES

1. Jarvious Cotton was a plaintiff in *Cotton v. Fordice*, 157 F.3d 388 (5th Cir. 1998), which held that Mississippi's felon disenfranchisement provision had lost its racially discriminatory taint. The information regarding Cotton's family tree was obtained by Emily Bolton on March 29, 1999, when she interviewed Cotton at Mississippi State Prison. Jarvious Cotton was released on parole in Mississippi, a state that denies voting rights to parolees.

2. The *New York Times* made the national media's first specific reference to crack in a story published in late 1985. Crack became known in a few impoverished neighborhoods in Los Angeles, New York, and Miami in early 1986. See Craig Reinarman and Harry Levine, "The Crack Attack: America's Latest Drug Scare, 1986–1992," in *Images of Issues: Typifying Contemporary Social Problems* (New York: Aldine De Gruyter, 1995), 152.

3. Clarence Page, "'The Plan': A Paranoid View of Black Problems," *Dover Herald* (Delaware), Feb. 23, 1990. See also Manning Marable, *Race, Reform, and Rebellions: The Second Reconstruction in Black America, 1945–1990* (Jackson: University Press of Mississippi, 1991), 212–13.

4. See Alexander Cockburn and Jeffrey St. Clair, *Whiteout: The CIA, Drugs, and the Press* (New York: Verso, 1999). See also Nick Shou, "The Truth in 'Dark Alliance,'" *Los Angeles Times*, Aug. 18, 2006; Peter Kornbluh, "CIA's Challenge in South Central," *Los Angeles Times* (Washington edition), Nov. 15, 1996; and Alexander Cockburn, "Why They Hated Gary Webb," *The Nation*, Dec. 16, 2004.

5. Katherine Beckett and Theodore Sasson, *The Politics of Injustice: Crime and Punishment in America* (Thousand Oaks, CA: Sage Publications, 2004), 163.

6. Marc Mauer, *Race to Incarcerate*, rev. ed. (New York: The New Press, 2006), 33.

7. PEW Center on the States, *One in 100: Behind Bars in America 2008* (Washington, DC: PEW Charitable Trusts, 2008), 5.

8. Donald Braman, *Doing Time on the Outside: Incarceration and Family Life in Urban America* (Ann Arbor: University of Michigan Press, 2004), 3, citing D.C. Department of Corrections data for 2000.

9. See, e.g., U.S. Department of Health and Human Services, Substance Abuse and Mental Health Services Administration, *Summary of Findings from the 2000 National Household Survey on Drug Abuse*, NHSDA series H-13, DHHS pub. no. SMA 01-3549 (Rockville, MD: 2001), reporting that 6.4 percent of whites, 6.4 percent of blacks, and 5.3 percent of Hispanics were current users of illegal drugs in 2000; *Results from the 2002 National Survey on Drug Use and Health: National Findings*, NHSDA series H-22, DHHS pub. no. SMA 03-3836 (2003), revealing nearly identical rates of illegal drug use among whites and blacks, only a single percentage point between them; and *Results from the 2007 National Survey on Drug Use and Health: National Findings*, NSDUH series H-34, DHHS pub. no. SMA 08-4343 (2007), showing essentially the same finding. See also Marc Mauer and Ryan S. King, *A 25-Year Quagmire: The "War on Drugs" and Its Impact on American Society* (Washington, DC: Sentencing Project, 2007), 19, citing a study suggesting that African Americans have slightly higher rates of illegal drug use than whites.

10. See, e.g., Howard N. Snyder and Melissa Sickmund, *Juvenile Offenders and Victims: 2006 National Report*, U.S. Department of Justice, Office of Justice Programs, Office of Juvenile Justice and Delinquency Prevention (Washington, DC: U.S. Department of Justice, 2006), reporting that white youth are more likely than black youth to engage in illegal drug sales. See also Lloyd D. Johnson, Patrick M. O'Malley, Jerald G. Bachman, and John E. Schulenberg, *Monitoring the Future, National Survey Results on Drug Use, 1975–2006*, vol. 1, *Secondary School Students*, U.S. Department of Health and Human Services, National Institute on Drug Abuse, NIH pub. no. 07-6205 (Bethesda, MD: 2007), 32, "African American 12th graders have consistently shown lower usage rates than White 12th graders for most drugs, both licit and illicit"; and Lloyd D. Johnston, Patrick M. O'Malley, and Jerald G. Bachman, *Monitoring the Future: National Results on Adolescent Drug Use: Overview of*

Key Findings 2002, U.S. Department of Health and Human Services, National Institute on Drug Abuse, NIH pub. no. 03-5374 (Bethesda, MD: 2003), presenting data showing that African American adolescents have slightly lower rates of illicit drug use than their white counterparts.

11. Human Rights Watch, *Punishment and Prejudice: Racial Disparities in the War on Drugs*, HRW Reports, vol. 12, no. 2 (New York, 2000).

12. See, e.g., Paul Street, *The Vicious Circle: Race, Prison, Jobs, and Community in Chicago, Illinois, and the Nation* (Chicago: Chicago Urban League, Department of Research and Planning, 2002).

All Words Matter: The Manipulation behind "All Lives Matter"

KELLY CORYELL

—⊡—

I'VE NEVER UNDERSTOOD THE POPULAR SAYING "Sticks
and stones may break my bones, but words will never hurt
me." I grew up as a tomboy; I've had more than my fair share
of scrapes, bruises, and stitches. But I've found that words
inflict the most painful injuries. On sleepless nights when
I toss and turn, I'm not replaying the time I broke my foot
over and over in my head—I'm thinking about some embarrassing thing I said that still makes me physically cringe or

---

KELLY CORYELL wrote this essay in her first-year writing course
at Diablo Valley College in Pleasant Hill, CA. Coryell, an English
major, works as a tutor in the college's learning center and serves as
a supplemental instruction leader for multilingual students. She plans
to become an English professor. This essay, which is documented in
MLA Style, was nominated for the Norton Writer's Prize.

a time someone said something hurtful to me. Broken bones heal—words stay with us.

This is because words have power. A skilled wordsmith can influence us by using evocative words that elicit an emotional response. The meanings of these "loaded" words aren't located in a dictionary. There is a context surrounding them that implies a meaning beyond the basic information they convey. Loaded words and phrases appeal to our emotions, not our logic—they enter our hearts, not our minds. They can manipulate, so sometimes people use loaded language to distract us from a flawed argument.

Such is the case when people use the phrase "all lives matter" to oppose the phrase "Black lives matter." In 2012, neighborhood watch coordinator George Zimmerman shot and killed Trayvon Martin, an unarmed African American teenager returning home from a late-night snack run. In 2013, Zimmerman was acquitted of all charges. This sparked the birth of the Black Lives Matter (BLM) movement, when activists Alicia Garza, Opal Tometi, and Patrisse Cullors, frustrated with the systemic inequality and oppression exemplified by Zimmerman's trial, started using the hashtag #BlackLivesMatter on *Twitter*. As more and more Black people died during police confrontations or in police custody—Eric Garner, Michael Brown, Tamir Rice, Walter Scott, Freddie Gray—the movement, chanting the phrase

Summarizes effectively (Chapter 2).

"Black lives matter," gained momentum and media coverage, eventually becoming a major talking point in the 2016 presidential election. And in the spring of 2020, the deaths of Ahmaud Arbery, Breonna Taylor, George Floyd, Rayshard Brooks, Dominique "Rem'mie" Fells, and Riah Milton re-ignited the BLM movement, leading to an overdue reckoning with racism in this country.

As a direct response, Americans who either disagreed with the BLM movement as a whole or who supported the movement but were uncomfortable with its slogan, began to chant their own phrase: "all lives matter." It should be acknowledged that some of those who have used the phrase "all lives matter" did so naïvely aiming to unify people in a time of division, thinking of the words as a positive affirmation to which no one could object. However, saying "all lives matter" as a response to "Black lives matter" is, in reality, sending a dangerous message: it steals attention from the systematic oppression of Black Americans and actively distorts the message behind the BLM movement, manipulating the American people into maintaining the oppressive status quo.

The phrase "all lives matter" belies the current racial 5 inequality in America by implying that all lives are at equal risk. The racism and prejudice endured by African Americans didn't end when slavery was abolished in 1865, it didn't

Entertains counterargument (Chapter 6).

end when Congress passed the Civil Rights Act of 1964, and it didn't end when a Black man was elected president of the United States in 2008. Racial inequality in America persists to this day, ingrained and interwoven so deeply in American society that our prison systems and manufacturing industries depend on it. It's so expertly hidden under layers of celebrity gossip in our media and blatant and bold lies from our politicians, and so "normalized" in our culture, that many people may not even be aware of the plight of Black Americans.

But the statistics speak for themselves. According to the NAACP, African Americans are incarcerated at six times the rate of white Americans for drug crimes ("Criminal Justice"). The Center for American Progress reported that in 2016, the median wealth of Black families was *only 10 percent* of the median wealth of white families (Hanks et al.). Police shoot and kill Black Americans at *two and a half times* the rate of white Americans, according to a 2016 report (Lowery). All these statistics point to the fact that Black lives are valued less than white lives in America. The BLM movement aims to change this depressing reality by insisting that "Black lives matter."

Responding to "Black lives matter" with "all lives matter" ignores the unique prejudices and discrimination Black

> Uses data (Chapter 18) and explains why we should care (Chapter 7).

Introduces quotation (Chapter 3).

people experience in America. Chimamanda Ngozi Adichie makes a parallel argument in her essay "I Decided to Call Myself a Happy Feminist." Adichie explains why she calls herself a feminist instead of a human-rights activist. She writes:

> Feminism is, of course, part of human rights in general—but to choose to use the vague expression *human rights* is to deny the specific and particular problem of gender. . . . For centuries, the world divided human beings into two groups and then proceeded to exclude and oppress one group. It is only fair that the solution to the problem should acknowledge that.

Explains quotation (Chapter 3).

Adichie's point is that not every human being suffers the oppression that women suffer. Therefore, campaigning for all humans, while noble, is irrelevant. It would ignore the specific plights of women, as well as the historical fact that those behind the oppression of women were other human beings—men. In the same way, emphasizing *all* lives takes much-needed focus away from the oppression specifically felt only by Black Americans—which is a direct result of the centuries of oppression at the hands of white Americans.

Later in her essay, Adichie recalls a conversation she once had about gender:

> A man said to me, "Why does it have to be you as a woman? Why not you as a human being?" This type of question is

a way of silencing a person's specific experiences. Of course I am a human being, but there are particular things that happen to me in the world because I am a woman.

Shifting attention away from the female gender to the entirety of humankind silences the hardships women face *simply because they are women.* Talking over them by questioning their commitment to the whole, and not allowing them to share their experiences, smothers their voices. The same is true when shifting focus from "Black lives" to "all lives." Saying "all lives matter" ignores the unique discrimination only Black Americans face, *simply because they are Black.* Dismissing the importance and relevance of their struggles because everyone has struggles misses the point entirely.

"All lives matter" implies that all lives endure an equal amount of hardship; therefore, the struggles of Black Americans deserve no more attention than the struggles of white Americans—which is demonstrably false statistically. Daniel Victor illustrates the harmful way the phrase "all lives matter" removes focus from the hardships of Black Americans in his article "Why 'All Lives Matter' Is Such a Perilous Phrase" for *The New York Times.* He writes:

> Those in the Black Lives Matter movement say black people are in immediate danger and need immediate attention. . . .

Saying "All Lives Matter" in response would suggest to them that all people are in equal danger, invalidating the specific concerns of black people.

"You're watering the house that's not burning, but you're choosing to leave the house that's burning unattended," said Allen Kwabena Frimpong, an organizer for the New York chapter of Black Lives Matter. "It's irresponsible."

To put it simply, focusing too much on the whole can divert much needed attention from crises affecting a specific group. As one *Twitter* user notes, "#AllLivesMatter is like I go to the Dr for a broken arm and he says 'All Bones Matter' ok but right now let's take care of this broken one" (SOAPbox). In this analogy, only one bone needs immediate attention—ignoring it because all bones are important to a person's health isn't an appropriate response to the situation. Nor would be putting the injured person in a full-body cast—though that would be treating every bone equally. "All lives matter" doesn't acknowledge that the lives of Black Americans are in greater danger due to the hundreds of years of systematic racism designed to devalue them. The point of saying "Black lives matter" is to bring attention to the fact that Black lives do not matter in our society. The BLM movement is not simply saying "Black people are shot and killed by the police," it's saying "Black people are shot and killed by the police *at two and a half times the rate of white people.*" Replying with "all races are shot and killed by the police" can be an acceptable response to the first statement, *but not the second.* Yet that is exactly what saying "all lives matter" does—it ignores the second statement, ignores the voices of BLM activists.

> Uses metacommentary to differentiate views (Chapter 10).

Using "all lives matter" as a response to "Black lives matter" perpetuates the misconception that BLM activists do not believe both sentiments. The core of the BLM movement is the belief that *all* lives matter—*including* Black lives, which are treated differently than white lives, not just by law enforcement but America as a whole. As J. Clara Chan explains in her article "What Is 'All Lives Matter'? A Short Explainer":

> BLM supporters stress that the movement isn't about believing no other races matter. Instead, the movement seeks to highlight and change how racism disproportionately affects the black community, in terms of police brutality, job security, socioeconomic status, educational opportunities, and more.

The BLM movement's focus on particular inequities doesn't mean other races don't matter, but the phrase "all lives matter" is loaded language that implies they don't. Dave Bry explains this manipulation in his article titled "'All Lives Matter' Is and Always Was Racist—and This Weekend's Trump Rally Proved It" for the UK paper *The Guardian*. He writes:

> Often people who say "all lives matter" say it pointedly, correctively under the veneer of the idea that "all men are created equal." It is meant to refute the idea that "only" black lives matter.
>
> But understanding "black lives matter" to mean "only" black lives matter has been a misinterpretation from the beginning, one made in ignorance of the intent of the statement and the statistical facts that led to it.

That is to say, "all lives matter" misinterprets the point the BLM movement is making—that all lives do matter; therefore, Black lives need to matter as much as white lives in American society. It isn't *only* Black lives matter"; it's "Black lives matter, *too*."

"All lives matter" manipulates people into believing those who say "Black lives matter" are against other lives. Jason Stanley explains the many ways language can be used as a tool for suppression in his *New York Times* opinion piece "The Ways of Silencing." Stanley writes, "Words

Connects
the parts
(Chapter 8).

are misappropriated and meanings twisted. I believe that these tactics are . . . if you will, linguistic strategies for stealing the voices of others." In other words, a group can be silenced if the language vital to their ability to express themselves and their beliefs is co-opted by another group. Supporters of "all lives matter" co-opted the language of the BLM movement, forcing a separation between the two phrases. As a result, BLM activists cannot say "all lives matter" without sounding like they oppose the views of the BLM movement, since "all lives matter" is no longer just a phrase but a rebuttal—a counterargument.

Saying "all lives matter" is premature, since it presupposes that equality has already been achieved. If Black lives really did matter as much as white lives in American society, then saying so would be as uncontroversial as stating any other fact. In fact, America is not a postracial society: poverty, education, health, incarceration rates—all are unequal between different races in America. We must acknowledge this ugly truth if we are ever going to change it. "All lives matter" invokes a naïve reality in which all races are holding hands in a great big circle, singing "This Land Is Your Land" as the sun smiles down on the world. "All lives matter," like the statement "I don't see race, I just see people," may, at first, seem like a beautiful sentiment. Those who say such things may truly do

Represents objections fairly (Chapter 6).

so with the intent of creating a world where everyone is treated equally—regardless of race, gender, creed, orientation, and so on.

But upon close examination, these phrases—however well-meaning—are harmful because, aside from robbing people of their racial identities, they ignore race-based discrimination. How can one notice racism when one does not "see race"? How can one point out discrimination against African Americans if the only response one gets is "everyone matters"? If one insists that a goal has already been met when it hasn't, why would anyone put in more effort toward reaching that goal? This is why "all lives matter" is so manipulative and damaging. It's an attempt to convince us we don't have to keep reaching for equality and justice, even though every fact around us tells us this is far from the case. Only by consciously acknowledging racial inequality will we ever be able to put an end to it.

The root of "all lives matter" boils down to one thing: 15 privilege, and the reluctance to give it up in the name of equality. As Chris Boeskool puts it: "Equality can *feel* like oppression. But it's not. What you're feeling is just the discomfort of losing a little bit of your privilege." Evening the playing field can feel like a bad thing to the person benefiting from the imbalance. In the 1960s, a white bus rider may have felt oppressed when she started having to compete with Black bus riders for the front seat—she lost the privilege of getting a guaranteed front seat because of her race. In the 1970s, a man might have complained that he could no longer "compliment" his female coworkers without them accusing him of sexual harassment—he lost the privilege of being able to say offensive things because of his gender. If American society starts to accept that Black lives matter as much as white lives, white Americans will lose some of the privileges afforded to them as a result of the oppression of Black Americans. Therefore, people who either do not realize they have this privilege, or people who simply don't want to give it up, chant "all lives matter" in an effort to hold on to that privilege. If the BLM movement is silenced, the status quo of racial inequality will be maintained. The privileged must resist this unethical temptation and not mistake oppression as equality.

Works Cited

Adichie, Chimamanda Ngozi. "I Decided to Call Myself a Happy Feminist." *The Guardian*, 17 Oct. 2014, www.theguardian .com/books/2014/oct/17/chimamanda-ngozi-adichie-extract -we-should-all-be-feminists.

Boeskool, Chris. "When You're Accustomed to Privilege, Equality Feels Like Oppression." *HuffPost*, 14 Mar. 2016, www.huffpost.com/entry/when-youre-accustomed-to -privilege_b_9460662.

Bry, Dave. "'All Lives Matter' Is and Always Was Racist—and This Weekend's Trump Rally Proved It." *The Guardian*, 23 Nov. 2015, www.theguardian.com/commentisfree/2015 /nov/23/all-lives-matter-racist-trump-weekend-campaign -rally-proved-it.

Chan, J. Clara. "What Is 'All Lives Matter'? A Short Explainer." *The Wrap*, 13 July 2016, www.thewrap.com/what-is-all-lives -matter-a-short-explainer.

"Criminal Justice Fact Sheet." NAACP, www.naacp.org /criminal-justice-fact-sheet. Accessed 12 Mar. 2019.

Hanks, Angela, et al. "Systematic Inequality: How America's Structural Racism Helped Create the Black–White Wealth Gap." *Center for American Progress*, 21 Feb. 2018, www .americanprogress.org/issues/race/reports/2018/02/21/447051 /systematic-inequality.

Lowery, Wesley. "Aren't More White People Than Black People Killed by Police? Yes, but No." *The Washington Post*, 11 July 2016, www.washingtonpost.com/news/post-nation /wp/2016/07/11/arent-more-white-people-than-black-people -killed-by-police-yes-but-no.

SOAPbox [@djsoap92]. "#AllLivesMatter is like I go to the Dr for a broken arm and he says 'All Bones Matter' ok but right now let's take care of this broken one." *Twitter*, 5 July 2016, twitter.com/djsoap92/status/750563460921057280.

Stanley, Jason. "The Ways of Silencing." *The New York Times*, 25 June 2011, opinionater.blogsnytimes.com/2011/06/25 /the-ways-of-silencing. Opinionator.

Victor, Daniel. "Why 'All Lives Matter' Is Such a Perilous Phrase." *The New York Times*, 15 July 2016, www.nytimes .com/2016/07/16/us/all-lives-matter-black-lives-matter.html.

"Rise of the Machines"
Is Not a Likely Future

MICHAEL LITTMAN

EVERY NEW TECHNOLOGY BRINGS its own nightmare scenarios. Artificial intelligence (AI) and robotics are no exceptions. Indeed, the word "robot" was coined for a 1920 play that dramatized just such a doomsday for humanity (Čapek).

Recently, an open letter about the future of AI, signed by a number of high-profile scientists and entrepreneurs, spurred a new round of harrowing headlines like "Top Scientists Have an Ominous Warning about Artificial Intelligence" (Sparkes), and "Artificial Intelligence Experts Sign Open Letter to Protect Mankind from Machines" (Statt). The implication is that the machines will one day displace humanity.

Let's get one thing straight: a world in which humans are enslaved or destroyed by superintelligent machines of our

MICHAEL LITTMAN is Royce Family Professor of Teaching Excellence in Computer Science at Brown University. With Dave Ackley, he is the host of the podcast *Computing Up*. This piece was originally published in *Live Science* on January 28, 2015, and it is documented in MLA style.

own creation is purely science fiction. Like every other technology, AI has risks and benefits, but we cannot let fear dominate the conversation or guide AI research. Nevertheless, the idea of dramatically changing the AI research agenda to focus on AI "safety" is the primary message of a group calling itself the Future of Life Institute (FLI). FLI includes a handful of deep thinkers and public figures such as Elon Musk and Stephen Hawking and worries about the day in which humanity is steamrolled by powerful programs run amuck.

As eloquently described in the book *Superintelligence: Paths, Dangers, Strategies* by FLI advisory board member and Oxford-based philosopher Nick Bostrom, the plot unfolds in three parts. In the first part—roughly where we are now—computational power and intelligent software develops at an increasing pace through the toil of scientists and engineers. Next, a breakthrough is made: programs are created that possess intelligence on par with humans. These programs, running on increasingly fast computers, improve themselves extremely rapidly, resulting in a runaway "intelligence explosion." In the third and final act, a singular super-intelligence takes hold—outsmarting, outmaneuvering, and ultimately outcompeting the entirety of humanity and perhaps life itself. End scene.

Let's take a closer look at this apocalyptic storyline. Of the three parts, the first is indeed happening now and Bostrom provides cogent and illuminating glimpses into current and near-future technology. The third part is a philosophical romp exploring the consequences of supersmart machines. It's that second part—the intelligence explosion—that demonstrably violates what we know of computer science and natural intelligence.

Runaway Intelligence?

The notion of the intelligence explosion arises from Moore's law, the observation that the speed of computers has been increasing exponentially since the 1950s. Project this trend forward and we'll see computers with the computational power of the entire human race within the next few decades. It's a leap to go from this idea to unchecked growth of machine intelligence, however.

See Chapter 18 for tips on presenting the prevailing theories.

First, ingenuity is not the sole bottleneck to developing faster computers. The machines need to actually be built, which requires real-world resources. Indeed, Moore's law comes with exponentially increasing production costs as well—mass production of precision electronics does not come cheap. Further, there are fundamental physical laws—quantum limits—that bound how quickly a transistor can do its work. Non-silicon technologies may overcome those limits, but such devices remain highly speculative.

In addition to physical laws, we know a lot about the fundamental nature of computation and its limits. For example, some computational puzzles, like figuring out how to factor a number and thereby crack online cryptography schemes, are generally believed to be unsolvable by any fast program. They are part of a class of mathematically defined problems that are "NP-complete," meaning that they are exactly as hard as any problem that can be solved non-deterministically (N) in polynomial time (P), and they have resisted any attempt at scalable solution. As it turns out, most computational problems that we associate with human intelligence are known to be in this class.

See Chapter 6 for tips on anticipating objections.

Wait a second, you might say. How does the human mind manage to solve mathematical problems that computer scientists believe can't be solved? We don't.

By and large, we cheat. We build a cartoonish mental model of the elements of the world that we're interested in and then probe the behavior of this invented miniworld. There's a trade-off between completeness and tractability in these imagined microcosms. Our ability to propose and ponder and project credible futures comes at the cost of accuracy. Even allowing for the possibility of the existence of considerably faster computers than we have today, it is a logical impossibility that these computers would be able to accurately simulate reality faster than reality itself.

Countering the Anti-AI Cause

In the face of general skepticism in the AI and computer science 10 communities about the possibility of an intelligence explosion, FLI still wants to win support for its cause. The group's letter calls for increased attention to maximizing the societal benefits of developing AI. Many of my esteemed colleagues signed the letter to show their support for the importance of avoiding potential pitfalls of the technology. But a few key phrases in the letter such as "our AI systems must do what we want them to do" (Tegmark et al.) are taken by the press as an admission that AI researchers believe they might be creating something that cannot be controlled. It also implies that AI researchers are asleep at the wheel, oblivious to the ominous possibilities, which is simply untrue.

To be clear, there are indeed concerns about the near-term future of AI—algorithmic traders crashing the economy, or sensitive power grids overreacting to fluctuations and shutting down electricity for large swaths of the population. There's also a concern that systemic biases within academia and industry prevent underrepresented minorities from participating and helping to steer the growth of information technology. These worries should play a central role in the development and deployment of new ideas. But dread predictions of computers suddenly waking up and turning on us are simply not realistic.

I welcome an open discussion about how AI can be made robust and beneficial, and how we can engineer intelligent machines and systems that make society better. But, let's please keep the discussion firmly within the realm of reason and leave the robot uprisings to Hollywood screenwriters.

Works Cited

Bostrom, Nick. *Superintelligence: Paths, Dangers, Strategies*. Oxford UP, 2014.

Čapek, Karel. *R. U. R.* Translated by David Wyllie, ebook ed., ebooks@Adelaide, 2010.

Sparkes, Matthew. "Top Scientists Have an Ominous Warning about Artificial Intelligence." *Business Insider*, 13 Jan. 2015, www.businessinsider.com /top-scientists-have-an-ominous-warning-about-artificial -intelligence-2015-1.

Statt, Nick. "Artificial Intelligence Experts Sign Open Letter to Protect Mankind from Machines." *CNET*, 11 Jan. 2015, www.cnet.com/news /artificial-intelligence-experts-sign-open-letter-to-protect-mankind -from-machines/.

Tegmark, Max, et al. "An Open Letter: Research Priorities for Robust and Beneficial Artificial Intelligence." *Future of Life Institute*, 2015, futureoflife.org/ai-open-letter.

The Electoral College Embodies American Ideals

GAVIN REID

IMAGINE THAT YOU'VE JUST CAST your vote for president, and you are now impatiently waiting for the election results to see who will be the next president of the United States of America. When the votes are counted, you are excited to see that the candidate you voted for won the majority of votes across the country . . . but then you realize that your candidate somehow lost in the Electoral College so will not become president. This was reality for many

GAVIN REID, a chemical engineering major, wrote this essay as a freshman at the University of Alabama. It was published in *Analog*, a collection of essays by the university's first-year students, and is written in APA style.

who voted in the US presidential elections of 1824, 1876, 1888, 2000, and 2016. It's strange that a candidate can win a majority of votes and yet still lose the presidential election. As a result, many people have argued that the Electoral College should be eliminated. However, the Electoral College should remain, because it was instated by the nation's founders for good reasons, it solidly embodies the ideals of the United States, and its benefits strongly outweigh possible shortcomings.

The Electoral College was created by our nation's founders to prevent one region from controlling the country. When the United States was founded, most of the population was concentrated within a few states, and those states would be able to dominate the country if the government were a pure democracy. Because of this population disparity, many small-population states feared that the larger ones would force them to conform to any laws and legislation that the larger states desired, creating a tyranny of the majority. So the founders put multiple measures in place to avoid this imbalance. One of those measures is the Electoral College, which gives each state a voice while also reflecting the opinion of the general population.

The Electoral College consists of groups of electors from each state. The number of electors for each state is equal to the sum of the number of the state's representatives in the House of Representatives and its two senators, so there is a total of 538 electors (and a candidate must earn 270 electoral votes to win the election). Each state legislature nominates the electors for the state, and all the electors in a state support a candidate based on how the general public in that state votes (National Archives, 2019). This strategy grants each state two electors regardless of population and grants additional electors based on each state's population. Without the Electoral College, urban areas could potentially dominate politics. If the president were simply decided by the popular vote, then vast regions of America wouldn't be properly represented.

> Says why it matters (Chapter 7).

The founders also appreciated the quality of votes as opposed to the quantity, an idea explored by Michael Uhlmann, a political science professor at Claremont Graduate University, and Richard Posner, a past judge on the United States Seventh Court of Appeals, a professor at the University of Chicago, and a Harvard Law School graduate. Uhlmann (2004) wrote that the Electoral College "teaches us that the character of a majority is more important than its size alone" (p. 29). Posner (2012) wrote that while a majority vote of the population could come solely from urban areas, "the Electoral College requires a presidential candidate to have trans-regional appeal." The president can't win the election by earning the support of simply one geographic area or

> Integrates quotations, blending them with the writer's own language (Chapter 3).

demographic of the population. The Electoral College forces the future president to appeal to people of various demographics, regions, and subcultures.

Many Americans believe that since the Electoral College does not always reflect the will of the majority it is, in effect, undemocratic. The short response to that comment is "yes," but the longer response requires a more thorough understanding of the founding of our nation. The framers of the Constitution formed a government with characteristics of a democracy, a republic, and a federalist system. While a democracy focuses solely on the will and desires of the majority of its population, a republic allows the people to elect representatives who will represent the population in legal matters by doing what those representatives believe is best for the nation. A federalist system, in turn, separates the powers of a government into multiple tiers to ensure that local areas are governed in a way that accurately represents the local population. While the Electoral College may seem to contradict some ideals of a democracy, it accomplishes goals set forth by a republic and federalist system. Representatives chosen by the public ultimately are the ones responsible for electing the president, and the state legislatures assume responsibility for nominating the members of the Electoral College. Thomas Jefferson is said to have stated, "Democracy is nothing more than mob rule,

5

Summarizes and answers a naysayer (Chapter 6).

where 51 percent of the people may take away the rights of the other 49 percent." The founders were wary of majority rule in a pure democracy and so ensured that the country was protected from itself by using principles of republic and federalist systems in the Electoral College. America is the great country that it is today because the founders promised American citizens certain unalienable rights through these systems, and we must be cautious of any political reform that could jeopardize those rights.

Some opponents of the Electoral College argue it should be removed because it has negative effects on campaigning strategy. Presidential campaigns tend to focus on certain key swing states and have "just taken a lot of states off of the presidential map" (Dotinga, 2016). Abolishing the Electoral College would supposedly "allow long-ignored states to get attention again in presidential campaigns" (Dotinga, 2016). While campaigns concentrating on certain states and not others is not ideal, it is unreasonable to assume that candidates would give equal attention to every region of the country if the Electoral College were abolished. In that case, it's more likely campaigns would instead focus on regions with concentrated population centers such as the Northeast and the West Coast. As a result, large sections of America, especially rural areas with low population density, would be ignored. So although it's fair to point out that presidential

> Summarizes and answers a second naysayer.

Connects
the parts
(Chapter 8).

campaigns focus on certain geographic areas and leave out others, removing the Electoral College would not fix this problem.

Another argument for abolishing the Electoral College is that every single vote would become more important and our political system would be more accommodating to third parties. Instead of ignoring the votes that do not align with the majority of voters in each state and the opinions of voters supporting third parties, every individual's vote would have an equal effect on the outcome of the election, allowing third parties the possibility to win. Uhlmann (2004) wrote, "What the people would get by choosing direct election is the disintegration of the state-based two-party system" (p. 28). Uhlmann also noted that removing the Electoral College would allow "the rise of numerous factional parties based on region, class, ideology, or cult of personality" (p. 28).

Summarizes
and answers
yet one more
naysayer.

Although this may be true and attractive, we must not lose sight of the initial purpose of the Electoral College and not let the appeal of the statement "Every vote counts" overshadow the purpose and intentions of the Electoral College. Just because a system has some flaws does not mean that extreme reform will lead us to a new system any more just and reasonable than what the founders designed. As long as government is organized by humans—and humans continue to be imperfect creatures—we must accept that our political system will include some flaws and carefully weigh whether or not reform would truly improve upon the founders' vision or leave us worse off. A single-vote system would leave us vulnerable to the "mob rule" that the founders worked to protect us against.

For these reasons, the United States of America should keep the Electoral College. Although the complaints against it are understandable, we must consider the profound reasons that it was initially created: to ensure a proper representation of each state, region, and people of the United States in the presidential election. The Electoral College prevents regional tyranny in our government, maintains our current government structure, and embodies the ideals that have helped our country survive and thrive. As appealing as a direct election may sound, we must remember what the founders had in mind for our country and that the institutions they put in place were created for the protection of our freedom and way of life.

> Recaps the author's central position while subtly acknowledging the counterview (Chapter 6).

REFERENCES

Dotinga, R. (2016, June 16). A backdoor plan to thwart the electoral college. *Christian Science Monitor*. https://www .csmonitor.com/2006/0616/p01s02-uspo.html

National Archives. (2019, December 23). *What is the Electoral College?* https://www.archives.gov/federal-register/electoral-college/about.html

Posner, R. A. (2012, November 12). *In defense of the Electoral College.* Slate. https://slate.com/news-and-politics/2012/11/defending-the-electoral-college.html

Uhlmann, M. M. (2004, November 8). The old (Electoral) College cheer: Why we have it; why we need it. *National Review,* 28–29.

GLORIA ANZALDÚA { *How to Tame a Wild Tongue*

GLORIA ANZALDÚA (1942–2004), a Chicana lesbian feminist, is a well-known early female voice in Chicana writing. Her first work, *This Bridge Called My Back* (1981), was co-authored with Cherríe Moraga. Her next book, *Borderlands / La Frontera: The New Mestiza* (1987) called attention not only to the difficulties she encountered growing up in the Rio Grande Valley of Texas, but also to the hardships faced by other women living along the U.S./Mexican border. Anzaldúa's other works include *Making Face, Making Soul / Haciendo Caras* (1990) and *Prietita and the Ghost Woman* (1996), a book for children.

In "How to Tame a Wild Tongue," an essay from *Borderlands*, Anzaldúa explores the linguistic borders between Mexico and the United States and the "border tongues" and ethnic identities that cross them. Her frequent use of Spanish will challenge those who do not read the language to find a dictionary or a Spanish speaker in order to discover the meaning not only of the words but also of the deeper ideas and emotions that English sometimes cannot convey for her. As you read, consider the reasons Anzaldúa might have for insisting that editors not translate her Spanish phrases for English readers. In this bilingual fashion, Anzaldúa allows her "wild tongue" to express itself fully and without constraint.

"WE'RE GOING TO HAVE TO control your tongue," the dentist says, pulling out all the metal from my mouth. Silver bits plop and tinkle into the basin. My mouth is a motherlode.

The dentist is cleaning out my roots. I get a whiff of the stench when I gasp. "I can't cap that tooth yet, you're still draining," he says.

"We're going to have to do something about your tongue," I hear the anger rising in his voice. My tongue keeps pushing out the wads of cotton, pushing back the drills, the long thin needles. "I've never seen anything as strong or as stubborn," he says. And I think, how do you tame a wild tongue, train it to be quiet, how do you bridle and saddle it? How do you make it lie down?

> *"Who is to say that robbing a people of its language is less violent than war?"*
>
> —Ray Gwyn Smith[1]

I remember being caught speaking Spanish at recess—that was good for three licks on the knuckles with a sharp ruler. I remember being sent to the corner of the classroom for "talking back" to the Anglo teacher when all I was trying to do was tell her how to pronounce my name. "If you want to be American, speak 'American.' If you don't like it, go back to Mexico where you belong."

"I want you to speak English. *Pa' hallar buen trabajo tienes que saber hablar el inglés bien. Qué vale toda tu educación si todavía hablas inglés con un* 'accent,'" my mother would say, mortified that I spoke English like a Mexican. At Pan American University, I, and all Chicano students were required to take two speech classes. Their purpose: to get rid of our accents.

Attacks on one's form of expression with the intent to censor are a violation of the First Amendment. *El Anglo con cara de inocente nos arrancó la lengua.* Wild tongues can't be tamed, they can only be cut out.

---

[1]Ray Gwyn Smith, *Moorland Is Cold Country*, unpublished book. [Unless otherwise indicated, notes are those of the author.]

OVERCOMING THE TRADITION OF SILENCE

Ahogadas, escupimos el oscuro.
Peleando con nuestra propia sombra
el silencio nos sepulta.

En boca cerrada no entran moscas. "Flies don't enter a closed mouth" is a saying I kept hearing when I was a child. *Ser habladora* was to be a gossip and a liar, to talk too much. *Muchachitas bien criadas,* well-bred girls don't answer back. *Es una falta de respeto* to talk back to one's mother or father. I remember one of the sins I'd recite to the priest in the confession box the few times I went to confession: talking back to my mother, *hablar pa' 'trás, repelar. Hocicona, repelona, chismosa,* having a big mouth, questioning, carrying tales are all signs of being *mal criada.* In my culture they are all words that are derogatory if applied to women—I've never heard them applied to men.

The first time I heard two women, a Puerto Rican and a Cuban, say the word *"nosotras,"* I was shocked. I had not known the word existed. Chicanas use *nosotros* whether we're male or female. We are robbed of our female being by the masculine plural. Language is a male discourse.

> And our tongues have become
> dry   the wilderness has
> dried out our tongues   and
> we have forgotten speech.
> —IRENA KLEPFISZ[2]

Even our own people, other Spanish speakers *nos quieren poner candados en la boca.* They would hold us back with their bag of *reglas de academia.*

---

[2]Irena Klepfisz, *"Di rayze aheym/*The Journey Home," in *The Tribe of Dina: A Jewish Women's Anthology,* Melanie Kaye/Kantrowitz and Irena Klepfisz, eds. (Montpelier, VT: Sinister Wisdom Books, 1986), 49.

OYÉ COMO LADRA: EL LENGUAJE DE LA FRONTERA

Quien tiene boca se equivoca.

—MEXICAN SAYING

"*Pocho,* cultural traitor, you're speaking the oppressor's language 10
by speaking English, you're ruining the Spanish language," I have
been accused by various Latinos and Latinas. Chicano Spanish is
considered by the purist and by most Latinos deficient, a mutilation
of Spanish.

But Chicano Spanish is a border tongue which developed naturally.
Change, *evolución, enriquecimiento de palabras nuevas por invención o
adopción* have created variants of Chicano Spanish, *un nuevo lenguaje.
Un lenguaje que corresponde a un modo de vivir.* Chicano Spanish is not
incorrect, it is a living language.

For a people who are neither Spanish nor live in a country in which
Spanish is the first language; for a people who live in a country in
which English is the reigning tongue but who are not Anglo; for a
people who cannot entirely identify with either standard (formal,
Castillian) Spanish nor standard English, what recourse is left to them
but to create their own language? A language which they can connect
their identity to, one capable of communicating the realities and values true to themselves—a language with terms that are neither *español
ni inglés,* but both. We speak a patois, a forked tongue, a variation of
two languages.

Chicano Spanish sprang out of the Chicanos' need to identify ourselves as a distinct people. We needed a language with which we could
communicate with ourselves, a secret language. For some of us, language is a homeland closer than the Southwest—for many Chicanos
today live in the Midwest and the East. And because we are a complex,
heterogeneous people, we speak many languages. Some of the languages we speak are:

1. Standard English
2. Working-class and slang English

3. Standard Spanish
4. Standard Mexican Spanish
5. North Mexican Spanish dialect
6. Chicano Spanish (Texas, New Mexico, Arizona and California have regional variations)
7. Tex-Mex
8. *Pachuco* (called *caló*)

My "home" tongues are the languages I speak with my sister and brothers, with my friends. They are the last five listed, with 6 and 7 being closest to my heart. From school, the media and job situations, I've picked up standard and working class English. From Mamagrande Locha and from reading Spanish and Mexican literature, I've picked up Standard Spanish and Standard Mexican Spanish. From *los recién llegados*, Mexican immigrants, and *braceros*, I learned the North Mexican dialect. With Mexicans I'll try to speak either Standard Mexican Spanish or the North Mexican dialect. From my parents and Chicanos living in the Valley, I picked up Chicano Texas Spanish, and I speak it with my mom, younger brother (who married a Mexican and who rarely mixes Spanish with English), aunts and older relatives.

With Chicanas from *Nuevo México* or *Arizona* I will speak Chicano 15 Spanish a little, but often they don't understand what I'm saying. With most California Chicanas I speak entirely in English (unless I forget). When I first moved to San Francisco, I'd rattle off something in Spanish, unintentionally embarrassing them. Often it is only with another Chicana *tejana* that I can talk freely.

Words distorted by English are known as anglicisms or *pochismos*. The *pocho* is an anglicized Mexican or American of Mexican origin who speaks Spanish with an accent characteristic of North Americans and who distorts and reconstructs the language according to the influence of English.[3] Tex-Mex, or Spanglish, comes most naturally to me. I may

[3]R. C. Ortega *Dialectología Del Barrio*, trans. Hortencia S. Alwan (Los Angeles, CA: R. C. Ortega Publisher & Bookseller, 1977), 132.

switch back and forth from English to Spanish in the same sentence or in the same word. With my sister and my brother Nune and with Chicano *tejano* contemporaries I speak in Tex-Mex.

From kids and people my own age I picked up *Pachuco. Pachuco* (the language of the zoot suiters) is a language of rebellion, both against Standard Spanish and Standard English. It is a secret language. Adults of the culture and outsiders cannot understand it. It is made up of slang words from both English and Spanish. *Ruca* means girl or woman, *vato* means guy or dude, *chale* means no, *simón* means yes, *churo* is sure, talk is *periquiar, pigionear* means petting, *que gacho* means how nerdy, *ponte águila* means watch out, death is called *la pelona.* Through lack of practice and not having others who can speak it, I've lost most of the *Pachuco* tongue.

CHICANO SPANISH

Chicanos, after 250 years of Spanish/Anglo colonization have developed significant differences in the Spanish we speak. We collapse two adjacent vowels into a single syllable and sometimes shift the stress in certain words such as *maíz/maiz, cohete/cuete.* We leave out certain consonants when they appear between vowels: *lado/lao, mojado/mojao.* Chicanos from South Texas pronounce *f* as *j* as in *jue (fue).* Chicanos use "archaisms," words that are no longer in the Spanish language, words that have been evolved out. We say *semos, truje, haiga, ansina,* and *naiden.* We retain the "archaic" *j,* as in *jalar,* that derives from an earlier *h,* (the French *halar* or the Germanic *halon* which was lost to standard Spanish in the 16th century), but which is still found in several regional dialects such as the one spoken in South Texas. (Due to geography, Chicanos from the Valley of South Texas were cut off linguistically from other Spanish speakers. We tend to use words that the Spaniards brought over from Medieval Spain. The majority of the Spanish colonizers in Mexico and the Southwest came from Extremadura[4]—Hernán Cortés was one of them—and Andalucía.

[4]Large region of southern Spain. *Hernán Cortés*: Spanish conquistador (1485–1547) who defeated the Aztec empire and claimed Mexico for Spain. [Editor's note.]

Andalucians pronounce *ll* like a *y*, and their *d*'s tend to be absorbed by adjacent vowels: *tirado* becomes *tirao*. They brought *el lenguaje popular, dialectos y regionalismos*.[5])

Chicanos and other Spanish speakers also shift *ll* to *y* and *z* to *s*.[6] We leave out initial syllables, saying *tar* for *estar, toy* for *estoy, hora* for *ahora* (*cubanos* and *puertorriqueños* also leave out initial letters of some words.) We also leave out the final syllable such as *pa* for *para*. The intervocalic *y*, the *ll* as in *tortilla, ella, botella*, gets replaced by *tortia* or *tortiya, ea, botea*. We add an additional syllable at the beginning of certain words: *atocar* for *tocar, agastar* for *gastar*. Sometimes we'll say *lavaste las vacijas*, other times *lavates* (substituting the *ates* verb endings for the *aste*).

We use anglicisms, words borrowed from English: *bola* from ball, 20 *carpeta* from carpet, *máchina de lavar* (instead of *lavadora*) from washing machine. Tex-Mex argot, created by adding a Spanish sound at the beginning or end of an English word such as *cookiar* for cook, *watchar* for watch, *parkiar* for park, and *rapiar* for rape, is the result of the pressures on Spanish speakers to adapt to English.

We don't use the word *vosotros/as* or its accompanying verb form. We don't say *claro* (to mean yes), *imagínate*, or *me emociona*, unless we picked up Spanish from Latinas[7], out of a book, or in a classroom. Other Spanish-speaking groups are going through the same, or similar, development in their Spanish.

LINGUISTIC TERRORISM

> *Deslenguadas. Somos los del español deficiente. We are your linguistic nightmare, your linguistic aberration, your linguistic mestizaje, the subject of your burla. Because we speak with tongues of fire we are culturally crucified. Racially, culturally and linguistically somos huérfanos— we speak an orphan tongue.*

---

[5]Eduardo Hernandéz-Chávez, Andrew D. Cohen, and Anthony F. Beltramo, *El Lenguaje de Chicanos: Regional and Social Characteristics of Language Used by Mexican Americans* (Arlington, VA: Center for Applied Linguistics, 1975), 39.

[6]Hernandéz-Chávez, xvii.

[7]That is, natives of Central and South America. [Ed.]

Chicanas who grew up speaking Chicano Spanish have internalized the belief that we speak poor Spanish. It is illegitimate, a bastard language. And because we internalize how our language has been used against us by the dominant culture, we use our language differences against each other.

Chicana feminists often skirt around each other with suspicion and hesitation. For the longest time I couldn't figure it out. Then it dawned on me. To be close to another Chicana is like looking into the mirror. We are afraid of what we'll see there. *Pena*. Shame. Low estimation of self. In childhood we are told that our language is wrong. Repeated attacks on our native tongue diminish our sense of self. The attacks continue throughout our lives.

Chicanas feel uncomfortable talking in Spanish to Latinas, afraid of their censure. Their language was not outlawed in their countries. They had a whole lifetime of being immersed in their native tongue; generations, centuries in which Spanish was a first language, taught in school, heard on radio and TV, and read in the newspaper.

If a person, Chicana or Latina, has a low estimation of my native tongue, she also has a low estimation of me. Often with *mexicanas y latinas* we'll speak English as a neutral language. Even among Chicanas we tend to speak English at parties or conferences. Yet, at the same time, we're afraid the other will think we're *agringadas* because we don't speak Chicano Spanish. We oppress each other trying to out-Chicano each other, vying to be the "real" Chicanas, to speak like Chicanos. There is no one Chicano language just as there is no one Chicano experience. A monolingual Chicana whose first language is English or Spanish is just as much a Chicana as one who speaks several variants of Spanish. A Chicana from Michigan or Chicago or Detroit is just as much a Chicana as one from the Southwest. Chicano Spanish is as diverse linguistically as it is regionally.

By the end of this century, Spanish speakers will comprise the biggest minority group in the U.S., a country where students in high schools and colleges are encouraged to take French classes because French is considered more "cultured." But for a language to remain alive it must be used.[8] By the end of this century English, and not Spanish, will be the mother tongue of most Chicanos and Latinos.

So, if you want to really hurt me, talk badly about my language. Ethnic identity is twin skin to linguistic identity—I am my language. Until I can take pride in my language, I cannot take pride in myself. Until I can accept as legitimate Chicano Texas Spanish, Tex-Mex and all the other languages I speak, I cannot accept the legitimacy of myself. Until I am free to write bilingually and to switch codes without having always to translate, while I still have to speak English or Spanish when I would rather speak Spanglish, and as long as I have to accommodate the English speakers rather than having them accommodate me, my tongue will be illegitimate.

I will no longer be made to feel ashamed of existing. I will have my voice: Indian, Spanish, white. I will have my serpent's tongue—my woman's voice, my sexual voice, my poet's voice. I will overcome the tradition of silence.

> *My fingers*
> *move sly against your palm,*
> *Like women everywhere, we speak in code. . . .*
> —MELANIE KAYE/KANTROWITZ[9]

"VISTAS," CORRIDOS, Y COMIDA: MY NATIVE TONGUE

In the 1960s, I read my first Chicano novel. It was *City of Night* by John Rechy, a gay Texan, son of a Scottish father and a Mexican mother. For days I walked around in stunned amazement that a Chicano could write and could get published. When I read *I Am*

---

[8]Irena Klepfisz, "Secular Jewish Identity: Yidishkayt in America," in *The Tribe of Dina*, Kaye/Kantrowitz and Klepfisz, eds., 43.

[9]Melanie Kaye/Kantrowitz, "Sign," in *We Speak in Code: Poems and Other Writings* (Pittsburgh, PA: Motheroot Publications, Inc., 1980), 85.

Joaquín[1] I was surprised to see a bilingual book by a Chicano in print. When I saw poetry written in Tex-Mex for the first time, a feeling of pure joy flashed through me. I felt like we really existed as a people. In 1971, when I started teaching High School English to Chicano students, I tried to supplement the required texts with works by Chicanos, only to be reprimanded and forbidden to do so by the principal. He claimed that I was supposed to teach "American" and English literature. At the risk of being fired, I swore my students to secrecy and slipped in Chicano short stories, poems, a play. In graduate school, while working toward a Ph.D., I had to "argue" with one advisor after the other, semester after semester, before I was allowed to make Chicano literature an area of focus.

Even before I read books by Chicanos or Mexicans, it was the 30 Mexican movies I saw at the drive-in—the Thursday night special of $1.00 a carload—that gave me a sense of belonging. *"Vámonos a las vistas,"* my mother would call out and we'd all—grandmother, brothers, sister and cousins—squeeze into the car. We'd wolf down cheese and bologna white bread sandwiches while watching Pedro Infante in melodramatic tear-jerkers like *Nosotros los pobres,* the first "real" Mexican movie (that was not an imitation of European movies). I remember seeing *Cuando los hijos se van* and surmising that all Mexican movies played up the love a mother has for her children and what ungrateful sons and daughters suffer when they are not devoted to their mothers. I remember the singing-type "westerns" of Jorge Negrete and Miguel Aceves Mejía. When watching Mexican movies, I felt a sense of homecoming as well as alienation. People who were to amount to something didn't go to Mexican movies, or *bailes* or tune their radios to *bolero, rancherita,* and *corrido* music.

The whole time I was growing up, there was *norteño* music sometimes called North Mexican border music, or Tex-Mex music, or Chicano music, or *cantina* (bar) music. I grew up listening to *conjuntos,* three- or four-piece bands made up of folk musicians playing guitar,

---

[1]Rodolfo Gonzales, *I Am Joaquín/Yo Soy Joaquín* (New York, NY: Bantam Books, 1972). It was first published in 1967.

bajo sexto, drums and button accordion, which Chicanos had borrowed from the German immigrants who had come to Central Texas and Mexico to farm and build breweries. In the Rio Grande Valley, Steve Jordan and Little Joe Hernández were popular, and Flaco Jiménez was the accordion king. The rhythms of Tex-Mex music are those of the polka, also adapted from the Germans, who in turn had borrowed the polka from the Czechs and Bohemians.

I remember the hot, sultry evenings when *corridos*—songs of love and death on the Texas-Mexican borderlands—reverberated out of cheap amplifiers from the local *cantinas* and wafted in through my bedroom window.

Corridos first became widely used along the South Texas/Mexican border during the early conflict between Chicanos and Anglos. The *corridos* are usually about Mexican heroes who do valiant deeds against the Anglo oppressors. Pancho Villa's song, *"La cucaracha,"* is the most famous one. *Corridos* of John F. Kennedy and his death are still very popular in the Valley. Older Chicanos remember Lydia Mendoza, one of the great border *corrido* singers who was called *la Gloria de Tejas.* Her *"El tango negro,"* sung during the Great Depression, made her a singer of the people. The everpresent *corridos* narrated one hundred years of border history, bringing news of events as well as entertaining. These folk musicians and folk songs are our chief cultural mythmakers, and they made our hard lives seem bearable.

I grew up feeling ambivalent about our music. Country-western and rock-and-roll had more status. In the 50s and 60s, for the slightly educated and *agringado* Chicanos, there existed a sense of shame at being caught listening to our music. Yet I couldn't stop my feet from thumping to the music, could not stop humming the words, nor hide from myself the exhilaration I felt when I heard it.

There are more subtle ways that we internalize identification, especially in the forms of images and emotions. For me food and certain smells are tied to my identity, to my homeland. Woodsmoke curling up to an immense blue sky; woodsmoke perfuming my grandmother's clothes, her skin. The stench of cow manure and the yellow patches on the ground; the crack of a .22 rifle and the reek of cordite. Homemade white cheese sizzling in a pan, melting inside a folded *tortilla*. My sister Hilda's hot, spicy *menudo, chile colorado* making it deep red, pieces of *panza* and hominy floating on top. My brother Carito barbecuing *fajitas* in the backyard. Even now and 3,000 miles away, I can see my mother spicing the ground beef, pork and venison with *chile*. My mouth salivates at the thought of the hot steaming *tamales* I would be eating if I were home.

SI LE PREGUNTAS A MI MAMÁ, "¿QUÉ ERES?"

"Identity is the essential core of who we are as individuals, the conscious experience of the self inside."

—Kaufman[2]

Nosotros los Chicanos straddle the borderlands. On one side of us, we are constantly exposed to the Spanish of the Mexicans, on the other side we hear the Anglos' incessant clamoring so that we forget our language. Among ourselves we don't say *nosotros los americanos, o nosotros los españoles, o nosotros los hispanos*. We say *nosotros los mexicanos* (by *mexicanos* we do not mean citizens of Mexico; we do not mean a national identity, but a racial one). We distinguish between *mexicanos del otro lado* and *mexicanos de este lado*. Deep in our hearts we believe that being Mexican has nothing to do with which country one lives in. Being Mexican is a state of soul—not one of mind, not one of citizenship. Neither eagle nor serpent, but both. And like the ocean, neither animal respects borders.

Dime con quien andas y te diré quien eres. *(Tell me who your friends are and I'll tell you who you are.)*

—Mexican saying

Si le preguntas a mi mamá, "¿Qué eres?" te dirá, "Soy mexicana." My brothers and sister say the same. I sometimes will answer *"soy mexi-*

[2]Kaufman, 68.

cana" and at others will say *"soy Chicana" o "soy tejana."* But I identified as *"Raza"* before I ever identified as *"mexicana"* or "Chicana."

As a culture, we call ourselves Spanish when referring to ourselves as a linguistic group and when copping out. It is then that we forget our predominant Indian genes. We are 70 to 80% Indian.[3] We call ourselves Hispanic[4] or Spanish-American or Latin American or Latin when linking ourselves to other Spanish-speaking peoples of the Western hemisphere and when copping out. We call ourselves Mexican-American[5] to signify we are neither Mexican nor American, but more the noun "American" than the adjective "Mexican" (and when copping out).

Chicanos and other people of color suffer economically for not acculturating. This voluntary (yet forced) alienation makes for psychological conflict, a kind of dual identity—we don't identify with the Anglo-American cultural values and we don't totally identify with the Mexican cultural values. We are a synergy of two cultures with various degrees of Mexicanness or Angloness. I have so internalized the borderland conflict that sometimes I feel like one cancels out the other and we are zero, nothing, no one. *A veces no soy nada ni nadie. Pero hasta cuando no lo soy, lo soy.*

When not copping out, when we know we are more than nothing, we call ourselves Mexican, referring to race and ancestry; *mestizo* when affirming both our Indian and Spanish (but we hardly ever own our Black ancestry); Chicano when referring to a politically aware people born and/or raised in the U.S.; *Raza* when referring to Chicanos; *tejanos* when we are Chicanos from Texas.   40

Chicanos did not know we were a people until 1965 when Cesar Chavez and the farmworkers united and *I Am Joaquín* was published and *la Raza Unida* party was formed in Texas. With that recognition, we became a distinct people. Something momentous happened to the Chicano soul—we became aware of our reality and acquired a name

---

[3]Chávez, 88–90.

[4]"Hispanic" is derived from *Hispanis (España*, a name given to the Iberian Peninsula in ancient times when it was a part of the Roman Empire) and is a term designated by the U.S. government to make it easier to handle us on paper.

[5]The treaty of Guadalupe Hidalgo created the Mexican-American in 1848.

and a language (Chicano Spanish) that reflected that reality. Now that we had a name, some of the fragmented pieces began to fall together— who we were, what we were, how we had evolved. We began to get glimpses of what we might eventually become.

Yet the struggle of identities continues, the struggle of borders is our reality still. One day the inner struggle will cease and a true integration take place. In the meantime, *tenemos que hacerla lucha, ¿Quién está protegiendo los ranchos de mi gente? ¿Quién está tratando de cerrar la fisura entre la india y el blanco en nuestra sangre? El Chicano, sí, el Chicano que anda como un ladron en su propia casa.*

Los Chicanos how patient we seem, how very patient. There is the quiet of the Indian about us.[6] We know how to survive. When other races have given up their tongue, we've kept ours. We know what it is to live under the hammer blow of the dominant *norteamericano* culture. But more than we count the blows, we count the days the weeks the years the centuries the eons until the white laws and commerce and customs will rot in the deserts they've created, lie bleached. *Humildes* yet proud, *quietos* yet wild, *nosotros los mexicanos*-Chicanos will walk by the crumbling ashes as we go about our business. Stubborn, persevering, impenetrable as stone, yet possessing a malleability that renders us unbreakable, we, the *mestizas* and *mestizos,* will remain.

---

[6]Anglos, in order to alleviate their guilt for dispossessing the Chicano, stressed the Spanish part of us and perpetrated the myth of the Spanish Southwest. We have accepted the fiction that we are Hispanic, that is Spanish, in order to accommoadate ourselves to the dominant culture and its abhorrence of Indians. Chávez, 88–91.

STUDY QUESTIONS

1. What is the "Pachuco" language? Explain how the various languages Anzaldúa discusses are related to the "wild tongue" reference in the title of her essay.

2. One of the RHETORICAL STRATEGIES Anzaldúa uses in her essay is DEFINITION, to ensure that the reader understands how the author will use a given term. Furthermore, the definition may be extended and clarified with examples. Find two examples of Anzaldúa's use of definition in this essay and explain how each functions in the overall essay.

3. Anzaldúa specified that when her work is reprinted, no footnotes be added to translate the Spanish and other foreign words and phrases she uses. What effect does this practice have on you as a reader? What do you think Anzaldúa is trying to achieve?

4. *For Writing.* Many speakers of other languages find it difficult to solely express themselves in English because it can be difficult to find the English word whose connotations best suit its meaning. For example, the Spanish words *cariño* and *amor* both mean *love* but are used for different situations. Write a PERSONAL NARRATIVE about an important situation in your life when it seemed as though English—or any other language—lacked the right words to convey effectively what you wanted to say.

MORTIMER J. ADLER { *How to Mark a Book*

MORTIMER J. ADLER (1902–2001), a native of New York City, dropped out of school at fourteen, to embark on a career in journalism. He began taking night courses at Columbia University to develop his writing skills and discovered a love of philosophy. By the late 1920s Adler was teaching at Columbia while pursuing his doctorate and writing his first book, *Dialectic* (1927). Along with Max Weismann, Adler founded The Center for the Study of Great Ideas to investigate such philosophical questions as "What ought we seek in life?" and "How ought we seek it?"

In "How to Mark a Book," Adler explains not only *how* to mark a book, but also *why* we should mark our books. Adler uses a range of rhetorical strategies—process analysis, description, definition, division and classification, and exemplification—to develop his ideas. Real ownership of books, Adler advises, comes from truly possessing the ideas, not just the pages, between the covers, and the point of reading is not to get through books but to get them through you.

YOU KNOW YOU HAVE TO read "between the lines" to get the most out of anything. I want to persuade you to do something equally important in the course of your reading. I want to persuade you to write between the lines. Unless you do, you are not likely to do the most efficient kind of reading.

I contend, quite bluntly, that marking up a book is not an act of mutilation but of love. You shouldn't mark up a book which isn't yours.

Librarians (or your friends) who lend you books expect you to keep them clean, and you should. If you decide that I am right about the usefulness of marking books, you will have to buy them. Most of the world's great books are available today, in reprint editions.

There are two ways in which one can own a book. The first is the property right you establish by paying for it, just as you pay for clothes and furniture. But this act of purchase is only the prelude to possession. Full ownership comes only when you have made it a part of yourself, and the best way to make yourself a part of it is by writing in it. An illustration may make the point clear. You buy a beefsteak and transfer it from the butcher's icebox to your own. But you do not own the beefsteak in the most important sense until you consume it and get it into your bloodstream. I am arguing that books, too, must be absorbed in your bloodstream to do you any good.

Confusion about what it means to "own" a book leads people to a 5 false reverence for paper, binding, and type—a respect for the physical thing—the craft of the printer rather than the genius of the author. They forget that it is possible for a man to acquire the idea, to possess the beauty, which a great book contains, without staking his claim by pasting his bookplate inside the cover. Having a fine library doesn't prove that its owner has a mind enriched by books; it proves nothing more than that he, his father, or his wife, was rich enough to buy them.

There are three kinds of book owners. The first has all the standard sets and best sellers—unread, untouched. (This deluded individual owns woodpulp and ink, not books.) The second has a great many books—a few of them read through, most of them dipped into, but all of them as clean and shiny as the day they were bought. (This person would probably like to make books his own, but is restrained by a false respect for their physical appearance.) The third has a few books or many—every one of them dog-eared and dilapidated, shaken and loosened by continual use, marked and scribbled in from front to back. (This man owns books.)

Is it false respect, you may ask, to preserve intact and unblemished a beautifully printed book, an elegantly bound edition? Of course not. I'd no more scribble all over a first edition of *Paradise Lost* than I'd give my baby a set of crayons and an original Rembrandt. I wouldn't mark up a painting or a statue. Its soul, so to speak, is inseparable from its body. And the beauty of a rare edition or of a richly manufactured volume is like that of a painting or a statue.

But the soul of a book "can" be separate from its body. A book is more like the score of a piece of music than it is like a painting. No great musician confuses a symphony with the printed sheets of music. Arturo Toscanini reveres Brahms,[1] but Toscanini's score of the G minor Symphony is so thoroughly marked up that no one but the maestro himself can read it. The reason why a great conductor makes notations on his musical scores—marks them up again and again each time he returns to study them—is the reason why you should mark your books. If your respect for magnificent binding or typography gets in the way, buy yourself a cheap edition and pay your respects to the author.

Why is marking up a book indispensable to reading? First, it keeps you awake. (And I don't mean merely conscious; I mean awake.) In the second place, reading, if it is active, is thinking, and thinking tends to express itself in words, spoken or written. The marked book is usually the thought-through book. Finally, writing helps you remember the thoughts you had, or the thoughts the author expressed. Let me develop these three points.

If reading is to accomplish anything more than passing time, it 10 must be active. You can't let your eyes glide across the lines of a book and come up with an understanding of what you have read. Now an ordinary piece of light fiction, like, say, *Gone With the Wind,*[2] doesn't require the most active kind of reading. The books you read for pleasure can be read in a state of relaxation, and nothing is lost. But a great book, rich in ideas and beauty, a book that raises and tries to answer great fundamental questions, demands the most active reading of which you are capable. You don't absorb the ideas of John Dewey the way you absorb the crooning of Mr. Vallée.[3] You have reach for them. That you cannot do while you're asleep.

[1]German composer (1833–97) of the Romantic era. *Arturo Toscanini* (1867–1957): Italian musician considered one of history's greatest orchestral conductors.

[2]Popular novel (1937) of the Civil War by Margaret Mitchell (1900–49).

[3]Rudy Vallée (1901–86), American singer and bandleader. *John Dewey* (1859–1952): American philosopher and educational reformer.

If, when you've finished reading a book, the pages are filled with your notes, you know that you read actively. The most famous "active" reader of great books I know is President Hutchins,[4] of the University of Chicago. He also has the hardest schedule of business activities of any man I know. He invariably reads with a pencil, and sometimes, when he picks up a book and pencil in the evening, he finds himself, instead of making intelligent notes, drawing what he calls "caviar factories" on the margins. When that happens, he puts the book down. He knows he's too tired to read, and he's just wasting time.

But, you may ask, why is writing necessary? Well, the physical act of writing, with your own hand, brings words and sentences more sharply before your mind and preserves them better in your memory. To set down your reaction to important words and sentences you have read, and the questions they have raised in your mind, is to preserve those reactions and sharpen those questions.

Even if you wrote on a scratch pad, and threw the paper away when you had finished writing, your grasp of the book would be surer. But you don't have to throw the paper away. The margins (top and bottom as well as side), the end-papers, the very space between the lines, are all available. They aren't sacred. And, best of all, your marks and notes become an integral part of the book and stay there forever. You can pick up the book the following week or year, and there are all your points of agreement, disagreement, doubt, and inquiry. It's like resuming an interrupted conversation with the advantage of being able to pick up where you left off.

And that is exactly what reading a book should be: a conversation between you and the author. Presumably he knows more about the subject than you do; naturally, you'll have the proper humility as you approach him. But don't let anybody tell you that a reader is supposed to be solely on the receiving end. Understanding is a two-way operation; learning doesn't consist in being an empty receptacle. The learner has to question himself and question the teacher. He even has to argue with the teacher, once he understands what the teacher is

---

[4]Robert Hutchins (1899–1977), educational philosopher and president of the University of Chicago, where he hired Mortimer Adler as a professor of the philosophy of law.

saying. And marking a book is literally an expression of differences, or agreements of opinion, with the author.

There are all kinds of devices for marking a book intelligently and 15 fruitfully. Here's the way I do it:

- **Underlining (or highlighting):** of major points, of important or forceful statements.

- **Vertical lines at the margin:** to emphasize a statement already underlined.

- **Star, asterisk, or other doo-dad at the margin:** to be used sparingly, to emphasize the ten or twenty most important statements in the book. (You may want to fold the bottom corner of each page on which you use such marks. It won't hurt the sturdy paper on which most modern books are printed, and you will be able take the book off the shelf at any time and, by opening it at the folded-corner page, refresh your recollection of the book.)

- **Numbers in the margin:** to indicate the sequence of points the author makes in developing a single argument.

- **Numbers of other pages in the margin:** to indicate where else in the book the author made points relevant to the point marked; to tie up the ideas in a book, which, though they may be separated by many pages, belong together.

- **Circling or highlighting of key words or phrases.**

- **Writing in the margin, or at the top or bottom of the page:** for the sake of recording questions (and perhaps answers) which a passage raised in your mind; reducing a complicated discussion to a simple statement; recording the sequence of major points right through the books. I use the end-papers at the back of the book to make a personal index of the author's points in the order of their appearance.

The front end-papers are to me the most important. Some people reserve them for a fancy bookplate. I reserve them for fancy thinking. After I have finished reading the book and making my personal index on the back end-papers, I turn to the front and try to outline the book, not page by page or point by point (I've already done that at the back), but as an integrated structure, with a basic unity and an order of parts. This outline is, to me, the measure of my understanding of the work.

If you're a die-hard anti-book-marker, you may object that the margins, the space between the lines, and the end-papers don't give you room enough. All right. How about using a scratch pad slightly smaller than the page-size of the book—so that the edges of the sheets won't protrude? Make your index, outlines, and even your notes on the pad, and then insert these sheets permanently inside the front and back covers of the book.

Or, you may say that this business of marking books is going to slow up your reading. It probably will. That's one of the reasons for doing it. Most of us have been taken in by the notion that speed of reading is a measure of our intelligence. There is no such thing as the right speed for intelligent reading. Some things should be read quickly and effortlessly and some should be read slowly and even laboriously. The sign of intelligence in reading is the ability to read different things differently according to their worth. In the case of good books, the point is not to see how many of them you can get through, but rather how many can get through you—how many you can make your own. A few friends are better than a thousand acquaintances. If this be your aim, as it should be, you will not be impatient if it takes more time and effort to read a great book than it does a newspaper.

You may have one final objection to marking books. You can't lend them to your friends because nobody else can read them without being distracted by your notes. Furthermore, you won't want to lend them because a marked copy is kind of intellectual diary, and lending it is almost like giving your mind away.

If your friend wishes to read your *Plutarch's Lives, Shakespeare,* or 20 *The Federalist Papers,* tell him gently but firmly to buy a copy. You will lend him your car or your coat—but your books are as much a part of you as your head or your heart.

STUDY QUESTIONS

1. Why does Adler advise against lending books to friends? What comparison does he use to explore the idea of owning a book, and how effective is it?

2. Numbering items in an essay is a rhetorical technique that can help guide readers through the development of an idea. Adler uses this TRANSITION technique several times in his article. Find these passages and explain what he enumerates. Does the strategy help you to follow his reasoning? Why or why not?

3. The "how to" in Adler's title indicates that he will present a process. Look carefully for the way Adler structures the process of marking a book. Find each step in the process and number them in the order in which they occur. Are there enough to guide someone through the process? Explain.

4. *For Writing.* Adler clearly cares very much about reading books and absorbing their content. Choose an activity for which you have a similar passion, and write a PROCESS ANALYSIS essay describing how best to enjoy that activity. Reread Adler's essay and make sure your essay covers all relevant aspects of participating in the activity, answers possible objections to doing it your way, and provides signposts and transitions for your reader to follow, as Adler's does.

GARY GUTTING   { *What Is College For?*

GARY GUTTING is an American academic and writer. He serves as a
professor and chairperson in the philosophy department at the University
of Notre Dame, having received his doctorate in philosophy from Saint
Louis University. Gutting's scholarship focuses on French philosophy and
the connections among faith, science, and society. He is the author of a
number of books, including *Religious Belief and Religious Skepticism*
(1982), *What Philosophers Know: Case Studies in Recent Analytical
Philosophy* (2009), and *Thinking the Impossible: French Philosophy Since
1960* (2011). In addition to his scholarly work, Gutting has written essays
and editorials on matters of education, philosophy, politics, and religion for
popular publications.

   "What Is College For?" was published in the *New York Times* in 2011. In
the essay, Gutting discusses the real importance of colleges and college
education, as well as the argument that college serves little useful purpose
for many students. While acknowledging that there are factors that can
limit some students' intellectual development during their college years,
Gutting argues that college can and should be a valuable experience for
students, provided that both they and their teachers approach classes with
the mindset that higher education is inherently "worth it," for students and
for the society at large. As you read, note the factors that hold some
students back, as well as those that can help students to thrive.

MOST AMERICAN COLLEGE STUDENTS ARE wrapping up yet another semester this week. For many of them, and their families, the past months or years in school have likely involved considerable time, commitment, effort and expense. Was it worth it?

Some evidence suggests that it was. A Pew Research survey this year found that 74 percent of graduates from four-year colleges say that their education was "very useful in helping them grow intellectually." Sixty-nine percent said that "it was very useful in helping them grow and mature as a person" and 55 percent claimed that "it was very useful in helping prepare them for a job or career." Moreover, 86 percent of these graduates think "college has been a good investment for them personally."

Nonetheless, there is incessant talk about the "failure" of higher education. (Anthony Grafton at The New York Review of Books provides an excellent survey of recent discussions.) Much of this has to do with access: it's too expensive, admissions policies are unfair, the drop-out rate is too high. There is also dismay at the exploitation of graduate students and part-time faculty members, the over-emphasis on frills such as semi-professional athletics or fancy dorms and student centers, and the proliferation of expensive and unneeded administrators. As important as they are, these criticisms don't contradict the Pew Survey's favorable picture of the fundamental value of students' core educational experience.

But, as Grafton's discussion also makes clear, there are serious concerns about the quality of this experience. In particular, the university curriculum leaves students disengaged from the material they are supposed to be learning. They see most of their courses as intrinsically "boring," of value only if they provide training relevant to future employment or if the teacher has a pleasing (amusing, exciting, "relevant") way of presenting the material. As a result, students spend only as much time as they need to get what they see as acceptable grades (on average, about 12 to 14 hour a week for all courses combined). Professors have ceased to expect genuine engagement from students and often give good grades (B or better) to work that is at best minimally adequate.

This lack of academic engagement is real, even among schools with the best students and the best teachers, and it increases dramatically 5 as the quality of the school decreases. But it results from a basic misunderstanding—by both students and teachers—of what colleges are for.

First of all, they are not simply for the education of students. This is an essential function, but the raison d'être of a college is to nourish a world of intellectual culture; that is, a world of ideas, dedicated to what we can know scientifically, understand humanistically, or express artistically. In our society, this world is mainly populated by members of college faculties: scientists, humanists, social scientists (who straddle the humanities and the sciences properly speaking), and those who study the fine arts. Law, medicine and engineering are included to the extent that they are still understood as "learned professions," deploying practical skills that are nonetheless deeply rooted in scientific knowledge or humanistic understanding. When, as is often the case in business education and teacher training, practical skills far outweigh theoretical understanding, we are moving beyond the intellectual culture that defines higher education.

Our support for higher education makes sense only if we regard this intellectual culture as essential to our society. Otherwise, we could provide job-training and basic social and moral formation for young adults far more efficiently and cheaply, through, say, a combination of professional and trade schools, and public service programs. There would be no need to support, at great expense, the highly specialized interests of, for example, physicists, philosophers, anthropologists and art historians. Colleges and universities have no point if we do not value the knowledge and understanding to which their faculties are dedicated.

This has important consequences for how we regard what goes on in college classrooms. Teachers need to see themselves as, first of all, intellectuals, dedicated to understanding poetry, history, human psychology, physics, biology—or whatever is the focus of their discipline. But they also need to realize that this dedication expresses not just their idiosyncratic interest in certain questions but a conviction that those questions have general human significance, even apart from immediately practical applications. This is why a discipline requires not just research but also teaching. Non-experts need access to what experts have learned, and experts need to make sure that their research remains in contact with general human concerns. The classroom is the primary locus of such contact.

Students, in turn, need to recognize that their college education is above all a matter of opening themselves up to new dimensions of knowledge and understanding. Teaching is not a matter of (as we too often say) "*making* a subject (poetry, physics, philosophy) interesting" to students but of students coming to see how such subjects are *intrinsically* interesting. It is more a matter of students moving beyond their interests than of teachers fitting their subjects to interests that students already have. Good teaching does not make a course's subject more interesting; it gives the students more interests—and so makes them more interesting.

Students readily accept the alleged wisdom that their most important learning at college takes place outside the classroom. Many faculty members—thinking of their labs, libraries or studies—would agree. But the truth is that, for both students and faculty members, the classroom is precisely where the most important learning occurs.

STUDY QUESTIONS

1. According to Gutting's essay, what are some factors that may hamper the college experience for some students, and what are some factors that can foster student engagement with their education?

2. What EVIDENCE does Gutting provide for why he thinks college is important and "worth it"?

3. How does Gutting DESCRIBE successful students and teachers? What are some of the qualities that members of the two groups possess?

4. *For Writing.* Gutting argues that for students to succeed they need to be engaged—and to engage themselves—with their subjects. Consider your own educational career to this point, and write a brief essay in which you examine your own level of engagement with your classes. In which classes do you find yourself most engaged, and how can you cultivate the same kind of enthusiasm for your work in other courses?

SARAH WILENSKY { *Generation Plagiarism*

SARAH WILENSKY (b. 1989) studies law at Columbia University. Prior
to attending Columbia, she worked as an executive assistant in the U.S.
Senate. Wilensky wrote the following essay while she was a student at
Indiana University, where she earned a bachelor's degree in political
science.

Published in the *Indiana Daily Student* in 2010, "Generation
Plagiarism" takes on the case of a young German novelist who defended
herself against accusations of plagiarism by arguing that her generation
is simply accustomed to taking material from online sources and using
that material in their own work, often without attribution—in other
words, that older definitions of intellectual property and plagiarism
simply do not work as well as they once did. Wilensky disputes this
notion, arguing that many people of her generation do not understand
the importance of intellectual and academic integrity, despite the fact
that professors take steps both to instruct students on the importance of
academic honesty and to catch students who cheat. As you read, note
how Wilensky connects concerns raised by the German case to the lives
and work of her audience of college students at Indiana University.

IN SOME WAYS, IT'S NO surprise that Helene Hegemann, whose first
novel was just chosen as a finalist for the Leipzig Book Fair prize for
fiction despite serious concerns about plagiarism, is only seventeen
years old.

"Generation Plagiarism" by Sarah Wilensky from Indiana Daily Student, Feb. 15, 2010.
Reprinted by permission.

While many more mature fiction writers aspire to receive the widespread acclaim that has characterized Hegemann's entrance to the literary world, a shift in generational attitudes and practices around plagiarism are what make it less surprising that the story revolves around such a young woman.

Most mature fiction writers have not stolen entire pages of prose from other authors and then defended their action.

The *New York Times* reports that Hegemann sees herself as part of "a different generation, one that freely mixes and matches from the whirring flood of information across new and old media, to create something new."

Plagiarism is nothing new, and it may be that as more and more 5
information becomes readily accessible to more people via the Internet, we are simply able to identify plagiarism that would have gone unnoticed in years past.

I think something else is going on—we are the generation of "copy-paste." We write papers with our sources open in neighboring windows on the same laptop screen, and we have access to more of other peoples' ideas than ever before—without even getting off the sofa.

In a 300-level political science class, we spent nearly an entire day of lecture reviewing how to effectively write without any risk of being accused of plagiarism.

No professor would spend that amount of time nailing home what should be a completely assumed skill, unless her students had shown a desperate need for a review.

It's tempting to say new technology has created a blurry zone around what used to be a more clear-cut line defining plagiarism. Helene Hegemann certainly seems to think so.

But technology hasn't changed one relatively noncontroversial soci- 10
etally held moral: stealing the words and ideas of others is wrong and cannot be permitted.

The Leipzig Book Fair should immediately rescind its consideration of Ms. Hegemann's novel, as the literary community should be a leader in condemning plagiarism. Professors around this university should crack down on cases of academic dishonesty.

My guess is that if a professor or teaching assistant actually gave the big old F every time they wondered about a very familiar paragraph in a paper, our copy-paste generation would quickly learn how to write originally and cite appropriately.

Technology, in fact, can be the key to encouraging authentic composition. Easy access to information makes it possible to verify whether that familiar passage is indeed some other scholar's work, or a case of déjà vu.

Web resources make citations simple, and where all else fails, Turnitin.com inspires exactly the kind of fear that forces students to interact with their sources appropriately.

Helene Hegemann's defense is indicative of a real problem that 15 must be addressed at every level of the writing community.

In our own university classrooms, ambiguity should not be tolerated, and plagiarism should be regarded for what it is—not, as Hegemann suggests "mixing," but theft, pure and simple.

STUDY QUESTIONS

1. According to Sarah Wilensky, why do many younger writers feel that PLAGIARISM is not a serious matter, and what should teachers and school administrators do about the situation?

2. Although she starts the essay by discussing the German plagiarism case, how does Wilensky help her AUDIENCE of students at an American college see how the issues raised in Germany relate to their own academic work?

3. What REASONS does Wilensky identify from each side of the argument— those that support traditional views on academic honesty versus those that oppose them?

4. *For Writing.* Think about your own experience as a student today. In a short essay, write about some of the ways in which technology affects how you research and write your papers—for instance, do you favor finding information online instead of going to the library to conduct research? Why? Do you find yourself using those resources in different ways?

NEIL POSTMAN AND
STEVE POWERS

{ *The Bias of Language, the Bias of Pictures*

NEIL POSTMAN (1931–2003) is best known for his book *Amusing Ourselves to Death* (1986), a critique of the medium of television. He received his BS from the State University of New York at Fredonia and his MA and EdD degrees from Columbia University. He taught at New York University and eventually chaired the Department of Culture and Communication there. His other books include *The Disappearance of Childhood* (1982), *How to Watch TV News* (1992), and *The End of Education* (1996).

STEVE POWERS (b. 1934), born in New York City, has led a wide-ranging life: he has worked as a disc jockey, played jazz with Dizzy Gillespie, served as a Coast Guard officer in Puerto Rico, earned a business degree from the City University of New York and a PhD from New York University, and was a reporter and anchor for New York's Channel 5 News from 1980 to 1993, for which he was awarded an Emmy in 1981. He has also anchored newscasts for New York Times Radio. Powers has taught at the Columbia School of Journalism, the New School, New York University, and St. John's University.

In 1992 Postman and Powers collaborated to write *How to Watch TV News*. In the following selection from that book, they explain how television news programs transform events into very different forms, how they choose what to show, and their failure to help viewers impose meaning on events. By demonstrating the almost inescapable biases of language and the way pictures can distort our sense of what is "news," Postman and Powers reveal how television news presents "the world as a series of unrelated, fragmentary moments . . . without meaning, connections, or continuity." As you read, think about how television news shows, and other sources of news, have changed—and stayed the same—in the decades since *How to Watch TV News* was published.

<hr>

WHEN A TELEVISION NEWS SHOW distorts the truth by altering or manufacturing facts (through re-creations), a television viewer is defenseless even if a re-creation is properly labeled. Viewers are still vulnerable to misinformation since they will not know (at least in the case of docudramas) what parts are fiction and what parts are not. But the problems of verisimilitude posed by re-creations pale to insignificance when compared to the problems viewers face when encountering a straight (no-monkey-business) show. All news shows, in a sense, are re-creations in that what we hear and see on them are attempts to represent actual events, and are not the events themselves. Perhaps, to avoid ambiguity, we might call all news shows "re-presentations" instead of "re-creations." These re-presentations come to us in two forms: language and pictures. The question then arises: what do viewers have to know about language and pictures in order to be properly armed to defend themselves against the seductions of eloquence (to use Bertrand Russell's[1] apt phrase)?

Let us take language first. Below are three principles that, in our opinion, are an essential part of the analytical equipment a viewer must bring to any encounter with a news show.

1. WHATEVER ANYONE SAYS SOMETHING IS, IT ISN'T.

This sounds more complex—and maybe more pretentious—than it actually is. What it means is that there is a difference between the world of events and the world of words about events. The job of an honest reporter is to try to find words and the appropriate tone in presenting them that will come as close to evoking the event as possible. But since no two people will use exactly the same words to describe an event, we

---

[1]Philosopher, mathematician, and writer (1872–1970), whose essay "On Denoting" (1905) had a great influence on the study of language and linguistics.

must acknowledge that for every verbal description of an event, there are multiple possible alternatives. You may demonstrate this to your own satisfaction by writing a two-paragraph description of a dinner you had with at least two other people, then asking the others who were present if each of them would also write, independently, a two-paragraph description of the "same" dinner. We should be very surprised if all of the descriptions include the same words, in the same order, emphasize the same things, and express the same feelings. In other words, "the dinner itself" is largely a nonverbal event. The words people use to describe this event are not the event itself and are only abstracted re-presentations of the event. What does this mean for a television viewer? It means that the viewer must never assume that the words spoken on a television news show are exactly what happened. Since there are so many alternative ways of describing what happened, the viewer must be on guard against assuming that he or she has heard "the absolute truth."

2. LANGUAGE OPERATES AT VARIOUS LEVELS OF ABSTRACTION.

This means that there is a level of language whose purpose is to *describe* an event. There is also a level of language whose purpose is to *evaluate* an event. Even more, there is a level of language whose purpose is to *infer* what is unknown on the basis of what is known. The usual way to make these distinctions clear is through sentences such as the following three:

Manny Freebus is 5'8" and weighs 235 pounds.

Manny Freebus is grossly fat.

Manny Freebus eats too much.

The first sentence may be said to be language as pure description. It involves no judgments and no inferences. The second sentence is a description of sorts, but is mainly a judgment that the speaker makes of

5

the "event" known as Manny Freebus. The third sentence is an inference based on observations the speaker has made. It is, in fact, a statement about the unknown based on the known. As it happens, we know Manny Freebus and can tell you that he eats no more than the average person but suffers from a glandular condition which keeps him overweight. Therefore, anyone who concluded from observing Manny's shape that he eats too much has made a false inference. A good guess, but false nonetheless.

You can watch television news programs from now until doomsday and never come across any statement about Manny Freebus. But you will constantly come across the three kinds of statements we have been discussing—descriptions, judgments, and inferences. And it is important for a viewer to distinguish among them. For example, you might hear an anchor introduce a story by saying: "Today Congress ordered an investigation of the explosive issue of whether Ronald Reagan's presidential campaign made a deal with Iran in 1980 to delay the release of American hostages until after the election."[2] This statement is, of course, largely descriptive, but includes the judgmental word "explosive" as part of the report. We need hardly point out that what is explosive to one person may seem trivial to another. We do not say that the news writer has no business to include his or her judgment of this investigation. We do say that the viewer has to be aware that a judgment has been made. In fact, even the phrase "made a deal" (why not "arranged with Iran"?) has a somewhat sleazy connotation that implies a judgment of sorts. If, in the same news report, we are told that the evidence for such a secret deal is weak and that only an investigation with subpoena power can establish the truth, we must know that we have left the arena of factual language and have moved into the land of inference. An investigation with subpoena power may be a good idea but

---

[2]A reference to the charge, never proven, that while a candidate for the presidency Ronald Reagan secretly negotiated with the revolutionary government of Iran, promising that he would divert a supply of American arms to Iran in return for the Iranians' delaying the release of fifty-two American hostages until Reagan had defeated President Jimmy Carter and assumed the office himself. Minutes after Reagan was inaugurated in 1981, the hostages were freed.

whether or not it can establish the truth is a guess on the journalist's part, and a viewer ought to know that.

3. ALMOST ALL WORDS HAVE CONNOTATIVE MEANINGS.

This suggests that even when attempting to use purely descriptive language, a journalist cannot avoid expressing an attitude about what he or she is saying. For example, here is the opening sentence of an anchor's report about national examinations: "For the first time in the nation's history, high-level education policymakers have designed the elements for a national examination system similar to the one advocated by President Bush."[3] This sentence certainly looks like it is pure description although it is filled with ambiguities. Is this the first time in our history that this has been done? Or only the first time that high-level education policymakers have done it? Or is it the first time something has been designed that is similar to what the President has advocated? But let us put those questions aside. (After all, there are limits to how analytical one ought to be.) Instead, we might concentrate on such words as "high-level," "policymakers," and "designed." Speaking for ourselves, we are by no means sure that we know what a "high-level policymaker" is, although it sounds awfully impressive. It is certainly better than a "low-level policymaker," although how one would distinguish between the two is a bit of a mystery. Come to think of it, a low-level "policymaker" must be pretty good, too, since anyone who makes policy must be important. It comes as no surprise, therefore, that what was done was "designed." To design something usually implies careful thought, preparation, organization, and coherence. People design buildings, bridges, and furniture. If your experience has been anything like ours, you will know that reports are almost never designed; they are usually "thrown together," and it is quite a compliment to say that a report was designed. The journalist who paid this compliment was certainly entitled to do it even though he may not have been aware of what he was doing. He probably thought he had made a simple description, avoiding any words that would imply favor or disfavor. But if so, he was

[3]That is, George H. W. Bush (b. 1924), forty-first president of the United States.

defeated in his effort because language tends to be emotion-laden. Because it is people who do the talking, the talk almost always includes a feeling, an attitude, a judgment. In a sense, every language contains the history of a people's feelings about the world. Our words are baskets of emotion. Smart journalists, of course, know this. And so do smart audiences. Smart audiences don't blame anyone for this state of affairs. They are, however, prepared for it.

It is not our intention to provide here a mini-course in semantics. Even if we could, we are well aware that no viewer could apply analytic principles all the time or even much of the time. Anchors and reporters talk too fast and too continuously for any of us to monitor most of their sentences. Besides, who would want to do that for most of the stories on a news show? If you have a sense of what is important, you will probably judge most news stories to be fluff, or nonsense, or irrelevancies, not worthy of your analytic weaponry. But there are times when stories appear that are of major significance from your point of view. These are the times when your level of attention will reach a peak and you must call upon your best powers of interpretation. In those moments, you need to draw on whatever you know about the relationship between language and reality; about the distinctions among statements of fact, judgment, and inference; about the connotative meanings of words. When this is done properly, viewers are no longer passive consumers of news but active participants in a kind of dialogue between a news show and themselves. A viewer may even find that he or she is "talking back to the television set" (which is the title of a book by former FCC commissioner Nicholas Johnson). In our view, nothing could be healthier for the sanity and well-being of our nation than to have ninety million viewers talking back to their television news shows every night and twice on Sunday.

Now we must turn to the problem of pictures. It is often said that a picture is worth a thousand words. Maybe so. But it is probably equally true that one word is worth a thousand pictures, at least sometimes—for example, when it comes to understanding the world we live in. Indeed, the whole problem with news on television comes down to this: all the words uttered in an hour of news coverage could be printed on one page of a newspaper. And the world cannot be understood in one page. Of course, there is a compensation: television offers pictures, and the pictures move. Moving pictures are a kind of language in themselves, but the language of pictures differs radically from oral and written language, and the differences are crucial for understanding television news.

To begin with, pictures, especially single pictures, speak only in particularities. Their vocabulary is limited to concrete representation. Unlike words and sentences, a picture does not present to us an idea or concept about the world, except as we use language itself to convert the image to idea. By itself, a picture cannot deal with the unseen, the remote, the internal, the abstract. It does not speak of "man," only of *a* man; not of "tree," only of *a* tree. You cannot produce an image of "nature," any more than an image of "the sea." You can only show a particular fragment of the here-and-now—a cliff of a certain terrain, in a certain condition of light; a wave at a moment in time, from a particular point of view. And just as "nature" and "the sea" cannot be photographed, such larger abstractions as truth, honor, love, and falsehood cannot be talked about in the lexicon of individual pictures. For "showing of" and "talking about" are two very different kinds of processes: individual pictures give us the world as object; language, the world as idea. There is no such thing in nature as "man" or "tree." The universe offers no such categories or simplifications; only flux and infinite variety. The picture documents and celebrates the particularities of the universe's infinite variety. Language makes them comprehensible.

Of course, moving pictures, video with sound, may bridge the gap by juxtaposing images, symbols, sound, and music. Such images can present emotions and rudimentary ideas. They can suggest the panorama of nature and the joys and miseries of humankind.

Picture—smoke pouring from the window, cut to people coughing, an ambulance racing to a hospital, a tombstone in a cemetery.

Picture—jet planes firing rockets, explosions, lines of foreign soldiers surrendering, the American flag waving in the wind.

Nonetheless, keep in mind that when terrorists want to prove to the world that their kidnap victims are still alive, they photograph them holding a copy of a recent newspaper. The dateline on the newspaper provides the proof that the photograph was taken on or after that date.

Without the help of the written word, film and videotape cannot portray temporal dimensions with any precision. Consider a film clip showing an aircraft carrier at sea. One might be able to identify the ship as Soviet or American, but there would be no way of telling where in the world the carrier was, where it was headed, or when the pictures were taken. It is only through language—words spoken over the pictures or reproduced in them—that the image of the aircraft carrier takes on specific meaning.

Still, it is possible to enjoy the image of the carrier for its own sake. One might find the hugeness of the vessel interesting; it signifies military power on the move. There is a certain drama in watching the planes come in at high speeds and skid to a stop on the deck. Suppose the ship were burning: that would be even more interesting. This leads to an important point about the language of pictures. Moving pictures favor images that change. That is why violence and dynamic destruction find their way onto television so often. When something is destroyed violently it is altered in a highly visible way; hence the entrancing power of fire. Fire gives visual form to the ideas of consumption, disappearance, death—the thing that burned is actually taken away by fire. It is at this very basic level that fires make a good subject for television news. Something was here, now it's gone, and the change is recorded on film.

Earthquakes and typhoons have the same power. Before the viewer's eyes the world is taken apart. If a television viewer has relatives in Mexico City and an earthquake occurs there, then he or she may take a special interest in the images of destruction as a report from a specific place and time; that is, one may look at television pictures for information about an important event. But film of an earthquake can be interesting even if the viewer cares nothing about the event itself. Which is only to say, as we noted earlier, that there is another way of participating in the news—as a spectator who desires to be entertained. Actually to see buildings topple is exciting, no matter where the buildings are. The world turns to dust before our eyes.

Those who produce television news in America know that their medium favors images that move. That is why they are wary of "talking heads," people who simply appear in front of a camera and speak.

When talking heads appear on television, there is nothing to record or document, no change in process. In the cinema the situation is somewhat different. On a movie screen, close-ups of a good actor speaking dramatically can sometimes be interesting to watch. When Clint Eastwood narrows his eyes and challenges his rival to shoot first, the spectator sees the cool rage of the Eastwood character take visual form, and the narrowing of the eyes is dramatic. But much of the effect of this small movement depends on the size of the movie screen and the darkness of the theater, which make Eastwood and his every action "larger than life."

The television screen is smaller than life. It occupies about 15 percent of the viewer's visual field (compared to about 70 percent for the movie screen). It is not set in a darkened theater closed off from the world but in the viewer's ordinary living space. This means that visual changes must be more extreme and more dramatic to be interesting on television. A narrowing of the eyes will not do. A car crash, an earthquake, a burning factory are much better.

With these principles in mind, let us examine more closely the structure of a typical newscast, and here we will include in the discussion not only the pictures but all the nonlinguistic symbols that make up a television news show. For example, in America, almost all news shows begin with music, the tone of which suggests important events about to unfold. The music is very important, for it equates the news with various forms of drama and ritual—the opera, for example, or a wedding procession—in which musical themes underscore the meaning of the event. Music takes us immediately into the realm of the symbolic, a world that is not to be taken literally. After all, when events unfold in the real world, they do so without musical accompaniment. More symbolism follows. The sound of teletype machines can be heard in the studio, not because it is impossible to screen this noise out, but because the sound is a kind of music in itself. It tells us that data are pouring in from all corners of the globe, a sensation reinforced by the world map in the background (or clocks noting the time on different continents). The fact is that teletype machines are rarely used in TV news rooms, having been replaced by silent computer terminals. When seen, they have only a symbolic function.

Already, then, before a single news item is introduced, a great deal 20
has been communicated. We know that we are in the presence of a
symbolic event, a form of theater in which the day's events are to be
dramatized. This theater takes the entire globe as its subject, although
it may look at the world from the perspective of a single nation. A certain tension is present, like the atmosphere in a theater just before the
curtain goes up. The tension is represented by the music, the staccato
beat of the teletype machines, and often the sight of news workers scur-
rying around typing reports and answering phones. As a technical matter, it would be no problem to build a set in which the newsroom staff
remained off camera, invisible to the viewer, but an important theatri-
cal effect would be lost. By being busy on camera, the workers help
communicate urgency about the events at hand, which suggests that
situations are changing so rapidly that constant revision of the news is
necessary.

The staff in the background also helps signal the importance of the
person in the center, the anchor, "in command" of both the staff and
the news. The anchor plays the role of host. He or she welcomes us to
the newscast and welcomes us back from the different locations we
visit during the filmed reports.

Many features of the newscast help the anchor to establish the
impression of control. These are usually equated with production values in broadcasting. They include such things as graphics that tell the
viewer what is being shown, or maps and charts that suddenly appear
on the screen and disappear on cue, or the orderly progression from
story to story. They also include the absence of gaps, or "dead time,"
during the broadcast, even the simple fact that the news starts and ends
at a certain hour. These common features are thought of as purely technical matters, which a professional crew handles as a matter of course.
But they are also symbols of a dominant theme of television news: the
imposition of an orderly world—called "the news"—upon the disor-
derly flow of events.

While the form of a news broadcast emphasizes tidiness and control, its content can best be described as fragmented. Because time is
so precious on television, because the nature of the medium favors
dynamic visual images, and because the pressures of a commercial

structure require the news to hold its audience above all else, there is rarely any attempt to explain issues in depth or place events in their proper context. The news moves nervously from a warehouse fire to a court decision, from a guerrilla war to a World Cup match, the quality of the film most often determining the length of the story. Certain stories show up only because they offer dramatic pictures. Bleachers collapse in South America: hundreds of people are crushed—a perfect television news story, for the cameras can record the face of disaster in all its anguish. Back in Washington, a new budget is approved by Congress. Here there is nothing to photograph because a budget is not a physical event; it is a document full of language and numbers. So the producers of the news will show a photo of the document itself, focusing on the cover where it says "Budget of the United States of America." Or sometimes they will send a camera crew to the government printing plant where copies of the budget are produced. That evening, while the contents of the budget are summarized by a voice-over, the viewer sees stacks of documents being loaded into boxes at the government printing plant. Then a few of the budget's more important provisions will be flashed on the screen in written form, but this is such a time-consuming process—using television as a printed page—that the producers keep it to a minimum. In short, the budget is not televisable, and for that reason its time on the news must be brief. The bleacher collapse will get more time that evening.

While appearing somewhat chaotic, these disparate stories are not just dropped in the news program helter-skelter. The appearance of a scattershot story order is really orchestrated to draw the audience from one story to the next—from one section to the next—through the commercial breaks to the end of the show. The story order is constructed to hold and build the viewership rather than place events in context or explain issues in depth.

Of course, it is a tendency of journalism in general to concentrate on the surface of events rather than underlying conditions; this is as true for the newspaper as it is for the newscast. But several features of television undermine whatever efforts journalists may make to give sense to the world. One is that a television broadcast is a series of events that occur in sequence, and the sequence is the same for all 25 viewers. This is not true for a newspaper page, which displays many items simultaneously, allowing readers to choose the order in which they read them. If newspaper readers want only a summary of the latest tax bill, they can read the headline and the first paragraph of an article, and if they want more, they can keep reading. In a sense, then, everyone reads a different newspaper, for no two readers will read (or ignore) the same items.

But all television viewers see the same broadcast. They have no choices. A report is either in the broadcast or out, which means that anything which is of narrow interest is unlikely to be included. As NBC News executive Reuven Frank once explained:

> A newspaper, for example, can easily afford to print an item of conceivable interest to only a fraction of its readers. A television news program must be put together with the assumption that each item will be of some interest to everyone that watches. Every time a newspaper includes a feature which will attract a specialized group it can assume it is adding at least a little bit to its circulation. To the degree a television news program includes an item of this sort . . . it must assume that its audience will diminish.

The need to "include everyone," an identifying feature of commercial television in all its forms, prevents journalists from offering lengthy or complex explanations, or from tracing the sequence of events leading up to today's headlines. One of the ironies of political life in modern democracies is that many problems which concern the "general welfare" are of interest only to specialized groups. Arms control, for example, is an issue that literally concerns everyone in the world, and yet the language of arms control and the complexity of the subject are so daunting that only a minority of people can actually follow the issue from week to week and month to month. If it wants to act responsibly, a newspaper can at least make available more information about arms control than most people want. Commercial television cannot afford to do so.

But even if commercial television could afford to do so, it wouldn't. The fact that television news is principally made up of moving pictures prevents it from offering lengthy, coherent explanations of events. A television news show reveals the world as a series of unrelated, fragmentary moments. It does not—and cannot be expected to—offer a sense of coherence or meaning. What does this suggest to a TV viewer? That the viewer must come with a prepared mind—information, opinions, a sense of proportion, an articulate value system. To the TV viewer lacking such mental equipment, a news program is only a kind of rousing light show. Here a falling building, there a five-alarm fire, everywhere the world as an object, much without meaning, connections, or continuity.

STUDY QUESTIONS

1. Explain the similarity, from the standpoint of television news, of fires, earthquakes, and typhoons. Why do such events interest viewers? What two functions can pictures of an earthquake serve? What is a "talking head"?

2. List several points of CONTRAST that Postman and Powers make between newspapers and television news. How does language play a part in each medium?

3. What is the authors' THESIS? Select several examples of CAUSE AND EFFECT found in the selection and explain how they support that thesis.

4. Consider news from media that Postman and Powers do not address, such as the radio and the Internet, and COMPARE how they present the news to how television news shows do. How would *you* ANALYZE the ways people process news from the radio? The Internet?

5. *For Writing.* Postman and Powers write about three different kinds of language: description, evaluation, and inference. (Description here does not refer to the same kind of DESCRIPTION that is often taught in writing classes, with its attention to detail and DOMINANT IMPRESSION.) Watch a television news program and take notes on the language that the reporters and anchors use. Then, write an essay in which you analyze their speech for these three kinds of language. Be sure to explain not only how they speak, but also why that matters and what it says about their reporting.

DAVID SHIPLEY { *How to Write*

AND WILL SCHWALBE { *(the Perfect) Email*

DAVID SHIPLEY (b. 1963) is the Op-Ed editor of the *New York Times*.
From 1995 to 1997 he served the Clinton administration as a special assistant to the president and speechwriter. Prior to his White House experience,
he was the executive editor of the *New Republic*.

WILL SCHWALBE (b. 1962) works in the field of new media and served as
senior vice president and editor-in-chief of both Hyperion Books and
William Morrow. He is on the board of governors of Yale University Press.
Schwalbe has a background in journalism and has written for such pub-
lications as the *New York Times*, *Ms.* magazine, and the *South China
Morning Post*.

Shipley and Schwalbe collaborated on *Send: Why People Email So
Badly and How to Do It Better* (2007). In the following selection from
that book, the authors instruct readers on how to write the "perfect"
e-mail, taking into account such elements as word choice, spelling, grammar,
and emoticons. The key, they say, is to consider carefully your relationship
to the person who will receive your message. As you read these instructions,
think about the kind of e-mails that you send and receive on a daily basis.
Do they follow Shipley and Schwalbe's guidelines? If not, why not?

THE FACT THAT EMAIL IS a searchable, storable medium means that
you have to compose your message with special care. And the fact that
you are writing—constructing sentences, choosing words, making
grammatical decisions, adding punctuation—with previously unimag-
inable swiftness makes the situation all the more vexed, as does the

delusion that email, because it's electronic, is somehow more ephemeral than, say, a letter.

Also, because it's *often* acceptable to be lax about the rules of grammar on email, there's the misconception that it's *always* acceptable to be lax about them. That's not the case. We aren't going to offer a guide to style and usage here—lots of books have done that already and done it well. What we are going to do, though, is outline the implications of taking risks with your English in emails and review the stylistic traps that are peculiar to the medium.

CHOOSING THE RIGHT WORDS

In Japanese, the status of the person you are addressing governs the words you use. A sentence directed toward a peer, for instance, requires different word forms from one directed to someone higher or lower than you on the social ladder. (You use one word form when speaking to your boss, another to a colleague, yet another to a child.) Learning Japanese, then, requires learning multiple ways of saying the same thing. The need to remember which kind of word form to use is one of the elements that makes it hard for native English speakers to master Japanese.

What many people don't consider, however, is that in this respect English is arguably more complicated than Japanese—precisely because English doesn't offer the convenience of different words to signal that you know the nature of your social relationship to the person with whom you are speaking. In lieu of specific words to show deference—or familiarity—English relies heavily on the delicate manipulation of tone.

More than anything else, vocabulary conveys tone and reveals you as boss or subordinate, buyer or seller, seeker or sage. The words you choose can be formal, casual, or somewhere in between; they can be literal or figurative; they can be precise or vague; understated, correct, or exaggerated; simple or complex; common or rare; prosaic or poetic; contracted or not.

Certainly, some words are inherently safer than others, but if you never venture beyond them you become yet another unmemorable correspondent, ceding the chance to make an impression in your email. Think of your own inbox. When wading through an ocean of emails, don't you yearn for one to jump out? After a hundred people email you that they "look forward to meeting you" so that they can share their "qualifications" or "describe the benefits of their product" or present you with a "business opportunity," you crave something by someone who took the time to choose words with personality, rather than simply cribbing phrases from the modern business lexicon. The trick is to be vivid and specific—even, perhaps, revealing—without forgetting your original relationship with the person to whom you're writing.

On the most elemental level, the deal is this. Before you set finger to keyboard, ask yourself one question (and don't write until you get the answer): *What is my relationship to the person I'm writing?* Then, make sure your word choice is appropriate.

* * *

MISSPELLINGS

If careful word choice is the ultimate goal, then accidental word choice is the ultimate pitfall. There is a big difference between poor spelling that reads as sloppiness and poor spelling that results in an entirely different word appearing from the one intended. As people have increasingly come to rely on computer spell-check programs, they've also become increasingly susceptible to creating documents where an entirely wrong, albeit correctly spelled, word has found its way into the text. When the word is obviously wrong ("sned," not "send"), then the recipient will probably guess correctly that you simply failed to proof the document. But when a word is more subtly wrong, then at best she may think you didn't know the meaning of the word you used; at worst she will assume the wrong word was the chosen one, and judge you accordingly.

A computer won't flag "affect" when you meant "effect." If you want your battery changed because it can no longer safely hold a charge, the ramifications if you accidentally ask for it to be charged instead of changed could be disastrous. Will once received an unintentionally humorous note about a film called *The Dangerous Lives of Alter Boys,* except that "Alter" was supposed to be "Altar." The sender intended the Subject line to refer to helpful Catholic children and not castrati.

A friend once received an email that said: 10

> am in Pqris trying to flog q book or 3—bugger French keyboqrds and forgive the ,istqkes: Will e,qil you over the weekend: Clips qrrived todqy qnd very many thqnks.

This is actually a charming example of what would otherwise be a disastrous piece of correspondence. It's saved because its meaning is still clear, it was among pals, and the misspellings are both ubiquitous and cheerfully acknowledged. The point is not that you should never misspell a word, but that you should be aware of how it will be received when you do.

GRAMMAR

Grammar is as important in determining tone as word choice is. The very same words, in different combinations, may or may not mean the same thing. But even if they mean the same thing, they may or may not convey the same tone. The examples used here aren't confined to email because good writing is good writing, no matter the medium.

Bad grammar isn't always wrong. "It ain't over till it's over" isn't right, but it's both memorable and effective. But even good grammar has its pitfalls. A simple sentence can be direct and unvarnished and perfectly appropriate. Or it can come across as childish or dictatorial. A complex sentence can sound conversational or elegant; it can also seem blathering or pompous.

Here's how simple grammar can be used to great effect.

On February 15, 1963, President John F. Kennedy wrote the following memo to Robert McNamara, his secretary of defense, after he had learned that the new military attaché to Laos, a former French colony, had only limited knowledge of French. The memo draws its power from a series of spare sentences, one after another, most sharing the same grammatical pattern, all but the last starting with a first-person pronoun.

I do not see how he can be effective in Laos without knowledge of the language. I would think that the Army must have many officers who have language facility. I would like to receive a report on whether attachés are expected to have a language facility in French or Spanish before they are sent to countries where these languages are spoken. I do not think we should expect an attaché to pick up the language upon his arrival there. Would you let me have your thoughts on this.

The president doesn't say he's annoyed, miffed, perplexed, or that he never wants this to happen again. He doesn't need to, because his disapproval is conveyed by the grammar. The structure is austere; the language is plain; the message is clear. The last sentence, "Would you let me have your thoughts on this," translates to "Please make sure this never happens again." 15

Obviously, this tone is appropriate for a subordinate and not a peer. But even presidents have peers. When Kennedy wrote to Soviet premier Nikita Khrushchev on the subject of space travel, his grammar turned expansive, complex, almost lyrical.

> Beyond these specific projects we are prepared now to discuss broader cooperation in the still more challenging projects which must be undertaken in the exploration of outer space. The tasks are so challenging, the costs so great, and the risks to the brave men who engage in space exploration so grave, that we must in all good conscience try every possibility of sharing these tasks and costs and of minimizing the risks.

In both cases, Kennedy knew who he wanted to be in relation to the person to whom he was writing—peeved boss to McNamara, visionary partner to fellow world leader Khrushchev.

But what if one of your peers gets out of line? Look at this letter from Kennedy to Khrushchev during the Cuban missile crisis, which echoes the note to McNamara in both structure and tone.

> I have taken careful note of your statement that the events in Cuba might affect peace in all parts of the world. I trust that this does not mean that

the Soviet government, using the situation in Cuba as a pretext, is planning to inflame other areas of the world. I would like to think that your government has too great a sense of responsibility to embark upon any enterprise so dangerous to general peace. . . . I believe, Mr. Chairman, that you should recognize that free peoples in all parts of the world do not accept the claim of historical inevitability for Communist revolution.

The Kennedy letters illustrate two surefire grammar guidelines, ones we'd all do well to keep in mind every time we dash off an email that's more than a sentence long:

1. Simple, short, repetitive grammar intensifies.

2. Complex, clause-filled, rhythmically varied sentences generally soften the message.

PUNCTUATION

It's OK to be lax so long as you're on email and on familiar terms with the person to whom you're writing. With handhelds and IMing, the rules are even looser. 20

It's useful to remind ourselves that punctuation originated as a reading tool. It was developed at a time when anyone who could write wrote by hand. Punctuation was a lifeline in a sea of poor handwriting and ink blotches. But email is completely legible. Generally, you can understand what someone is trying to tell you—even if periods and commas are dropped and paragraphs are littered with dashes.

Still, relaxed punctuation can do damage in a way that heedless uppercasing and lowercasing cannot. Punctuation is in some measure governed by your relationship to the person you're writing. If it's someone senior to you, punctuate correctly. If the email you received was properly punctuated, your correspondent deserves the same. This is something that's easy to forget. The speed, fluidity, and back-and-forth of email make it easier for all sorts of punctuation tics to creep into our writing. Witness, for example, the (confounding) growth in the use of trailing punctuation. "See you next summer . . ." or "We can just discuss this in the meeting . . ."

or "I lost my balloon . . ." We realize that email is often an ongoing conversation, but what's so bad about a period?

And note: any kind of relaxed punctuation is not appropriate in letters or memos. Also, keep in mind that even in email, if you drop, for example, an important comma, you can change the meaning of a sentence 180 degrees.

THE DANGERS OF MISSING PUNCTUATION

A friend of ours worked in an office where an email flame war erupted over a missing period. The email in question read:

No thanks to you.

It was supposed to say:

No. Thanks to you.

PARAGRAPHS

Keep them short.

Otherwise, people won't be able to read your emails easily on a computer screen.

Make sure you break a paragraph when you shift topics.

The key point or instruction should never be buried in a long paragraph.

Don't fear white space.

CONTRACTIONS

Our language comes with an option for paring the fat out of a sentence: contractions. But many people who constantly use contractions in speech will avoid them in writing. The colleague who says, "I don't know whether to get a cappuccino or a latte today," will minutes later write an email stating, "I do not know whether we should send the shipment today or tomorrow." The tone of the latter is more formal and can strike the ear as awkward or fussy; in addition, because it places more emphasis on the "not," it sounds more severe. Email—flat, informal, democratic email—should encourage us to use contractions in a way we'd never use them in formal letters.

In email, *not* contracting comes with a risk. As with so much else, it 30 all goes back to childhood. Parents tend to avoid contractions when teaching small children a lesson. "Do NOT put your fingers in the soup bowl, Elliott (or Ben or Natalie or Sophie); I am telling you that for the last time and I am NOT going to tell you again." The word "don't" is a warning; the phrase "do not" is both a warning and a reprimand. The uncontracted form puts the reader in young Elliott's place, and makes him feel as if he's being lectured by an authority figure. This can be useful when the warning you are giving is dire: the directive "Do not let the nuclear reactor overheat" is strengthened by the use of the freestanding "not." But "Do not make extra copies of the report" would probably be better served by a "don't," unless you mean to suggest that there will be dire consequences for doing so.

And this point isn't confined to contractions of the word "not." Many noncontractions manage to make the recipient feel scolded. The person who says, "I am upset," is probably more upset than the one who says, "I'm upset." In most general email correspondence, the contraction should be the default, the uncontracted form used for special emphasis.

CAPITALS

When words are written in CAPITAL LETTERS, it means that THE WRITER IS SHOUTING AT YOU. Since no one likes to be yelled at, and people generally shout when they feel that they can win only by intimidation and not by reason, it's a good rule never to compose entire emails in capitals, even cheery ones. For one thing, they're just that much harder to read because we aren't used to reading large blocks of capitalized text. And rarely is it a good idea to capitalize pejorative words—IDIOT, for example. These words are that much harsher when capitalized.

(You can, however, shout a word or two in joy or celebration. HOORAY is a word that is appropriately capitalized. It's a loud word that no one minds hearing louder. Ditto for CONGRATULATIONS and BON APPETIT.)

If you really want to aggravate someone, using all caps is an effective way to do it. A study of email users in the United States and Britain found that overuse of capitals was the thing that most irritated email recipients. (Emails that conveyed an overly friendly tone also made the most-annoying list, but only in the United Kingdom.)

Oddly, writing only in lowercase doesn't indicate the opposite of shouting—no one thinks you are whispering when you abstain from using capital letters. They just think you are too lazy to hit the Shift key from time to time. As with typos and abbreviations, people are more forgiving of this when they know you are sending them a message from a mobile device than when you are clearly at a desktop. There is, however, an implied casualness to all-lowercase communication. Generally, it's acceptable from an employer to an employee but not the other way around, among friends or colleagues, and especially in very short replies. But it's industry-specific—at many companies it's more the rule than the exception. When in doubt, though, capitalize normally, especially if someone wrote to you that way.

EMOTICONS

Even though we're well out of junior high, we like emoticons and think there are good uses for them. Pictographic smiling faces and those created out of punctuation marks—☺ and :)—bug many people but they make us smile. (So, of course, does sunshine on our shoulders.) Emoticons are an attempt to put a human face on faceless, quick communication. We also love the whole emoticon family, though we must admit that some of the more baroque manifestations can leave us perplexed—by what they are supposed to be and by when we'd use them. For example, =) :–)= is Abraham Lincoln and :OI is mouth full.

Emoticons are handy for the following:

1. They're great for text and instant messages and rapid-fire emails because they're really just a kind of shorthand.

2. They're helpful if you want to be cute, ironic, or tongue-in-cheek when writing those with whom you've already established a comfortable electronic correspondence. Certainly, you can use them with others who have used them with you.

However, emoticons should never be deployed when:

1. You're writing any kind of formal email or electronic message.

2. You're trying to compensate for a barb, a risky joke, or a sarcastic comment; the addition of an emoticon doesn't guarantee that there won't be hurt feelings.

* * *

ABBREVIATIONS

Abbreviations are like emoticons. They have an important function. FWIW (for what it's worth), PCM (please call me), W8 (wait)—all these facilitate communication, and in some cases they either help to bond people together in a shared language or are simply taken for granted. Whether an abbreviation seems silly or outlandish depends on where you sit. After all, is LOL, which some people sneer at, really inherently more opaque than FYI?

Of course, when the conversation is formal or you're not sure the other person knows the code, spell words out. 40

* * *

STUDY QUESTIONS

1. The authors list a number of elements that comprise a "perfect" e-mail. Which do you think are the most important? The least important? Why? They also list a number of e-mail hazards. Which are the worst? Why?

2. Consider this selection as a piece of advice. Evaluate its TONE, as well as the quality and quantity of examples provided. Are they effective? Are you likely to follow these authors' advice? Why or why not?

3. *For Writing.* Review a week's worth of e-mails that you have sent to your friends, instructors, and family. In an essay, ANALYZE your writing STYLE in each kind of e-mail. Do you see any kinds of patterns? How do you write differently for your different AUDIENCES? Does this analysis make you reconsider the way you write e-mail?

DEREK BOK { *Preparing for a Career*

DEREK BOK (b. 1930) earned his BA at Stanford University in 1951, his law degree at Harvard Law School in 1954, and his MA at George Washington University in 1958. After teaching law at Harvard, he served as the dean of the law school from 1968 until 1971, when he became the university's president, a position he held for twenty years. His books on education include *Beyond the Ivory Tower* (1984), *Universities and the Future of America* (1990), and *Universities in the Marketplace* (2003).

In "Preparing for a Career," Bok challenges what he considers to be the elitist notion that vocational training has no place in a liberal arts curriculum. In fact, he argues, the vocational and the liberal arts could merge, producing a student who is better prepared for the world of work. As you read, consider Bok's ethos as the president of one of the most elite liberal arts colleges in the United States. How persuasive is his argument? Should the vocational and the liberal arts be integrated?

VOCATIONAL COURSES HAVE LONG BEEN a burr under the saddle of those who teach the liberal arts. According to one survey, 60 percent of Arts and Sciences professors do not even think that preparing for a good job is a particularly important goal for undergraduates. In sharp contrast, almost three-fourths entering freshmen regard it as the *most* important reason for going to college. One can easily understand why students feel this way. Most of them will spend more time making a living over the next several decades than they will doing anything else. The careers they choose and the success they achieve at work will have a great deal to do with defining who they are, how satisfied they feel about their lives, and how comfortably they will live. No wonder they take their careers so seriously. The puzzle is that so few liberal arts teachers seem to agree.

Why are these professors so cool to the vocational needs of their students? How can they educate young people in so many ways and for so many purposes yet refuse to help prepare them for the work that will shape their future lives so profoundly?

Part of the explanation, surely, is the tendency of much vocational education to offer training without intellectual depth.[1] However worthy their place in the economic order, hotel management, mortuary science, and public relations do not engage the frontiers of thought in the same way as mathematics, physics, or philosophy. Much of what students need to prepare for these callings takes the form of practical skills rather than the kinds of knowledge that are the intellectual's stock in trade. To many liberal arts professors, such competencies should be either learned on the job or taught in some kind of trade school, but surely not studied in a university under the tutelage of scholars.

Another contributing cause is the fear that students will be so concerned about their careers that, once vocational education gains a foothold in the college, it will spread like crabgrass and eventually take over the entire curriculum. Money and commercialization already exert undue influence over university behavior. Making room for vocational training will arguably exacerbate these worrisome trends. Undergraduates are deeply preoccupied with succeeding in their careers, especially in a world they perceive as increasingly competitive and in constant flux. Given the opportunity, they may well neglect other purposes of undergraduate education in their eagerness to take any course that promises to give them a competitive edge in the struggle for success and financial security.

---

[1] It should be noted that evidence is mixed on whether the vocational emphasis of a college either helps or hinders the development of cognitive ability (including critical thinking skills); Ernest T. Pascarella and Patrick T. Terenzini, *How College Affects Students*, Vol. 2, pp. 172–73. [Author's note.]

At the same time, the threat posed by vocational courses cannot be 5 removed by simply ignoring their existence. Denying vocational concerns any place in the curriculum will diminish the chance to help undergraduates think about their careers in terms broader than simply making money. Moreover, such opposition is impractical in any event. Since students can choose which college to attend, market pressures force institutions to give them the practical training they desire. University officials who worry about filling the seats in the college cannot afford the fantasy that finding a job is a matter of little consequence. They understand full well the depth of student desire to prepare for a career. As a result, apart from a few score institutions that remain wholly dedicated to the liberal arts, virtually all colleges have established vocational majors, often separated from Arts and Sciences in schools of their own.

The question, then, is not whether to banish all vocational courses but whether to join in giving students a larger view of the professions that goes beyond mere skills training. Unfortunately, in universities with both liberal arts and vocational faculties, cooperation has been conspicuous by its absence. According to one report, "In many colleges and universities, a lamentable chasm separates the liberal arts college and professional departments. Competition for resources is keen, autonomy is jealously guarded, and cross-disciplinary discourse is fraught with difficulty."

Liberal arts faculties have paid a heavy price for their ostrich-like response to the demand for practical courses. Given a choice, students have deserted the traditional disciplines in droves. Today 60 percent of all college seniors are majoring in a vocational program. Whereas substantial majorities once chose a liberal arts concentration, only about one-third do so now. The rest must often make their way through programs that receive little help from Arts and Sciences faculties to ensure that the courses students take outside their vocational majors afford them the full benefit of a first-rate liberal education.

These disadvantages have finally begun to persuade some Arts and Sciences faculties to reexamine their connections with vocational education and think about responding to students' employment concerns in new and creative ways. The challenge is critical, and not just for practical reasons. Successfully met, it could invigorate both the liberal arts and vocational programs while accomplishing much to serve the needs of undergraduates.

* * *

VOCATIONAL MAJORS

Most college seniors do not move directly to an advanced degree program after they graduate; they look for work. Since the average length of time people stay in their first job has shrunk dramatically, more and more employers want their employees to "hit the ground running" without having to receive costly training from the company. As a result, undergraduates today are more likely than ever to feel that they must not only choose a career but also prepare themselves for a job while still in college. Spurred by competition for students, university officials have responded by mounting a wide array of vocational majors ranging from traditional staples, such as business and engineering, to such exotic entries as prison administration, sports management, and even video game design.

There has long been disagreement over whether vocational majors 10 are actually better preparation for a career than a liberal arts degree. In most cases, the answer depends on the line of work a student wishes to pursue. Undergraduates who plan to move directly into a highly specialized or technical career had best enroll in vocational programs. No employer looking for an engineer or a hospital technician will be eager to hire someone with a major in English literature. On the other hand, students who expect to take a professional degree in law or medicine will be well advised to follow a liberal arts program in college and leave their vocational training for later. The choice is not so clear, however, for undergraduates who want to find some sort of managerial or supervisory job in business without acquiring an M.B.A. Should such students select a business major or take a traditional liberal arts degree? Since many thousands of undergraduates face this choice every year, the question has considerable practical importance.

A number of researchers have tried to supply an answer. Their work seems to show that vocational majors have an easier time than liberal arts graduates in finding an initial job in business and tend to advance faster and earn more money during their first 10 years of work. After 10 years, the picture becomes more complicated. As time goes on, the technical and practical skills that vocational majors learn in college become less important to continued success. Such abilities as communication skills, human relations, creativity, and "big-picture thinking" matter more. Since liberal arts faculties appear to do a better job than their vocational colleagues in fostering these qualities, graduates with traditional Arts and Sciences majors begin to gain ground. Within the ranks of top management, neither liberal arts nor vocational majors have an advantage.

Studies also show that the nature of one's education has a bearing on *what kind* of position one will occupy in business. Management and engineering majors tend to gravitate toward careers in accounting, production, and finance. Their comparative advantage seems to lie in manufacturing companies. Liberal arts majors are more likely to specialize in marketing, human resources, or public affairs and to move into companies in the service sector.

Future trends are harder to predict. Corporations are becoming more technical and science based, trends that favor business and engineering majors. On the other hand, companies also seem destined to witness faster change, more frequent career shifts, increasingly diverse workforces, and expanding global operations, all of which favor a broad liberal arts education.

In light of these findings, what can one say about the choice between liberal arts and vocational degrees? All in all, though many undergraduates may be excessively concerned with getting a job and earning money, it is hard to fault them for choosing vocational programs. The degrees they earn are essential for many technical jobs and offer advantages in business for at least a decade following graduation. Even in the longer run, there is little indication that students with business degrees will suffer a disadvantage. The practical question, then, is not whether many students are unwisely choosing vocational majors but whether *both* liberal arts *and* vocational programs could do a better job of reconciling the career needs of students with the other goals of a rounded undergraduate education.

How should vocational majors be constructed to respect the other 15 important aims of college? In principle, the guidelines seem fairly clear. Like all majors, vocational programs should not take up so much space in the curriculum that other important educational goals must be sacrificed. Professors should not spend valuable time teaching skills better learned at work, nor ought they to be excessively preoccupied with teaching competencies that may be relevant to a first job but will soon become obsolete. Since critical thinking is as important to almost every occupation as it is to the liberal arts, instructors should try to use active methods of teaching with appropriate feedback. Moreover, because there is more to a calling than making money, vocational concentrations should offer breadth and perspective by including material on the history of the profession, its current role in society, and the recurring moral dilemmas that practitioners face in carrying out their work. Finally, like all majors, vocational programs should include some sort of culminating project that gives students an opportunity to increase their powers of reasoning and analysis by exploring a challenging problem in depth.

How successful are the more prominent occupational majors in meeting these specifications?[2]

* * *

[2] In a section omitted here because of space concerns, Bok details the requirements of the three most prominent occupational majors. Of these, engineering is considered the most academically rigorous because of the many required math, science, and technical courses. However, engineering programs are often criticized for doing little to help their students develop communication skills, cultural sensitivity, ethical guidelines, or the ability to collaborate—all important components of a well-rounded education. Education programs, on the other hand, while meeting many of the requirements of a well-rounded education because of their recommended course work in the liberal arts, are criticized for not being rigorous enough. Courses in education history, pedagogy, and curriculum planning are perceived as poorly conceived and shallow. Finally, business schools offer the most popular occupational degree, but here too there is concern over curricular breadth and depth. While business colleges do require students to take a number of liberal arts courses, employers have found that business graduates have poor writing and speaking skills, poor critical thinking skills, and poor leadership skills, and lack "ethical sensitivity."

LIBERAL ARTS MAJORS

Many undergraduates who plan to move directly to a job and know what sort of job they want still seek a liberal arts degree. What, if anything, should colleges do to prepare these students for their careers? This issue rarely arises in debates about liberal education. While participants often question whether vocational programs are consistent with a suitably rounded education, they seldom inquire whether liberal arts programs are sufficiently respectful of undergraduates' desire for a successful, satisfying career. More's the pity. A well-crafted college curriculum, even if it offers no vocational majors, can do much to help students find jobs and fare well in their chosen careers.

The most important step that Arts and Sciences faculties can take is simply to do a better job of achieving the traditional goals of liberal education. As previously noted, when business leaders describe what they most need from the young managers and engineers they employ, they regularly stress not only strong communications skills and an ability to think critically and solve problems, but also a capacity to collaborate with others and work with diverse populations, a sensitivity to ethical problems, a strong self-discipline, and—for increasing numbers of companies—an appreciation of global issues and an ability to understand foreign cultures. These are all important aims of a liberal education and are accepted by almost every college faculty. As previous chapters have pointed out, however, many students graduate having made only modest progress in acquiring these capabilities. That is why employers who complain about the college graduates they hire grumble not only about the lack of sufficient technical and vocational skills but also about deficiencies in speaking, writing, and other competencies long associated with a traditional college education.

A very different complaint from employers is that many of the young B.A. recipients they hire are lacking in self-discipline. According to their superiors, they often have difficulty being on time, working hard enough to do each job well, or listening carefully and following instructions. In view of these concerns, it is worth asking whether faculties themselves are not partially to blame by permitting a certain laxity to become entrenched on many campuses. Colleges have allowed widespread grade inflation and shown increased tolerance of late or incomplete work. As George Kuh points out after surveying hundreds of colleges, "There seems to be a breakdown of shared responsibility for learning—on the part of faculty members who allow students to get by with far less than maximal effort, and on the part of students who are not taking full advantage of the resources institutions provide." If undergraduates can receive high marks for sloppy work, routinely get extensions for assignments not completed on time, and escape being penalized for various forms of minor misconduct, it is hardly a surprise that employers find them lacking in self-discipline. Doing something to remedy this problem is not a crass concession to commercial interests but a useful reform that serves the interests of faculties and students as well as employers.

A much more controversial step would be to allow undergraduates   20
to take a small number of elective courses in practical vocational subjects, such as accounting, marketing, or finance. Arguably even two or three courses of this kind would help undergraduates decide what kind of business career to pursue and improve their prospects for employment. Recognizing these advantages, a number of colleges have already begun to provide this opportunity, but some liberal arts faculties still resist, fearing that any vocational courses they provide will become a beachhead for undermining the entire liberal arts curriculum and subverting the larger purposes it serves.

Barring all vocational courses makes little difference in colleges where almost all seniors go on to graduate or professional school. The consequences are more serious, however, for the majority of colleges in which most liberal arts students go directly into the workforce. Some companies have begun paying business schools to give a summer "crash course" in the basics of management for the new liberal arts graduates they have hired. While this step may solve the problem for some undergraduates, it does nothing for seniors seeking employment in companies that cannot or will not sponsor a program of this kind. Without any exposure to the skills and knowledge of the business world, such students could easily find themselves at a disadvantage in competing for jobs when they graduate.

At present, most business majors take at least half their courses in the liberal arts. In contrast, liberal arts majors have traditionally taken an average of less than 2 percent of their total courses in business. In effect, therefore, many undergraduates are choosing between a curriculum entirely devoted to the liberal arts and a vocational program that reserves half the curriculum for the liberal arts and half for courses specifically related to a career. It is not at all clear that such a choice is helpful for students or even in the best interest of Arts and Sciences faculties. A mere two or three elective courses in business or some other practical pursuit could help many undergraduates prepare for work without interfering significantly with the broader values of a liberal education. By encouraging such courses, faculties might even attract some undergraduates who would prefer a liberal arts curriculum but fear the consequences when they have to look for a job.

THE CRITICAL CHALLENGE

Efforts to prepare students for a career are pulled in different directions by the two most powerful forces shaping American undergraduate education: the views of the faculty, on the one hand, and, on the other, the market pressures that students exert through their power to choose which institutions to attend. A few colleges have enough prestige that their faculties are not much bound by student opinion, leaving them reasonably free to build their educational programs according to their own ideas of what is appropriate. At most colleges, however, faculties must pay close heed to what prospective students want in order to attract enough applicants to fill their classrooms with undergraduates of adequate ability and promise.

Unfortunately neither faculty nor students can be counted upon to make fully appropriate choices about the role of vocation in a rounded undergraduate education. Arts and Sciences professors tend to attach too little importance to student career needs. Undergraduates, and the vocational faculties that prepare them for work, often neglect educational goals that serve the larger community, such as moral sensitivity and civic responsibility, and take too narrow a view of the competencies needed to succeed in a career. Achieving an ideal balance, then, requires a collaborative effort on the part of everyone involved.

Most universities have not yet managed to reconcile these two con- 25 flicting tendencies. Liberal arts programs seldom take adequate account of the crucial importance of students' careers—careers that will inevitably affect what kind of persons they become, how well they balance the claims of work and family, and what opportunities they have to serve others besides themselves. Vocational faculties, either by choice or because they have been rebuffed by their liberal arts colleagues, do not collaborate enough with Arts and Sciences faculties to prepare their students well for purposes other than performing the tasks demanded by their jobs.

The pressure to respond appropriately to vocational needs will not diminish in the foreseeable future. Liberal arts professors are unlikely to find their students becoming less preoccupied with their careers. The growing numbers of older and part-time students and the continuing high priority freshmen place on making money promise to keep vocational concerns at the forefront of their minds. At the same time, vocational faculties do not merely encounter pressure to pay more attention to specific practical skills; instead they are being urged to do a better job of developing precisely the competencies and qualities of mind traditionally associated with a liberal education.

The evolving priorities of employers make it easier for vocational programs and Arts and Sciences departments to collaborate, since the needs they serve increasingly overlap. Both faculties have good reason to cooperate. Without the help of liberal arts colleagues, vocational programs are likely to fall far short both in meeting the needs of employers and in preparing students for a rich, fulfilling life outside of work. Without paying greater attention to the career needs of their students, Arts and Sciences faculties seem destined to go on serving a minority of undergraduates while leaving the rest to vocational programs that deny them the full benefits of a rounded college education. Only if both faculties recognize the cost of going their separate ways will they achieve the full potential of both the liberal arts and vocational education in serving all the needs of their students.

STUDY QUESTIONS

1. Why, according to Bok, has vocational training been dismissed by instructors at liberal arts colleges? What role does Bok think that it *should* play in higher education?

2. Identify Bok's THESIS. Is it stated directly or implied?

3. How does Bok attempt to persuade his readers that vocational training can and should be integrated into the liberal arts curriculum? Are his ARGUMENTS convincing? Why or why not?

4. What rhetorical STRATEGIES does Bok use to lay out his argument? What purpose do the subheadings in the essay serve?

5. *For Writing.* Write an essay in which you argue for or against—or both— Bok's thesis, drawing on personal experience and using concrete EXAMPLES to support your ideas.

SCOTT RUSSELL SANDERS (b. 1945), born in Memphis, Tennessee, grew up mainly in Ohio. He graduated from Brown University in 1967 and received his PhD from Cambridge University in 1971. He has taught at Indiana University since 1971. The author of eight novels and eleven works of nonfiction, he has written widely on environmental issues, social justice, and community.

In "The Inheritance of Tools," Sanders meditates on the proper use of tools and the virtue and morality of building with one's hands, knowledge that has been passed down through the generations of Sanders men. He brings together past and present as he describes passing on his own knowledge to his children. By the end of his essay, Sanders has described not only his tools and their history, but also what those tools represent—purpose, timelessness, and love.

AT JUST ABOUT THE HOUR when my father died, soon after dawn one February morning when ice coated the windows like cataracts, I banged my thumb with a hammer. Naturally I swore at the hammer, the reckless thing, and in the moment of swearing I thought of what my father would say: "If you'd try hitting the nail it would go in a whole lot faster. Don't you know your thumb's not as hard as that hammer?" We both were doing carpentry that day, but far apart. He was building cupboards at my brother's place in Oklahoma; I was at home in Indiana putting up a wall in the basement to make a bedroom for my daughter. By the time my mother called with news of his death—the long-distance wires whittling her voice until it seemed too thin to bear the weight of what she had to say—my thumb was swollen. A week or so later a white scar in the shape of a crescent moon began to show above the cuticle, and month by month it rose across the pink sky of my thumbnail. It took the better part of a year for the scar to disappear, and every time I noticed it I thought of my father.

The hammer had belonged to him, and to his father before him. The three of us have used it to build houses and barns and chicken coops, to upholster chairs and crack walnuts, to make doll furniture and bookshelves and jewelry boxes. The head is scratched and pock-marked, like an old plowshare that has been working rocky fields, and it gives off the sort of dull sheen you see on fast creek water in the shade. It is a finishing hammer, about the weight of a bread loaf, too light really for framing walls, too heavy for cabinetwork, with a curved claw for pulling nails, a rounded head for pounding, a fluted neck for looks, and a hickory handle for strength.

The present handle is my third one, bought from a lumberyard in Tennessee down the road from where my brother and I were helping my father build his retirement house. I broke the previous one by trying to pull sixteen penny nails out of floor joists—a foolish thing to do with a finishing hammer, as my father pointed out. "You ever hear of a crowbar?" he said. No telling how many handles he and my grandfather had gone through before me. My grandfather used to cut down hickory trees on his farm, saw them into slabs, cure the planks in his hayloft, and carve handles with a drawknife. The grain in hickory is crooked and knotty, and therefore tough, hard to split, like the grain in the two men who owned this hammer before me.

After proposing marriage to a neighbor girl, my grandfather used this hammer to build a house for his bride on a stretch of river bottom in northern Mississippi. The lumber for the place, like the hickory for the handle, was cut on his own land. By the day of the wedding he had not quite finished the house, and so right after the ceremony he took his wife home and put her to work. My grandmother had worn her Sunday dress for the wedding, with a fringe of lace tacked on around the hem in honor of the occasion. She removed this lace and folded it away before going out to help my grandfather nail siding on the house.

"There she was in her good dress," he told me some fifty-odd years after that wedding day, "holding up them long pieces of clapboard while I hammered, and together we got the place covered up before dark." As the family grew to four, six, eight, and eventually thirteen, my grandfather used this hammer to enlarge his house room by room, like a chambered nautilus expanding his shell.

By and by the hammer was passed along to my father. One day he 5 was up on the roof of our pony barn nailing shingles with it, when I stepped out the kitchen door to call him for supper. Before I could yell, something about the sight of him straddling the spine of that roof and swinging the hammer caught my eye and made me hold my tongue. I was five or six years old, and the world's commonplaces were still news to me. He would pull a nail from the pouch at his wrist, bring the hammer down, and a moment later the *thunk* of the blow would reach my ears. And that is what had stopped me in my tracks and stilled my tongue, that momentary gap between seeing and hearing the blow. Instead of yelling from the kitchen door, I ran to the barn and climbed two rungs up the ladder—as far as I was allowed to go—and spoke quietly to my father. On our walk to the house he explained that sound takes time to make its way through air. Suddenly the world seemed larger, the air more dense, if sound could be held back like any ordinary traveler.

By the time I started using this hammer, at about the age when I discovered the speed of sound, it already contained houses and mysteries for me. The smooth handle was one my grandfather had made. In those days I needed both hands to swing it. My father would start a nail in a scrap of wood, and I would pound away until I bent it over.

"Looks like you got ahold of some of those rubber nails," he would tell me. "Here, let me see if I can find you some stiff ones." And he would rummage in a drawer until he came up with a fistful of more cooperative nails. "Look at the head," he would tell me. "Don't look at your hands, don't look at the hammer. Just look at the head of that nail and pretty soon you'll learn to hit it square."

Pretty soon I did learn. While he worked in the garage cutting dovetail joints for a drawer or skinning a deer or tuning an engine, I would hammer nails. I made innocent blocks of wood look like porcupines.

He did not talk much in the midst of his tools, but he kept up a nearly ceaseless humming, slipping in and out of a dozen tunes in an afternoon, often running back over the same stretch of melody again and again, as if searching for a way out. When the humming did cease, I knew he was faced with a task requiring great delicacy or concentration, and I took care not to distract him.

He kept scraps of wood in a cardboard box—the ends of two-by-fours, slabs of shelving and plywood, odd pieces of molding—and everything in it was fair game. I nailed scraps together to fashion what I called boats or houses, but the results usually bore only faint resemblance to the visions I carried in my head. I would hold up these constructions to show my father, and he would turn them over in his hands admiringly, speculating about what they might be. My cobbled-together guitars might have been alien spaceships, my barns might have been models of Aztec temples, each wooden contraption might have been anything but what I had set out to make.

Now and again I would feel the need to have a chunk of wood shaped or shortened before I riddled it with nails, and I would clamp it in a vice and scrape at it with a handsaw. My father would let me lacerate the board until my arm gave out, and then he would wrap his hand around mine and help me finish the cut, showing me how to use my thumb to guide the blade, how to pull back on the saw to keep it from binding, how to let my shoulder do the work.

"Don't force it," he would say, "just drag it easy and give the teeth a chance to bite."

As the saw teeth bit down the wood released its smell, each kind with its own fragrance, oak or walnut or cherry or pine—usually pine, because it was the softest and the easiest for a child to work. No matter how weathered and gray the board, no matter how warped and cracked, inside there was this smell waiting, as of something freshly baked. I gathered every smidgen of sawdust and stored it away in coffee cans, which I kept in a drawer of the workbench. When I did not feel like hammering nails I would dump my sawdust on the concrete floor of the garage and landscape it into highways and farms and towns, running miniature cars and trucks along miniature roads. Looming as huge as a colossus, my father worked over and around me, now and again bend-

10

ing down to inspect my work, careful not to trample my creations. It was a landscape that smelled dizzyingly of wood. Even after a bath my skin would carry the smell, and so would my father's hair, when he lifted me for a bedtime hug.

I tell these things not only from memory but also from recent observation, because my own son now turns blocks of wood into nailed porcupines, dumps cans full of sawdust at my feet and sculpts highways on the floor. He learns how to swing a hammer from the elbow instead of the wrist, how to lay his thumb beside the blade to guide a saw, how to tap a chisel with a wooden mallet, how to mark a hole with an awl before starting a drill bit. My daughter did the same before him, and even now, on the brink of teenage aloofness, she will occasionally drag out my box of wood scraps and carpenter something. So I have seen my apprenticeship to wood and tools reenacted in each of my children, as my father saw his own apprenticeship renewed in me.

The saw I use belonged to him, as did my level and both of my squares, and all four tools had belonged to his father. The blade of the saw is the bluish color of gun barrels, and the maple handle, dark from the sweat of hands, is inscribed with curving leaf designs. The level is a shaft of walnut two feet long, edged with brass and pierced by three round windows in which air bubbles float in oil-filled tubes of glass. The middle window serves for testing whether a surface is horizontal, the others for testing whether it is plumb or vertical. My grandfather used to carry this level on the gun rack behind the seat in his pickup, and when I rode with him I would turn around to watch the bubbles dance. The larger of the two squares is called a framing square, a flat steel elbow so beat up and tarnished you can barely make out the rows of numbers that show how to figure the cuts on rafters. The smaller one is called a try square, for marking right angles, with a blued steel blade for the shank and a brass-faced block of cherry for the head.

I was taught early on that a saw is not to be used apart from a square: 15 "If you're going to cut a piece of wood," my father insisted, "you owe it to the tree to cut it straight."

Long before studying geometry, I learned there is a mystical virtue in right angles. There is an unspoken morality in seeking the level and the plumb. A house will stand, a table will bear weight, the sides of a box will hold together only if the joints are square and the members upright. When the bubble is lined up between two marks etched in the glass tube of a level, you have aligned yourself with the forces that hold the universe together. When you miter the corners of a picture frame, each angle must be exactly forty-five degrees, as they are in the perfect triangles of Pythagoras, not a degree more or less. Otherwise the frame will hang crookedly, as if ashamed of itself and of its maker. No matter if the joints you are cutting do not show. Even if you are butting two pieces of wood together inside a cabinet, where no one except a wrecking crew will ever see them, you must take pains to insure that the ends are square and the studs are plumb.

I took pains over the wall I was building on the day my father died. Not long after that wall was finished—paneled with tongue-and-groove boards of yellow pine, the nail holes filled with putty and the wood all stained and sealed—I came close to wrecking it one afternoon when my daughter ran howling up the stairs to announce that her gerbils had escaped from their cage and were hiding in my brand-new wall. She could hear them scratching and squeaking behind her bed. Impossible! I said. How on earth could they get inside my drum-tight wall? Through the heating vent, she answered. I went downstairs, pressed my ear to the honey-colored wood, and heard the scritch scritch of tiny feet.

"What can we do?" my daughter wailed. "They'll starve to death, they'll die of thirst, they'll suffocate." "Hold on," I soothed. "I'll think of something."

While I thought and she fretted, the radio on her bedside table delivered us the headlines. Several thousand people had died in a city in India from a poisonous cloud that had leaked overnight from a chemical plant. A nuclear-powered submarine had been launched. Rioting continued in South Africa. An airplane had been hijacked in the Mediterranean. Authorities calculated that several thousand homeless people slept on the streets within sight of the Washington Monument. I felt my usual helplessness in face of all these calamities. But here was my daughter weeping because her gerbils were holed up in a wall. This calamity I could handle.

"Don't worry," I told her. "We'll set food and water by the heating   20 vent and lure them out. And if that doesn't do the trick, I'll tear the wall apart until we find them."

She stopped crying and gazed at me. "You'd really tear it apart? Just for my gerbils? The *wall*?" Astonishment slowed her down only for a second, however, before she ran to the workbench and began tugging at drawers, saying, "Let's see, what'll we need? Crowbar. Hammer. Chisels. I hope we don't have to use them—but just in case."

We didn't need the wrecking tools. I never had to assault my handsome wall, because the gerbils eventually came out to nibble at a dish of popcorn. But for several hours I studied the tongue-and-groove skin I had nailed up on the day of my father's death, considering where to begin prying. There were no gaps in that wall, no crooked joints.

I had botched a great many pieces of wood before I mastered the right angle with a saw, botched even more before I learned to miter a joint. The knowledge of these things resides in my hands and eyes and the webwork of muscles, not in the tools. There are machines for sale— powered miter boxes and radial arm saws, for instance—that will enable any casual soul to cut proper angles in boards. The skill is invested in the gadget instead of the person who uses it, and this is what distinguishes a machine from a tool. If I had to earn my keep by making furniture or building houses, I suppose I would buy powered saws and pneumatic nailers; the need for speed would drive me to it. But since I carpenter only for my own pleasure or to help neighbors or to remake the house around the ears of my family, I stick with hand tools. Most of the ones I own were given to me by my father, who also taught me how to wield them. The tools in my workbench are a double inheritance, for each hammer and level and saw is wrapped in a cloud of knowing.

All of these tools are a pleasure to look at and to hold. Merchants would never paste NEW NEW NEW! signs on them in stores. Their designs are old because they work, because they serve their purpose well. Like folksongs and aphorisms and the grainy bits of language, these tools have been pared down to essentials. I look at my claw hammer, the distillation of a hundred generations of carpenters, and consider that it holds up well beside those other classics—Greek vases, Gregorian chants, *Don Quixote,* barbed fishhooks, candles, spoons.

Knowledge of hammering stretches back to the earliest humans who squatted beside fires chipping flints. Anthropologists have a lovely name for those unworked rocks that served as the earliest hammers. "Dawn stones" they are called. Their only qualification for the work, aside from hardness, is that they fit the hand. Our ancestors used them for grinding corn, tapping awls, smashing bones. From dawn stones to this claw hammer is a great leap in time, but no great distance in design or imagination.

On that iced-over February morning when I smashed my thumb 25 with the hammer, I was down in the basement framing the wall that my daughter's gerbils would later hide in. I was thinking of my father, as I always did whenever I built anything, thinking how he would have gone about the work, hearing in memory what he would have said about the wisdom of hitting the nail instead of my thumb. I had the studs and plates nailed together all square and trim, and was lifting the wall into place when the phone rang upstairs. My wife answered, and in a moment she came to the basement door and called down softly to me. The stillness in her voice made me drop the framed wall and hurry upstairs. She told me my father was dead. Then I heard the details over the phone from my mother. Building a set of cupboards for my brother in Oklahoma, he had knocked off work early the previous afternoon because of cramps in his stomach. Early this morning, on his way into the kitchen of my brother's trailer, maybe going for a glass of water, so early that no one else was awake, he slumped down on the linoleum and his heart quit.

For several hours I paced around inside my house, upstairs and down, in and out of every room, looking for the right door to open and knowing there was no such door. My wife and children followed me and wrapped me in arms and backed away again, circling and staring as if I were on fire. Where was the door, the door, the door? I kept wondering. My smashed thumb turned purple and throbbed, making me furious. I wanted to cut it off and rush outside and scrape away the snow and hack a hole in the frozen earth and bury the shameful thing.

I went down into the basement, opened a drawer in my workbench, and stared at the ranks of chisels and knives. Oiled and sharp, as my father would have kept them, they gleamed at me like teeth. I took up a clasp knife, pried out the longest blade, and tested the edge on the hair of my forearm. A tuft came away cleanly, and I saw my father testing the sharpness of tools on his own skin, the blades of axes and knives and gouges and hoes, saw the red hair shaved off in patches from his arms and the backs of his hands. "That will cut bear," he would say. He never cut a bear with his blades, now my blades, but he cut deer, dirt, wood. I closed the knife and put it away. Then I took up the hammer and went back to work on my daughter's wall, snugging the bottom place against a chalkline on the floor, shimming the top plate against the joists overhead, plumbing the studs with my level, making sure before I drove the first nail that every line was square and true.

STUDY QUESTIONS

1. What advice did Sanders's father give him about hammering nails? What did Sanders make from the various chunks of wood his father gave him? What was Sanders's greatest achievement as a builder?

2. ANALYZE Sander's DESCRIPTION of his hammer (paragraphs 2–6). How does the hammer look, sound, and feel? How does this description contribute to Sander's overall NARRATIVE?

3. Sanders begins and ends his MEMOIR of his father by recounting what he is doing just before and just after he learns of his father's death. Why do you think he chose to frame the narrative in this way? What is the significance to this essay of using this rhetorical strategy? How does the word "frame" fit both the strategy and the subject?

4. *For Writing.* Choose a person who is special in your life, and make a list of some experiences that you have shared. Select the experience that stirs the most emotions, that best displays your relationship with this person, and that you can write about. Using DESCRIPTION, PATHOS, and any other rhetorical strategies that will give your AUDIENCE a full picture of your subject, write a memoir of this special person.

BARAK OBAMA   { *Inaugural Address*

BARACK OBAMA (b. 1961) was born in Honolulu, Hawaii, to Stanley Ann
Dunham, a native of Kansas, and Barack Obama Sr., a native of Kenya. His
parents divorced in 1964, and his father returned to Africa. Obama's mother
eventually married Lolo Soetoro, an Indonesian student, and the family lived
in Jakarta, Indonesia, for four years. When he was ten, Obama returned to
the United States, where he lived with his mother's parents in Hawaii and
completed his schooling. He began his postsecondary education in 1979 at
Occidental College in Los Angeles, transferring to Columbia University in
1981. He received his BA in political science, with a focus on international
relations, in 1983. Obama began to make his mark when he took a job in
1985 as a community organizer with the Developing Communities Project in
Chicago, where he introduced a job training program, a college preparatory
program, and a tenants' rights group. In 1988 he left to enter Harvard Law
School, graduating in 1991. He taught constitutional law at the University of
Chicago Law School for twelve years and then ran for and won a seat in the
Illinois Senate in 1997, a seat he held until he was elected to the U.S.
Senate in 2005. Following his tenure in the Senate, in 2008 Obama was
elected the forty-fourth president of the United States, the first African
American to hold that office. In 2009 he was awarded the Nobel Peace
Prize "for his extraordinary efforts to strengthen international diplomacy
and cooperation between peoples."

President Barack Obama's Inaugural Address, delivered on January 21,
2009, outlines his hopes for the future and charts the process that he feels
the United States must follow if it is to retain its greatness. His positive tone
echoes the optimism of his campaign slogan, "Yes we can." In calling for
the American people to come together, how does he speak to both those
who elected him and those who did not vote for him?

MY FELLOW CITIZENS: I STAND here today humbled by the task before us, grateful for the trust you've bestowed, mindful of the sacrifices borne by our ancestors.

I thank President Bush for his service to our nation—[applause]— as well as the generosity and cooperation he has shown throughout this transition.

Forty-four Americans have now taken the presidential oath. The words have been spoken during rising tides of prosperity and the still waters of peace. Yet, every so often, the oath is taken amidst gathering clouds and raging storms. At these moments, America has carried on not simply because of the skill or vision of those in high office, but because we, the people, have remained faithful to the ideals of our fore-bears and true to our founding documents.

So it has been: so it must be with this generation of Americans.

That we are in the midst of crisis is now well understood. Our nation 5 is at war against a far-reaching network of violence and hatred. Our economy is badly weakened, a consequence of greed and irresponsibility on the part of some, but also our collective failure to make hard choices and prepare the nation for a new age. Homes have been lost, jobs shed, businesses shuttered. Our health care is too costly, our schools fail too many—and each day brings further evidence that the ways we use energy strengthen our adversaries and threaten our planet.

These are the indicators of crisis, subject to data and statistics. Less measurable, but no less profound, is a sapping of confidence across our land: a nagging fear that America's decline is inevitable, that the next generation must lower its sights.

Today I say to you that the challenges we face are real. They are serious and they are many. They will not be met easily or in a short span of time. But know this America: They will be met. [Applause.]

On this day, we gather because we have chosen hope over fear, unity of purpose over conflict and discord. On this day, we come to pro-claim an end to the petty grievances and false promises, the recrimina-tions and worn-out dogmas that for far too long have strangled our politics. We remain a young nation. But in the words of Scripture, the time has come to set aside childish things.[1] The time has come to reaffirm our enduring spirit; to choose our better history: to carry forward that precious gift, that noble idea passed on from generation to generation: the God-given promise that all are equal, all are free, and all deserve a chance to pursue their full measure of happiness. [Applause.]

In reaffirming the greatness of our nation we understand that greatness is never a given. It must be earned. Our journey has never been one of short-cuts or settling for less. It has not been the path for the faint-hearted, for those that prefer leisure over work or seek only the pleasures of riches and fame. Rather, it has been the risk-takers, the doers, the makers of things—some celebrated, but more often men and women obscure in their labor—who have carried us up the long rugged path towards prosperity and freedom.

For us, they packed up their few worldly possessions and traveled across oceans in search of a new life. For us, they toiled in sweatshops, and settled the West, endured the lash of the whip, and plowed the hard earth. For us, they fought and died in places like Concord and Gettysburg, Normandy and Khe Sahn.

Time and again these men and women struggled and sacrificed and worked till their hands were raw so that we might live a better life. They saw America as bigger than the sum of our individual ambitions, greater than all the differences of birth or wealth or faction.

This is the journey we continue today. We remain the most prosperous, powerful nation on Earth. Our workers are no less productive than when this crisis began. Our minds are no less inventive, our goods and services no less needed than they were last week, or last month, or last year. Our capacity remains undiminished. But our time of standing pat, of protecting narrow interests and putting off unpleasant decisions— that time has surely passed. Starting today, we must pick ourselves up, dust ourselves off, and begin again the work of remaking America. [Applause.]

For everywhere we look, there is work to be done. The state of our economy calls for action, bold and swift. And we will act, not only to

[1] 1 Corinthians 13:11.

create new jobs, but to lay a new foundation for growth. We will build the roads and bridges, the electric grids and digital lines that feed our commerce and bind us together. We'll restore science to its rightful place, and wield technology's wonders to raise health care's quality and lower its cost. We will harness the sun and the winds and the soil to fuel our cars and run our factories. And we will transform our schools and colleges and universities to meet the demands of a new age. All this we can do. All this we will do.

Now, there are some who question the scale of our ambitions, who suggest that our system cannot tolerate too many big plans. Their memories are short, for they have forgotten what this country has already done, what free men and women can achieve when imagination is joined to common purpose, and necessity to courage. What the cynics fail to understand is that the ground has shifted beneath them, that the stale political arguments that have consumed us for so long no longer apply.

The question we ask today is not whether our government is too big 15 or too small, but whether it works—whether it helps families find jobs at a decent wage, care they can afford, a retirement that is dignified. Where the answer is yes, we intend to move forward. Where the answer is no, programs will end. And those of us who manage the public's dollars will be held to account, to spend wisely, reform bad habits, and do our business in the light of day, because only then can we restore the vital trust between a people and their government.

Nor is the question before us whether the market is a force for good or ill. Its power to generate wealth and expand freedom is unmatched. But this crisis has reminded us that without a watchful eye, the market can spin out of control. The nation cannot prosper long when it favors only the prosperous. The success of our economy has always depended not just on the size of our gross domestic product, but on the reach of our prosperity, on the ability to extend opportunity to every willing heart—not out of charity, but because it is the surest route to our common good. [Applause.]

As for our common defense, we reject as false the choice between our safety and our ideals. Our Founding Fathers—[applause]—our Founding Fathers, faced with perils that we can scarcely imagine, drafted a charter to assure the rule of law and the rights of man—a charter expanded by the blood of generations. Those ideals still light the world, and we will not give them up for expedience sake. [Applause.]

And so, to all the other peoples and governments who are watching today, from the grandest capitals to the small village where my father was born, know that America is a friend of each nation, and every man, woman and child who seeks a future of peace and dignity. And we are ready to lead once more. [Applause.]

Recall that earlier generations faced down fascism and communism not just with missiles and tanks, but with the sturdy alliances and enduring convictions. They understood that our power alone cannot protect us, nor does it entitle us to do as we please. Instead they knew that our power grows through its prudent use; our security emanates from the justness of our cause, the force of our example, the tempering qualities of humility and restraint.

We are the keepers of this legacy. Guided by these principles once 20 more we can meet those new threats that demand even greater effort, even greater cooperation and understanding between nations. We will begin to responsibly leave Iraq to its people and forge a hard-earned peace in Afghanistan. With old friends and former foes, we'll work tirelessly to lessen the nuclear threat, and roll back the specter of a warming planet.

We will not apologize for our way of life, nor will we waver in its defense. And for those who seek to advance their aims by inducing terror and slaughtering innocents, we say to you now that our spirit is stronger and cannot be broken—you cannot outlast us, and we will defeat you. [Applause.]

For we know that our patchwork heritage is a strength, not a weakness. We are a nation of Christians and Muslims, Jews and Hindus, and non-believers. We are shaped by every language and culture, drawn from every end of this Earth; and because we have tasted the bitter swill of civil war and segregation, and emerged from that dark chapter stronger and more united, we cannot help but believe that the old hatreds shall someday pass; that the lines of tribe shall soon dissolve: that as the world grows smaller, our common humanity shall reveal itself; and that America must play its role in ushering in a new era of peace.

To the Muslim world, we seek a new way forward, based on mutual interest and mutual respect. To those leaders around the globe who seek to sow conflict, or blame their society's ills on the West, know that your people will judge you on what you can build, not what you destroy. [Applause.]

To those who cling to power through corruption and deceit and the silencing of dissent, know that you are on the wrong side of history, but that we will extend a hand if you are willing to unclench your fist. [Applause.]

To the people of poor nations, we pledge to work alongside you to 25 make your farms flourish and let clean waters flow: to nourish starved bodies and feed hungry minds. And to those nations like ours that enjoy relative plenty, we say we can no longer afford indifference to the suffering outside our borders, nor can we consume the world's resources without regard to effect. For the world has changed, and we must change with it.

As we consider the role that unfolds before us, we remember with humble gratitude those brave Americans who at this very hour patrol far-off deserts and distant mountains. They have something to tell us, just as the fallen heroes who lie in Arlington whisper through the ages.

We honor them not only because they are the guardians of our liberty, but because they embody the spirit of service—a willingness to find meaning in something greater than themselves.

And yet at this moment, a moment that will define a generation, it is precisely this spirit that must inhabit us all. For as much as government can do, and must do, it is ultimately the faith and determination of the American people upon which this nation relies. It is the kindness to take in a stranger when the levees break, the selflessness of workers who would rather cut their hours than see a friend lose their job which sees us through our darkest hours. It is the firefighter's courage to storm a stairway filled with smoke, but also a parent's willingness to nurture a child that finally decides our fate.

Our challenges may be new. The instruments with which we meet them may be new. But those values upon which our success depends— honesty and hard work, courage and fair play, tolerance and curiosity, loyalty and patriotism—these things are old. These things are true. They have been the quiet force of progress throughout our history.

What is demanded, then, is a return to these truths. What is required 30 of us now is a new era of responsibility—a recognition on the part of every American that we have duties to ourselves, our nation and the world; duties that we do not grudgingly accept, but rather seize gladly, firm in the knowledge that there is nothing so satisfying to the spirit, so defining of our character than giving our all to a difficult task.

This is the price and the promise of citizenship. This is the source of our confidence—the knowledge that God calls on us to shape an uncertain destiny. This is the meaning of our liberty and our creed, why men and women and children of every race and every faith can join in celebration across this magnificent mall; and why a man whose father less than 60 years ago might not have been served in a local restaurant can now stand before you to take a most sacred oath. [Applause.]

So let us mark this day with remembrance of who we are and how far we have traveled. In the year of America's birth, in the coldest of months, a small band of patriots huddled by dying campfires on the shores of an icy river. The capital was abandoned. The enemy was advancing. The snow was stained with blood. At the moment when the outcome of our revolution was most in doubt, the father of our nation ordered these words to be read to the people:

"Let it be told to the future world . . . that in the depth of winter, when nothing but hope and virtue could survive . . . that the city and the country, alarmed at one common danger, came forth to meet [it]."

America: In the face of our common dangers, in this winter of our hardship, let us remember these timeless words. With hope and virtue, let us brave once more the icy currents, and endure what storms may come. Let it be said by our children's children that when we were tested we refused to let this journey end, that we did not turn back nor did we falter; and with eyes fixed on the horizon and God's grace upon us, we carried forth that great gift of freedom and delivered it safely to future generations.

Thank you. God bless you. And God bless the United States of America. [Applause.]

STUDY QUESTIONS

1. According to the incoming president, what are the challenges that the United States faces?

2. What is the process that Americans must follow in order to surmount these various challenges?

3. Find examples of parallel structure within and across sentences in this speech. Why might such structures be effective in the GENRE of a speech? Can you think of other orators who used this technique?

4. *For Writing.* President Obama says that the country requires a "new era of responsibility." How does he attempt to PERSUADE his listeners in this PROPOSAL to accept and act on that responsibility? Evaluate his ARGU-MENT and the examples he offers for support. How does he speak to both the people who voted for him and those who did not?

NINETEEN

COMPOSITION AT UNCW
Introduction

—▫—

WELCOME TO UNCW's Composition Program. Although we are housed in the English Department, we serve students from all over campus, and we are attentive to the wide range of writing you'll need to do throughout your time here at UNCW and beyond. This section of the book will help familiarize you with the university's composition requirements, explain what "composition" is and why each student is required to take courses in it, and provide some examples of award-winning writing from past students in our program. It includes sections highlighting campus resources, including Writing Services and the Randall Library, as well as short chapters on reading and design strategies to help make your experience as a composition student as successful and productive as possible.

In brief, our program exists to help prepare you to write in other courses, in other academic fields, and in the professional and public contexts you'll enter after college. It exists because effective communication—whether you want to head a corporation or start a revolution—is an essential skill. Much of the writing you will do in composition courses is known as *academic discourse*, but you will also explore different genres inside and outside of the university environment. You will conduct library research, use digital technologies, and work collaboratively with your classmates. You will address a variety of writing situations, paying particular attention to what we call the 'rhetorical situation'—the particular occasion for which a piece of writing is intended, including audience, purpose, context, and medium. While no single class (or even two classes) can fully prepare you for every communicative situation you'll encounter in the future, a composition class can help you gain some important basic skills to draw from in navigating all situations.

Think of a composition course like a total body workout: just as general exercise doesn't train you specifically to play tennis or basketball or golf, a composition course doesn't train you specifically for success in any single one of your classes or in a particular job. But just as having good general fitness gives you a starting place for mastering each of those sports, a rigorous composition course will help you "get in shape" for whatever writing tasks come your way. And just like fitness, composition is not a topic to be mastered, but a skill that must be maintained through consistent and focused practice—both during your time in our program and beyond.

For these reasons, we hope you'll understand your composition courses not as a series of boxes to check off on your list of requirements for graduation, but as opportunities to develop and refine skills you can use throughout your life.

What courses will I take?

Most students at UNCW will spend two semesters in our composition program, taking first English 101 (College Reading and Writing I) and then English 201 (College Reading and Writing II. A few students with exceptional scores on the AP English Language test, the SAT, or the university's English Placement test will take one course only, English 103 (Advanced College Reading and Writing).

English 101 (College Reading and Writing I) provides you with a solid foundation for thinking about how writing strategies evolve depending on your circumstances and goals. If you want to describe a personal experience in a warm, funny way, for example, you'll use different language and draw from different kinds of research than if you want to persuade the general public to take a side on a serious political issue. In a similar way, your writing strategies should evolve when writing in different media or genres: a piece written to be read aloud should have particular qualities, as should a memo written to be read quickly in the workplace.

Although we all intuit these different situational approaches to writing, it helps to practice, analyze, and discuss them in a dedicated class. In English 101 you'll do just that, undertaking three to four projects that require you to experiment with and critique different purposes and audiences for writing. These projects will vary by class, but they will generally include the following:

- A personal or descriptive essay

- A rhetorical analysis of a piece of non-fiction prose, so that you can examine and critique different types of rhetorical and stylistic appeals in action

- A multimodal project requiring you to expand your sense of what it means to "compose" to include elements of design as well as authoring text

Importantly, completing these projects will not just be a matter of pulling an all-nighter and submitting a final draft. A big part of English 101 is its commitment to helping students approach writing and research as an ongoing process in which effective polished drafts emerge slowly, over the course of several weeks of informal writing exercises, drafting, peer review, and revision. So expect to write many more words than actually make it into your final drafts, to learn from responding to others' work, and take into account feedback from others in making choices about how to revise.

Each student in English 101 should expect to conference individually with instructors during the semester. Additionally, many students will work collaboratively with peers on projects, visit the library for guidance in conducting research for their projects, or even complete a service-learning project to assist a campus or community organization.

Students who successfully complete English 101 will partially fulfill their University Studies Composition requirement.

English 201 (College Reading and Writing II) builds on the rhetorical skills you developed in English 101, focusing more intensely on sustained research and argument-based writing suitable for academic contexts.

You will continue to develop a sense of writing as an ongoing and often recursive process that includes invention or brainstorming strategies, drafting, peer review, revision, and editing (and maybe multiple rounds of each). Additionally, you will gain an understanding of how to articulate a question and conduct thorough research, evaluating and integrating sources into your work and putting yourself in conversation with those sources. You won't simply be "using" sources so much as "engaging" with them—accounting for them as projects with both uses and limits, and integrating them into your own arguments accordingly.

In English 201 you will write three to four major essays or projects that will require you to learn how to argue effectively and to critique the arguments of others. These essays will vary by class, but they will generally include the following:

- Two critical or rhetorical analyses of an assigned text, emphasizing literary conventions, purpose, and audience

- At least one persuasive or argumentative essay grounded in research

- A multimodal project requiring you to expand your sense of what it means to "compose" to include elements of design as well as authoring text

Each student in English 201 should expect to conference with instructors during the semester. Additionally, as in English 101, many students will work collaboratively with peers on projects or complete a service-learning project with a community or campus partner.

Students who successfully complete English 201 will fulfill their University Studies Composition requirement and partially fulfill their University Studies Information Literacy requirement.

English 103 Advanced College Reading and Writing is an accelerated, one-semester version of UNCW's composition sequence. In this course, you will practice writing in a variety of forms, attending especially to writing for academic purposes. That is, in your essays you will work to develop a balanced and tolerant, but also decisive, intellectual stance in making arguments. Though specific assignments will vary, you will likely complete the following sequence of assignments:

- An essay that draws upon personal experience to support a generalization

- A critical analysis of an assigned text, emphasizing literary conventions, purpose, and audience

- At least one persuasive or argumentative essay grounded in research

- A multimodal project requiring you to expand your sense of what it means to "compose" to include elements of design as well as authoring text

Additionally, many students will work collaboratively with peers on projects or even complete a service-learning project to assist a local or campus organization.

As in all of our composition courses, essays should be completed over a series of drafts, as well as through several informal writing exercises: journals, blogs, brainstorming, etc. You'll receive feedback from your peers and your instructor on your writing, and you'll be responsible for offering intelligent, substantive feedback to your peers.

Students who successfully complete English 103 will fulfill their University Studies Composition requirement and partially fulfill their University Studies Information Literacy requirement.

TERMS TO REMEMBER

In your composition classes at UNCW, you are likely to hear some or all of the terms below, as well as numerous others that will help inform your sense of how to approach a writing task. Use these terms to help you develop your own, more robust theory of how writing works and of what strategies are especially useful to you. Having a vocabulary to describe how writing works not only at the sentence level, but as part of a larger system, is an important first step in becoming a competent, self-reliant writer.

Though we feel that the terms below offer help navigating our composition classes, this list is by no means exhaustive. In formulating your own vocabulary for talking about writing, please feel free to draw from past courses, textbooks, and experiences.

AUDIENCE: Of course, on the surface, "audience" refers simply to the readership for a piece of writing. Who will be reading what you've written? As a writer, you have to consider what that person is likely to already know about your topic, what opinions they already have, and what their expectations are for reading.

But you also need to think about audience more broadly—not only as the group or individual who will actually, literally be reading your writing, but as a general profile for an intended group of prospective readers. Try not to assume that your audience is simply your instructor, even if it is the case that they will be reading and grading your project. Rather, consider the genre in which you've been asked to write and what sort of audience that genre generally invites. Try to keep that audience in mind as you write, whether it be the UNCW student body or the U.S. Congress or a group of prospective voters in your hometown.

To the extent that you are comfortable doing so, let your perceptions of that audience's preferences shape your content, tone, organization, and vocabulary; if you aren't sure whether a decision you made based on your imagined audience is appropriate, ask your professor, classmates, or outside readers for guidance.

DIGITAL LITERACY: In this cultural moment, university education must strive to keep pace with the tremendous change that has accompanied the rise of digital culture and circulation. How can universities prepare students to communicate effectively and ethically in public forums and workplaces if we do not acknowledge the dramatic changes that have taken place in the ways that people today interact, argue, and inform one another? How can we help students cultivate the digital literacy skills they will need in order to be full citizens of the world they are inheriting? The composition program is committed to helping make digital literacy a part of Seahawk students' experience here at UNCW.

Of course, at face value, one might think that "digital literacy" refers only to one's ability to navigate digital environments as a user (functional literacy)—a skill that many college students possess in abundance. However, we understand digital literacy as also encompassing two other realms: rhetorical literacy (the ability to create or intervene productively in digital environments) and critical literacy (a general critical awareness of how these sites function within the broader culture).

Depending on how your instructor structures projects for your class, you may find yourself examining the concept of digital literacy in your readings, reflections, or larger assignments. For instance, in your class you may strengthen your digital literacy skills by reading, creating, and analyzing the circulation of social media posts, or you may be asked to explore how relatively new digital genres are altering the forums and mechanisms by which public discourse and social change occur.

GENRE: You may already be familiar with the concept of the *literary* genre, which refers to such different textual groupings as mystery, science fiction, romance, and lyric poem. *Rhetorical* genres are similar in that they, too, refer to loose categories of texts: memos, videos, tweets, opinion letters, etc. These real-world genres not only share certain structural features, but (more importantly) also strive to accomplish similar ends and are shaped by a relatively stable audience, purpose, and context.

Although you can't (and shouldn't) attempt to memorize the standard format for every genre you encounter in your daily life, understanding the concept of genre and the ways it shapes how you approach a writing task will help you negotiate new situations in which you may find yourself. In your composition class, you'll be exposed to several different genres and may be asked to select an appropriate genre for a writing task in which you're engaging. To do so, you'll have to not only study its features, but also analyze who will read it, how they will receive it, what expectations they will bring to it, and so forth.

Both in your composition classes and beyond, you'll benefit from thinking of unfamiliar writing tasks in terms of genre, seeking out examples of genre, and balancing the somewhat stable expectations of genre with the very particular ones of the situation to which you're responding.

GLOBAL VERSUS LOCAL REVISIONS: Your instructor may use these terms to differentiate between two types of revisions: big (global) and small (local). If you decide to make a significant change to your thesis statement and it affects the argument that follows, for instance, you've made a global revision. If you are tinkering with your word choices or correcting your MLA format, meanwhile, you're making a local change.

Many students have it backwards: they focus on the local issues right away, and then—because they've spent so much time perfecting sentences—hesitate to make larger, more substantive global changes that could substantially improve the paper. In order to avoid this problem, resist the urge to zero in on local issues until you're sure your paper is organized and argued exactly as you'd like it to be.

PURPOSE: Understanding the concept of purpose is useful both in analyzing and in producing texts. Simply put, the purpose of a text refers to what the author or authors intended for it to accomplish. Most texts have multiple purposes, some of which seem obvious from the start and others of which require more careful reading. For instance, an advertisement's purpose is not only to sell a product, but often to promote a particular image of the company that made the product, or to encourage the audience to identify with the product or company in some way. A literature review, similarly, may be intended not only to review relevant materials, but also to signal to a select group of expert readers that the author or authors share their expertise and way of organizing the field of study under consideration.

RHETORICAL APPEALS: Also known as Aristotle's artistic proofs or as the modes of persuasion, the triumvirate of logos, pathos, and ethos is likely to cross your path during your time in composition. The appeals generally work together in any persuasive situation, formal or informal, and you may be asked to analyze how they are operating in a text.

Logos is the use of logical appeals supported by evidence to make a case. Often, students understand logos strictly as the inclusion of facts and statistics, but the term refers more broadly to a sequence of conclusions that the audience understands to follow one another. Logos can be inductive (proceeding from the specific to the general) or deductive (proceeding from the general to the specific). A deductive argument might read as follows: "If the university has promised to listen to the student body's requests, and UNCW students are currently lobbying for free transportation to the beach, then it follows that the university should listen to this request." An inductive argument, meanwhile, might begin with the notion that the university has heeded student requests for past initiatives (such as recycling or expanded library hours), so it might be predicted to heed future student requests as well.

Pathos is the use of emotional appeals to make a case. Whether these appeals produce sorrow, happiness, fear, or some other emotion, they all help push the audience toward caring about the cause or issue in question. To return to the example involving UNCW students lobbying for beach transportation, an arguer who shares an anecdote about the joys of the beach (or the dangerous choices students might be forced to make to get there) would be drawing on pathos to influence the audience.

Ethos is the use of ethical appeals, or appeals to one's credibility with the intended audience, to make a case. Credibility can come from celebrity (as when a distinguished alum stands behind students in their efforts to lobby for beach transportation), expertise (as when a transportation expert weighs in on the issue), or simple goodwill and competence (as when the students themselves are able to convey their noble reasons for making the transportation request).

RHETORICAL EXIGENCE: This fancy term simply refers to the immediate need for a piece of writing or communication. What is prompting you to write about a particular topic or issue at a given time? A friend's birthday is an occasion that, many feel, demands a card—a straightforward exigence to which you have a clear reason for responding. Other situations—political controversies, for instance—are more complicated in that they require a writer to make a convincing claim of the need for a response.

Some professors may ask you to clarify the exigence for a particular research topic or project. Why write about the legalization of marijuana right now? They might ask: how is this already common paper topic fresh and important right now, as opposed to five or ten years ago? How will your argument be shaped by the particulars of the present moment, and how does the present moment demand a response? If you have a good sense of the answers to questions like these and can convey that sense in your essay, you understand rhetorical exigence.

TRANSFER: In scholarship by education researchers, psychologists, and others, the concept of "transfer" refers to the ability of students to transfer what they learn in one context to other, similar situations.

Since composition is a foundational course, students should strive consciously to transfer what they learn in that class to other classes and even workplaces. In order to help you with this process, your professor might ask you to reflect often on your reading and writing strategies, to consider how your approach to writing has changed since high school or changes for different classes and assignments, or even to articulate your own theory of writing (in which you might draw from some of the terms listed here).

Some Questions to Consider:

1. What terms from above resonate with you as a writer? Use one or two of the terms to describe a writing situation you've encountered recently, whether in this class or another. Consider how your awareness or lack of awareness of the term informed or shaped the way you responded to the situation.
2. What is a genre that you are very familiar with? What would you say its purpose is: what does it strive to accomplish? Who is its audience, and under what conditions do they encounter this genre? Speculate about how the features of the genre are shaped by purpose, audience, and context.
3. Name a time when you had to compose in a genre or for a situation that was wholly unfamiliar. Perhaps you were writing your first lab report or memo, or you visited a new social media site for the first time. What skills or strategies did you transfer from your previous writing experiences? How successful were you in navigating the new situation?

READING STRATEGIES: 6 TIPS

SOME STUDENTS STRUGGLE with the amount and density of reading that is required at the college level. Often, instructors expect students to read assigned readings and never cover the material in class, pull test questions from the book, or merely begin discussing the content without preamble. Sometimes, too, an instructor may ask you to do your own research for a paper, and you'll be expected to work through several difficult texts entirely on your own in order to develop an argument or synthesis of the content.

The tips below are intended to help you work through these situations and others you may encounter in composition and beyond. The more you experiment with different strategies for tackling your reading load successfully, the better off you'll be in navigating each new situation that arises.

TIP 1: MANAGE YOUR ENVIRONMENT

Studies have proven that the more complex the environment, the less the brain can process efficiently and effectively because it is trying to understand all the sensory stimuli happening around it. Limit your distractions, including music. Find a quiet place to read, like the second floor of Randall Library, a coffee shop, or some comfortable place on campus. Then, limit your multi-tasking. Set your phone alarm for a set period of time, and then unplug. Ear plugs and noise-cancelling headphones also may help.

TIP 2: MANAGE YOUR TIME

If a task is important, put it in your planner. If you have material to read, assess the density of the material and plan your day and week accordingly. Study your reading when you are most refreshed, and if you have trouble concentrating or are facing your most difficult subject, exercise beforehand.

In fact, frequent breaks (walking, yoga, stretching) improve your concentration and allow your brain to process information.

Set your alarm to remind you to move a little every 30 minutes, then return to the page and review what you read before the break. Test for comprehension. If you do not understand it, review the material before reading further.

TIP 3: GET READY TO READ

As you sit down to read, do some preliminary work. This wise investment of time aids comprehension, especially if the material is very dense.

Begin by reviewing your previous class notes, as well as any handouts, homework questions, or prompts before starting. If you are doing independent research, you might review the notes you have already taken or even freewrite to review what you know already and what you are hoping to learn about your topic. These kinds of activities allow you to begin to gather information to which you can connect new information, a process known as scaffolding.

Next, consider how the genre you are being asked to read might influence how you read the text. For instance, if you are reading a scholarly article, you might start by attending carefully to the abstract to get a sense of the question or problem that the authors are tackling, as well as their overall claims or findings. You might also identify the year of publication and assess the reputation of the journal. In the sciences, the body of the article may be organized in an IMRD format: introduction, methods, results, discussion. Simply being familiar with the standard purpose and format of a genre will help you develop expectations and strategies for how to proceed. The same is true for other genres: textbooks, literary essays, blog posts, and even course materials.

Finally, spend some time surveying the material as a whole: read the introductory material, headings and subheadings, bolded terms, photos and captions, charts and other visuals, summaries, and study questions. Identify genre-specific features, such as the IMRD format mentioned above.

To increase comprehension, especially when encountering dense explanatory material such as that found in textbooks, you may want to use the First and Last Method. The First and Last Method has three easy steps:

1. After preliminary skimming and reviewing activities, read the entire first paragraph. (Make sure to note the background information, context and, in most cases, thesis.)
2. Read the first line of each paragraph. (The first line is often the topic sentence which directly relates to the thesis.)
3. Read the entire concluding paragraph. (The conclusion will often restate the thesis and key ideas and reveal how the writer drew his or her conclusions.)

Now you will have an outline of the text, which will improve comprehension.

The First and Last method is also good for skimming, reviewing, and in timed tests, such as the SAT, GRE, MCAT, LSAT, and others.

NOTE: the First and Last Method works well for material (like a textbook) that is difficult, but that as a student you will be expected to understand fully. It might be frustrating for scholarly texts you encounter in your own research, however. Because you are an outsider to the fields for which these texts were written, you should strive to understand the big picture: the research questions, the overall claims or findings, the nature of the conversation to which the authors are responding. Rather than reading by paragraph, you might focus on attending carefully to the beginning and ending of the text as a whole.

TIP 4: CONNECT WITH THE TEXT (QUESTION)

After you have skimmed and performed prereading activities, stop and reflect on what you already know about the topics discussed in the selection. Consider what you need to know and understand. Connecting previous knowledge with what you are reading also helps you to process the new information and to increase comprehension.

TIP 5: ACTIVELY READ THE TEXT (READ)

Now that you have done some preliminary preparation, you are ready to start reading. However, there is a difference between reading and active reading.

Active Reading

Active reading means that you will stay engaged with the text throughout the reading experience. You may want to open a search engine like Google and an online dictionary like Dictionary.com. As you read, stop when an unfamiliar concept, word, or idea occurs, and then quickly reference it and write this information in your notes.

This engagement may take many forms.

Annotating

Don't be afraid to mark in your books! As long as you do not go crazy, the bookstore will buy back annotated texts, even rentals. As you read you may want to underline or highlight key phrases and concepts. The idea, however, is to limit what you underline or highlight to essential information, so that later, you can quickly skim a page, reading only the highlighted/ underlined parts and be able to recall the information.

If you have bought a used textbook, you will often find that what is "essential" to one person may not be essential to you. Also, as you reread a text, you will start connecting to new information that you may have missed the first time.

Chapter Notes

If you know you'll be expected to write a paper about a text or will be tested on the material, you should take notes as you read, identifying key ideas within each section to highlight and keeping track of page or paragraph numbers as you go. You might do this after annotating, using your annotations to provide a map of what to transfer to notepaper or type on your computer.

Some students, such as visual learners, may even color code their annotations; however, others find marking their books too distracting. You may find Post-it Notes that you place in the text with your marginal notes more effective.

Another technique involves numbering the paragraphs in the book and then entering your notes into your course notebook, which allows you a quick way to review and reference material.

Be mindful, though, of the context for your reading when you take notes; how you interact with a text depends on what you'll do with the knowledge later (will it be fodder for a discussion? Useful in a future paper?); you'll want to allot your time and energy in accordance with what the situation demands.

Margin Notes

Margin notes provide an opportunity not only to think critically about the text, but also to summarize, note concepts and key ideas, or pinpoint important information. Your margin notes give you a wonderful road map of the text and increase your connection to your earlier preliminary activities.

TIP 6: REVIEW AND REREAD

Strong readers use a technique known as "chunking." This strategy involves breaking the text down into smaller sections. The more you struggle with reading comprehension, get "lost" when reading, or the more complex the text, the smaller the "chunks."

You will read a section, stop, summarize, and evaluate comprehension. This short break also offers an opportunity to make notes in your notebook or margins and highlight/underline important information, to take a break and refresh your mind for a few minutes, or to take notes what the last section has offered.

TO SUM IT UP . . . .

Although we talk about it a lot less, developing good strategies for reading is a lot like developing good strategies for writing. Just as everyone experiences the writing process a little differently (with some people using outlines, for instance, and others drawing diagrams or freewriting), everyone has a slightly different array of reading activities that works for them. In both cases, the only way to find out how you work best is to experiment with ways of comprehending and relating to the material. We hope that the five tips above will provide you with a good start.

Questions to Consider:

1. How do you approach a difficult text? Have you used any of the above strategies in the past, or are there others that you find particularly helpful?
2. What was one difficult text—story, article, poem, website, etc.—you had to read carefully? What did you do, and how well do you think your strategy would work in other situations or with other genres?

3. What do you do when you are an outsider to a discourse community, such as a community of scholars, and you are tasked with reading a text intended for that community (a scholarly article or book)? How can you gain something from that reading even as an outsider who cannot hope to engage as fully as an expert might?

PRINCIPLES OF VISUAL
DESIGN AND RHETORIC

—▣—

IN YOUR COMPOSITION class, you may be asked to compose not only traditional essays, but also genres—such as blog posts, infographics, brochures, or presentations—that will require you to make meaning through a host of design choices. What color background should you use? Which fonts and what font sizes? How much white space and where should it be located? These are the sorts of questions you'll need to navigate competently, and having a basic sense of design will help you find success in your project.

It is important to think of design not simply as aesthetic, but also as functional: the way you design your content may assist or impede your audience in reading the document. It may affect how well they understand the content, what importance they assign to different points or pieces of information you've included, and even where their eyes linger as they scan the page. Good design may help to persuade them of your claims or heighten your ethos as a credible author.

THE CRAP PRINCIPLES

CRAP is a (somewhat unfortunate, but highly memorable) acronym coined by visual designer Robin Williams (no, not the comedian Robin Williams). It stands for the four basic design elements of Contrast, Repetition, Alignment, and Proximity, which interact in every genre from the résumé to the scientific poster to enhance readability and aesthetics alike. Read below to get a basic sense of how each of these terms operates in different kinds of documents.

Contrast

Simply put, contrast refers to differences in visual elements of the presentation: different font sizes, different colors, different styles of font, etc. Generally, higher contrast in all these areas is better; as Robin Williams says, "If you're going to make two things different, make them really different!" For instance, if you want to use a larger font size for a heading than your standard 11pt font body text, make it significantly larger (14 pt font at least). To heighten the contrast further, play with font color or style, making use of two very different fonts for your headings and body text. The same goes with color, generally—don't use orange and red as your color scheme; use red and blue, as the contrast is much greater.

Repetition

Repetition refers to the repeating occurrence of the same or similar elements throughout a text, whether that text be a set of presentation slides, a textbook, a blog post, or a brochure. Heading fonts should remain the same size, font, and alignment throughout a text, for instance. Or if the topic of your project is endangered plant species, repeated use of similar plant images can bring a subtle sense of cohesiveness to the whole.

Alignment

According to Williams, the point of the alignment principle is to ensure that nothing looks like it was placed at random. Every element of your page, infographic, or presentation slide should be aligned visually to other elements, as though there were invisible grid lines dictating the placement of elements throughout. For instance, every chunk on this page is aligned to the left margin, creating the sense of an invisible line down the left side of the page. If the text was centered throughout, no such line would exist, making the document look and feel chaotic to read.

Proximity

As with alignment, proximity is concerned with how objects are placed in a text. Here the focus is on grouping: items that are meant to be grouped together should be placed close together; those that are not meant to be grouped together should be separated by an extra bit of white (or blank) space. For instance, each of the CRAP principles listed here is separated from the others by an extra space, visually reinforcing the sense that they are each separate and worthy of independent consideration.

Questions to Consider:

1. Look at a poster in your classroom or out on a bulletin board in the hallway. Or leaf through this textbook. How well do these texts demonstrate the principles of contrast, repetition, alignment, and proximity?

2. What role do you think design principles play in persuasion? Can you think of particular texts (advertisements, books, posters, etc) with a design that pleases you? What is it you like about the design, and can you see the CRAP principles at work in the design?

WRITING SERVICES

Will Wilkinson

—▫—

DePaolo Hall, first floor
910-962-7857

All writers need readers, and the more readers you have while drafting a paper, the better your paper can become. Writing Services provides experienced peer readers for all UNCW students as they develop and improve their writing skills. Writing Services are not remedial, but designed for all student writers who want to improve their papers. Students can get help with their writing in three ways:

- The Writing Center provides one-on-one writing sessions led by faculty-recommended peer writing consultants who are trained to help students identify areas to improve and develop specific revision plans.

- Students can also receive electronic responses to their developing papers through our Online Writing & Learning (OWL) program. Visit our website for a variety of writing resources: handouts, guides, useful links, and the Online Consultation link.

- Students can drop in at our Writing Lab for help with quick questions about their developing papers. The Writing Lab is staffed with a writing consultant, and has a few computers and other writing resources for students.

What to Expect:

During typical face-to-face appointments, you can expect the writing consultant to:

- Talk with you about the assignment (it is helpful to have a copy of the prompt).

- Ask you what you want to work on during the appointment.

- Ask you to read through your draft aloud (it is helpful to have a printed copy of your draft).

- Respond to your questions and concerns, while making other suggestions or asking questions about other parts of your paper.

- Suggest ways to continue working on your paper after the appointment.

How to make the most of your writing consultation:

We ask that students take responsibility for preparing for each consultation. We can't "fix" your writing, but we can help you learn to become a better and more confident writer.

The Responsibilities of Students:

- Make appointments well before your paper is due. Writing consultants won't be able to provide much help if you don't have time to revise your paper after the consultation.

- Prior to your visit, think about what you want out of your consultation, and tell the writing consultant what you want to work on.

- Bring a copy of your assignment with you.

- Bring your notes, ideas, and rough drafts.

- Bring a flashdrive if you want to use a computer.

The Responsibilities of Writing Consultants:

- Writing consultants will begin by focusing on what *you* think needs work in your paper.

- Writing consultants will make suggestions, not lecture or grade you.

- Writing consultants will ask you questions to help you imagine ways to revise your draft.

- Writing consultants will talk with you about focus, content development, organization, and audience.

- Writing consultants will help you learn about punctuation, grammar, and usage.

When Responding to Online Submissions (OWLs), Writing Consultants:

- Will only respond to "global" revision concerns (i.e. focus, development, organization, etc.). If you want assistance with "local" revision concerns (how to edit, MLA or APA citation, etc.), you need to set an appointment to meet face to face with a writing consultant.

- Will use Word's comment function to respond to drafts, posing questions and making suggestions.

- Papers that are 10 pages or longer must be "broken" into more than one submission. A peer writing consultant cannot get through more than 10 pages during a typical online response session.

- You should receive your response within 2-3 business days, but this is not guaranteed.

What Writing Consultants Will Not Do:

- Writing consultants will not correct or proofread your paper.

- Writing consultants will not write the paper for you.

- Writing consultants will not guess what grade the paper might receive.

WILLIAM MADISON RANDALL LIBRARY

Tammy E. Ivins, Lisa R. Coats, and
Anne E. Pemberton

—⊡—

Randall Library
910-962-3750
http://library.uncw.edu/

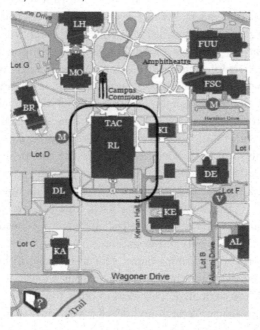

As a UNCW student, you will probably be asked to write many research papers. In order to write good papers, you need to develop good research skills. Much of your research will involve the library in some way. UNCW's William Madison Randall Library offers information through online collections as well as through physical collections of books, films, journals, and more. Randall Library is the main library for the UNCW community. Through the library, you have access to almost 800,000 books (both in print and online formats), more than 62,000 journals (primarily online through the library's databases), and close to 360,000 media items (DVDs, VHS tapes, online streaming video, CDs, streaming audio, etc.). Even if you do not do your research in the library building itself, you will probably use the library's online resources, especially when you need to find articles from journals and magazines.

As you begin writing a paper, your instructor will likely ask you to review what scholars and experts say about a topic, and then ask you to analyze their ideas in order to help you synthesize the available research and develop your own thoughts. So good research skills begin with the ability to develop a research question. Once you've determined the question you're going to investigate, you will then find what others have said about it, or how others have answered it. The library provides access to the books and articles that are the results of other people's investigations into a topic. These books and articles are the information sources that you will use to develop your research papers.

Once you identify your research topic or question, it is important that you:

1. Know how to search for and find relevant information on your topic,
2. Evaluate the information to determine the reliability of your sources and the validity of their information,
3. And, if you use the words or ideas of other people in your paper, you will need to cite, or give credit to, the original authors in order to acknowledge their work and to distinguish your ideas from theirs.

All of the steps above are part of the research process. Since much of your research will begin with Randall Library resources, the information below will help you when you need to do research.

SEARCHING FOR INFORMATION: TYPES OF INFORMATION SOURCES AND HOW TO FIND THEM

Articles

Articles are writings published in magazines, newspapers, or scholarly journals. Journalists write articles in magazines and newspapers, and these articles typically range from just a few paragraphs to two to three pages in length. Professors, researchers, and people with advanced degrees in a particular field write scholarly journal articles. Scholarly articles are usually much longer, ranging from five pages to fifty pages in length, cite other works in a list of references at the end of the article, and usually involve an in-depth review by other experts in the field in a process called peer review.

If you were researching the use and prescription of psychiatric drugs among children, you should expect to find that different article types will handle the topic differently. For example:

- A Dallas *newspaper*, focusing on local news, reports on how a legislative bill in Texas might prevent children on Medicaid from receiving antidepressants.

- A *magazine* article might highlight results of a national poll surveying people in the United States about the number of children who take antipsychotic drugs.

- A *scholarly journal* article might present results of a study comparing the overall health of people who took psychotropic drugs as children to those who did not take psychotropic drugs; the research study finds that people who took psychotropic drugs as children are at a higher risk of experiencing cardiovascular problems as adults.

To find any of these types of articles, a good place to start is using the search box on the library's homepage: http://library .uncw.edu. This box searches through the library's biggest article database. You can also search other specific databases, such as *ProQuest Central, JSTOR,* or *ScienceDirect.* You can find these databases by name (A-Z) or by subject on the library website: https://library.uncw.edu/articles_on_topic.

Only UNCW students, faculty, and staff have access to these online collections of articles. People not affiliated with UNCW can access these collections only if they come into Randall Library and use one of the guest computers. Access to these databases is paid for by the library through subscriptions. Since subscriptions are paid for using some of your tuition dollars, you will be prompted to log in to these resources if you're not on campus.

Keyword Searches

In order to search effectively, you will need to create an appropriate keyword search. Instead of using a whole phrase to search, like:

The effects of psychiatric drugs on children

the search is more effective if you search only with keywords, placing an "and" between keywords or keyword phrases. With this strategy, your keyword search could be:

psychiatric drugs and children

Since the search above is only looking for exact matches on the words you type in, you would also want to come up with a list of related words, or synonyms, to use in your search. Each of the searches below uses related words, but will bring back different results than the first search above.

antidepressants and adolescents
antipsychotics and pediatrics
pyschotropic drugs and children

To get more practice with developing a search, you can use the "My Research Strategy" website: http://library.uncw.edu/instruction/research_strategy. It will walk you through each step of creating an effective keyword search.

Many articles will be available in PDF or HTML full-text. If you would like to read an article that doesn't have a full-text link, just ask a librarian for help. You can get help from Randall Library librarians by text, chat, email, phone, or in person. Go to http://library.uncw.edu/ask to ask a librarian for assistance.

Books

A nonfiction book may have a single author or several different authors. For example, in a book about child psychiatry, one author might write a chapter about how doctors diagnose depression and bipolar disorders in children. That chapter might be followed by another chapter, written by a different author who describes how treatments for children with bipolar disorder vary between European and American psychiatrists.

Searching for Books

To search for books in the library, you can use the search box on the library homepage. You can even limit your search to only "Books & eBooks" using the drop-down menu to the left of the search box. Just as you search for articles using keywords, you also want to search for books using keywords. Keep in mind that articles are about something very specific, while books generally cover a topic with greater breadth. You might not find a book specifically about childhood depression, but you'll find many books about child psychiatry in general, each of which may have several chapters about childhood depression.

You might start with a search for:

antidepressants and children

If only a few of the books look relevant, you might broaden your search and use more general keywords. You might search a couple more times, again using synonyms to try to find more matches.

children and psychiatry
children and psychoactive drugs
children and pyschopharmacology

Remember, if you ever have trouble coming up with keywords to search, you can ask a librarian: http://library.uncw.edu/ask.

If you're searching for a particular book, you can search by title or by author. Make sure to put titles in quotation marks ("The Hunger Games"). When you click on the title of the book, you're taken to a page with more detailed information about the book. The chapter titles from the table of contents are often on this page.

Locating Books and Other Materials in Randall

To find out if something is available for checkout, click on the title of the book. If the book is available online as an eBook, you'll be provided with a link to read the book online. If the book is in print and UNCW owns a copy you'll see a "Location," "Call number," and "Status" for the item. Items noted as "AVAILABLE" are on the shelf and ready to be checked out. Books currently checked out have the due date listed.

To retrieve an available item on the shelf, take note of the location and the entire call number. The location is like the neighborhood in the library where something is shelved, and the call number is like the item's address.

If you wanted to locate the book *No Child Left Different*, the location (or "neighborhood") is the "UNCW General Collection." Most books in Randall Library are in the UNCW General Collection, which is on the second floor. If you aren't sure where a particular location is within Randall Library, floor maps are available under "Use the Library" on the library's website.

The call number, or the item's "address," matches a spot on the shelf in the item's location where the book is stored; in this case, the "address" you're looking for is RJ 504.7.N6 2006.

Be sure to note all the letters and numbers of the call number, or "address," to help you find the book you want.

DVDs

Recreational and documentary DVDs are located on the first floor of the library. Movies are organized by genres (comedy, horror, science fiction, etc.). The library also has television series on DVD as well as documentary videos. There is also a collection of documentary videos in VHS format on the second floor.

You can find specific videos using the library's search box. Once you complete a search using an actor's name, director's name, or film title, you can look at the results under the heading "Videos & Music" on the search results page. Again, the location is similar to the "neighborhood" where an item is located, and the call number is its "address" in that neighborhood or location.

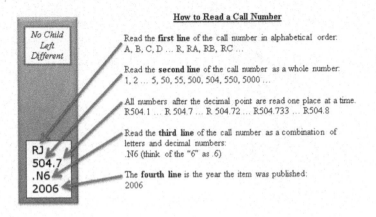

How to Read a Call Number

Read the **first line** of the call number in alphabetical order:
A, B, C, D ... R, RA, RB, RC ...

Read the **second line** of the call number as a whole number:
1, 2 ... 5, 50, 55, 500, 504, 550, 5000 ...

All numbers after the decimal point are read one place at a time.
R504.1 ... R 504.7 ... R 504.72 ... R504.733 ... R504.8

Read the **third line** of the call number as a combination of
letters and decimal numbers:
.N6 (think of the "6" as .6)

The **fourth line** is the year the item was published:
2006

RJ
504.7
.N6
2006

Websites

You are probably used to using *Google*, or another search engine, to search for information online. Finding information is important in being a good researcher, but it is just as important to evaluate information, especially regarding information you find on the Internet. This is because authorship and reliability are not always easy to determine on Internet sites. See the section "Evaluating Information Sources" below for more information.

There are a few things you should know about using search engines. First, you can increase your ability to find reliable information if you limit your searches to specific domains on the Internet. For example, you can limit your results to web pages stored on college and university servers—meaning that those pages have been authored by faculty, staff, or students at a college or university—if you end your search in *Google* with *site: .edu*. For example, the search for *children psychiatric drugs site:.edu* will retrieve results only from colleges and universities in the United States.

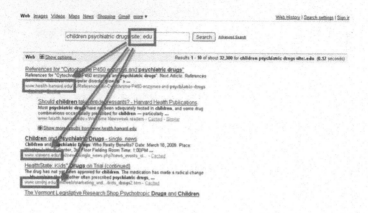

You can do the same thing with any Internet domain in *Google*; searching for *adolescent depression site:.gov* will return web pages from government agencies such as the National Institutes of Health, the Surgeon General's office, and the U.S. Department of Health and Human Services. Searching *Google* for *children psychotropic drugs site:.ac.uk* will retrieve web pages from colleges and universities in the United Kingdom.

Second, in your list of results in *Google*, you might find a relevant article, but you won't necessarily have access to the full article. The publisher might ask you to pay to download the article. Do not pay! The library may already have a subscription to the publication you need, and a librarian can help you find the article in one of the library's databases. If the library does not subscribe to the publication, the library will find the article for you using a service called Interlibrary Loan (ILL) which is free for you, though it may take a few days to get the article. You should never pay for an article because Randall Library will generally find a copy at no cost to you.

Finally, use the library's subject guides to direct you to useful resources on your topic. Librarians have selected particular databases and websites that have credible authors and reliable information. You can find them in any subject guide on the Randall Library Website: http://library.uncw.edu/guides.

EVALUATING INFORMATION SOURCES

When you are doing research, it is not enough to find a source to quote in your paper. You must also evaluate the source. Articles, scientific reports, studies, books, and letters to the editor all have possible flaws or limitations, if not flat-out inaccuracies. It can also be difficult to tell what you are looking at in an electronic format. For example, scholarly journals publish not only research-based articles but also opinion pieces, such as book reviews and letters to the editor. Just because something is published doesn't make it true. As a researcher, you must critically examine the information you receive and determine whether or not it is reliable and accurate.

Being a researcher is like being a detective—and your sources are your evidence. When you're deciding what sources to use for your paper, think about what evidence will help you solve your case. You'll ask yourself three questions:

QUESTION 1: DO I TRUST THIS SOURCE?

If a child had chocolate all over their face but insisted that they didn't eat candy, you'd be a little skeptical. Detectives regularly have to decide how reliable a witness is based on clues about them. It's exactly the same for research: you have to examine the source carefully. Consider the person, people, or publications that produced a source to decide if it's credible, reliable, and trustworthy enough. Watch out for things like uninformed authors who are not credible experts, bias and intentional misinformation, and unprofessional publication platforms (like a blog) that do insufficient vetting and editing.

So, how can you spot those red flags? One key is looking outside of the source. Think about it this way: if you were investigating a crime, would you trust a suspect automatically if they said, "I didn't do it?" Probably not. You'd question other people and try to find out how likely it is that the suspect is telling the truth. It's the same with research. Just because a source or platform claims something doesn't mean that you should believe them. You often have to explore other sources in order to piece together different bits of information and get an accurate picture of a source's validity.

QUESTION 2: IS THIS SOURCE GOOD ENOUGH?

Not all evidence is of the same quality. Is yours good enough to rely on to solve your case, or to present in court? In this case, "good" means up-to-date, informative, and accurate. We determine that by asking when, why, and how the information was created.

First: when was the source written? Not everything old is bad! An older source can provide valuable insight, but up-to-date information can include important content missing in older sources. Think about solving a crime. It may be useful to know that six months ago, the suspect was driving a white sedan. However, it is likely more useful to know that two days ago the suspect was seen in a blue van. In research, the publication date can be more or less important, depending on what discipline you are in and what angle you are taking for your research.

Next: why was the source created? Think of witnesses in a case. If someone stood to inherit a lot of money in a court case, you would keep that in mind while reviewing their testimony. The same is true for research—ask yourself, why did the author write this piece, make this video, etc.? Is the intent of the author to inform, to explore, to convince or persuade, to entertain, or to sell? For example, news is usually meant to inform the reader, while scholarly articles and books are meant to explore a topic in more depth.

Finally, imagine you are a detective, and each source is a folder of evidence being handed to you. You probably wouldn't trust an evidence file if the junior detective who put it together wouldn't tell you where or how they got the evidence, or said they'd just written down some gossip they'd overheard. Be sure the sources you're using were researched and assembled in a way that makes it more likely to be accurate.

QUESTION 3: DOES THIS SOURCE HELP ME?

If you were a detective working a case, it wouldn't matter how reliable or good a tip is if that tip isn't useful. You could have a very reliable witness providing in-depth information, but if that information is about the suspect's pet cat, it won't be very useful in assembling evidence of tax fraud. It's the same with research.

First, consider the assignment guidelines and your specific thesis to decide what information do you need. You'll need different kinds of evidence depending on your case. Then, consider what information (aka: evidence) is in this source. Sometimes we get excited when a source is on our topic, and we don't stop to think about whether it is actually useful to us. Once you have an idea of what kind of information is in a source, stop and consider carefully whether it is the evidence that you need for the assignment and to support your thesis.

A good shortcut to remember is BEAM, which breaks down four different ways you could use information in a paper:

- **B**ackground = general information or factual evidence that you can use to provide context in your paper.

- **E**xhibits = evidence that you will analyze or interpret in your paper.

- **A**rgument = examples of what experts are saying about your topic; you will engage with their comments (refute, refine, build off of, affirm, etc.).

- **M**ethod = definitions of terminology & concepts, manner of thinking/analysis.

Evaluation is an art, not a science, and there is no "one size fits all" set of guidelines for this important activity. As always, if you have questions or need a hand, just ask a librarian at http://library.uncw.edu/ask.

USING SOURCES: CREATING CITATIONS AND AVOIDING PLAGIARISM

Research builds off of the work of others. Your own research will involve reviewing the thoughts and experiments of others in order to develop your own understanding. It is important to differentiate your thoughts and words from others' so that you do not give the impression that these thoughts or words are your own. You should give proper credit where credit is due.

Giving credit to others is as easy as citing them. Using citation styles, such as the American Psychological Association (APA) or Modern Language Association (MLA) citation styles, you can quote, paraphrase, or summarize the work of others appropriately if you use quotation marks, parenthetical citations, and include a list of references cited at the end of your paper. Proper citation ensures that you will not engage in academic dishonesty. At UNCW, cheating and plagiarism are forms of academic dishonesty and violate the Academic Honor Code. Engaging in such behavior may result in you receiving an "F" in a course, or worse.

Plagiarism can be avoided by using citations, bur sometimes citation styles can seem tricky. Be careful when searching the open web for citation assistance, as many websites may contain errors and/or not be updated to the latest edition of a citation style. Randall Library has a list of reliable guides on how to cite at http://library.uncw.edu/citations. In addition, although the University Learning Center is not part of the library, you should know about their helpful services. The Writing Center, part of the University Learning Center in DePaolo Hall, sets up appointments with students who would like help with citations. For more information, visit their web site: https://uncw.edu/ulc/services/writing/center.html

ABOUT RANDALL LIBRARY

- Many UNCW students study late, so Randall Library has extensive hours of service. Hours are listed on the library's website http://library.uncw.edu/hours. You can search from your own computer 24/7.

- If you visit the library after 10:00 p.m., you must bring your UNCW ID card to swipe in order to enter the building.

- The second floor of Randall Library is reserved for quiet study. There is also a "Quiet Zone" room available on the second floor.

- In the Learning Commons on the library's first floor, you'll find:

  - research assistance

  - ~150 desktop computers

  - printers

  - copiers

  - scanners

- Also located on the first floor is the Technology Assistance Center (TAC). TAC provides technical assistance, video editing stations, laptop checkout, and much more.

- Near TAC in the back of the first floor is the iPrint Business Center. They provide a variety of services including printing and laminating. iPrint allows you to send print jobs from any computer to any iPrint release station on campus. Randall Library has several iPrint release stations on the first floor and a few on the second floor.

- Also near TAC is the Digital Makerspace, which offers access to emerging technologies such as VR, 3D printing, and more. https://digitalmakerspace.uncw.edu/

- UNCW undergraduate students can check out an unlimited number of books. For DVDs, VHS tapes, CDs, and New and Popular Books, undergraduates can check out a total of 7 items at one time, in any combination (for example, 4 DVDs and 3 CDs). Most books can be checked out for 28 days.

- Group study rooms are available throughout the library for groups to use to study or practice presentations. To see locations and reserve a group study room online, visit: http://library.uncw.edu/room_reservations.

- Port City Java (PCJ) is the coffee shop in Randall Library and serves a full array of snacks and beverages.

- The Center for Southeast North Carolina Archives and History includes Randall Library's Special Collections and the UNCW Archives. http://library.uncw.edu /archives_special

  - Special Collections holds materials dating back to the 16th Century and actively builds its many collections, including a collection on southeast North Carolina history.

  - UNCW Archives, housed in Randall Library, has documents and materials from UNCW's history, including photographs and memorabilia.

- Randall Library contains a large collection of both state and federal government documents. To learn more, visit: http://library.uncw.edu/gov_docs.

- You can find out more about the library here: http://library. uncw.edu/about_library

- Librarians and library staff are here to help you. So please ask if you have any questions. To get help in person, visit the Research Help Desk, or to get help virtually, visit: http:// library.uncw.edu/ask.

HELPFUL SERVICES FROM THE LIBRARY'S WEBSITE

- **Get Help** (chat, email, call, or get in person assistance from a librarian) http://library.uncw.edu/ask

- **Interlibrary Loan** (get books and articles Randall Library doesn't have at no cost to you) http://library.uncw.edu/ill

- **My Library Account** (renew online the DVDs, CDs, or books you have checked out) https://libcat.uncw.edu/patroninfo

- **Online Tutorials** http://library.uncw.edu/tutorials

Whether you use our online resources, or visit the building for a study break, research help, or to collaborate with other students, the librarians and staff at Randall Library hope you find what you need to make your UNCW career successful. If you aren't sure how to find something or are not sure where to go, please don't hesitate to ask a librarian by visiting: http:// library.uncw.edu/ask.

TWENTY

AWARD-WINNING ESSAYS FROM
UNCW STUDENTS

———◻———

THE FOLLOWING IS a small sample of the many excellent essays students write each year in their UNCW composition classes. These examples are all recent award winners from the Composition Program's Jo Ann Seiple Composition Contest, and are reprinted here to provide you with a better sense of the range of work students produce in our program. They represent each of the annual contest's three categories: personal narratives, rhetorical or textual analysis, and researched argumentative essays. Links to excellent multimodal projects—also award winners— are available on the English Department's website on the Composition page.

Keep in mind that these essays are not intended to be perfectly representative of what you will do in your classes. Specific requirements vary by teacher, and different skills will be emphasized in different assignments. Also, there is no such thing as an objective "A" paper; all writing is situated. This means that a particular essay's success is not determined by an essential, transcendent quality, but rather by how well it responds to the occasion articulated through prompts, rubrics, class discussion, conferences, peer review, etc. (This is true for all forms of writing—for example, there is no such thing as a perfect résumé for all possible jobs.) Because of this, we have included excerpts from the corresponding assignment prompts, and we encourage you to read these essays not as perfect models for what you ought to do, but as examples of effective, engaging, and nuanced student writing that responds well to its particular situation.

We encourage you to submit work from your composition classes to the Jo Ann Seiple Composition Contest, so that your essay might appear in this book or on our website in a future year. Authors of selected entries receive gift certificates to merchants of their choice, valued at up to $100. For more information about the contest, please visit the Composition page on the UNCW English Department website.

Fair Trade

HUNTER SMITH

EXCERPTED PROMPT

Research Essay

In your final essay, you will develop and support a well-researched argument of your own that responds to a conceptual or practical problem that you formulate for yourself. Unless you have changed topics, this will be a continuation of the research you began in your review of literature. You should think of this essay as a way of working on a problem that is of interest to you and that should be of interest to your readers. There are a few required elements, listed below, but you should also think of this essay as demonstrating your use of the principles and "moves" described in *They Say, I Say*.

Research essay written for English 103 with Dr. Nathan Ragain.

Requirements

Length: 8 pages, double spaced, plus Works Cited/References.

Introduction/Claim: Your introduction should accomplish all the moves of a "problem frame," although this does not mean that it must be only one paragraph. It should, however, end with a strong claim. A strong claim should be contestable, supportable, specific, and interesting (in the sense that it is at least somewhat unique and that it helps us solve a problem that we should care about).

Sources: There is no set number of total sources. The total number of sources will be dictated by what you feel you need in order to make your argument and to frame it as part of a conversation. However, you must have at least four scholarly sources, and all of your sources must be included in a works cited/references page and given proper internal citation.

Acknowledgement & Response: You must have at least one full paragraph in which you engage in a sustained acknowledgement/response regarding a competing view of some aspect of your argument. In most cases, it will be best to frame this acknowledgement/response in dialogue with at least one of your sources.

FAIR TRADE

When shopping online or in person, it's rare that customers consider the environment in which their products are made, by whom they were made, and how much those people were paid. Generally, a customer's main concern is what they receive, not the process it took to get there. Even if consumers were concerned about the maker-to-market journey of the product they're purchasing, they'd likely get distracted by the competitive pricing and trendy addiction of fast fashion. In general, customers assume their clothes, jewelry, electronics, and everyday life products are ethically made by appropriately paid wage workers. However, even if the truth is carefully hidden behind flashy ad campaigns and ripped jeans worn by attractive models, many brands and even entire markets are based on unfair trade. There's a lack of international legislation enforcing acceptable conditions, payment, and treatment of workers in order to protect from companies that take advantage of their already flimsy rights. Not only are people being harmed, but entire economies and companies as a whole are unknowingly or willingly remaining ignorant to the fact that they're being burdened with economic consequences as well. And people aren't the only ones paying the price, the planet is too: many companies' unfair trade practices take a large toll on the already vulnerable environment. In order to help all parties—workers who are treated unfairly, companies that participate in unfair trade and therefore lose money, and the planet—international organizations like the United Nations need to pass legislation that bans these unethical practices and establishes requisites for companies to function and workers to enjoy safety, reasonable hours, and decent pay. In the meantime, people can help by spreading awareness, boycotting companies, pushing for change via outlets like social media, and pressing politicians to protect workers and aid companies.

In order to understand how to fix the problem of unfair labor practices it's imperative to understand the objective— fair trade. Fair trade is the exchange of goods from developing to developed countries based on ethical practices throughout each step from maker to market. The intent of organizations like Fair Trade Certified is to "support responsible companies, empower farmers, workers, and fishermen, and protect the environment" (Fair Trade Certified 2020). Similarly, Fair Trade America's standards serve as an appropriate baseline for how a fair-trade company functions. They set standards in a variety of categories within the company's structure; for example, within the social aspect of companies lies regulations against child labor and discrimination-based hiring, and minimums for working conditions and labor practices like the ability for workers to create unions, organize, and have employment contracts. Standards for economic practices of companies are established as well, according to their published standards summary, Fair Trade America sets requirements for measures like "paying the Fairtrade Minimum Price as well as the Premium, requiring traceability of the product through record-keeping as well as transparency in trade relations and providing pre-finance if requested by producers" (Fairtrade America 2020). The final portion of Fair Trade America's standards covers protections on the environment that minimize the negative effect of companies' manufacturing on the planet and include bans on harmful pesticides and GMO seeds while incentivizing eco-friendly practices through increased premiums (Fairtrade America 2020). These standards give an idea of what fair trade looks like in action: companies that treat their workers well and abide by their rights, both socially and economically, and practice eco-friendly production and commerce in order to reduce harmful consequences to the environment. However, only about 1.66 million farmers and 2,400 companies qualify as fair trade under these and similar fair trade organizations' standards and whilst this number may seem like a large amount, the entire state of Pennsylvania includes 2.6 million companies alone, according to the Pennsylvania Business Department of State (A Guide to Business registration in Pennsylvania, 2018). This disparity proves how little business cares about being known as fair trade. And although a lack of certification from Fair Trade organizations doesn't automatically mean that these companies treat their workers poorly and have total disregard for the environment (they still have to follow the laws), it makes it easy for these companies to behave in ways that would not fall under definitions or regulations of fair trade and hurt their workers without being held accountable.

However, the appeal to business practices that would not fall under fair trade is obvious, with benefits for both the producer and consumer. Businesses are able to produce their goods at a lower price and customers reap the benefits of cheaper sales of products. The fashion industry, and specifically "fast fashion," provides a powerful example of companies taking advantage of workers and participating in production that's extremely harmful to the environment. The definition of fast fashion is "cheaply produced and priced garments that copy the latest catwalk styles and get pumped quickly through stores in order to maximise on current trends" (Maiti 2020). Researchers Gérard P. Cachon and Robert Swinney analyzed the economic impacts of fast fashion and found that when quick response methods are combined with enhanced design practices profits for clothing companies are increased. The authors described quick response methods as having "design abilities [that] are standard but a production time [that] is fast" (Cachon & Swinney 2011). This way companies are able to produce the majority of the product after the demand level has been accurately gaged and are able to deliver it to customers without having to pay for expedited production procedures. Enhanced design occurs when production time is longer, but the firm invests in improved design efforts that the customer values and can be charged more for. When working in cooperation, these two practices allow for the most desirable, most valued product for the consumer and most efficient, most profitable manufacturing for the producer. The tactic of enhanced design can be incorporated with quick response via the upcharging for better quality items, but kept at competitive prices since the companies save money on not needing to pay for exhibited shipping and commerce. Apparently, a win for the manufacturing companies, and a win for the consumer.

But what about workers? The basic human rights violations occurring in order to fulfill fast fashion needs like the enhanced design and quick response systems are largely made possible by sweatshops which continue to be a big problem in many developing countries, even though they are considered abhorrent by the consumers who unknowingly support them. Business Ethics researchers Tara J. Radlin and Martin Calkins attempt to explain why sweatshops still exist and the best way to get rid of them. Because there's no specific definition of a sweatshop and no clear standards for regulation, they argue, these spaces are difficult to ban. Essentially, if there isn't a consensus on what something is, how can you say it's not allowed? When attempting to define "sweatshop," other troubling definitions arise when trying to apply commonly cited words. For example, most definitions of sweatshop include exploitation of workers. However, if a worker signs up for a job and continues to work are they genuinely being exploited or not because they continue to choose to stay? Now of course there's the argument that workers don't have the choice to leave because they need to afford basic necessities, but many companies continue to make the excuse that at least they're providing opportunities and money for work that workers might not have had otherwise and therefore they're not exploiting them, but helping them. Instead of coming to an explicit definition for sweatshop, many have accepted that the term is ambiguous but useful as a general or category expression" (Radlin & Calkins 2006).

The prominent notion of utilitarianism, the philosophy that good is measured in how much happiness something brings, also gets in the way of banning sweatshops. When this philosophy is applied to sweatshops, the miserable lives of a few can be outweighed by the joy brought to many by the shirts and jeans produced by those workers. Finally, companies defend their practices by pointing to the social and economic conditions in the developing countries where their sweatshops are located. Due to the poor national state of these places, workers lack education and skill that make them eligible for any other type of job, and in a way these jobs are better than nothing. The overwhelming argument being made is that the lack of opportunity in these countries, coupled with the broader happiness they bring, are an excuse for the continuation of sweatshop. However, basic moral reasoning suggests that the sweatshop, as we generally define it, needs to be shuttered in order to save and improve lives.

The inhumane treatment of fashion and textile manufacturing workers is proof that people continue to work in sweatshops which are sustaining the fast fashion industry. According to the European Union (EU), the working conditions in many Asian countries qualify as slave labor due to workers' long hours, low wages, lack of regular contracts, and systematically hazardous conditions. Problematically, 70% of textiles in the EU were produced in Asia (D'Ambrogio 2014). Beginning with working hours, the daily average working hours for a worker in most manufacturing countries is 14–16 hours, about double that of an average American work day, which also only spans a five-day period per week, not seven. Many times these workers are refused overtime pay and are fired if they choose to leave early, which they can't afford. For these exhausting hours they get paid extremely low wages, for example in Bangladesh the living wage is 259.8 euros, but minimum wage is 49.56 euros, that's a fifth of the amount of money these workers need to live. On top of the exploitative hours and low wages, the conditions in which workers spend their 14-hour days are brutal. They lack basic safety materials, are constantly prone to injury from factory machines, and fall ill to toxins they breathe in through the air. And there's no way for the workers to fight for themselves because they don't have the right to unionize and therefore almost never have steady contracts (Sustain 2020).

Not only are human beings being harmed, but so is the planet. The biggest environmental problem with fast fashion is the "fast" part of it. Clothing is pumped into the market at extremely high rates, replaced by new trends every few months, and old clothes are thrown away as waste. At the pace that clothing completes its minute life cycle combined with the amount of water used to make the materials, carbon emissions produced by the clothes, and waste from the clothes in the trash dumps, the impact it has on the environment is astronomical. In order to produce cheaper clothes, companies use materials like nylon and polyester which are not biodegradable and the microplastics that come from them make up around "31% of plastic pollution in the ocean" (Mfall-Johnsen 2019). Not only does fast-fashion pollute the Earth's water, but it also consumes it; according to *Business Insider*, the fashion industry is the second largest consumer of water in the world

(Mcfall-Johnsen 2019). It's also responsible for 10% of the world's carbon emissions, which is only exacerbated by using the above mentioned polyesters, which creates two to three times more carbon when used in clothing production. Finally, 85% of textiles end up in dumps each year. These are just a few of endless examples of how negative an impact fast-fashion, an example of extremely unfair trading practices, has on the environment.

Despite the general agreement that human rights and environmental protections are justifiable enough for enforcement of fair-trade practices, there's economic arguments for fair trade that favor businesses as well. According to the World Health Organization, worker's health lacks priority and standards in many countries which results in injury, disease, overall unwellness, and death for workers in these unfortunate conditions. Occupational health standards are especially lacking in small enterprises and agricultural companies where there's no health services to regulate or help improve these conditions. As a result of complications due to poor working conditions (which include heat, dust, dangerous chemicals and machines, and psychological stress) there is a 4–6% economic downfall each year, and the price for proper healthcare for one worker is on average between $16–$80. Specialized occupational health services assess risks and provide processes to fix conditions and help workers, which allows for better working environments, increases worker's health conditions, gives companies economic advantage because they have healthier, more efficient workers, and creates a more stabilized economy and healthier workforce overall. Data that proves these claims shows that "health initiatives can help reduce sick leave absenteeism by 27% and health-care costs for companies by 26% (WHO)." The health of people is largely dependent on their working conditions, and when companies look out for their workers' health and safety they are able to save money and employees are able to lead healthier and happier lives. The economic benefits for business and the explications of the horror that unfair trade practices incurs reasonably and justly incites the need for a solution—for the people, for the planet, and the companies. In his essay "What if all trade was fair trade? The potential of a social clause to achieve the goals of fair trade," business researcher Carmen Valor suggests the possibility that including social clause in trade agreements would help to protect labor rights internationally. A social clause is a regulation on "any non-economic aspect of trade exchanges ... [and] are commonly used to protect labour rights," and when enforced, would curtail exports by any company not following labor standards (Valor 2006). This method of enforcing human rights is seen as an economic sanction on violating labor regulations internationally. There are two categories of theoretical debate that foster the idea of a social clause: an economic debate and moral debate. The economic debate focuses on whether or not worker protection mandates that are deemed "ethical" have a real economic benefit, which is true when considering worker's health which was previously explained. In addition, the incorporation of a social clause would not raise labour costs an exorbitant amount because they lack a minimum wage. The moral debate is fueled by the argument that a social clause is protecting human rights and that no matter the economic advantage or disadvantage these laws are necessary. The effectiveness of fair trade is dependent on worker's rights and social clauses will work to protect those rights.

The environmental side of fair trade is dependent on enforcement of regulations of international organizations like the United Nations. Jeremic Vuk and Jeffrey Sachs list some of the important environmental goals published by the United Nations in *The United Nations in the Age of Sustainable Development*. Two of these goals that are the most important when pertaining to the planet's well-being are one: "Curb Human-Induced Climate Change and Ensure Sustainable Energy" by ensuring clean-energy for all, improve practices in agriculture, forestry, waste management, and industry in order to curb carbon emissions, and pricing green-house gas emissions (Vuk and Sachs). The other goal established in order to aid in the health of the Earth is "Secure Ecosystem

Services and Biodiversity, and Ensure Good Management of Water and Other Natural Resources" by adopting legislation and policies that halt the degradation of the ecosystems, monitoring these ecosystems in order to keep track of their health, and having all business committed to sustainable management of resources. Both of these sustainable development goals and their methodology back up the regulations set by fair trade organizations in order to protect the environment and its resources as well as diminished carbon emissions. In the context of industries like fast fashion that use a large portion of the planet's non-replenishable resources and produce many irreversible negative effects, the passing and enforcement of legislation that reaches these goals would be an undeniably large step in the right direction toward environmental sustainability and enforcing fair trade practices on a large scale in order to save the planet.

Although these changes—internationally enforced worker's rights, fixing economic disparity caused by unfair trade, and environmental aid—are necessary, the enforcement of objectives this widely spanning takes time that could be used effectively by the general public in ways that would push fair trade toward the forefront of the economy and establish it as the business norm. Since fast fashion is generally a problem caused by generation z the solution needs to start with generation z. Trends spread among this group via outlets like social media, which thrives off the most consumable, most relevant content at the time, and due to the short attention span of this generation, relevancy comes to and fades by the same trend quickly. This relevance also pertains to fashion trends, which is how fast fashion remains so successful, because it satisfies generation z's ever changing style and is affordable due to the nature of their production system. A way to replace fast fashion with fair trade, in the minds of generation z consumers, is to pump it out via social media. People of influence on social media choose to make certain trends, products, or lifestyle choices popular and promote them on their platform when they receive a sponsorship. If social media influencers are approached by organizations that promote fair trade and are offered sponsorships, these influencers could come to their followers with ways to help push fair trade. Influencers could set a trend to boycott businesses that exploit their workers and the environment, which would be very effective due to the foundation already established within social media activism. Influencers could also promote second-hand shopping, which aligns with other trends like thrift store shopping.

It's also well known how much social media can influence politics, which can be seen when analyzing movements like the Black Lives Matter movement. According to PEW Research "23% of adult social media users in the United States—and 17% of adults overall—say they have changed their views about a political or social issue because of something they saw on social media in the past year. ... And when asked to elaborate on the things they have changed their views about, these adults often mention the Black Lives Matter movement and police brutality" (Perrin 2020). Following the death of George Floyd on May 25th the Black Lives Matter movement took off on social media and by June 20th, legislation was passed in Minneapolis, New York, Los Angeles, Kentucky, and the United Kingdom reforming police force structure and function, which exemplifies how social media influences politics and legislation. If this logic is applied to fair trade, legislation could be passed in order to enforce regulations internationally if a large movement gained traction on social media. The benefits and importance of fair trade are far more important than the interests of greedy manufacturers and trendy customers. The need to produce goods that don't depend on immoral labor practices and work toward conserving the planet is growing rapidly and is dependent on international laws and trading regulations. People are being treated inhumanely due to the lack of enforcement of human rights and Earth is spiraling toward an environment full of irreversible damage. Although companies suggest that industries like fast fashion benefit the economy and produce high profit margins, the negative effects of these production firms are not made up for by these selfish benefits. Going forward, fair trade needs to be more heavily and widely enforced in order to maintain a peaceful, healthy, sustainable ecosystem, economy, and human race.

Sources

Cachon, Gérard P., and Robert Swinney. "The Value of Fast Fashion: Quick Response, Enhanced Design, and Strategic Consumer Behavior." *Management Science*, vol. 57, no. 4, 2011, pp. 778–95. JSTOR, www.jstor.org.liblink.uncw.edu /stable/25835736. Accessed 20 Nov. 2020.

D'ambrogio, Enrico. *Workers' Conditions in the Textile and Clothing Sector: Just an Asian Affair? Issues at Stake after the Rana Plaza Tragedy.* Technical report no. 538.222, European Parliament, Aug. 2014. *European Parliament*, www.europarl.europa.eu /EPRS/140841REV1 Workers-conditions-in-the-textile-and -clothing-sector-just an Asian affair FINAL pdf

"Fairtrade Standards." *Fairtrade America*, 2020, www .fairtradeamerica.org/the-standards/. Accessed 20 Nov. 2020.

"Inhumane Working Conditions." *Sustain Your Style*, www.sustainyourstyle.org/old-working-conditions#:~:text =Accidents%2C%20fires%2C%20injuries%2C%20 and,not%20allowed%20to%20drink%20water. Accessed 20 Nov. 2020.

Jeremic, Vuk, and Jeffrey D. Sachs. "The United Nations in the Age of Sustainable Development." *The Economic and Social Review*, vol. 45, no. 2, Summer 2014, pp. 161–88. *ProQuest Central*, search-proquest-com.liblink.uncw.edu/docview /1545341719?accountid=14606.

Maiti, Rashmila. "Fast Fashion: Its Detrimental Effect on the Environment." *Earth.Org*, 29 Jan. 2020, earth.org /fast-fashions-detrimental-effect-on-the-environment/. Accessed 20 Nov. 2020.

Mcfall-Johnsen, Morgan. "The Fashion Industry Emits More Carbon than International Flights and Maritime Shipping

Combined. Here Are the Biggest Ways It Impacts the Planet."
Business Insider, Insider, 21 Oct. 2019, www.businessinsider
.com/fast-fashion-environmental-impact-pollution-emissions
-waste-water-2019-10#the-dyeing-process-uses-enough-water
-to-fill-2-million-olympic-sized-swimming-pools-each-year-20.
Accessed 20 Nov. 2020.

Pennsylvania State, General Assembly, Assembly, Department
of State. *A Guide to Business Registration in Pennsylvania.*
Pennsylvania Department of State, 2018, www.dos.pa.gov
/BusinessCharities/Business/Documents/FEB2018
%2021460%20Guide%20to%20Business%20Registration.pdf.
Accessed 20 Nov. 2020. 2018 General Assembly, Assembly
Document 21460.

Perrin, Andrew. "23% Of Users in U.S. Say Social Media Led
Them to Change Views on an Issue; Some Cite Black
Lives Matter." Pew Research Center, 15 Oct. 2020,
www.pewresearch.org/fact-tank/.

Radin, Tara J., and Martin Calkins. "The Struggle against
Sweatshops: Moving toward Responsible Global Business:
JBE." *Journal of Business Ethics*, vol. 66, nos. 2–3,
Jun 2006, pp. 261–72. *PAIS Index; ProQuest Central*,
http://dx.doi.org.liblink.uncw.edu/10.1007
/s10551-005-5597-8.

Subramanian, Samanth. "Is Fair Trade Finished?" *The Guardian*,
Guardian News and Media, July 2019, www.theguardian.com
/business/2019/jul/23/fairtrade-ethical-certification
-supermarkets-sainsburys. Accessed 20 Nov. 2020.

Valor, Carmen. "What If All Trade Was Fair Trade? The Potential
of a Social Clause to Achieve the Goals of Fair Trade." *Journal
of Strategic Marketing*, vol. 14, no. 3, Sep 2006, pp. 263–275.
ProQuest Central, search-proquest-com.liblink.uncw.edu
/docview/197447514?accountid=14606.

Vuk, Jeremic, and Jeffrey Sachs. *The United Nations in the Age
of Sustainable Development.* Presented by the Office of the
President of the 76th session of the United Nations General
Assembly. 2013.

Why Teens Take Risks

CAMRYN BROCKMAN

The adolescent brain has always been the most puzzling stage in developmental psychology to comprehend. According to neuroscientists, the teenaged brain is much more developed than an infant's or child's, however not as complex as a full-grown adult brain. Why teenagers do crazy things like drink alcohol, take drugs, or attempt life-threatening dares are always in question. To find out, Kashfia Rahman, a freshman at Harvard University majoring in cognitive science and global health policy, conducted her own study to understand an adolescent's brain. She presents her discovery through a moving and effective TED Talk, "Why Teenagers Take Risks," which owes its success to her description of her personal background, her inspired credibility as a Harvard student, and the purpose and methods of her study.

Rahman begins the speech by telling her personal story of how her experiment came to be. Rahman was only sixteen

Rhetorical analysis written for English 201 with Professor Caroline Powers.

when she started her study, which made her talk more inter-esting and inspiring, considering she began as a normal high school student in South Dakota. Rahman observed her peers around her curiously, watching them do silly pranks and taking unknown substances, all while holding student leadership positions and making good grades. She noticed the more students took risks, the more inclined they were to repeat or worsen their actions. As she states in her TED Talk, "This made me incredibly curious. So, as someone with a name which literally means "to explore knowledge", I started searching for a scientific explanation" (Rahman 00:01:09-00:01:17). Utilizing such humorous emotional appeals helps make her talk more engaging and accessible, considering that she is about to describe a scientific experiment. Sharing her story captivates her audience and draws their attention from the start, creating an empathetic connection to her perspec-tive, making her speech powerful yet trustworthy. It leaves her audience on the edge of their seats, eager to learn more about her study.

Rahman foreshadows her procedure by explaining the habituation process, a notion in the brain which blunts nega-tive and cautionary emotions, such as fear, guilt, or discom-fort during and after risk-taking behaviors and eventually causes "repetition of an ongoing action" (00:02:16-00:02:40). Once again, she renders her experiment more relatable by creating an emotional connection through her personal story, mentioning that she used her own money to purchase the EEG (electroencephalogram) machines students used while being tested by the simulator to measure neurological signals. As she puts it in her speech, "I bought a portable EEG head set with my own money, instead of buying the new iPhone X that a lot of kids my age were saving up for" (00:05:19-00:05:26). Additionally, this admission verifies her commitment to her project and gives her reason to move forward with her study. After weeks of analysis of her data, Rahman came to her results: habituation to risk changes a teen's brain by altering their emotional level and fading their ability to control themselves, physically changing their brains and drawing them toward dangerous behaviors (00:06:37-00:08:37). Her hypothesis was correct, which could, according to Rahman, help transform high schools, parenting strategies, the field of adolescent psychology, and even teenagers themselves.

Understanding the teen brain can help maintain a safe environment for teenagers. Rahman proves her study to be significant through logic by explaining her entire methods and results, but also showing how they can be useful when applied to the real world. She says, "These results are a wake-up call for teens . . . [They show . .] that the natural and necessary fear and guilt that protect them from unsafe situations actually become numb when they repeatedly choose risky behaviors" (00:08:50-00:09:00). With the knowledge gained from her study, teens can be kept safer and more informed about how their brains work, giving them reason to second guess risky behaviors. This use of logic further demonstrates the sophistication and credibility of Rahman's study and her speech.

Following her experiment, Rahman brought her study to the International Science and Engineering Fair, or as she humorously calls it, "the Olympics of Science Fairs," where she won first place in the category of Behavioral and Social Sciences. Her study was replicated by psychologists and neuroscientists, enhancing her credibility and leading her to Harvard University. In her speech, she never mentions her accomplishments of getting into the Ivy League school, yet the TED Talk mentions it in her introduction in order to validate her sincerity towards her speech; there's a sense of respect for anyone who has the ability to work or study at an Ivy League school in American society. It takes hard work and a lot of dedication, and the fact she did not care to mention it shows she was not boasting or bragging, but simply sharing her story. Additionally, she expresses how she was surprised she won by stating, "I was in such disbelief I questioned myself: was this another "La la land" blunder, like the Oscars?" (00:09:38-00:09:44). Together with this moment of humor, Rahman's humbleness in receiving her award strengthens the effectiveness of her speech through her credibility. She does not care about the fame, she does not take pride in herself, only in her accomplishments and discoveries. Rahman only mentions the award she received to prove the reliability of the study itself, not her reputation. This enhances Rahman's credibility, and suddenly her pride is spread to her audience through the knowledge that she truly did this out of curiosity, and never once for greed.

Overall, Kashfia Rahman presents her logical reasoning, her emotional appeals, and her credibility as a driven student to propel an effective TED Talk to her audience. By the end, the audience seems convinced and motivated as they stand and clap for her, which seems to be the most appropriate response. She seemed confident and excited the entire speech and ends with her hopes for the future. Knowing how she affects society and contributes to it, the audience can then take the trusted information they learned from her and use it to revolutionize the way society sees the adolescent brain and its function. Adolescent psychology has always been understood as a difficult area of study, but thanks to Rahman's motivational presentation, psychologists are one step closer to comprehending it.

Works Cited

Rahman, Kashfia. "How Risk-Taking Changes a Teenager's Brain."
     TED, www.ted.com/talks/kashfia_rahman_how_risk_taking
     _changes_a_teenager_s_brain?language=en#t-75437.

Allbirds *"Tread Lighter"* Commercial Rhetorical Analysis

JORDAN LAMOREUX

—◻—

EXCERPTED PROMPT

For your second essay, you will analyze a commercial in a three- to four-page essay. When choosing your commercial, I encourage you to choose one that advertises for a product/ cause you care about and may want to research in the next essay. For example, you may view a video ad on Instagram for sustainable cleaning products; if you want to research sustainability in the next essay because it is an area of interest for you, this could work! That being said, you can choose a commercial you view on YouTube, social media, or television. Your choice.

Rhetorical analysis written for Professor Caroline Powers, 21 October 2020.

As you write this essay, you will not only consider the rhetorical appeals we have covered in class (pathos, ethos, logos), but also visual, written, and verbal elements as well.

The appeals and other elements that are in (or not in) your website or video will be some of the methods you will use to determine the effectiveness (or ineffectiveness) of the source's message. Throughout your essay, you should address the source's purpose (the point or argument of the source), what the source addresses (is it in response to anything?), the intended audience, and how the source uses rhetorical appeals to convey its point effectively or ineffectively to the intended audience. You must address all three rhetorical appeals. If an appeal is lacking, you should address why that appeal might not be present. Points will be deducted if you simply say that a source does not contain an appeal. Consider why the source would not make use of an appeal.

ALLBIRDS "TREAD LIGHTER" COMMERCIAL RHETORICAL ANALYSIS

Allbirds created their "Tread Lighter" commercial to high-light the importance of living sustainably and reducing their carbon footprint. Allbirds offers environmentally friendly products, such as shoes and clothes, that are made out of recycled materials, wool, and trees. All of these materials, the commercial explains, are part of their efforts to explain and reduce their carbon footprint. Allbirds lets viewers and pos-sible consumers know that "knowing our impact and sharing it with the world is the first step towards a solution" when it comes to solving the problem of pollution and the climate crisis (00:00:33-00:00:39). Allbirds effectively shows how sustainable their products are through credibly emphasizing how important it is to be environmentally conscious of carbon footprints and keeping planet Earth safe.

The Allbirds "Tread Lighter" commercial begins with a quote from Franklin D. Roosevelt that states, "courage is not the absence of fear, but rather the assessment that something else is more important than fear" (00:00:00-00:00:04). It then cuts to a clip of a news reporter presenting information about the first Earth Day, followed by clips of citizens with signs at a protest against the pollution of the environment. The narrator of the Allbirds commercial describes how audiences need to measure the choices they make to see how they add up, which begins with knowing "our" carbon footprint, as well as reducing it "as much as we possibly can" (00:00:20-00:00:30). The narrator then promises that the company is going to add its carbon footprint information to every product they make, so "the world can see how much carbon is emitted when an Allbirds product is created" (00:00:48-00:00:52). The commercial then shows the different types of natural materials Allbirds uses to make their products and what the process looks like as well. The commercial ends with Allbirds expressing how their carbon footprint isn't zero yet, but "it can be, and so can everyone else's" (00:01:09-00:01:11). Through all of these individual details that Allbirds highlights in their commercial, they effectively inform viewers of the importance of being environmentally conscious by the way they create their products.

There are a few purposes behind the Allbirds "Tread Lighter" commercial. First, they clarify that their products are unique as compared to other products on their market, as Allbirds products are made in an environmentally friendly way. They also emphasize their dedication to sustainability and saving the planet one step at a time, while creating a high-quality product that encapsulates both of these important points. The commercial, as well as Allbirds as a company, addresses the importance of being aware of carbon footprints and the ever-changing planet Earth as more and more waste is produced day by day. They are dedicated to using sustainable and natural materials to reduce this waste. Allbirds the company also emphasizes the importance of reducing their own carbon footprint, and hopefully making an impact on their audience to reduce theirs as well.

The Allbirds "Tread Lighter" commercial uses ethos by expressing how much they care about sustainability. They also give proof that they are measuring their carbon footprint as they create their products while being mindful of the environment and its state. Allbirds lets viewers know that they are going to be adding their carbon footprint to every product that they make, because they "want the world to see how much carbon is emitted when an Allbirds product is created" (00:00:48-00:00:52). This conveys in itself how confident they are in being the most environmentally conscious as they can be when creating their products, as they strive to have a low carbon footprint. Allbirds also includes a quote from Franklin D. Roosevelt, as this is a credible source with wise words to further back up their claims. This commercial effectively uses ethos through all of these ways to further convey their point that they are truly confident in their environmental consciousness.

Allbirds uses pathos in their commercial by adding clips of Earth Day information and history while highlighting the protests against the increase in pollution of the environment. They also include a quote that highlights sustainability. When the commercial opens up with the quote from Franklin D. Roosevelt, it sets the tone for the fact that although the Earth is experiencing a climate crisis, citizens cannot be fearful, but rather be courageous and stand for change. This sets the stage for emotion in the next clips that follow about Earth Day. Signs are shown that say "the world stinks" and signs that spell out "pollution" as they are protesting against the pollution of the environment (00:00:12-00:00:15). Allbirds also includes clips of oil spillage, glaciers/icebergs melting, and pollution and toxic waste spilling from pipes, which truly makes viewers realize what is going on in the world right now (00:00:20-00:00:27). More clips of citizens holding signs containing messages such as "save our mother earth," "our children need a home," and "the world is in our hands" also appeal to emotion and effectively make viewers become aware of how serious this climate crisis is (00:00:31-00:00:38). Allbirds use of pathos in this commercial adds personal touches that leave an emotional mark on their audience through how viewers may feel towards the images of pollution and protests.

Allbirds "Tread Lighter" commercial also uses logos, or logic, as the company explains what exactly a carbon footprint is and how viewers can reduce their own, while Allbirds is doing the same. They demonstrate that they are measuring their carbon footprint by including a clip of a specific shoe, the Wool Runner, moving through its life cycle from manufacturing through use alongside numeric measures of carbon emitted for consumers to see (00:00:48-00:00:51). Additionally, Allbirds provides scientific-looking visuals of how they actually measure their carbon footprint with graphs and measurements, from "sourcing materials, designing, manufacturing, care, and disposal" (00:00:55-00:01:04). The commercial also uses a metaphor when they state that they will be adding their carbon footprint onto every product "like nutrition labels on food" so the world can truly see how much carbon is emitted when creating their products (00:00:44-00:00:47). The company does an effective job with their use of logos with their extensive use of statistics and metaphor to further prove their point of being as environmentally friendly as they possibly can be.

Allbirds's use of ethos, pathos, and logos in their "Tread Lighter" commercial is effective for many reasons. The commercial makes use of credible information to demonstrate that the company supports science and sustainability. It also calls on the reader to grasp the true importance of sustainability. Allbirds does an effective job when expressing their dedication to creating their products in an environmentally conscious way. Even if viewers do not purchase their products, Allbirds strives to make them more environmentally conscious as well.

Work Cited

Allbirds. "Tread Lighter | Allbirds." *YouTube*, 31 April 2020, https://www.youtube.com/watch?v=cIxlZSw8LxQ.

The Gift of Life

JAHNIYA KILIRU

—▢—

EXCERPTED PROMPT

For your first paper, you will explore a familiar subject: yourself. A paper that explores one's own life, telling a story or
focusing on a series of related or seemingly unrelated events,
and then drawing conclusions about those events, is called
a personal narrative. Your personal narrative asks you, as a
writer, to explore how events or place has shaped your identity
and reflect on why you care about a particular issue.

For the past several years, you have been discouraged from
using the personal pronoun "I" in papers. It may be helpful
to think of using the "I" as in "eyewitness." In other words,
merely incorporating the phrases "I think that," "I feel that,"
or "I believe that" do not constitute a personal narrative. In
fact, omit these qualifiers from your writing entirely.

Instead, focus on placing the reader in your story by focusing on the five senses and the details that reveal setting and

plot— showing and not telling. As you write journal entries for your integrative seminar, write in personal diaries, or write free writes and other reflection papers, you are creating potential paper topics; however, personal narratives differ from these highly personal, sometimes, and often very private writings meant for the self, because personal narratives use revision and editing to hone the piece for a public audience. Of course, private writing can become public if one chooses to fine tune the work into an essay.

THE GIFT OF LIFE

It was one of those hot and sticky kinds of days in late March of 2014. The windows were open, and the fans were blowing as they tried to cool the hot African air. It was a good thing we had already planned a day at the pool to celebrate a birthday. This was the second year that birthdays would happen on the other side of the world, away from friends and family. Living in a different country had its perks, but it was days like today that we wished our loved ones were around. My family didn't realize how real that wish would be later that afternoon and for the months to follow.

My mother was in the kitchen packing a picnic as my father called the driver. My sister and I sat on the couch, our eyes glued to the TV. My eyes left the screen, and my head turned towards the window as I heard a car coming down the dirt road. I looked at my phone and saw it was twenty minutes past the time we were supposed to leave. After living abroad for two years, I still wasn't used to what was referred to as "Ghana Time." Unlike me, people here had their own flow of things and were never in a hurry to be on time. Here, punctuality wasn't a necessity, but to me, it was a must. As I stepped onto the balcony, I noticed the car drove by our house and continued up the road. I heard my dad yell from the kitchen to come back inside because we were leaving. I made my way through the house and saw my mother and younger sister by the door, ready to go.

When I asked where our driver Kojo was, my father explained there had been a family emergency, and we would have to catch a taxi. We made our way out the gate and down the road. We waited as my father hailed a cab, and we finally piled into the back. The taxi was a dark green color, with an extended hatchback and old leather seats. There was a man in front next to the driver, who kept glancing back at my father. My father caught the attention of many people as he was a white man in an African country and was often referred to as Father Christmas due to his sizeable graying beard. We drove along the road lined by coconut trees. I sat behind the driver. My mother was next to me with my father to her right and my sister on his lap. As we drove, I looked out the half-rolled down window, feeling the warm breeze on my face, smelling the salty ocean air, and watching the business of life. Fishermen pulling in their nets, women with baskets on their heads full of fabric, vegetables, and firewood, young children running with a soccer ball. Every one of them was smiling.

After ten minutes, we made it to the last turn. We slowed at the T junction with the left turn signal flashing as we waited for the cars on the opposite side of the road to pass. All at once, I felt a woosh as a large bright blue bus went around us on the right side shoulder. I remember this moment so clearly and thinking, "Wow, that was close." Not a second after that thought crossed my mind, I heard the loud crunch of metal hitting metal, and my body lurched forward. From that point, everything started to go in slow motion. I heard screaming; as I turned my head, I saw my mother's eyes shut tight, mouth open, and each hand flung across my sister and me. I remember telling myself, "It's okay, Jahniya, you have just been in a car accident." We were spinning. Seven times we spun around. We turned right into oncoming traffic, and that's when the second crunching sound exploded through my ears. I shut my eyes tight as I saw my window burst into a thousand pieces of glass. Then, just as quickly as it happened, it stopped, and I felt still.

When I opened my eyes, I could see people running over to us. I felt like I was in a movie where there's no sound except the characters' breath even though people were shouting and yelling. Their mouths move, but no sound is heard. Right here, my memory becomes hazy. I remember my sister crying, my mother's face twisted in pain, and the man in the front seat getting out and walking away. I don't know how long I sat in the car. I watched as people tried to pull my mother out as she yelled in protest not to touch her because her back was in so much pain. It wasn't until someone tried to open my door that I finally looked down at myself. I was trapped.

When the car had spun onto the opposite side of the road, another car hit my door. The force had also caused the driver's seat to be pushed back onto my legs. There I sat with glass on my lap, the car door jammed into my left thigh, and both legs stuck under the seat in front of me. The bystanders that were helping couldn't get my door open, so they started yanking at the seat in front of me, and that's when I felt it. The pain of 100 knives jabbing into my legs, shooting up my thighs. Then I realized I felt the pain, but I couldn't feel my legs. I don't remember how I got out of the car; the last thing I remember before being taken to the hospital was looking back as we drove away. The crashed car had landed right in between a large tree and a billboard two inches to either side. This could have been a very different story.

The panic of not being able to feel my legs consumed me. I remember little bits about that first night at the hospital. Laying in a bed next to my mother, the doctor giving me injections for the pain, my father's black eye, my sister curled up in a chair. My tears as they cleaned out my foot that had been sliced open from all the glass, tears for my mother as she lay there in so much pain, but most of all my tears were because I was afraid. During the first few hours that we were there, many people came to see us, friends from school, their families, my teachers, neighbors, and so many others.

I spent five days in the hospital. The feeling in my legs came back, but my x rays showed much more damage. I had ribs and my spine out of place. The whiplash caused my neck to go forward so much that it dislocated, and now I have a bump from the regrown scar tissue. My mother spent two weeks in the hospital before she moved home, still bedridden. The axle of the car had gone into my mother's back and shifted her spinal disks. It took over three months of physical therapy for her to learn how to walk again. My sister and father both fractured their necks but healed quickly.

For the first few weeks after the accident, I would have nightmares, I could hear the crunching of metal, the screams, and I refused to get into a car. We were lucky Kojo hadn't been driving; his small car that barely had a trunk would have killed us on impact. To this day, driving gives me some anxiety. I couldn't drive on the highway for a while because all I could think about was cars hitting me while I merged. When my turn signal goes on, my hands start to grip the steering wheel, and my palms get sweaty as I brace myself for impact. But the crunching sound and spinning don't come. Hospitals are even worse, and I do everything I can to avoid them. Since the wreck, I have been in the hospital four times, but for sports injuries, not car accidents. However, it does not change my body's reaction to stepping in through those automatic glass doors. My heart beats faster, my breathing comes out more labored, and my hands shake. The clean chemical smell, the scrubs, the white coats, and hospital gowns all send me back to the hospital bed in Ghana, unable to move.

PTSD, post-traumatic stress disorder, is what they call it. My flashbacks, my nightmares, my triggers, all from witnessing and experiencing a traumatic event. Many people have PTSD but don't know what to do about it; I don't even know. Like many other disorders our society likes to sweep under the rug, there is no open education on PTSD. Many people aren't taken seriously when they are suffering from instances of trauma. These memories of trauma can take over and prevent people from living their lives. PTSD can be big or small, short-term, or long-term. I managed to get back into a car, but some things I still can't do. I loved gymnastics, being able to flip, tumble, and spin on the bar. Since the accident,

I haven't been able to do cartwheels, round-offs, handsprings, or anything on the bar. The motion is too similar to how I felt when our car was spinning. The man who hit us was drunk and didn't have a license. Drunk drivers have ended so many lives, and my family was very fortunate. We were in court for over three years, but that is a small price to pay to be able to walk and breathe. When the calendar rolls around to that day in March, there isn't only the celebration of a birthday, but the celebration of all our lives.

How a Bracelet Shaped My Views on My Mother

GRACEE LAUB

Personal essay written for English 101 with Professor Caroline Powers.

EXCERPTED PROMPT

For your first large assignment, you will write a two- to four-page personal narrative essay. Usually, stronger essays are around three pages, so keep that in mind. A personal narrative is a place for you to discuss important moments, events, or items, from your life, and how those important things have impacted you. A personal narrative essay might ask you to explore something from your life, and how that "something" has shaped your identity or values. For your topic, you will choose one of the two journals you have completed, and extend your chosen topic into a full essay. See below for journal topics and important notes.

Journal/Essay Topics

Reflect on an item from your life that is specific to you. This can take shape in many different forms. For instance, you may focus on a gift from a loved one, your first car, an award from childhood, etc. Throughout the essay, you should describe the item as well as reasons (memories, for example), that show how and why the item is significant to you. Consider how the object represents a part of your identity or one of your values.

Reflect on a time in your life where you have been challenged. This challenge may have been a physical challenge, a situation that challenged you, etc. Throughout your essay, you should focus on the challenge itself, but also on how the challenge ultimately impacted you and why it is/was significant. Consider how you are today with the challenge in mind.

HOW A BRACELET SHAPED MY VIEWS ON MY MOTHER

How can one sentimental item influence your values and keep you grounded throughout the different phases of life? Gifts from loved ones can teach you about what really matters to you and create foundational values which you can build upon for years to come.

Earlier this year, my mom gifted me with a beaded marble bracelet that matched the one she always wore. It was an unexpected, yet thought-provoking gift. She had never really given me anything with a lot of meaning, usually just old pairs of shoes or fragrances. But this item was very different from the others because she had the exact same one, and it grew to represent the connection we now hold. I wondered why she chose to give this gift to me, and why now. Not only has this bracelet taught me how valuable relationships truly are, but this item now symbolizes my newfound relationship with my mother and the growth we've experienced as we have overcome many hurdles and grown closer as mother and daughter.

My mother and I have always had trouble finding common ground. Ever since my parents divorced for the third time when I was in the 6th grade, I have lived with my dad. My father ran his own construction business, so he was a great leader, and did other things such as teach me more about faith and provide for me. Over time, I came to see him as the prominent parent, regardless of my mother's efforts to connect with me. She has never lived with a sense of stability, so I was always drawn to my dad's lifestyle and found comfort in his presence. I failed to realize that these things did not matter, and that my mom will always be the woman who gave birth to me and who supports me no matter what. I needed to rethink what was important to me, work on my connection with her, and put more time into our relationship.

Everything changed a few years ago when she was diagnosed with Lyme disease and had life-threatening symptoms. She was immediately hospitalized, and the doctors didn't know how she was affected so badly by this disease. After seeing many, many doctors, we found one who had finally discovered the root of everything, which happened to be a much deeper problem. Her right heart valve was infected, and her heart was being brutally attacked by bacteria. Before my siblings and I could see her, she was rushed into open heart surgery to replace her heart valve. Having to do such a drastic surgery unexpectedly was unheard of. During her year of recovery, she was extraordinarily weak and couldn't sit up, let alone do anything on her own. My dad, my brothers, and I had to be with her during this process, and let me say, it was so painful to see my mom like this. However, there was some good that came out of it. Our family dynamic has always been so broken and disconnected because we each live our lives separately and never do things like eat dinner together as a family. My dad would occasionally take us to a monthly movie, but the majority of my time as a child consisted of being locked in my room or with my friends. As a result, seeing my family come together, share meals, and spend quality time with one another while we cared for my mom was a very different experience to say the least. Even though this situation was incredibly unfortunate, it changed my perspective on family and opened my eyes to the reality of my weakened relationship with my mother.

That's why the bracelet she gave me is so powerful: receiving it reignited my love for her and reminds me how far we have both come. Having to start from the beginning and learn about who she was from the ground up was the only way I saw any change occurring. I began to know her as a different woman than before. I learned to love the strong woman my mother is and appreciate her powerful and caring nature. I realize now that she would do anything for me. Once I started going out for lunch and casually getting coffee with her, I started to learn more about who she was. She wasn't just any average person in my life, she turned into the person who motivates me daily. She made me realize that people don't live forever, and I was able to gain a sense of accountability in terms of focusing on the people in my life who care about me. I used to be selfish in a way, only focusing on what I thought benefitted me most and only allowing in people who have something to offer into my life. Because of my mother and the connection we share through the bracelet, I am now much more devoted to everyone in my life and I care about other people's feelings. Every person has so much more to them and can change you for the better if you take time to listen and understand who they are, and then go on to learn from that.

This bracelet has erased my previous views of my mother. It represents the woman I know now, who is the woman I've known since 2016. Without this bracelet, I wouldn't have anything to represent our union and I wouldn't have such a strong love for family. Obtaining this bracelet has shown me how "bad" experiences can allow you to examine your ways of being and shape yourself into the person that you strive to be. I now have a strong belief that family is important because it provides love and support, and because it sets the stage for personal growth. After reevaluating my relationship with my mother, I have turned into a better person. Receiving this sentimental gift unexpectedly showed me how much I mean to my mom now and changed my previously loose fundamental values to more meaningful ones. I know the amount of personal growth that I've experienced is immense because I can now influence others to appreciate their families by sharing my story.

All in all, I came to realize that an item as small and seemingly unimportant as a marble bracelet can change the way I look at and think about life. It represents my mother's strength, my values, and the bond we hold. Experiencing her at her lowest point somehow brought us both to our strongest point. I feel like this bracelet gives an accurate representation of the person I've become through my mom. It symbolizes her love for me, and wearing it brings me back to my values. This bracelet represents growth, family, and reminds me of the person I am today because of my mom.

CREDITS

TEXT

Michelle Alexander: Excerpt from *The New Jim Crow*—Copyright © 2010, 2012 by Michelle Alexander. Reprinted by permission of The New Press. www.thenewpress.com

Camryn Brockman: "Why Teens Take Risks" by Camryn Brockman. Reprinted by permission of the author.

Editorial Staff of *The Eagle Eye*: Excerpt from "Our Manifesto to Fix America's Gun Laws," *The Guardian*, March 23, 2018. Copyright Guardian News & Media Ltd 2020. www.theguardian.com. Used with permission.

Christopher J. Ferguson and Patrick Markey: Excerpt from "Video Games Aren't Addictive" from *The New York Times*. © 2017 The New York Times Company. All rights reserved. Used under license.

Kenneth Goldsmith: "Go Ahead: Waste Time on the Internet," *The Los Angeles Times*, August 12, 2016. Reprinted courtesy of Kenneth Goldsmith.

Gerald Graff: "Hidden Intellectualism," adapted from *Clueless in Academe: How Schooling Obscures the Life of the Mind*. Copyright © 2003 Yale University. Reprinted by permission of Yale University Press.

Jahniya Kiliru: "The Gift of Life" by Jahniya Kiliru. Reprinted by permission of the author.

Jordan Lamoreux: "Allbirds 'Tread Lighter' Commercial Rhetorical Analysis" by Jordan Lamoreux. Reprinted by permission of the author.

PHOTOGRAPHS

ACKNOWLEDGMENTS

THIS BOOK WOULD NEVER HAVE seen print if it weren't for Marilyn Moller, our superb editor at Norton, and the extraordinary job she has done of inspiring, commenting on, and rewriting (and then rewriting and rewriting again) our many drafts. Our friendship with Marilyn is one of the most cherished things to have developed from this project.

We are also particularly thankful to our current Norton editor Sarah Touborg, whose exemplary counsel, criticism, and hands-on intervention shaped the changes we have made to this edition. We are grateful for Sarah's unflagging patience with a couple of sometimes-recalcitrant authors. Assistant editor Emma Peters skillfully and cheerfully coordinated the many details involved in preparing our manuscript.

Our thanks go as well to Roby Harrington for his encouragement and astute suggestions (and great dinners) on his annual visits to Chicago. We extend our gratitude to Christine D'Antonio and Elizabeth Marotta for their superb work managing the editing and production of this edition; and to Joy Cranshaw and Katie Bolger for their energetic work creating the many digital resources that accompany the book. We appreciate Patricia Wong's excellent work as permissions editor and Ted Szczepanski's management of the photos for both versions of the book.

Thanks to John Darger, our Norton representative, who offered early encouragement to write this book; to Debra Morton Hoyt and Mike Wood for their excellent work on the cover. Special thanks to Michele Dobbins, Elizabeth Pieslor, Kim Bowers, Emily Rowin, Lib Triplett, and the incomparable Norton travelers for the superb work they've done on behalf of our book.

We extend our deep thanks to Laura J. Panning Davies for her many contributions to this edition, including the new exercises, the new readings in *"They Say / I Say" with Readings*, and updating of the instructor's guide for the book, and for her ongoing work on **theysayiblog.com**. We owe a special debt of gratitude to Erin Ackerman for her expert contributions to the new chapter on research and for her chapter on writing in the social sciences. We also thank Chris Gillen for his chapter on writing in the sciences. Working with Erin and Chris proved to be an exhilarating experience; we learned a great deal by seeing how they applied our ideas to their disciplines.

A very special thanks goes to those who provided in-depth reviews of the new chapters on research and revising: Steven Bailey (Central Michigan University), Ana Cooke (Penn State University), Courtney Danforth (College of Southern Nevada), Africa Fine (Palm Beach State College), and Traci Klass (Palm Beach State College); and to those who provided detailed evaluations of the fourth edition: Joe Bizup (Boston University), Laura J. Panning Davies (SUNY Cortland), Karen Gocsik (University of California at San Diego), and Kelly Ritter (University of Illinois at Urbana–Champaign).

We are grateful to all of the instructors whose feedback was invaluable in shaping this fifth edition: Catherine Agar (Keuka College); Craig Albin (Missouri State University, West Plains Campus); Jason Barrett-Fox (Weber State); Jade Bittle

(Rowan-Cabarrus Community College); Roberta Brown (Western New Mexico University); William Burgos (LIU Brooklyn); Jackson Connor (University of Rio Grande); Charles Cook (Red Creek High School/Finger Lakes Community College); Amanda Corcoran (American River College); Linda Cowling (North Central Missouri College); Ginny Crisco (California State University, Fresno); Tamera Davis, (Northern Oklahoma College, Stillwater); Matt Dube (William Woods University); Mei Mei Evans (Alaska Pacific University); Anna Eyre (Merrimack College); Audrey Fessler (Appalachian State University); Jane Focht-Hansen (San Antonio College); Susan Gentry (Tunxis Community College); Sean Glassberg (Horry-Georgetown Technical College); Sarah Hallenbeck (University of North Carolina Wilmington); LewEllyn Hallett (University of Arkansas, Fayetteville); Natalie Hewitt (Hope International University); Lori Hughes (Lone Star College, Montgomery); Mark Hughes (Community College of Philadelphia); Elizabeth Inness-Brown (Saint Michael's College); Tim Jensen (Oregon State University); Alyssa Johnson (Horry-Georgetown Technical College); Gregory Johnson (Wake Technical Community College); Rhonda Jackson Joseph (Lone Star University Park); Alan Lindsay (New Hampshire Technical Institute); Jade Lynch-Greenberg (Purdue University Northwest); Gina MacKenzie (Holy Family University); Andrew Marvin (Three Rivers Community College); James Matthews (Fairmont State University); Gena McKinley (Rappahannock Community College, Warsaw Campus); Kelsey McNiff (Endicott College); Jeremy Meyer (Arizona State University, Tempe Campus); Jeannine Morgan (St. John's River State College); Janine Morris (Nova Southeastern University); Nichole Oechslin (Piedmont Valley Community College); Jessica Santini (Lake Region State College); Dagmar Scharold (University of Houston, Downtown);

Greta Skogseth (Montcalm Community College); Joshua Smith (University of North Carolina at Chapel Hill); Christian Smith (Coastal Carolina University); Kristen Snoddy (Indiana University Kokomo); Nicholas Vick (Pitt Community College); Tobin von der Nuell (University of Colorado Boulder); Sarah White (Purdue University Northwest); Lacey Wootton (American University); and Ali Zimmerman Zuckerman (University of Minnesota).

We owe a special thanks to our colleagues in the English department at the University of Illinois at Chicago: Mark Canuel, our former department head, for supporting our earlier efforts overseeing the university's Writing in the Disciplines requirement; Walter Benn Michaels, another former department head; and Ann Feldman, former director of university writing programs, for encouraging us to teach first-year composition courses at UIC in which we could try out ideas and drafts of our manuscript; Tom Moss, Diane Chin, Vainis Aleksa, and Matt Pavesich, who have also been very supportive of our efforts; and Matt Oakes, our former research assistant. We are also grateful to Ann Feldman, Diane Chin, and Mark Bennett for bringing us into their graduate course on the teaching of writing; and to Lisa Freeman, John Huntington, Walter Benn Michaels, and Ralph Cintron for inviting us to present our ideas in the keynote lecture at UIC's 2013 Composition Matters conference.

We are also especially grateful to Steve Benton and Nadya Pittendrigh, who taught a section of composition with us using an early draft of this book. Steve made many helpful suggestions, particularly regarding the exercises. We are grateful to Andy Young, a lecturer at UIC who has tested our book in his courses and who continues to give us extremely helpful feedback. And we thank Vershawn A. Young, whose work on code-meshing influenced our argument in Chapter 9, and Hillel Crandus, who inspired the chapter on "Entering Classroom Discussions."

We are grateful to the many colleagues and friends who've let us talk our ideas out with them and given extremely helpful responses. UIC's former dean, Stanley Fish, has been central in this respect, both in personal conversations and in his incisive articles calling for greater focus on form in the teaching of writing. Our conversations with Jane Tompkins have also been integral to this book, as was the composition course that Jane cotaught with Gerald, titled "Can We Talk?" Lenny Davis, too, offered both intellectual insight and emotional support, as did Heather Arnet, Jennifer Ashton, Janet Atwill, Kyra Auslander, Noel Barker, Mark Bauerlein, Jim Benton, Jack Brereton, Jim Burke, Tim Cantrick, Marsha Cassidy, David Chinitz, Lisa Chinitz, Pat Chu, Harry J. Cook, Duane Davis, Bridget O'Rourke Flick, Steve Flisk, Judy Gardiner, Howard Gardner, Rich Gelb, Gwynne Gertz, Jeff Gore, Bill Haddad, Ben Hale, Scott Hammerl, Patricia Harkin, Andy Hoberek, John Huntington, Carol Jago, Joe Janangelo, Paul Jay, David Jolliffe, Nancy Kohn, Don Lazere, Sarah Levine, Jo Liebermann, Les Lynn, Steven Mailloux, Deirdre McCloskey, Maurice J. Meilleur, Alan Meyers, Greg Meyerson, Anna Minkov, Chris Newfield, Randy Olson, Jim Phelan, Paul Psilos, Bruce Robbins, Charles Ross, Eileen Seifert, Evan Seymour, David Shumway, Herb Simons, Jim Sosnoski, Kyle Stedman, David Steiner, Harold Aram Veeser, Chuck Venegoni, Marla Weeg, Jerry Wexler, Joyce Wexler, Virginia Wexman, Jeffrey Williams, Lynn Woodbury, Art Young, Vershawn Young, and the late Wayne Booth, whose friendship we dearly miss.

We are grateful for having had the opportunity to present our ideas to a number of colleges and high schools: University of

Arkansas at Little Rock, Augustana College, Brandeis University, Brigham Young University, Bryn Mawr College, California State University at Bakersfield, California State University at Northridge, University of California at Riverside, Case Western University, Central Michigan University, Clemson University, Columbia University, Community College of Philadelphia, Daemen College, Davidson College, University of Delaware, DePauw University, Drew University, Duke University, Duquesne University, Elmhurst College, Emory University, Fairfield University, Fontbonne University, Furman University, Gettysburg College, Harper College, Harvard University, Haverford College, Hawaii Office of Secondary School Curriculum Instruction, Hunter College, University of Illinois College of Medicine, Illinois State University, Illinois Wesleyan University, John Carroll University, Kansas State University, Lawrence University, the Lawrenceville School, University of Louisiana at Lafayette, MacEwan University, University of Maryland at College Park, Massachusetts Institute of Technology, University of Memphis, Miami University, Mills College, University of Missouri at Columbia, New Trier High School, North Carolina A&T University, University of North Florida, Northern Michigan University, Northwestern University Division of Continuing Studies, Norwalk Community College, University of Notre Dame, Ohio State University, Ohio Wesleyan University, Oregon State University, University of Portland, Purdue University at Calumet, University of Rochester, Rockford University, St. Ambrose University, St. Andrew's School, St. Charles High School, St. Francis University at Joliet, State University of New York at Geneseo, State University of New York at Stony Brook, Seattle University, South Elgin High School, University of South Florida, Southern Connecticut State University, University of Southern Mississippi, Stanford

University, Swarthmore College, Teachers College, University of Tennessee at Knoxville, University of Texas at Arlington, Tulane University, Union College, Ursinus College, Wabash College, Washington College, University of Washington, University of West Virginia at Morgantown, Western Michigan University, Westinghouse/Kenwood High Schools, Wheaton North High School, Wheaton Warrenville English Chairs, Winona State University, and the University of Wisconsin at Whitewater.

We particularly thank those who helped arrange these visits and discussed writing issues with us: Jeff Abernathy, Herman Asarnow, John Austin, Greg Barnheisel, John Bean, Crystal Benedicks, Joe Bizup, Sheridan Blau, Dagne Bloland, Chris Breu, Elizabeth Brockman, Mark Brouwer, Lizabeth Bryant, Joan Johnson Bube, John Caldwell, Gregory Clark, Irene Clark, Dean Philip Cohen, Cathy D'Agostino, Tom Deans, Gaurav Desai, Lisa Dresdner, Kathleen Dudden Rowlands, Lisa Ede, Alexia Ellett, Emory Elliott, Anthony Ellis, Kim Flachmann, Ronald Fortune, Rosanna Fukuda, George Haggerty, Donald Hall, Joe Harris, Gary Hatch, Elizabeth Hatmaker, Donna Heiland, Harry Hellenbrand, Nicole Henderson, Doug Hesse, Van Hillard, Andrew Hoberek, Michael Hustedde, Sara Jameson, T. R. Johnson, David Jones, Ann Kaplan, Don Kartiganer, Linda Kinnahan, Dean Georg Kleine, Albert Labriola, Craig Lawrence, Lori Lopez, Tom Liam Lynch, Hiram Maxim, Michael Mays, Elizabeth McDermott, Thomas McFadden, Sean Meehan, Connie Mick, Robert Morace, Joseph Musser, Margaret Oakes, John O'Connor, Gary Olson, Tom Pace, Amy Pearson, Les Perelman, Jim Phelan, Emily Poe, Dominick Randolph, Clancy Ratliff, Monica Rico, Kelly Ritter, Jack Robinson, Warren Rosenberg, Laura Rosenthal, Dean Howard Ross, Deborah Rossen-Knill, Paul Schacht, Petra Schatz, Evan Seymour, Rose

Shapiro, Mike Shea, Cecilia M. Shore, Erec Smith, Kelly Smith, Nancy Sommers, Stephen Spector, Timothy Spurgin, Ron Strickland, Marcy Taylor, Michael Theune, Trig Thoreson, Josh Toth, Judy Trost, Aiman Tulamait, Charles Tung, John Webster, Robert Weisbuch, Sandi Weisenberg, Karin Westman, Martha Woodmansee, and Lynn Worsham.

We also wish to extend particular thanks to two Chicago-area educators who have worked closely with us: Eileen Murphy of CERCA and Les Lynn, formerly of the Chicago Debate League and now director of our joint organization, Argument-Centered Education. Lastly, we wish to thank two high school teachers for their excellent and inventive adaptations of our work: Mark Gozonsky in his *YouTube* video clip "Building Blocks," and Dave Stuart Jr. in his blogs, *Teaching the Core* and *Let's Make Teaching Better*.

We would also like to express our gratitude to several people who have published recent interviews with us about *"They Say / I Say"*: Dave Stuart Jr., "A Conversation with Gerald Graff and Cathy Birkenstein" at **www.davestuartjr.com**; Erica Meltzer, "The Critical Reader Conversation with Gerald Graff and Cathy Birkenstein" at **www.thecriticalreader.com**; Park Howell, "How the Teaching of Argument Can Save American Education" at **www.businessofstory.com**; and Harold Aram Veeser, ed., in *The Rebirth of American Literary Theory and Criticism: Scholars Discuss Intellectual Origins and Turning Points* (2020).

For inviting us to present our ideas at their conferences, we are grateful to John Brereton and Richard Wendorf at the Boston Athenaeum; Wendy Katkin of the Reinvention Center of State University of New York at Stony Brook; Luchen Li of the Michigan English Association; Lisa Lee and Barbara Ransby of the Public Square in Chicago; Don Lazere of the University of Tennessee at Knoxville; Dennis Baron of the University of Illinois at Urbana–Champaign; Alfie Guy of Yale University; Irene Clark of the California State University of Northridge; George Crandell and Steve Hubbard, codirectors of the ACETA conference at Auburn University; Mary Beth Rose of the Humanities Institute at the University of Illinois at Chicago; Diana Smith of St. Anne's Belfield School and the University of Virginia; Jim Maddox and Victor Luftig of the Bread Loaf School of English; Jan Fitzsimmons and Jerry Berberet of the Associated Colleges of Illinois; Rosemary Feal, executive director of the Modern Language Association; Les Perelman of the Massachusetts Institute of Technology; and Bruce Herzberg of Bentley College and Chris Gallagher of Northeastern University.

We wish to thank several reviewers not already mentioned who provided feedback on the material for Chapter 9: Ana Cooke (Carnegie Mellon University); Elias Dominguez-Barajas (University of Arkansas); Douglas Kern (University of Maryland); Janine Morris (Nova Southeastern University); and Keith Walters (Portland State University).

Our thanks also go to those who helped develop the ideas for the chapter on online discussions: Karen Bruce (Ohio State University); Nick Carbone; Ana Cooke (Carnegie Mellon); Courtney Danforth (University of Southern Nevada); Lyra Hilliard (University of Maryland); Janine Morris (Nova Southeastern University); and Ilknur Sancak-Marusa (West Chester University).

A very special thanks goes to those who reviewed materials for the fourth edition: Teresa Alto (Itasca Community College); Darla Anderson (California State University, Northridge); Jan Andres (Riverside City College); Steven Bailey (Central Michigan University); Valerie Bell (Loras College); Tamara

Benson (Kent State University); Jade Bittle (Rowan-Cabarrus Community College); Jill Bonds (University of Phoenix); William Cantrell (Johnson Central High School); David Chase (Raritan Valley Community College); Barbara Cook (Mount Aloysius College); Jonathan Cook (Durham Technical Community College); Carol Lynne Lana Dalley (California State University, Fullerton); D'Arcangelis (Memorial University of Newfoundland); Nicholas DeArmas (Seminole State College of Florida); Elias Dominguez-Barajas (University of Arkansas); Ember Dooling (St. Joseph High School); Andrew Dunphy (Massasoit Community College); Justin Eells (Minnesota State University, Mankato); Africa Fine (Palm Beach State College); Valerie Fong (Foothill College); Reese Fuller (Episcopal School of Acadiana); Karen Gaffney (Raritan Valley Community College); Jacquelyn Geiger (Bucks County Community College); Joshua Geist (College of the Sequoias); Ashley Gendek (Kentucky Wesleyan College); Sean George (Dixie State University); Karen Gocsik (University of California, San Diego); Sarah Gray (Middle Tennessee State University); George Grinnell (University of British Columbia Okanagan); Lindsay Haney (Bellevue College); Catherine Hayter (Saddleback College); Stephen V. Hoyt (Obridge Academy/St. Joseph's College); Timothy Jackson (Rosemont College); Julie Jung-Kim (Trinity International University); Hannah Keller (Campbell University); Michael Keller (South Dakota State University); Nina Kutty (DePaul University); Lisa Lipani (University of Georgia); Judi Mack (Joliet Junior College); Anna Maheshwari (Schoolcraft College); Sarah F. McGinley (Wright State University); James McGovern (Germanna Community College); Liz McLemore (Minneapolis Community and Technical College) Jason Melton (Sacramento State University); Michael Mendoza (Seminole State College of Florida); Carey

Millsap-Spears (Moraine Valley Community College); Nicole Morris (Emory University); Shelley Palmer (Central Piedmont Community College); Jeff Pruchnic (Wayne State University); Tammy Ramsey (Bluegrass Community and Technical College); Cynthia Cox Richardson (Sinclair Community College); Rachel Rinehart (St. Edward's University); Kelly Ritter (University of Illinois Urbana–Champaign); Deborah Rossen-Knill (University of Rochester); Laura Rossi-Le (Endicott College); Julie Shattuck (Frederick Community College); Ellen Sorg (Owens Community College); Jennifer Stefaniak (Springfield Technical Community College); Heather Stringham (College of Southern Nevada); Stuart Swirsky (Seminole State College of Florida); Star Taylor (Riverside City College); Stephanie Tran (Foothill College); Alicia Trotman (Mercy College); Robert Williams (St. Edward's University); and Benjamin Woo (Carleton University)

A very special thanks goes to those who reviewed materials for the third edition: Carrie Bailey (Clark College); Heather Barrett (Boston University); Amy Bennett-Zendzian (Boston University); Seth Blumenthal (Boston University); Ron Brooks (Oklahoma State University); Jonathan Cook (Durham Technical Community College); Tessa Croker (Boston University); Perry Cumbie (Durham Technical Community College); Robert Danberg (Binghamton University); Elias Dominguez-Barajas (University of Arkansas); Nancy Enright (Seton Hall University); Jason Evans (Prairie State College); Ted Fitts (Boston University); Karen Gaffney (Raritan Valley Community College); Karen Gardiner (University of Alabama); Stephen Hodin (Boston University); Michael Horwitz (University of Hartford); John Hyman (American University); Claire Kervin (Boston University); Melinda Kreth (Central Michigan University); Heather Marcovitch (Red Deer College);

ACKNOWLEDGMENTS

Christina Michaud (Boston University); Marisa Milanese (Boston University); Theresa Mooney (Austin Community College); Roxanne Munch (Joliet Junior College); Sarah Quirk (Waubonsee Community College); Lauri Ramey (California State University, Los Angeles); David Shawn (Boston University); Jennifer Sia (Boston University); Laura Sonderman (Marshall University); Katherine Stebbins McCaffrey (Boston University); K. Sullivan (Lane Community College); Anne-Marie Thomas (Austin Community College at Riverside); Eliot Treichel (Lane Community College); Rosanna Walker (Lane Community College); and Mary Erica Zimmer (Boston University). We also thank those who reviewed the literature chapter: Julie Bowman (Carnegie Mellon University); Jim Burke (Burlingame High School); Ana Cooke (Carnegie Mellon University); Thomas Cooley (Ohio State University); Lisa Ede (Oregon State University); Priscilla Glanville (State College of Florida); Melissa Goldthwaite (Saint Joseph's University); Rafey Habib (Rutgers University at Camden); Michael Hennessy (Texas State University); and Alexis Teagarden (Carnegie Mellon University).

Thanks to those who reviewed the materials for the second edition: Erin Ackerman (City University of New York–John Jay College); Mary Angeline (University of Northern Colorado); Ned Bachus (Community College of Philadelphia); Michelle Ballif (University of Georgia); Jonathan Barz (University of Dubuque); Mary Bauer Morley (University of North Dakota); Benjamin Bennett-Carpenter (Oakland University); Michelle Boswell (University of Maryland); Laura Bowles (University of Central Arkansas); E. Brand (Broome Community College); Beth Buyserie (Washington State University); Dana Cairns Watson (University of California, Los Angeles); Genevieve Carminati (Montgomery College); Brent Chesley (Aquinas

College); Joseph Colavito (Butler University); Tara DaPra (University of Minnesota); Emily Detmer-Goebel (Northern Kentucky University); J. Michael Duvall (College of Charleston); Adriana Estill (Carleton College); Ralph Faris (Community College of Philadelphia); Chris Gillen (Kenyon College); Patricia Gillikin (University of New Mexico Valencia Campus); Kenneth Grant (University of Wisconsin–Baraboo/Sauk County); Kevin Griffith (Capital University); Annemarie Hamlin (Central Oregon Community College); Rick Hansen (California State University, Fresno); John Hare (Montgomery College); Wendy Hayden (Hunter College of the City University of New York); Karen Head (Georgia Institute of Technology); Chene Heady (Longwood University); Nels Highberg (University of Hartford); Victoria Holladay (California State University, Los Angeles); D. Kern Holoman (University of California, Davis); Elizabeth Huergo (Montgomery College); Sara Jameson (Oregon State University); Joseph Jones (University of Memphis); Andrew Keitt (University of Alabama at Birmingham); Kurt Koenigsberger (Case Western Reserve University); Gary Leising (Utica College); Gary Lewandowski (Monmouth University); Michelle Maher (La Roche College); Lisa Martin (University of Wisconsin–Baraboo/Sauk County); Miles McCrimmon (J. Sargeant Reynolds Community College); Jacqueline Megow (Oklahoma State University); Bruce Michelson (University of Illinois at Urbana–Champaign); Megan Morton (Purdue University); Steven Muhlberger (Nipissing University); Lori Muntz (Iowa Wesleyan College); Ann Murphy (Assumption College); Sarah Perrault (University of Nevada, Reno); Christine Pipitone-Herron (Raritan Valley Community College); David Samper (University of Oklahoma); Rose Shapiro (Fontbonne University); Jennifer Stewart (Indiana University–Purdue University Fort Wayne);

Sandra Stollman (Broward College); Linda Sturtz (Beloit College); Mark Sutton (Kean University); Tobin von der Nuell (University of Colorado at Boulder); Brody Waybrant (Bay Mills Community College); Gina Weaver (Southern Nazarene University); Amy Whitson (Missouri State University); and Susan Wright (Montclair State University).

Thanks also to those who reviewed the manuscript for the original version of *They Say*; their suggestions contributed enormously to this book: Alan Ainsworth (Houston Community College); Rise Axelrod (University of California, Riverside); Bob Baron (Mesa Community College); David Bartholomae (University of Pittsburgh); Diane Belcher (Georgia State University); Michel De Benedictis (Miami Dade College); Joseph Bizup (Boston University); Patricia Bizzell (College of the Holy Cross); John Brereton (Harvard University); Richard Bullock (Wright State University); Charles Cooper (University of California, San Diego); Christine Cozzens (Agnes Scott College); Sarah Duerden (Arizona State University); Russel Durst (University of Cincinnati); Joseph Harris (Duke University); Paul Heilker (Virginia Polytechnic Institute); Michael Hennessy (Texas State University); Karen Lunsford (University of California, Santa Barbara); Libby Miles (University of Rhode Island); Mike Rose (University of California, Los Angeles); William H. Smith (Weatherford College); Scott Stevens (Western Washington University); Patricia Sullivan (University of Colorado); Pamela Wright (University of California, San Diego); and Daniel Zimmerman (Middlesex Community College).

Finally, a special thank you to David Bartholomae for suggesting the phrase that became the subtitle of this book.

INDEX OF TEMPLATES

LISTEN BEFORE YOU LEAP
(pp. 10–11)

▸ While I understand the impulse to _____, my own view
is _____.

▸ While I agree with X that _____, I cannot accept her overall conclusion that _____.

▸ While X argues _____, and I argue _____, in a way
we're both right.

THE TEMPLATE OF TEMPLATES
(p. 11)

▸ In recent discussions of _____, a controversial issue has
been whether _____. On the one hand, some argue
that _____. From this perspective, _____. On the other
hand, however, others argue that _____. In the words of
_____, one of this view's main proponents, "_____."
According to this view, _____. In sum, then, the issue is
whether _____ or _____.

My own view is that _____. Though I concede that
_____, I still maintain that _____. For example,
_____. Although some might object that _____, I would
reply that _____. The issue is important because _____.

INTRODUCING WHAT "THEY SAY"
(p. 23)

▸ A number of _____ have recently suggested that
_____.

▸ It has become common today to dismiss _____.

▸ In their recent work, Y and Z have offered harsh critiques of
_____ for _____.

INTRODUCING "STANDARD VIEWS"
(pp. 23–24)

▸ Americans have always believed that _____.

▸ Conventional wisdom has it that _____.

▸ Common sense seems to dictate that _____.

▸ The standard way of thinking about topic X has it that _____.

▸ It is often said that _____.

▸ My whole life I have heard it said that _____.

▸ You would think that _____.

▸ Many people assume that _____.

Index of Templates

MAKING WHAT "THEY SAY" SOMETHING *YOU* SAY
(pp. 24–25)

▸ I've always believed that _____.

▸ When I was a child, I used to think that _____.

▸ Although I should know better by now, I cannot help thinking that _____.

▸ At the same time that I believe _____, I also believe _____.

INTRODUCING SOMETHING IMPLIED OR ASSUMED
(p. 25)

▸ Although none of them have ever said so directly, my teachers have often given me the impression that _____.

▸ One implication of X's treatment of _____ is that _____.

▸ Although X does not say so directly, she apparently assumes that _____.

▸ While they rarely admit as much, _____ often take for granted that _____.

INTRODUCING AN ONGOING DEBATE
(pp. 25–28)

▸ In discussions of X, one controversial issue has been _____. On the one hand, _____ argues _____. On the other hand, _____ contends _____. Others even maintain _____. My own view is _____.

▸ When it comes to the topic of _____, most of us will readily agree that _____. Where this agreement usually ends, however, is on the question of _____. Whereas some are convinced that _____, others maintain that _____.

▸ In conclusion, then, as I suggested earlier, defenders of _____ can't have it both ways. Their assertion that _____ is contradicted by their claim that _____.

CAPTURING AUTHORIAL ACTION
(pp. 41–44)

▸ X acknowledges that _____.

▸ X agrees that _____.

▸ X argues that _____.

▸ X believes that _____.

▸ X celebrates the fact that _____.

▸ X claims that _____.

▸ X complains that _____.

▸ X concedes that _____.

▸ X demonstrates that _____.

▸ X denies/does not deny that _____.

▸ X deplores the tendency to _____.

▸ X emphasizes that _____.

- ▸ X insists that _____.

- ▸ X observes that _____.

- ▸ X questions whether _____.

- ▸ X refutes the claim that _____.

- ▸ X reminds us that _____.

- ▸ X reports that _____.

- ▸ X suggests that _____.

- ▸ X urges us to _____.

INTRODUCING QUOTATIONS
(p. 51)

- ▸ X states, "_____."

- ▸ As the prominent philosopher X puts it, "_____."

- ▸ According to X, "_____."

- ▸ X himself writes, "_____."

- ▸ In her book, _____, X maintains that "_____."

- ▸ Writing in the journal _____, X complains that "_____."

- ▸ In X's view, "_____."

- ▸ X agrees when she writes, "_____."

- ▸ X disagrees when he writes, "_____."

- ▸ X complicates matters further when he writes, "_____."

INDEX OF TEMPLATES

EXPLAINING QUOTATIONS
(p. 52)

▸ Basically, X is warning _____.

▸ In other words, X believes _____.

▸ In making this comment, X urges us to _____.

▸ X is corroborating the age-old adage that _____.

▸ X's point is that _____.

▸ The essence of X's argument is that _____.

DISAGREEING, WITH REASONS
(p. 62)

▸ I think X is mistaken because she overlooks _____.

▸ X's claim that _____ rests upon the questionable assumption that _____.

▸ I disagree with X's view that _____ because, as recent research has shown, _____.

▸ X contradicts herself / can't have it both ways. On the one hand, she argues _____. On the other hand, she also says _____.

▸ By focusing on _____, X overlooks the deeper problem of _____.

AGREEING
(pp. 64–66)

▸ I agree that _____ because my experience _____ confirms it.

▸ X surely is right about _____ because, as she may not be aware, recent studies have shown that _____.

▸ X's theory of _____ is extremely useful because it sheds insight on the difficult problem of _____.

▸ Those unfamiliar with this school of thought may be interested to know that it basically boils down to _____.

▸ I agree that _____, a point that needs emphasizing since so many people believe _____.

▸ If group X is right that _____, as I think they are, then we need to reassess the popular assumption that _____.

AGREEING AND DISAGREEING SIMULTANEOUSLY
(pp. 68–69)

▸ Although I agree with X up to a point, I cannot accept his overall conclusion that _____.

▸ Although I disagree with much that X says, I fully endorse his final conclusion that _____.

▸ Though I concede that _____, I still insist that _____.

▸ X is right that _____, but she seems on more dubious ground when she claims that _____.

▶ While X is probably wrong when she claims that _____, she is right that _____.

▶ Whereas X provides ample evidence that _____, Y and Z's research on _____ and _____ convinces me that _____ instead.

▶ I'm of two minds about X's claim that _____. On the one hand, I agree that _____. On the other hand, I'm not sure if _____.

▶ My feelings on the issue are mixed. I do support X's position that _____, but I find Y's argument about _____ and Z's research on _____ to be equally persuasive.

SIGNALING WHO IS SAYING WHAT
(pp. 75–76)

▶ X argues _____.

▶ According to both X and Y, _____.

▶ Politicians, X argues, should _____.

▶ Most athletes will tell you that _____.

▶ My own view, however, is that _____.

▶ I agree, as X may not realize, that _____.

▶ But _____ are real and, arguably, the most significant factor in _____.

▶ But X is wrong that _____.

▶ However, it is simply not true that _____.

▶ Indeed, it is highly likely that _____.

▶ X's assertion that _____ does not fit the facts.

▸ X is right that _____.

▸ X is wrong that _____.

▸ X is both right and wrong that _____.

▸ Yet a sober analysis of the matter reveals _____.

▸ Nevertheless, new research shows _____.

▸ Anyone familiar with _____ ____ should agree that _____.

EMBEDDING VOICE MARKERS
(p. 79)

▸ X overlooks what I consider an important point about _____.

▸ My own view is that what X insists is a _____ is in fact a _____.

▸ I wholeheartedly endorse what X calls _____.

▸ These conclusions, which X discusses in _____, add weight to the argument that _____.

ENTERTAINING OBJECTIONS
(p. 86)

▸ At this point I would like to raise some objections that have been inspired by the skeptic in me. She feels that I have been ignoring _____.

▸ Yet some readers may challenge the view that _____.

▸ Of course, many will probably disagree with this assertion that _____.

NAMING YOUR NAYSAYERS
(pp. 87–88)

▶ Here many _____ would probably object that _____.

▶ But _____ would certainly take issue with the argument that _____.

▶ _____, of course, may want to question whether _____.

▶ Nevertheless, both followers and critics of _____ will probably argue that _____.

▶ Although not all _____ think alike, some of them will probably dispute my claim that _____.

▶ _____ are so diverse in their views that it's hard to generalize about them, but some are likely to object on the grounds that _____.

INTRODUCING OBJECTIONS INFORMALLY
(pp. 88–89)

▶ But is my proposal realistic? What are the chances of its actually being adopted?

▶ Yet is it always true that _____? Is it always the case, as I have been suggesting, that _____?

▶ However, does the evidence I've cited prove conclusively that _____?

▶ "Impossible," some will say. "You must be reading the research selectively."

MAKING CONCESSIONS WHILE STILL
STANDING YOUR GROUND (p. 93)

▸ Although I grant that _____, I still maintain that _____.

▸ Proponents of X are right to argue that _____. But they exaggerate when they claim that _____.

▸ While it is true that _____, it does not necessarily follow that _____.

▸ On the one hand, I agree with X that _____. But on the other hand, I still insist that _____.

INDICATING WHO CARES
(pp. 99–100)

▸ _____ used to think _____. But recently [or within the past few decades] _____ suggests that _____.

▸ These findings challenge the work of earlier researchers, who tended to assume that _____.

▸ Recent studies like these shed new light on _____, which previous studies had not addressed.

▸ Researchers have long assumed that _____. For instance, one eminent scholar of cell biology, _____, assumed in _____, her seminal work on cell structures and functions, that fat cells _____. As _____ herself put it, "_____" (2012). Another leading scientist, _____, argued that fat cells "_____" (2011). Ultimately, when it came to the nature of fat, the basic assumption was that _____.

But a new body of research shows that fat cells are far more complex and that _____ .

▸ If sports enthusiasts stopped to think about it, many of them might simply assume that the most successful athletes _____ . However, new research shows _____ .

▸ These findings challenge neoliberals' common assumptions that _____ .

▸ At first glance, teenagers appear to _____ . But on closer inspection _____ .

ESTABLISHING WHY YOUR CLAIMS MATTER
(pp. 102–3)

▸ X matters / is important because _____ .

▸ Although X may seem trivial, it is in fact crucial in terms of today's concern over _____ .

▸ Ultimately, what is at stake here is _____ .

▸ These findings have important consequences for the broader domain of _____ .

▸ My discussion of X is in fact addressing the larger matter of _____ .

▸ These conclusions / This discovery will have significant applications in _____ as well as in _____ .

▸ Although X may seem of concern to only a small group of _____ , it should in fact concern anyone who cares about _____ .

COMMONLY USED TRANSITIONS
(pp. 111–12)

ADDITION

also	in fact
and	indeed
besides	moreover
furthermore	so too
in addition	

ELABORATION

actually	to put it another way
by extension	to put it bluntly
in other words	to put it succinctly
in short	ultimately
that is	

EXAMPLE

after all	for instance
as an illustration	specifically
consider	to take a case in point
for example	

CAUSE AND EFFECT

accordingly	so
as a result	then
consequently	therefore
hence	thus
since	

COMPARISON

along the same lines	likewise
in the same way	similarly

CONTRAST

although	nevertheless
but	nonetheless
by contrast	on the contrary
conversely	on the other hand
despite	regardless
even though	whereas
however	while
in contrast	yet

CONCESSION

admittedly	of course
although it is true that	naturally
granted	to be sure

CONCLUSION

as a result	in sum
consequently	therefore
hence	thus
in conclusion	to sum up
in short	to summarize

Index of Templates

TRANSLATION RECIPES
(pp. 126–27)

- Scholar X argues, "_____." In other words, _____.

- Essentially, X argues _____.

- X's point, succinctly put, is that _____.

- Plainly put, _____.

ADDING METACOMMENTARY
(pp. 140–46)

- In other words, _____.

- What _____ really means by this is _____.

- My point is not _____, but _____.

- Ultimately, my goal is to demonstrate that _____.

- To put it another way, _____.

- Chapter 2 explores _____, while Chapter 3 examines _____.

- Even more important, _____.

- Incidentally, _____.

- In sum, then, _____.

- My conclusion, then, is that, _____.

- In short, _____.

- Having just argued that _____, let us now turn our attention to _____.

- Although some readers may object that _____, I would answer that _____.

LINKING TO WHAT "THEY SAY"
(p. 182)

▸ As X mentions in <u>this article,</u> " _____."

▸ In making <u>this comment,</u> X warns that _____.

▸ Economists often assume _____; however, <u>new research</u> by X suggests _____.

DEVELOPING GOOD RESEARCH QUESTIONS
(pp. 205–8)

▸ Why did X happen? Was it, as _____ argues, because of _____ or, as _____ contends, because of _____?

▸ What should we do about X? Should we _____, as _____ urges, or _____, as _____ argues?

▸ Is X as harmful as _____ insists, or does it have benefits, as _____ claims?

▸ Is it true, as some assert, that _____?

▸ What is the relationship between _____ and _____? Is it X, as most assume, or could it be Y, as one source suggests?

▸ Throughout the many years that I have taken an interest in _____, I, probably like most people, have assumed that _____. When I researched the topic for this essay, however, I was surprised to discover that _____.

▸ X argues _____. In my experience, however, _____.

Index of Templates

LET ONE GOOD SOURCE LEAD TO ANOTHER
(p. 209)

▸ X is far too pessimistic in her prediction that _____.

▸ Authors X and Y focus on the wrong issue. The issue is not _____ but _____.

▸ I agree with X in her critique of the view that _____, but _____.

STARTING WITH WHAT OTHERS SAY
ABOUT A LITERARY WORK
(pp. 234–36)

▸ Critic X complains that author Y's story is compromised by his _____. While there's some truth to this critique, I argue that critic X overlooks _____.

▸ According to critic A, novel X suggests _____. I agree, but would add that _____.

▸ Several members of our class have suggested that the final message of play X is _____. I agree up to a point, but I still think that _____.

▸ On first reading play Z, I thought it was an uncritical celebration of _____. After rereading the play and discussing it in class, however, I see that it is more critical of _____ than I originally thought.

▸ It might be said that poem Y is chiefly about _____. But the problem with this reading, in my view, is _____.

▶ Though religious readers might be tempted to analyze poem X as a parable about _____, a closer examination suggests that the poem is in fact about _____.

RESPONDING TO OTHER INTERPRETATIONS
OF A LITERARY WORK
(p. 239)

▶ It might be argued that in the clash between character X and Y in play Z, the author wants us to favor character Y, since she is presented as the play's heroine. I contend, however, that _____.

▶ Several critics seem to assume that poem X endorses the values of _____ represented by the image of _____ over those of _____ represented by the image of _____. I agree, but with the following caveat: _____.

SHOWING EVIDENCE WHEN WRITING
ABOUT A LITERARY WORK
(p. 244)

▶ Although some might read the metaphor of _____ in this poem as evidence, that for author X, _____, I see it as _____.

▶ Some might claim that evidence X suggests _____, but I argue that, on the contrary, it suggests _____.

▶ I agree with my classmate _____ that the image of _____ in novel Y is evidence of _____. Unlike _____, however, I think _____.

EXPLAIN WHAT THE DATA MEAN
(p. 258–59)

▸ Our data *support / confirm / verify* the work of X by showing that
_____.

▸ By demonstrating _____, X's work *extends* the findings
of Y.

▸ The results of X *contradict / refute* Y's conclusion that _____.

▸ X's findings *call into question* the widely accepted theory that
_____.

▸ Our data *are consistent with* X's hypothesis that _____.

EXPLAINING AN EXPERIMENTAL RESULT
(p. 262)

▸ One explanation for X's finding of _____ is that _____.
An alternative explanation is _____.

▸ The difference between _____ and _____ is probably due to _____.

INTRODUCING GAPS IN THE EXISTING RESEARCH
(p. 277)

▸ Studies of X have indicated _____. It is not clear, however,
that this conclusion applies to _____.

▸ _____ often take for granted that _____. Few have
investigated this assumption, however.

▸ X's work tells us a great deal about _____. Can this work be generalized to _____?

▸ Our understanding of _____ remains incomplete because previous work has not examined _____.

GERALD GRAFF, Emeritus Professor of English and Education at the University of Illinois at Chicago and the 2008 President of the Modern Language Association of America, has had a major impact on teachers through such books as *Professing Literature: An Institutional History*, *Beyond the Culture Wars: How Teaching the Conflicts Can Revitalize American Education*, and *Clueless in Academe: How Schooling Obscures the Life of the Mind*. The Common Core State Standards for K–12 cite his work on the importance of argument literacy for college and career readiness. **CATHY BIRKENSTEIN**, a lecturer at the University of Illinois at Chicago, has published essays on writing, most recently in *College English*, and, with Gerald, in *The Chronicle of Higher Education, Academe*, and *College Composition and Communication*. She and Gerald have given over a hundred lectures and workshops at colleges, conferences, and high schools—and are at present working on a book contending that our currently confusing school and college curriculum needs to be clarified by making the practice of argument the common thread across all disciplines.